Photoshop® Elements 2
Complete Course

Jan Kabili

WILEY

Wiley Publishing, Inc.

Photoshop® Elements 2 Complete Course

Published by:

Wiley Publishing, Inc.
111 River Street
Hoboken, NJ 07030
www.wiley.com/compbooks

Published simultaneously in Canada

For general information on our other products and services or to obtain technical support please contact our Customer Care Department within the U.S. at 800-762-2974, outside the U.S. at 317-572-3993 or fax 317-572-4002.

Library of Congress Cataloging-in-Publication Data: 2003105641

ISBN: 0-7645-4093-9

Manufactured in the United States of America

10 9 8 7 6 5 4 3 2 1

Credits

Publisher: Barry Pruett

Project Editor: Cricket Krengel

Acquisitions Editor: Michael Roney

Editorial Manager: Robyn Siesky

Technical Editor: Dennis Cohen

Copy Editor: Gwenette Gaddis Goshert

Production Coordinator: Courtney MacIntyre

Cover Designer: Anthony Bunyan

Layout: Beth Brooks, Carrie Foster, Jennifer Heleine, Lynsey Osborn, Heather Pope

Proofreader: Vicki Broyles

Quality Control: John Greenough, Susan Moritz, Angel Perez, Rob Springer, Charles Spencer

» Dedication

To my children Ben Kabili, Coby Kabili, and Kate Kabili.

» Acknowledgements

Personal thanks to my agent Neil Salkind at Stufio B, my mentor Lynda Weinman at lynda.com, and my inspiration David Van de Water at Artfact Design. I'd also like to thank Al Lewis and Dan Russelman at IndexStock stock agency.

» About the Author

Jan Kabili has been writing about, teaching, and creating with Photoshop since 1996. Jan wrote and oversaw the Adobe curriculum at Lynda Weinman's Digital Arts Center, where she taught hundreds of students how to use Photoshop, ImageReady, and other Adobe programs. She's spoken at national Web design conferences and taught at several universities. Jan is also the author of the very successful Photoshop 7 Complete Course.

Jan is currently an author and educator. She is a regu-lar columnist for Mac Design magazine, and an Adobe Certified Expert in Photoshop and ImageReady. She has a Master of Fine Arts degree in Electronic Media from the University of Colorado at Boulder, a law degree from Stanford Law School, a Phi Beta Kappa key, three kids, a black lab, and a home in Boulder, Colorado.

» Table of Contents

Introduction

This book and its subject, Adobe Photoshop Elements 2, are for real people. You, like many others, may not have the time, inclination, or bank account to invest in learning a high-end digital imaging program. Yet you want the ability to correct and manipulate your digital photographs, add text to your photos, create a slide show of your work, or display your portfolio on the Web. This book teaches you how to do all that and more with Adobe's popular image-editing program Photoshop Elements 2.

You've probably heard that Photoshop Elements 2 is a bargain, but don't be fooled by its low cost. This program offers many of the features found in the world-class image-editing program Adobe Photoshop, as well as unique features that make Photoshop Elements 2 easier to use than Photoshop. Although Photoshop Elements 2 has special features geared toward digital photographers, it is not limited to simple photo-editing tasks. After you know the program, you can use it to create sophisticated photo-based artwork. That's where this book comes in.

In these pages, you use a tried and true, step-by-step method to learn Photoshop Elements 2 as you create a professional-looking design project. This is a complete, structured course that leads you through a progressive series of tutorials. Each lesson builds on those that have gone before, giving you a chance to practice and expand on what you've learned. Content is just as important as technique. So this book teaches Photoshop Elements 2 in the context of a design project—a series of sophisticated greeting cards with a singular theme, action sports. As you work through this project, you get a sense of what you can create with Photoshop Elements 2, as well as a thorough understanding of how to use the program.

Is This Book for You?

This book is perfect for you if you are a hobbyist, a creative professional, or an educator interested in digital photography or digital imaging. You'll get the most out of this book if you're new to Photoshop Elements 2 or if you have some experience with this or similar programs and simply want to learn more. The book assumes that you are familiar with your computer's operating system and any digital camera or scanner you may have.

How Should You Approach This Book?

I strongly suggest that you not only read this book, but work through it at your computer using the tutorial files from the CD-ROM at the back of the book. I've taught many people how to use digital imaging tools, and I've found that the most effective method for most people is to learn by doing.

Start with the Confidence Builder to warm up and familiarize yourself with the basic features of Photoshop Elements 2. Then dive into the action-packed sessions that follow. If you're a beginner, work through the progressive tutorials in order. If you get stuck at any point, look back to preceding sessions where you are most likely find the information you need. Above all, enjoy yourself as you work through this complete course. You can find nuts-and-bolts information about the course in the Project Overview and instructions for installing tutorial files and software in the CD Appendix.

What's in This Book?

» Confidence Builder. Get your feet wet by working through this introductory step-by-step tutorial that gives you a taste of some of the tools and features in Photoshop Elements 2.

» **Part I: Course Setup.** This section contains introductory material about Photoshop Elements 2 and this course.

» Photoshop Elements 2 Basics offers an overview of the program and what you can use it for.

» Project Overview explains the project you work on throughout this book.

» **Part II: Understanding Basic Features.** This is where you find the first of the tutorials that make up the bulk of the book. This part contains three sessions (chapters):

» Session 1, "Creating and Saving Images," covers how to create a document in Photoshop Elements 2, and how to import images into the program from a digital camera, a scanner, a video, and a PDF (Portable Document Format) file. It explains resolution and file formats, and teaches how to save files.

» Session 2, "Getting Comfortable with the Interface," includes tutorials that show you how to use the basic program elements—tools, menu bars, and palettes. You learn about program preferences, color management features, and the user-friendly Help system.

» Session 3, "Handling Documents," covers accessing information about a document, using Rulers and Grids for positioning, zooming in and out of the document window, navigating in a document window, changing image size, image resolution, and canvas size, and cropping an image.

» Session 4, "Fixing Mistakes," shows you multiple ways of retracing your steps as you work on an image. It includes tutorials on the eraser tools, the Undo commands, the Undo History palette, and reverting to the last saved version of a file.

» **Part III: Mastering Selections and Layers.** This part concerns the heart of image-editing in Photoshop Elements 2—working with selections and layers.

» Session 5, "Making Selections," addresses the most efficient ways of selecting part of an image so that you can edit its content. You learn how and when to use various selection tools, what anti-aliasing means, and how to modify, move, and edit selections.

» Session 6, "Working with Layers," includes a discussion on layer basics, along with tutorials on generating, copying, and managing layers. You learn about layer blending modes, layer opacity, special fill and adjustment layers, layer styles, and merging layers. You even discover a useful work-around for creating layer masks, which are otherwise not accessible in Photoshop Elements 2.

» **Part IV: Fixing Photographs.** This part zeros in on editing photographs in Photoshop Elements 2. It covers photo retouching, adjusting tonal values, and color correcting.

» Session 7, "Retouching and Adjusting Photographs," offers a photo-adjustment workflow you can use to improve the look of your photographs. It covers straightening and cropping a scanned photo, eliminating stains from a photograph, removing dust and damage, adjusting tonal values and exposure, cloning and manipulating content, and sharpening. You learn about the Quick Fix approach built in to the program, as well as more advanced retouching and adjustment techniques.

» Session 8, "Color Correcting Photographs." This session covers how to correct color in a photograph. You learn step-by-step how to improve color and contrast using Levels, the Color Cast command, the Auto Color Correction command, and the Color Variations feature. You fix lighting problems using the Adjust Backlighting command, the Fill Flash feature, and the Red Eye Brush tool. You also learn about adjusting color saturation and some efficient methods of replacing one color with another.

» **Part V: Using Text and Shapes.** This part focuses on the vector-based features in the program that allow you to create text and graphic shapes.

» Session 9, "Adding Shapes." This session is all about shapes, the shape tools you use to create them, and the special qualities of shape layers.

» Session 10, "Creating and Editing Text." Here you learn to create and edit text. You work with text formatting, warping text into unusual shapes, and using text as a mask for images.

» **Part VI: Outputting.** This part addresses how to output your digital work to print, Web, and other other on-screen formats.

» Session 11, "Printing." Here you prepare the greeting cards you created throughout the book for printing on a desktop printer. You also learn how to make a contact sheet to index your images, and a print Picture Package of images of various sizes. And you join several photographs into a wide, panoramic document using the Photomerge feature in Photoshop Elements 2.

» Session 12, "Outputting for the Web and Screen." This session teaches how to optimize photographs, graphics, and text for publication on the World Wide Web. You make artwork for rollover buttons, create an animated GIF, and generate a full Web Photo Gallery site. You also learn how to create a PDF slideshow, and automatically attach an image to e-mail from Photoshop Elements 2.

» **Bonus Material (On the CD-ROM): Enhancing Images.** These bonus sessions employ tutorials to teach you how to enhance your images using filters and effects.

» Bonus Session 1, "Using Filters" (CD-ROM). In this session you use filters to embellish text, add texture, and create sketches and painterly looks in photographs.

» Bonus Session 2, "Applying Effects" (CD-ROM). Here you learn to use special effects built into Photoshop Elements 2 to add dimensionality and framing to images.

What Conventions Are Used in This Book?

Here's a key to the conventions of structure and style used in this book:

» Tutorials are the heart of this book. Each tutorial contains numbered steps. The bolded portion of a step is an instruction for you to perform. Some steps include unbolded text that explains the step.

» Discussions cover more complex issues, like image resolution and color management, in depth. These are narrative parts of the book.

» Some tutorial steps have hot pink numbers, indicating that the step is illustrated. Look for a corresponding hot pink number on a nearby illustration.

» Extra information is provided in the form of short Notes, Tips, and Cautions in magenta type sprinkled throughout the tutorials. You'll also see some blue boxes, called Sidebars, containing background or extra information.

» The first set of instructions in a tutorial is based on the Windows XP operating system. If there are different instructions for Macintosh users, those appear in parentheses and reflect the Macintosh OS X operating system. Photoshop Elements 2 is virtually the same across operating systems. The primary differences are some key commands, including those listed in table Intro-1.

Table Intro-1: Cross-Platform Equivalents

Windows Command	Macintosh Equivalent
Ctrl+click	⌘+click
Alt+click	Option+click
Right click	Ctrl+click
Enter	Return

» Most illustrations were made in Windows XP, with the Windows XP desktop theme slightly modified so that it is easier to read in print. You see a few illustrations made in Macintosh OS X where there is a cross-platform difference to illustrate.

» Filenames (like `climber.psd`) are distinguished with a special monofont typeface.

» When you are instructed to type in text, what you should type appears in bold if it appears in a nonbolded line of text. It appears as nonbold text if it is in a line of bold text.

» Small arrows (→) are shorthand for "go to and choose." For example, the instruction File→Open means go to the File menu and choose Open.

» Ctrl+click is shorthand for "press and hold the Control key while clicking the mouse." Shift+click, Alt+click, Option+click, and ⌘+click are similar. Right-click means "click the button on the right side of the mouse."

Now that you're aware of the conventions you'll encounter, you should be ready to try your hand at the Confidence Builder that follows. Good luck!

Confidence Builder

Introduction

The purpose of this Confidence Builder is to give you a taste of what you learn in the sessions that follow. You try out some of the basic tools and commands in Photoshop Elements 2 and get a first look at features that are addressed in more detail later in the course. Keep in mind that this is just a warm up; don't worry about getting every last detail under your belt. You revisit all the features touched on here in future sessions. Enjoy this chance to limber up while you create a dynamic image for the first card in the Complete Course project.

TOOLS YOU'LL USE
Welcome Screen, New dialog box, Gradient tool, Crop tool, Rotate command, Auto Contrast command, Save commands, Palette Well, Layers palette, Move tool, Hand tool, Clone Stamp tool, Type tool, Effects palette, Layer Style palette, Pencil tool.

CD-ROM FILES NEEDED
globe.psd, cliff.psd, climber_end.psd

TIME REQUIRED
40 minutes

Tutorial

» Creating a New Document

In this tutorial you create and save a new document.

1. **Launch Photoshop Elements 2, pressing Alt+Ctrl+Shift (Macintosh: Option+⌘+Shift) as the program starts.**
   Pressing this key combination as you start Photoshop Elements 2 resets the program's Preferences, which are the settings that allow you to customize basic behaviors. Resetting your preferences to their defaults ensures that your copy of Photoshop Elements 2 behaves just like the copy used in this course.

< NOTE >
The first time you launch the program, you see the Registration Choice window. If you want to register your copy of the program now, click Continue. If you want to register later, select Do not display this dialog again and click Continue. This keeps the registration window from popping up repeatedly. When you're ready to register later, choose Help→Registration.

< NOTE >
When Photoshop Elements 2 opens, you see the colorful Welcome Screen. Although the Welcome Screen looks impressive, it's nothing more than a collection of shortcuts to features that you can also access from menu commands. If you don't want to see the Welcome Screen each time you open the program, deselect Show this screen at startup at the bottom of the Welcome Screen.

2. **Click the New File button in the Welcome Screen.**
   This opens the New dialog box.

< TIP >
The width, height, and other numbers you see in your New dialog box reflect the size of whatever item is currently in your Clipboard (the size of the last item that you copied or cut). If nothing is in the Clipboard, these numbers reflect the size of the last document you created. If you want to make a series of documents that are the same size, ignore the Clipboard by holding the Alt key (Macintosh: Option key) each time you choose File→New, or empty the Clipboard by going to Edit→Preferences→General, deselecting Export Clipboard, and restarting the program.

3. **Set the fields in the New dialog box as follows:**

   » Name: Type **climber**.

   » Width: Choose inches from the menu. Then type **6.25**.

   » Height: Choose inches from the menu. Then type **4.625**.

   » Resolution: Choose pixels/inch (pixels per inch) from the menu, and type **240**.

   » Mode: Choose RGB Color from the menu.

   » Contents: Select the radio button for White.

   These settings determine the attributes of the new file you create, which is an RGB color file with a white background that is 6.25 inches wide and 4.625 inches high when printed at a resolution of 240 pixels per inch. You learn all about size, resolution, and color mode in Part II of the course.

4. **Click OK to close the New dialog box.**
   A document window opens, displaying your new white image.

5. **Choose File→Save As to open the Save As window. In the Save in (Macintosh: the Where) field of that window navigate to the** ccproject **folder on your desktop. Leave the other options at their defaults and click Save.**
   Notice in the File name field that Photoshop Elements 2 automatically adds a .psd suffix to the file name climber. This identifies the file as being in photoshop document (PSD) format, which is the native file format of Photoshop Elements 2, as well as of Adobe Photoshop. It's good practice to save the original of any document in PSD format to preserve the document's layers and other attributes.

<TIP>
The first time you save an image, the Save command is not available. So you have to use Save As.

<CAUTION>
Don't be fooled into thinking that creating a new file makes that file permanent. If you don't save a new file at least once before closing it, the file will be lost. So get in the habit of saving immediately after creating a new file and saving frequently as you work to preserve changes.

6. **Leave this image open and move on to the next tutorial.**

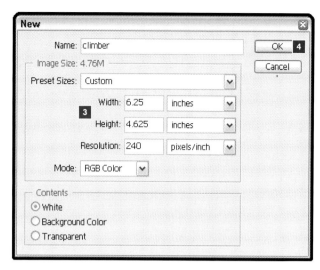

<TIP>
You set the dimensions of this document to a custom size in order to create a card that fits neatly into a standard A6 envelope. Photoshop Elements 2 also has a long list of preconfigured document sizes that may come in handy in some situations. Click in the Preset Sizes field of the New dialog box to see a list of document sizes organized by paper type (for print), inches (for standard-sized photographs), pixels (for Web pages and other screen formats), and paper size (for print).

Tutorial
» Choosing and Using Color

Here you get a taste of some basic techniques for choosing and applying color. You set the background color to black automatically, choose a vibrant foreground color in the Color Picker, and create a color gradient using these foreground and background colors.

1. **Click the default colors icon (the tiny black and white squares at the bottom of the toolbox) to set the foreground and background color boxes to black and white respectively.**

   The foreground and background color boxes determine the color of brushes, fills, gradients, and erasures.

   <NOTE>

   The file `climber.psd` should be open from the last tutorial. If it's not, open it from your ccproject folder.

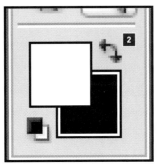

2. **Click the double-pointed arrow above the color boxes to switch the foreground and background colors.**

   The foreground color box should now be white and the background color box black, as in the illustration.

3. **Click the white Foreground Color box in the toolbox to open the Color Picker.**

4. **In the Color Picker, make sure that Only Web Colors is unchecked so that the color field on the left side of the Color Picker is not limited to displaying Web-safe colors.**

5. **Type the following values in the R, G, and B (red, green, and blue) fields in the Color Picker: R:** 234, **G:** 140, **B:** 37 **to select a shade of gold as the foreground color.**

6. **Click OK to close the Color Picker.**

   Notice that the Foreground Color box in the toolbox is now set to gold. You use the foreground and background colors to create a color gradient in the following steps.

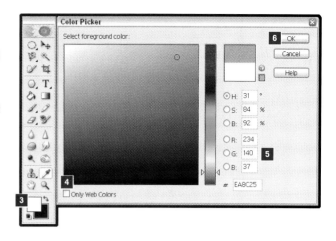

7. **Choose View→Rulers to display horizontal and vertical rulers along the top and left edges of the document window.**

   Rulers come in handy when you need to reproduce an image or place an item precisely in the document window. You use them to reproduce a color gradient in the next steps.

<TIP>

You can hide the rulers at any time by again choosing View→Rulers.

<TIP>

If you were creating a graphic for the Web rather than for print, the rulers would be more useful if they displayed pixels rather than inches. You can change the rulers' unit of measurement to pixels at any time by double-clicking inside either ruler to open the Units and Rulers Preferences window and choosing pixels in the Rulers field. Leave the rulers in inches for now because you're creating images for print.

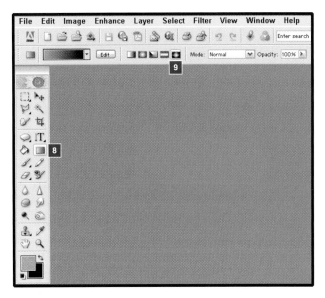

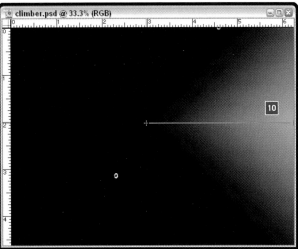

8. **Click the Gradient tool in the toolbox to select that tool.**

   Notice that the Options bar now displays options specific to the Gradient tool, including a foreground color to background color (gold to black) gradient.

<**N O T E**>

The context-sensitive Options bar changes with each tool you select in the toolbox, offering settings for that particular tool.

<**T I P**>

If you're not sure which is the Gradient tool, Tool Tips can help you. Hold your mouse over any tool until a Tool Tip appears, displaying the tool name and a shortcut key that's a quick alternative for selecting the tool.

9. **Click the Diamond Gradient button on the Options bar to set the gradient tool to create a diamond-shaped gradient, rather than the linear gradient that it creates by default.**

10. **To create a gold to black diamond-shaped gradient like the one shown in the figure, place your cursor just inside the right edge of the document window. (The dotted lines should be at the 2-inch mark on the vertical ruler.) Click and drag to the left in a straight, horizontal line, releasing the cursor when you reach the 3-inch mark on the horizontal ruler.**

   The small dotted lines on the vertical ruler that runs down the left side of the document window mark your vertical position. They also show the position of the cursor as you drag. If you're not happy with your first attempt, you can click and drag again to redraw the gradient without having to undo the first gradient.

<**N O T E**>

Don't worry about replicating the gradient in the illustration exactly. Your gradient may look a little different because the length and direction of the line you drag is what determines the shape of a gradient. The point is to try out the Gradient tool and to get a sense that you can create content from scratch in Photoshop Elements 2. In other words, this is not just a photo-editing program!

11. **Choose File→Save to preserve the changes you made to** `climber.psd` **and leave this document open for the next tutorial.**

   The Save command is now available because you made changes to the image since saving it initially. The Save command automatically saves to the same location as the last save, your ccproject folder, and replaces the last saved version of the file.

Tutorial
» Preparing Images for Compositing

Before combining multiple images, you should prepare them so that they match in terms of size, orientation, tone, lighting, and color. In this tutorial, you prepare an image to be added to your climber.psd document. You change the magnification at which you view the new image, crop it to size, flip it horizontally, and adjust its contrast so that it fits and blends in with climber.psd.

1. **Choose File→Open from the menu bar and navigate to the Confidence Builder folder in the Tutorial Files folder on your hard drive. Select** globe.psd **and click Open.**

   If you can't remember where on your hard drive you installed the tutorial files, use your operating system's search tools to find the path to the Confidence Builder folder.

<NOTE>

You now should have two images open, globe.psd and climber.psd. If climber.psd is not still open, open it from your ccproject folder. Your first task is to view these two images at the same magnification so that you can accurately compare their size.

2. **Select the Zoom tool in the toolbox.**

3. **Look at the percentage in the title bar at the top of the** globe.psd **document window. If that percentage is greater than 25%, select the Zoom Out button (the minus sign) in the Options bar. If that percentage is less than 25%, select the Zoom In button (the plus sign) in the Options bar.**

4. **Click anywhere in the** globe.psd **document window to zoom in or out until the title bar at the top of the document window reads 25%.**

   You may have to click more than once.

<NOTE>

The Zoom tool, just like an adjustable telescope or the zoom lens on a camera, changes only the magnification at which you view an image; it does not change the actual size of the image. Zooming out reduces magnification and makes the image appear smaller; zooming in increases magnification and makes the image appear bigger. But neither affects real image size.

5. **Repeat steps 3 and 4 in the** climber.psd **document window so that its title bar also reads 25%.**

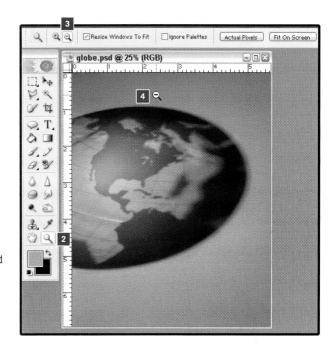

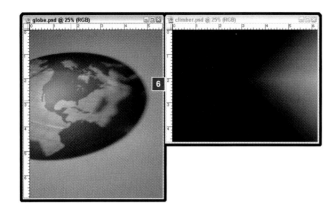

6. **Compare the two images and notice that** globe.psd **is quite a bit taller than** climber.psd.

   With the images at the same magnification, you can see that only part of globe.psd fits into climber.psd. Resizing either image does not resolve the mismatch; sizing globe.psd down makes the subject matter too small for your collage, and sizing climber.psd up could cause unwanted image distortion. So leave both images at their current size. In the next step you use the Crop tool to isolate a portion of globe.psd to combine with the other image.

<TIP>

Comparing image sizes is easier if the rulers are visible in both document windows. If you don't see rulers in either document window, click in that window and choose View➔Rulers.

<NOTE>

A realistic comparison of the size of multiple images requires that they share the same magnification and the same resolution (number of pixels per inch). The complex subject of resolution is covered in depth in future sessions. For now, you can accept that these two images have the same resolution of 240 pixels per inch.

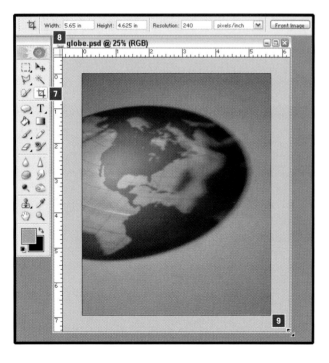

7. **Select the Crop tool in the toolbox.**

8. **In the Crop tool's Options bar, type** 5.65 **in the Width field,** 4.625 **in the Height field, and** 240 **in the Resolution field. Make sure that the Resolution field is set to pixels/inch (pixels per inch).**

   This sets a fixed size for the area to be cropped in globe.psd. If you wonder where these numbers came from, the dimensions are estimates arrived at by eyeballing climber.psd with its rulers on and deciding how much of that image to cover with the image of the globe. The resolution is the actual resolution of both images.

9. **Click on the bottom-right corner of the** globe.psd **document window, and drag to increase the gray canvas area around the image.**

   This is a convenience to give you more room to maneuver with the Crop tool.

<NOTE>

Expanding the canvas around an image has no effect on the image size. The canvas is just blank space surrounding an image.

10. Click with the Crop tool in the gray canvas just to the left of the image and drag as far to the right as your fixed-size crop setting allows to define the area to be cropped.

11. Click and drag inside the crop marquee (the dotted lines) to adjust the location of the crop marquee to match the illustration.

12. Press Enter (Macintosh: Return) on your keyboard to execute the crop.

    The area outside the crop marquee is eliminated by the crop and the area inside the crop marquee is now the same size as the other image, climber.psd. The two images will now fit together when you combine them in the next tutorial.

<NOTE>

If you don't like the way the crop turns out, choose Edit→Step Backward and repeat the preceding step. Edit→Step Backward lets you undo up to 20 operations by default. The shortcut for this command, Ctrl+Z (Macintosh: ⌘+Z) is one that you may want to commit to memory. You learn more about how to correct mistakes in Session 3.

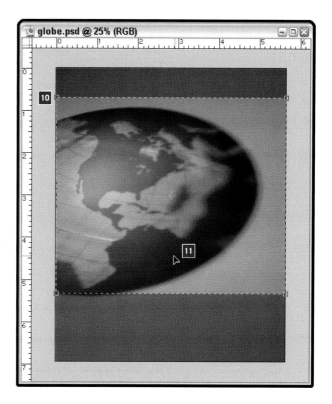

Auto Adjustment versus Manual Adjustment for Contrast

Auto Contrast is a simple tool for adjusting tone in an image. You just execute one command, and you're good to go. The trade-offs are that Auto Contrast, like the other auto adjustment features in Photoshop Elements 2, doesn't give you control over the results, doesn't account for your aesthetic tastes, and doesn't always do the best job on every image. For example, I was able to get better results adjusting the tonality of globe.psd manually using controls in the Levels dialog box than by using simple Auto Contrast.

On the other hand, auto adjustment features come in handy for quick results like those you might apply to snapshots, drafts, or design layouts. Adjusting tone and correcting color in photographs are important skills for a Photoshop Elements 2 user. You just get your feet wet here. You spend lots more time learning how to use adjustment methods, from auto controls to more complex manual features, in Part IV of this course.

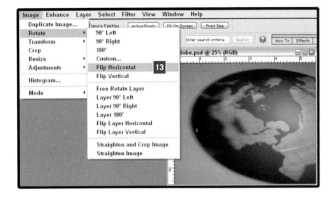

13. **Choose Image→Rotate→Flip Horizontal.**

    This inverts the image, flipping the globe to the right side of the document window so that it fits the final design.

14. **Click anywhere in globe.psd to ensure that it is still the active image on your screen and then choose Enhance→Auto Contrast.**

    You see a subtle change in contrast in globe.psd (the dark areas are a little darker, the light areas lighter, and there's a slightly less uniform gray tone across the image). To prove to yourself that there is a difference, press Ctrl+Z (Macintosh: ⌘+Z) to undo the contrast adjustment and then Ctrl+Y (Macintosh: ⌘+Y) to redo it. You should see a slight change as you toggle back and forth between these commands, particularly if you squint a little.

15. **Choose File→Save As, navigate to your ccproject folder, and click Save to save globe.psd with its changes.**

    There's no need to resave climber.psd because you haven't substantively changed the image since last saving it. Leave globe.psd and climber.psd open for the next tutorial. The image globe.psd is now sized and adjusted so that it's ready to be combined with climber.psd, which you do in the next tutorial.

    <TIP>

    If you accidentally save over a version of a file that you meant to keep, you can take advantage of the safety net built in to Photoshop Elements 2. You can restore your document to the way things were before the inadvertent save by choosing Edit→Step Backwards. Undoing after a save is a trick that has gotten many users out of a jam.

Tutorial
» Combining Images

In this tutorial you combine two images by dragging one image into another and positioning the relocated image with the Move tool. This is how digital collages are made in Photoshop Elements 2.

1. **Choose Window→Reset Palette Locations.**
   This resets all the palettes in Photoshop Elements 2 to their default locations and states so that your work space is set up like the one in these illustrations. Palettes are tabbed panes that contain various editing features.

2. **Move your cursor over the tabs in the Palette Well on the right side of the Shortcuts bar at the top of the screen. When the Layers tab comes forward, click and drag that tab out of the Palette Well to open the Layers palette in the application window (Macintosh: on the desktop).**
   The Palette Well is a convenient place for storing and accessing palettes.

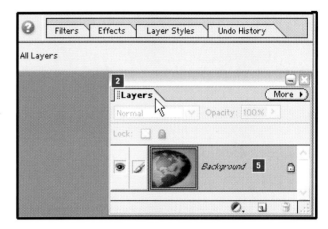

<CAUTION>
Make sure that you drag the Layers palette out of the Palette Well as instructed in step 2. If you leave the Layers palette open but docked in the Palette Well, it zips itself up and disappears back into the Palette Well as soon as you click anywhere else on the screen. If you want a frequently used palette to remain open as you work, drag it out of the Palette Well. On the other hand, it makes sense to open an infrequently used palette inside the Palette Well (by just clicking the palette tab), so that the palette closes automatically after use, freeing up your work space.

3. **Check that both** globe.psd **and** climber.psd **are still open and that neither is completely obscured by other items on your screen.**
   If either is closed, open it from your ccproject folder.

4. **Click anywhere in the** climber.psd **document window to make that document active.**

5. **Take a look at the Layers palette and notice that** climber.psd **currently has just one layer called** *Background*.

<TIP>
Every new image starts out with a layer called ***Background*** that has special properties. An official ***Background*** layer cannot be erased, moved in the layer stack, or made transparent like other layers. If you ever try to perform an action on a ***Background*** layer that doesn't work, try converting it to a regular layer by double-clicking the ***Background*** layer in the Layers palette and typing in a new name for that layer.

<NOTE>
Layers are the heart of the editing system in Photoshop Elements 2. Each layer is like a piece of transparent glass arranged in a stack with other layers. That stack is represented by the Layers palette. You can see down through the transparent areas of the stacked layers to whatever artwork has been placed on layers below. If you place important items on separate layers, you have the freedom to delete, move, or change each of those items without affecting the rest of your image. You learn more about layers and the Layers palette in Session 6.

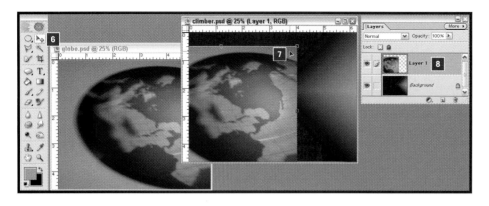

6. **Select the Move tool in the toolbox.**

7. **Click anywhere inside the** `globe.psd` **document window and drag that image into the** `climber.psd` **document window.**
   The Layers palette indicates that `climber.psd` now has two layers—***Background*** and **Layer 1**.

8. **Double-click the name** Layer 1 **in the** `climber.psd` **Layers palette, and type a more meaningful layer name**—globe.

9. **With the** globe **layer selected, click with the Move tool inside the** `climber.psd` **document window and drag the globe image into position to match the illustration.**
   The right edge of the globe image should be at about the 5-inch mark on the horizontal ruler; the left side of the image should be cut off by the left edge of the document window.

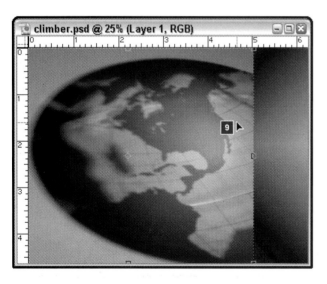

10. **Choose File→Save to save** `climber.psd` **with the changes. Leave this document open.**

11. **Click anywhere in** `globe.psd` **to make that document window active, and choose File→Close. You won't use this file again.**
    If you're asked whether to save changes to the document, select No. Take a minute to review what you've done so far in the Confidence Builder. You created a new image, `climber.psd`, and filled it with a color gradient. Then you prepared another image, `globe.psd`, for compositing by resizing and adjusting contrast. You combined the two images by dragging `globe.psd` into `climber.psd` and positioning the globe image with the move tool.

Tutorial
» Manipulating Image Content

You can change the content of photographs and other images in Photoshop Elements 2 by adding, deleting, or moving items in the image. In this tutorial you use the Clone Stamp tool to cover an area of discoloration in a photograph. You also select and copy part of that photograph to your `climber.psd` image.

1. **Choose File→Open and navigate to the Tutorial Files→Confidence Builder folder on your hard drive. Select** `cliff.psd` **and click Open.**
   This is a great image, but it has a flaw—the blue reflection in the rock, which needs to be eliminated.

2. **Double-click the Zoom tool in the toolbox to set the image magnification to 100%.**
   This is a shortcut for changing image magnification to 100%. It makes sense to use 100% magnification for basic photo retouching because that's the way your viewers see the image when you're finished.

3. **If the whole image does not fit on your screen at this magnification, click and drag the scroll bars until you see the blue reflection on the rock in your document window.**
   The scroll bars appear at the right and bottom edges of the document window.

4. **Select the Clone Stamp tool in the toolbox.**
   This is one of a number of tools that is applied with a brush. In the next step you choose a brush type and brush size to use with the Clone Stamp tool.

5. **To choose a brush to use with the Clone Stamp tool, click the Brush Presets field on the Options bar, which opens the Brush Presets palette.**
   Notice that the Options bar has changed to show options for the Clone Stamp tool. The Brush Presets palette is an option for all of the tools that are applied with a brush.

6. **Use the arrows on the Brush Presets palette to scroll down the menu of brush strokes in the palette. Choose the Soft Round 27 pixel brush. Leave the other Options settings at their defaults as in the illustration.**

7. **To select clean source pixels to cover the blue reflection, hold the Alt key (Macintosh: Option key) while you click in a nonblemished area near the blue reflection.**
   Holding the Alt (Macintosh: Option) key changes the cursor to a target symbol.

< T I P >

To see the name of any brush, hover over its brush stroke in the Brush Presets palette until a Tool Tip appears.

8. **To cover the blue reflection with pixels cloned from the source pixels, release the Alt key (Macintosh: Option key), and click in a random pattern on and around the blue pixels seven or eight times.**

Notice that the source area (which is under the plus symbol) moves with your cursor (the circle symbol).

< T I P >

It's important to click in a random fashion, rather than click and drag, or you create a telltale repeating pattern of cloned pixels in your image.

9. **Select the Zoom tool in the toolbox, and click the Zoom Out (minus) button in the Options bar. Click in the document window to zoom out until you can see the entire image.**

In the next steps, you select the foreground elements of cliff.psd and copy them to climber.psd. You use selections often in Photoshop Elements 2 to isolate pixels on which to perform all kinds of editing tasks.

< T I P >

A selection limits the area affected by copying, moving, deleting, coloring, filtering, and styling pixels.

10. **To select the foreground elements of cliff.psd using a pre-built selection, choose Select→Load Selection from the menu bar at the top of the screen.**

This opens the Load Selection dialog box.

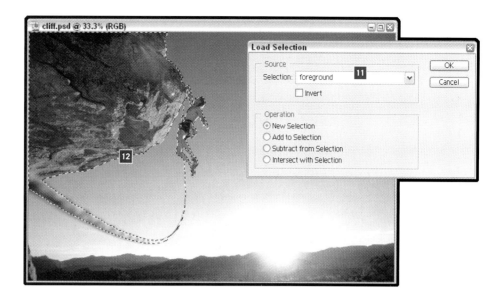

11. **In the Load Selection dialog box, make sure that the Selection Source is set to foreground and click OK.**

    This loads a prebuilt selection around the foreground elements in the image.

12. **Notice the animated dotted lines around the cliff, the climber, and the rope.**

    These are called marching ants. They delineate the boundary of the selection.

13. **A second image, climber.psd, should still be open from the last tutorial. If it's not, open it from your ccproject folder. Make sure the globe layer is selected in the climber.psd layers palette.**

< N O T E >

Making a clean selection of a complex shape like this can be time-consuming, so I made this selection for you. I selected large areas of the sky with the Magic Wand tool. I added the landscape to the selection with the Lasso tool. Then I inverted the selection with the Select→Inverse command, and cleaned up its edges using the Selection Brush tool. When I was finished creating the selection, I named and saved it with the image. You learn to use these and other selection features in Session 5.

< T I P >

While a selection is active you can save it with an image by choosing Select→Save Selection. You can reload the selection at any time and use it for any purpose for which you normally use a selection.

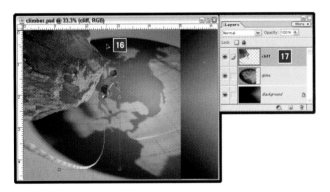

14. **Select the Move tool in the toolbox.**

15. **Click inside the selection in** cliff.psd, **and drag the selected pixels into the** climber.psd **document window.**
    A copy of the selected area from cliff.psd appears in climber.psd. This trick is often used to switch out backgrounds on photographs.

16. **Use the Move tool to drag the copied selection into position to match the illustration (the right border of the bounding box around the selection should be at the 3-inch mark on the horizontal ruler, and the lower border of the bounding box should be several ticks up from the bottom on the vertical ruler).**
    You can move this artwork separately because it was automatically placed on its own layer when you dragged it into the document.

17. **Double-click on the new layer in the Layers palette, and type** cliff **to give the layer a meaningful name.**

18. **Choose File→Save to resave** climber.psd **to your ccproject folder with these changes. Leave this image open for the next tutorial.**

19. **Click in the** cliff.psd **document window, and select File→Close without saving changes.**
    You won't use this image again.

Tutorial
» Adding Text

In this short tutorial you add a layer of editable type to your `climber.psd` image.

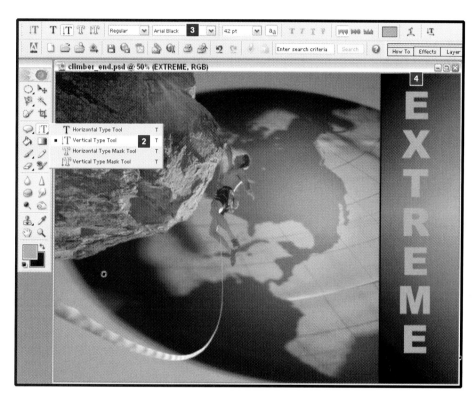

1. Make sure that `climber.psd` is still open from the last tutorial. If it's not, open it from your ccproject folder.

2. Click and hold the Horizontal Type tool in the toolbox to display a flyout tool menu, and select the Vertical Type tool from that menu.

3. The Options bar now displays options specific to the type tools. In the Options bar, type 42 pt in the Font Size field and choose Arial Black in the Font Family field.

   Type color doesn't matter because you override the type color with a type effect later in this tutorial.

4. Add text by clicking in the vertical bar on the right side of the image, holding the caps lock key on your keyboard, and typing EXTREME.

   This creates a new layer in the Layers palette. The T symbol indicates that this is an editable type layer. This means that you can change the properties or content of this layer at any time by selecting and editing part or all of the type.

5. Select the Move tool, and center the text vertically.

   You can move the text independently because it is on a separate layer.

< T I P >

The Move tool displays a bounding box around the artwork on a selected layer. You can hide the bounding box, if it bothers you, by deselecting Show Bounding Box on the Move tool Options bar.

6. Choose File→Save, and leave this file open for the last tutorial in the Confidence Builder, in which you add special effects to the text in this image.

Tutorial
» Applying Special Effects

Photoshop Elements 2 offers several kinds of special effects—Layer Styles, Effects, and Filters—that you can apply to text or artwork. In this tutorial you add selections from the Effects palette and the Layer Styles palette to the text in climber.psd.

1. **If** climber.psd **is not still open from the last tutorial, open it from your ccproject folder.**

2. **Select the EXTREME type layer in the Layers palette.**
   This limits the special effects you apply in this tutorial to this layer.

3. **Choose a foreground color for the text effect you apply in the next steps. Click in the Foreground Color Box in the toolbox, choose a gold color in the Color Picker (try R: 237, G: 141, B: 28), and click OK.**

4. **Click the Effects tab in the Palette Well to open the Effects palette.**

5. **Click the button at the top left of the Effects palette to open a menu of text effect categories. Choose Text Effects from that menu.**
   Effects in the Text Effects category can only be applied to a type layer. Other kinds of effects can be applied to image or type.

6. **To apply the Sprayed Stencil text effect, scroll down in the Effects palette until you see the thumbnail labeled Sprayed Stencil, and double-click that thumbnail.**
   This effect creates a copy of the type layer and simplifies that layer, changing it from an editable type layer to a regular layer named **EXTREME copy**. The effect creates a color glow around the text and knocks out the text itself.

<TIP>
Once an effect is applied, it cannot be edited.

<NOTE>
The Layer Styles palette offers another kind of special effect that applies to all of the artwork on a layer. In the next steps, you add a layer style to the **EXTREME copy** layer.

7. **Click on the Layer Styles tab in the Palette Well to open the Layer Styles palette.**

8. **Click the button at the top left of the Layer Styles palette to display a menu of layer style categories, and choose Image Effects from that menu.**

9. **To apply the Puzzle layer style, scroll down in the Layer Styles palette until you see the Puzzle thumbnail, and double-click that thumbnail.**

   The *f* icon that appears on the **EXTREME copy** layer in the Layers palette indicates that this layer contains a layer style.

<NOTE>

Layer Styles differ from Effects in that Layer Styles are editable. To modify a Layer Style after it's been applied, double-click the *f* icon on the affected layer in the Layers palette and modify the style to your liking in the Style Settings dialog box that appears.

<NOTE>

To finish off the image, you draw a decorative line with the Pencil tool in the next steps.

10. **Select the globe layer in the Layers palette.**

11. **Select the Pencil tool in the toolbox.**
    The Options bar now shows options for the Pencil tool.

12. **In the Options bar, leave the Brush Presets palette set to the default brush (Hard Round 1 Pixel), but increase the size of that brush by clicking the arrow to the right of the Size field and dragging the slider to 6 px. Leave the other Pencil tool options at their defaults.**

13. **To select a color for the line you draw, click the small default colors icon at the bottom of the toolbox. This changes the Foreground Color to black.**

14. **To draw a straight vertical line, hold the Shift key, click at the top of the document window between the globe image and the text area, and drag to the bottom of the image.**
    The Shift key restrains the Pencil tool to a straight line.

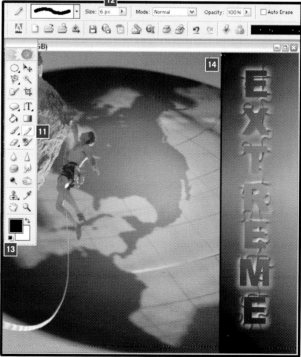

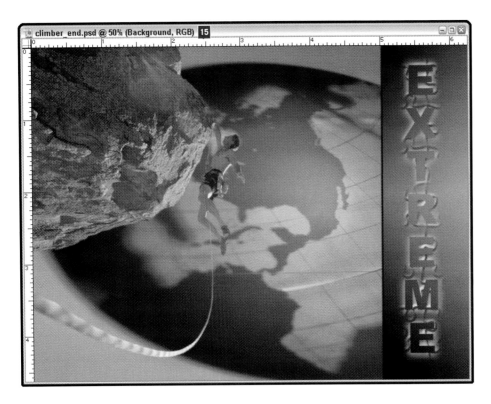

15. **Choose File→Save As, and name your final image**
    climber_end.psd. **Navigate to the ccproject folder you
    created on your desktop, and click Save.**

    Congratulations. You completed the Confidence Builder and
    created a dynamic image for your first greeting card, as you
    can see in the figure. Along the way you were introduced to a
    variety of basic techniques, including how to create and save
    an image, choose and apply color, combine images, edit con-
    tent, add text, and apply special effects. In the sessions that
    follow, you learn more about the features you tried out here.
    A copy of the completed image, climber_end.psd, is
    located in the Tutorial Files→Confidence Builder folder.

Part I
Course Setup

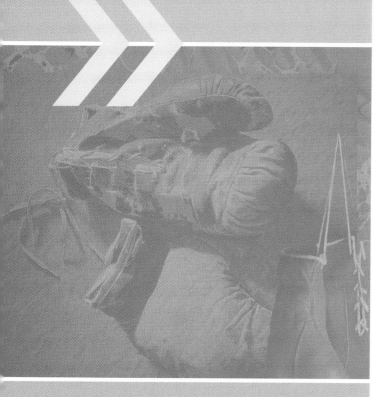

Photoshop Elements 2 Basics

Not so long ago, digital imaging was inaccessible to most people. Hardware and software costs were prohibitive, learning curves were steep, and the equipment available did not work well together. That picture has changed. A thriving market now exists for digital cameras, scanners, printers, CDd and DVD burners, and more. As the equipment gets better and cheaper, more people are getting involved in digital imaging. And the involvement of all kinds of people—creative professionals, hobbyists, educators, students, and just plain folks—has increased the need for smart, creative, accessible imaging software.

Ideally, that software should be relatively easy to learn and use, but not dumbed down. It should offer practical applications, but be versatile and deep enough to support creative explorations. It should integrate with the current and expected crop of digital cameras and scanners, but it shouldn't be so expensive that only institutions can afford it. But wait—I'm describing software that's already available! That software is Adobe Photoshop Elements 2.

Take a minute to read through this brief chapter for an overview of what Photoshop Elements 2 offers, what you can use it for, and how it differs from its progenitor, Adobe Photoshop.

Overview of Photoshop Elements 2

Photoshop Elements 2 is digital-imaging software. In the broadest sense, it is a collection of tools for editing bitmap (pixel-based) digital images. The particulars of what you can do with this software tell more of the story.

The program is best known for its ability to help digital photographers in all stages of their workflow: input, editing, and output. Photoshop Elements 2 has features that can be used for:

» Connecting with and importing images from digital cameras and scanners

» Batch processing, including renaming, converting format, resizing, and rotating collections of images

» Browsing, sorting, and organizing images

» Cropping, straightening, and rotating scans

» Fixing flash-related problems, such as red eye, lack of fill flash, and lack of backlighting

» Removing dust and scratches

» Repairing tears and retouching blemishes

» Fixing exposure and contrast automatically and with manual controls

» Correcting color automatically and with manual controls

» Sharpening and blurring

» Adding text in creative ways

» Colorizing

» Digitally framing photos

» Enhancing with filters, effects, and layer styles

» Removing distracting content

» Replacing and adding content

» Creating composite images

» Laying out contact sheets and picture packages

» Merging images into panoramas

» Building Web photo galleries

» Making slide shows in PDF format

» Preparing photographs for email distribution

An important point, and one that I think the official publicists don't make strongly enough, is that Photoshop Elements 2 is not just for photographers. All of its features can be used in other contexts, making it just as valuable to someone whose goal is to generate art, illustrations, educational materials, designs and layouts, promotional materials, brochures, portfolios, or any graphic creation.

Yes, the program can be used to create personal projects, and it includes recipes for performing common tasks, hints, and some automatic features that make it accessible to the non-professional. At the same time, in the hands of a professional, it produces professional results. The bottom line is that if you know how to use Photoshop Elements 2, as you will by the end of this Complete Course, the possibilities are limited only by your imagination.

How Photoshop Elements 2 Compares to Photoshop

The Adobe Photoshop Elements feature set and interface are based on those in the full version of Adobe Photoshop. In addition to the features mentioned above, Photoshop Elements 2 includes drawing and painting tools, vector-based type and shape tools, customizable brushes, selection tools, layers, filters, adjustments, tool options, Web-related features, and lots more.

The first question many people ask about Photoshop Elements 2 is how it compares to Photoshop, the flagship of digital image editing. The answer is that there are some features that are unique to Photoshop and some that are unique to Photoshop Elements.

For the most part, the Photoshop features that you won't find in Photoshop Elements are higher-end tools and functions, like curves, paths, and controls for accessing channels and masks. After all, Adobe has to justify the significant price difference between these programs.

Don't let the lack of some high-end features discourage you. Workarounds can achieve what some of these absent features would offer. For example, as you work through this course, you learn workarounds for accessing layer masks and information in hidden channels.

A fair comparison of Photoshop Elements to Photoshop is by no means a one-way street. Photoshop Elements 2 has features that are not included in the current version of Photoshop (Photoshop 7), most of which are aimed at making the interface easier to use and understand. Unique features of Photoshop Elements 2 include the following:

» Selection brush for quickly selecting pixels

» Quick Fix window for correcting photographs

» Red Eye brush

» Fill Flash adjustment

» Backlighting adjustment

» Shortcuts bar

» How To palette of image-editing recipes

» Hints palette with tool and palette explanations

» Thumbnails that visually describe each filter, effect, and layer style

» PDF Slidemaker

» Photomerge for making panoramas

This is just an overview of what Photoshop Elements 2 has to offer. You learn much more about its features, functions, and potential as you work through this book.

Project Overview

The Complete Course Project

What you have in your hands is not just a book. It is a full-blown, tutorial-based curriculum for learning Adobe Photoshop Elements 2. The thrust of this course is to teach you the features and functions of the program and to do so in a real-world context. That context is a design project that runs throughout the book— the creation of images for a line of greeting cards with the central theme of action sports.

You create a sophisticated image for each card as you work through the tutorials in the book. The images are designed to be printable on your desktop printer, so that at the end of the course you have a series of cards in hand. Use them to show off your digital-imaging skills, to remind yourself of techniques you learned in these pages, and to stimulate ideas for future projects.This short chapter familiarizes you with the course project and with the hardware, software, and files you need to get started.

Stepping Through the Project

This course is based on step-by-step tutorials, each of which does two things. The tutorials teach you a set of related program features and imaging techniques. At the same time, they walk you through the steps of creating the course project, which is a series of greeting cards with a sports theme.

It's important to understand that each tutorial builds on and assumes that you know the skills taught in the preceding tutorials. This means that as you move through the course, you might occasionally have to flip back to an earlier tutorial to remind yourself of a detail you learned there. Beginners fare best by moving through the tutorials in order.

The tutorials are made up of progressive steps, many of which are accompanied by a sentence or two to explain the reasons for or results of taking that step. Tutorials are peppered with occasional notes, tips, cautions, and sidebars that contain extra information, but are not as crucial to completing the tutorial as the steps themselves. Here and there, you find discussions that explain larger issues, like image resolution or file formats. As you can tell, this book contains lots of information. I suggest that you focus on the tutorials and their steps, and view the rest as a readily available source of information that you can reference when you're working on this or your own projects.

The larger organization of the book is simple. Tutorials are grouped into sessions (chapters), each of which concerns a subject common to its tutorials. Sessions are grouped into logical parts. A quick look through the Table of Contents gives you an idea of what each session and part covers.

Let me emphasize that this course is designed to be hands-on. I encourage you not only to read this book, but also to perform it at your computer. I've taught many people how to use digital-imaging software, so I can say with some authority that most people learn best by doing. So after you get your hardware set up and your software and tutorial files installed, as explained next, go ahead and start 'doing' by working through the Confidence Builder and then Session 1, Creating and Saving Images.

The Tutorial Files

The tutorial files, which are on a CD-ROM at the back of the book, are an important part of this course. Install the tutorial files onto your hard drive before you get started, following the instructions for either Windows or Macintosh computers in Appendix A. After installation, some Windows users may have a few more steps to follow to change the read-only status of the installed files and to make the file extensions visible. All of that is covered in Appendix A. You use the tutorial files frequently, so make sure they're installed in an easily accessible place on your hard drive. You should run all tutorial files from your computer, rather than from the CD-ROM.

The Tutorial Files folder that you install on your hard drive includes a subfolder for each session, which contains the source files you use for the tutorials in that session. Each subfolder contains at least one file with the word _end in the filename. The _end file is an example of how a particular image that you create looks when at the end of a session. You also find iteration files in some of the Tutorial Files subfolders. These are fresh versions of those files that are used in more than one session. The text instructs you when you have the choice of using an iteration file instead of the file you've been building. This gives you an option if you get lost, mess up a file, or just want to skip ahead.

I strongly suggest that you create a new folder on your hard drive called ccproject (for Complete Course project). This is the folder into which you save all your working files as you go through the tutorials. It's also where you save the final version of each greeting card you create. Whenever you're prompted to save, navigate to the ccproject folder. Don't save your working files over your tutorial files because you're likely to get confused about which file is which. If you ever need a fresh copy of a tutorial file, you can always reinstall it from the CD-ROM.

Software Requirements

You need a copy of Adobe Photoshop Elements 2 for Windows or Macintosh. If the first version of the program, which was called Adobe Photoshop Elements, is already installed on your computer, remove it. I don't suggest you use that first version for this course because some of its features are different than those in Adobe Photoshop Elements 2. Install your copy of Adobe Photoshop Elements 2 following the manufacturer's instructions.

If you don't have a copy of Photoshop Elements 2, you can use a tryout version of the program. The tryout version is currently available as a free download from the Adobe Systems, Inc. Web site: www.adobe.com. If you recently purchased a scanner, check the disks that came with it to see if a copy of Photoshop Elements 2 is included there. Some manufacturers and distributors are bundling the program with their hardware.

You probably already have a Web browser installed on your computer. Adobe recommends Internet Explorer 5.0, 5.5, or 6.0 (updated with applicable Service Packs) for Windows users, but no particular browser for Macintosh users. Internet Explorer can be downloaded from www.microsoft.com, Netscape Navigator from www.netscape.com, and Apple Safari from www.apple.com.

You can also download a free copy of Adobe Reader from www.adobe.com. It is useful for viewing the results of the tutorial on creating a PDF slide show.

System Requirements

Adobe's recommended system requirements for Photoshop Elements 2.0 are as follows.

Windows

» Intel Pentium processor

» Microsoft Windows 98, Windows 98 Second Edition, Windows Millennium Edition, Windows 2000, or Windows XP Home/Professional

» 128MB of RAM

» 150MB of available hard-disk space

» Color monitor capable of displaying thousands of colors at a resolution of 800x600 or greater

» Internet Explorer 5.0, 5.5, or 6.0 (updated with applicable Service Packs)

» CD-ROM drive

Macintosh

» PowerPC processor

» Mac OS 9.1, 9.2.x, or Mac OS X v.10.1.3 or later

» 128MB of RAM with virtual memory on

» 350MB of available hard-disk space

» Color monitor capable of displaying thousands of colors at a resolution of 800x600 or greater

» CD-ROM drive

Other hardware requirements

Hardware requirements for this course are minimal. They include the following:

CD-ROM drive. You need a CD-ROM drive to install the tutorial files from the CD-ROM at the back of the book. The CD-ROM and its files can be read on both Windows and Macintosh platforms.

Optional digital camera, memory card reader, and scanner. Neither a digital camera, a memory card reader, nor a scanner is required to work through the tutorials in this book. However, if you have access to any of this equipment and the software that it comes with, it comes in handy in Session 1, which covers importing digital photographs and scans into Photoshop Elements 2.

Part II
Understanding
Basic Features

Session 1

Creating and Saving Images

Session Introduction

This session is about the ins and outs of Photoshop Elements 2—getting images into the program so that you can work with them and saving content out of the program. Photoshop Elements 2 helps simplify the potentially frustrating process of acquiring content from a variety of sources. It has features that you can use to find and open photographs, to scan documents and objects, and even to import still frames from video footage. In this session, you learn all about these features as you create a greeting card that starts with a new file and includes a scanned image, a photograph, an image imported from a PDF file, and video frames. Along the way, you learn critical information about file resolution, scanning, integration with digital cameras, file formats, and saving your work.

TOOLS YOU'LL USE
Welcome Screen, New command, Save commands, Import command, Move tool, Layers palette, File Browser, Batch Processing command, Rectangular Marquee tool, Import Video Frames command, Import PDF Image command, Magic Eraser tool

CD-ROM FILES NEEDED
01_scan_2.psd, 01_photo.jpg, 01_boxmovie.mpg, 01_boxmovie1.psd, 01_boxmovie2.psd, 01boxmovie3.psd, 01_calendar.pdf, all files in the biking folder, 01_boxing_end.psd

TIME REQUIRED
45 minutes

Tutorial
» Creating a Document from Scratch

The first step in creating this session's greeting card is to generate a brand new file with a solid color background. This is also where you learn about file size and color mode.

1. **Launch or restart Photoshop Elements 2.**

   If you did not reset the program's preferences to their defaults in the Confidence Builder chapter, do so now by pressing Alt+Ctrl+Shift (Macintosh: Option+⌘+Shift) as the program starts up and clicking Yes when prompted to delete the Settings file. If this is the first time you've opened Photoshop Elements 2 after installing, you are prompted to choose color settings. Click Cancel. You come back to color settings later.

2. **Click the New File button on the Welcome Screen to open the New dialog box.**

   The Welcome Screen opens automatically when you launch the program. If it's not showing, choose Window→Welcome from the Photoshop Elements 2 Menu bar.

The Welcome Screen

The Welcome Screen is one of several ways to access commands and features that you might use when you begin working on a project. The Welcome Screen closes automatically when you choose one of its options. You can reach all the same commands from menus and shortcuts in the program, so you probably won't use the Welcome Screen much after its brief initial appearance. If you want to bring back the Welcome Screen at any time, choose Window→Welcome. Here's a summary of what each of the buttons on the Welcome Screen does.

» The New File button opens the New dialog box, used for creating documents from scratch. This button is a shortcut for choosing File→New.

» The Browse for File button opens the File Browser, from which you can visually find, open, and manage files. This is a shortcut for choosing File→Browse.

» The Connect to Camera or Scanner button opens a menu of cameras, scanners, and other devices installed on your system from which you can import images. It's a shortcut for choosing File→Import.

» The Common Issues button opens the How To palette, in which you can view step-by-step recipes for doing common tasks, like removing red eye. This button is a shortcut for choosing Window→How To and selecting Common Issues.

» The Tutorial button opens the Photoshop Elements 2 on-screen Help system to a page that offers illustrated tutorials about how to accomplish particular tasks, such as fixing a scanned image. This is a shortcut for choosing Help→Photoshop Elements Help and scrolling down to Photoshop Elements 2.0 Tutorials in the menu on the left side of the browser window.

» You can deselect the Show this screen at startup check box to stop the Welcome Screen from automatically appearing every time you launch the program.

» The Exit Welcome Screen button closes the Welcome Screen.

<**N O T E**>

Photoshop Elements 2, like other programs, opens in an application window on Windows computers and on the desktop on Macintosh computers. The menu bar is located at the top of the application window on Windows and at the top of the desktop on Macintosh. The menu bar holds menus from which you access program commands.

3. **Type** 01_boxing **in the Name field of the New dialog box.**
   You do not have to type a file extension (like .psd). This is added automatically when you save the file.

4. **Choose inches from the menus to the right of the Width and Height fields.**
   Do this prior to entering dimensions into the Width and Height fields, because if these unit-of-measurement fields are set to pixels rather than inches, the program won't allow you to type in anything other than integers.

5. **Type** 6.25 **in the Width field and** 4.625 **in the Height field.**
   Notice that the Preset Sizes field is set to Custom. That's because you typed your own dimensions into the Width and Height fields, rather than choosing preset dimensions from the Preset Sizes menu.

6. **Make sure the menu to the right of the Resolution field is set to pixels/inch (pixels per inch). Type** 240 **into the Resolution field.**
   See the discussion on Understanding Resolution that follows this tutorial to learn more about what resolution means and how to choose an appropriate resolution for a new file.

7. **Choose RGB Color from the Mode menu.**

8. **Select the radio button for White in the Contents area, and click OK.**
   A document window opens containing a 6.25-inch-wide x 4.625-inch-high single layer image filled with solid white.

<**N O T E**>

If you have not yet made a ccproject folder on your desktop, do so now by clicking the Create New Folder icon (Macintosh: New Folder button) in the Save As dialog box. You use the ccproject folder as a place to store all the files you generate as you work through this book.

9. **Choose File→Save As to save the new file for the first time.**
   This opens the Save As dialog box.

<**N O T E**>

You may have noticed that the Save item on the File menu was grayed out. You can't use the Save command until you use Save As at least once, because Save just replaces the last version of a file without asking for new file information. This makes Save a handy command to use frequently as you work.

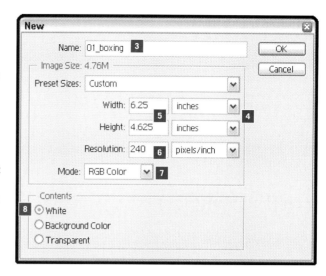

Color Modes

Color mode means a color model that describes a system of colors. RGB (red, green, blue) is the only color mode in which you can create a new file in Photoshop Elements 2. Photoshop Elements 2 does not offer CMYK mode, which is the color mode used most often in commercial printing. Each pixel in an RGB file is composed of a combination of red, green, and blue color values. There are 16.7 million color combinations (24-bit color) to choose from, resulting from 256 brightness values for each of the three primary colors. RGB is the appropriate color mode for image editing in Photoshop Elements 2 for a number of reasons: Computer monitors display color in RGB mode, most digital cameras and scanners produce images in RGB mode, and most desktop printers (even those with CMYK ink cartridges) use RGB drivers. That's not to mention the wide range of RGB colors available and the ability to save RGB images in many file formats.

You use the other color modes in Photoshop Elements 2 less often. Grayscale mode has no color; it is composed of 256 values of gray, black, and white. Bitmap mode also has no color; it uses only pure black and white dots to simulate grays. Indexed Color mode, which has a very limited palette of 256 colors, is used primarily to prepare GIF images for the Internet. You can convert an image from one color mode to another by choosing Image→Mode from the Menu bar.

< N O T E >
The Save As dialog box is one of the few places where there is a noticeable cross-platform difference in the Photoshop Elements 2 interface. For that reason, I've included both the Windows and Macintosh versions of this dialog box in this illustration. As you can see, the differences are cosmetic only. Some fields have slightly different names and are located in different positions in the dialog box in the two platforms.

10. **In the Save As dialog box, click in the Save In (Macintosh: the Where) field and navigate to the ccproject folder you created on your desktop.**

11. **Make sure that the Format field in the Save As dialog box is set to Photoshop (*.PSD, *.PDD) (Macintosh: Photoshop). Leave the other selections at their defaults for now.**

< N O T E >
PSD (Photoshop) format is the native file format for Adobe Photoshop Elements 2 and Adobe Photoshop. I suggest that you do all your editing work in PSD format and save the final product as a PSD, because that format honors and retains all features of Photoshop Elements 2 and Photoshop. If you need a copy of the image in another format, you have a couple of options: File→Save As→As a Copy or File→Save a Copy.

12. **Click the Save button in the Save As dialog box to save the file and close the dialog box.**
    Notice that saving a file with the Save As command does not close the document. It remains open on your desktop.

Preset Document Sizes

If you are creating a standard-sized document (which I don't do very often), you can choose from a menu of Preset Sizes in the New dialog box to have the program set the dimensions and resolution of the document for you. Items in this menu that are intended for print are measured in inches and are set to a default resolution of 300 pixels per inch. You can change this default resolution in Photoshop Elements 2 preferences. (Edit [Macintosh: Photoshop Elements]→Preferences→Units & Rulers→Print Resolution). So, for example, my Epson desktop printer does a good job of printing at 240 pixels per inch. To save on file size, I changed my Document Preset Print Resolution preference to 240.

Items in the Preset Sizes menu that are intended for the screen (for example, for use on the Web, in video, or in on-screen presentations) are measured in pixels rather than inches. The Preferences dialog box sets Document Preset Screen Resolution to 72 pixels per inch. You can ignore this setting (don't worry about whether you should change it) because resolution has no real effect on a document destined for screen rather than print. Resolution is nothing more than the number of pixels in a printed inch of a document, so resolution is not an issue when printing is not involved.

13. **Click the Foreground Color Box at the bottom of the toolbox to open the Color Picker.**

14. **In the Color Picker make sure that the Only Web Colors check box is deselected, and type the following values in the RGB fields—R:** 134, **G:** 69, **B:** 17.

    The cursor moves to the defined color in the Color field on the left side of the Color Picker. The newly selected color appears above the existing Foreground color in the color box to the right of the Color slider. You can ignore the small cube to the right of that box, which indicates that the selected color is not Web-safe.

15. **Click OK to change the Foreground Color box in the toolbox to a tobacco color and to close the Color Picker.**

16. **Choose Edit→Fill from the menu bar at the top of the screen.**

    This opens the Fill dialog box.

17. **In the Fill dialog box, select Use: Foreground Color, and click OK.**

    The image background fills with a tobacco color and the Fill dialog box closes.

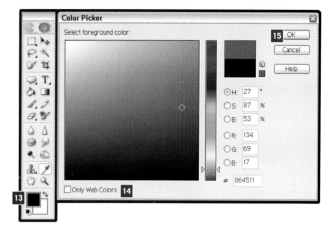

<NOTE>

You frequently fill layers and selections with color, pattern, or gradient. So you may want to remember the keyboard shortcut for filling with the foreground color, which is Alt+Backspace (Macintosh: Option+Delete).

<NOTE>

Another way to create a solid color document from scratch is to select a Background color before creating the image, by clicking the Background Color box in the toolbox and choosing a color in the Color Picker. Then create a new image, but select the radio button for Background Color in the New dialog box.

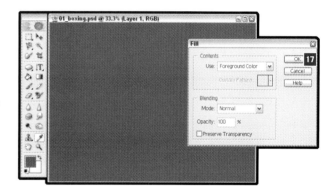

18. **Choose File→Save to save** 01_boxing.psd **with its changes, and leave it open for the next tutorial.**

    You now have a document with a solid color background that you created from scratch. You add more artwork to this document from other sources in the tutorials to come.

Discussion

Understanding Resolution

Resolution is not as complex a subject as you may think. It is simply a way of talking about one unit of measurement (pixels) in terms of another (inches). You use pixels to measure an image when it is on screen. You use inches to measure a printed document. Resolution is the number of pixels of information in an image that would make up each inch of the image if the image were printed.

Pixel stands for picture element—a tiny rectangle of color information that is the basic unit from which many digital images are built. An on-screen image is defined by the number of pixels it contains. A 1600-pixel-wide x 1200-pixel-high image is wider and taller on a computer screen than an 800 x 600 pixel image. If your monitor is set to display only 800 x 600 pixels, you are able to see all of the second image, but only part of the first unless you scroll around or reduce the magnification of the image.

The pixel dimensions of an image and the display resolution of the computer on which the image is viewed are all you need to know to estimate how big an image will be on a particular monitor. However, the number of pixels alone does not tell you how big an image will be when printed. That depends on the number of pixels assigned to each printed inch of the image. The higher this print resolution (the more pixels per printed inch of an image), the better the printed image looks, but only up to a limit. That limit is the highest resolution that your particular printer can reproduce.

For example, my Epson printer can't reproduce much more than 240 pixels per inch. So there's no reason to create a file to send to that printer that has more than 240 pixels/inch resolution. Choosing a higher resolution would unnecessarily increase the total size of the file with the following consequences: The file would take up more storage space, it would be slower to transmit electronically and perhaps slower to print, and it might be slower to work with in editing programs like Photoshop Elements 2. On the other hand, if I set the resolution too low, say 72 pixels per inch, the printed file would probably look pixilated or blurry because it wouldn't have enough information to satisfy my printer's capability. (By the way, that's why low-resolution files downloaded from the Internet look so bad when printed.)

So how should you use all this information when you are creating a new file in Photoshop Elements 2 or scanning an image to bring into the program? First, find out from your printer's manufacturer the real print resolution of your printer, and set the resolution of the files you create to that number. Second, don't be fooled by inflated claims of resolution. Most desktop inkjet printers use around three dots of ink to reproduce every pixel. If the advertised maximum resolution of a desktop inkjet printer is in the thousands, that is probably a reference to dots per inch (dpi)—triple the actual printer resolution. Current desktop inkjet printers offer optimal resolution of 240 to 300 pixels per inch. Third, don't wait until after a file is created to address its resolution. It's usually okay to reduce a file's resolution, but it's decidedly not okay to increase file resolution, because your software or hardware has to fabricate information to fill in nonexistent pixels. If an image is likely to be output in several ways, create it with enough resolution for the most demanding of those outputs and downsize if necessary.

Tutorial

» Scanning into Photoshop Elements 2

Scanners are useful for making digital images of photographic prints and slides, flat art, and even three-dimensional objects. Photoshop Elements 2 makes the process easier by providing an interface for scanning images directly into the program. If you have a flatbed scanner, you can follow along with this tutorial by scanning a dark textured object with an antique look, like the marbled frontispiece of a book, a scrap of dark leather, a piece of old screen, or a weathered plank. If you have no scanner or item to scan, read through the tutorial. You can join in at Step 7 using 01_scan_2.psd, a pre-scanned image in the Tutorial Files→Session 01 folder on your hard drive.

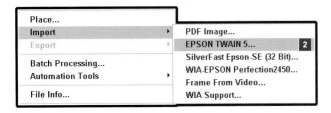

1. **Make sure that you've installed any software, drivers, and plug-ins that may have come with your scanner, and that the scanner is connected to your computer according to the manufacturer's instructions.**

   In order for your scanner to show up in the Import menu in Photoshop Elements 2, a compatible plug-in must be installed in the Photoshop Elements 2 import-export plug-ins folder on your computer. If you're lucky, your scanner's software automatically installed such a plug-in in the correct spot.

2. **Choose File→Import to reveal a menu of scanners, cameras, and other acquisition devices that are connected to your computer and for which a compatible import-export plug-in is installed.**

   Choose the name of your scanner from that menu if you see it there. If you do not see your scanner in this menu, read the Help, No Scanner! sidebar. If you do see your scanner, continue to the next step.

Help, No Scanner!

If you do not see your properly connected scanner in the File→Import menu in Photoshop Elements 2, try to locate a plug-in for your scanner. Check the CD-ROM or other media that came with your scanner, the scanner manufacturer's Web site, and third-party download sites such as www.versiontracker.com. Look for a plug-in specific to your scanner's software or a TWAIN plug-in that works with your scanner. (TWAIN is standard for drivers that connect scanners and digital cameras to applications.) If you find a promising plug-in, copy and paste it into C:→Program Files→Adobe→Photoshop Elements 2→Plug-Ins→Import-Export (Macintosh: copy and drag it to Applications→Adobe→Photoshop Elements 2→Plug-Ins→Import/Export.) If you're using Windows, you must restart your computer in order to load the plug-in. Restarting isn't necessary if you're using a Mac. Then go back to Step 2.

If you can't find an appropriate plug-in, you have several other options. If you're using Windows XP or Windows Me, you can scan directly into Photoshop Elements 2 using WIA support (Windows Image Acquisition support). WIA is an architecture that facilitates communication between scanners and digital cameras on the one hand and imaging applications like Photoshop Elements 2 on the other. Unfortunately, WIA interfaces are barebones. They lack the detailed settings found in other scanning interfaces that allow you to control the dimensions, resolution, bit depth, and other parameters of your scans. If you're using Macintosh OX 10.2 or later, you can try using the similar built-in Image Capture utility that is compatible with some scanners.

If none of these solutions work for you, consider scanning independently of Photoshop Elements 2 using your scanner's proprietary software. Save the resulting scan as a TIFF file. In Photoshop Elements 2, find and open the scanned file using the File Browser or the File→Open command. Choose File→Save As and resave the scan in PSD format. You can then incorporate the scan into your project like any other existing file. This method involves a few more steps than scanning directly into Photoshop Elements 2, but it may prove to be the best solution for you.

<TIP>
You can also access the Import menu by clicking the Import button on the Toolbar or bringing back the Welcome Screen and choosing Connect to Camera or Scanner. This opens the Select Import Source dialog box from which you can access the Import menu.

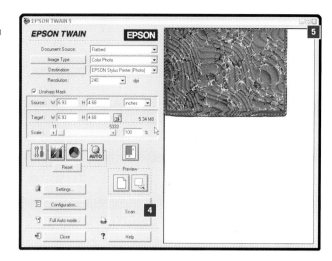

3. **Set the controls in your scanning software, making sure that the resulting file will be at least 6.25 inches wide by 4.625 inches high with a resolution of 240 pixels per inch, so that it fits the design of this project.**

4. **Start the scan in your scanning software.**

   Most scanning software includes a Scan button that you can click. If you scanned directly into Photoshop Elements 2, your scanned image opens in a Photoshop Elements document window.

5. **When the scan is completed, close the scanning software by clicking the red button at the top right (Macintosh: top left) of the application window.**

   The image remains open, but unsaved, in Photoshop Elements 2.

6. **Choose File➔Save As to save the scanned image for the first time. In the Save in (Macintosh: Where) field of the Save As dialog box, navigate to the ccproject folder on your hard drive. Type 01_scan.psd in the File Name (Macintosh: Save As) field, and click Save.**

<NOTE>
You don't have to spend time straightening, cropping, and touching up this scan, as you normally would do to a new scan, because this is a background image, much of which will be hidden from view. Its function is to provide pattern and texture, rather than to appear flawless.

<NOTE>
Leave the scanned file 01_scan.psd open. In the following steps you combine it with the document you created from scratch in the last tutorial—01_boxing.psd.

7. **Make sure 01_boxing.psd is still open from the first tutorial in this session.**

   If it is not, reopen it now from its location in your ccproject folder.

<NOTE>
Although your particular scanning software may look different than the Epson TWAIN scanning interface in the illustration, its elements are instructive. It's typical to begin with a prescan. In this interface, you click the Preview button to invoke a prescan. Then click the green Image Location button to isolate the previewed object with marching ants. Set the Document Source (flatbed, slide, or negative scanner), the Image Type (which determines the bit-depth, or number of potential colors, in the scan), and the Destination (which determines the default resolution of the scan). The physical dimensions of the original object are set automatically in the Source fields by the location of the marching ants. The Target and Scale fields can be used to make the scanned image bigger or smaller than the original object. Leave Scale at 100% and target at the same size as Source to scan your object at 100%. I recommend leaving the rest of the settings at their defaults, so that you have an uncorrected scan to edit in Photoshop Elements 2.

<TIP>
It's better to create a scan that's too big for your design than one that is too small. You usually can perform a post-scan file size reduction without negative consequence, but increasing a document's size is likely to result in a blurry, low-quality image as your editing software struggles to fill in missing information and stretch existing pixels.

<NOTE>
If for any reason you did not create the scanned file 01_scan.psd, you can continue this tutorial using a prebuilt replica, 01_scan_2.psd. Choose File➔Open, navigate to the Tutorial Files➔Session 01 folder on your hard drive, select 01_scan_2.psd, and click Open. Remember that the instructions will continue to refer to 01 scan.psd.

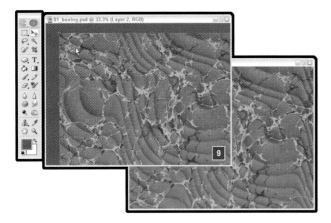

Using Photoshop Elements 2 as a Scanning Calculator

If your scanning software doesn't have separate controls for dpi, physical dimensions, scale, or other settings, you can still make an appropriately sized scan as long as the scanning software displays the overall file size of the scan. The trick is to use Photoshop Elements as a calculator to determine the overall file size that you need, following these instructions:

Choose File→New in Photoshop Elements 2 to open the New dialog box. In the New dialog box, set the Width and Height fields to inches and type in the physical dimensions of the largest print you want to make from your scan. Set the resolution field to pixels/inch and type in the resolution of your printer. (Read the Discussion: Understanding Resolution to learn about ink jet printer resolution.) Set Color Mode to RGB if you want to print in color. Photoshop Elements 2 calculates the total file size you need to print the scan with these dimensions and displays it in the Image Size field of the New dialog box. For example, a 6.25-inch x 4.625-inch file at 240 pixels per inch requires a 4.76 Megabyte file. Jot down the Image Size calculation and close the New dialog box.

When you return to your scanning software, manipulate whatever controls are available so that the total file size readout in the scanning software is at least as big as the Image Size number Photoshop Elements 2 calculated for you. It doesn't matter which scanning controls you adjust to get to that number because you can alter the physical dimensions and resolution of the resulting image in Photoshop Elements 2 after you make the scan, as long as it contains enough overall file information for your print requirements.

8. **Set** 01_boxing.psd **and** 01_scan.psd **to the same magnification so that you can see whether their sizes will match when you combine them. Select the Zoom tool in the toolbox. Select the Zoom Out button (the icon with the minus sign) in the Options bar at the top of the screen. Click inside both of the open images,** 01_boxing.psd **and** 01_scan.psd, **until the magnification of each is reduced to 33.3%.**

The amount of reduction is reported in the title bar at the top of each document window. With the two documents at the same magnification, you can see that they are approximately the same size, so they fit together nicely.

<CAUTION>

In the next step you combine the two images, 01_scan.psd and 01_boxing.psd. It may take some practice to coordinate the movements in the next step. Take it slow, and if you make a mistake, click Edit→Step Backward and try again.

9. **Arrange the two open images,** 01_scan.psd **and** 01_boxing.psd, **so that you can see part of both. With the Move tool selected, click and hold Ctrl+Shift (Macintosh: ⌘+Shift) while you click anywhere inside the scanned pattern** 01_scan.psd **and drag into the solid brown image** 01_boxing.psd. **Release the mouse only first. Then release the keys.**

This makes a copy of the scanned pattern in the solid brown image. Holding the Ctrl and Shift keys deposits the scanned pattern in exactly the same position in the solid brown document window that it had in its own document window. The scanned pattern should completely obscure the solid brown color in 01_boxing.psd. If it does not, click the scanned pattern in 01_boxing.psd and drag it into place with the Move tool.

10. **Click on** 01_scan.psd **to activate that image, and choose File→Close. You won't use this image again.**

11. **Click on** 01_boxing.psd, **and choose File→Save to save the combined image. Leave this image open.**

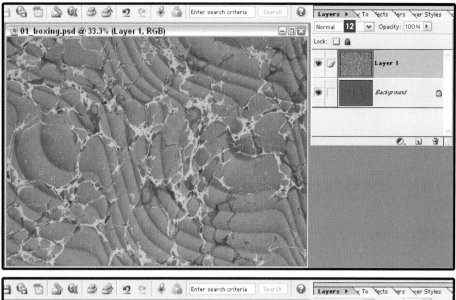

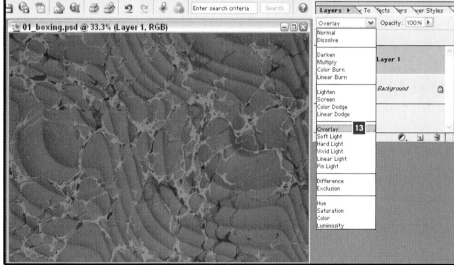

12. **Move your cursor over the tabs in the Palette Well on the right side of the Shortcut bar, and when the Layers tab comes to the front, click on that tab.**

This opens the Layers palette. Notice that there are two layers in the Layers palette: the brown *Background* layer, and the pattern **Layer 1**.

< C A U T I O N >

If you click anywhere else on the screen, the Layers palette closes back into the Palette Well and you have to open it again.

13. **Click in the gray (Macintosh: white) area of** Layer 1 **to select that layer. Click the Blending Modes button at the top left of the Layers palette (which currently reads Normal), and choose Overlay from that menu.**

This changes the way the colors on **Layer 1** blend with the colors on the *Background* layer below.

14. **Choose File→Save to resave** 01_boxing.psd **with these changes. Leave this image open.**

In this tutorial you created an image by scanning an object. You combined the scan with the brown background image you cre-ated from scratch earlier, using a layer blending mode to blend the two images together to make a unique patterned background.

> **49**

Discussion

Getting Digital Photographs into Photoshop Elements 2

You can use several methods to get photographs out of a digital camera and directly into Photoshop Elements 2, or at least into your computer where you can open and edit them in Photoshop Elements 2. These methods include using the Import command in Photoshop Elements 2, mounting a card or camera as a mass storage device, using a USB card reader, and importing files with third-party software.

The Import command in Photoshop Elements 2

The Import menu (accessed from the File menu, the Import shortcut on the Shortcuts bar, or the Welcome Screen) works the same way with digital cameras as it does with scanners. If you connect a digital camera to your computer and install the software and drivers that came with the camera, that camera theoretically should show up in the Import menu in Photoshop Elements 2. By clicking that item on the Import menu, you can open images in the camera from within Photoshop Elements 2, choose the images you want to edit, and save them to your hard drive.

In Windows XP and ME, you can accomplish all of this by accessing WIA support from the Import menu, and selecting the check box labeled Open Acquired Elements in Photoshop Elements.

Unfortunately, photographers are often heard to complain that their particular digital cameras do not show up in the program's Import menu. So this method is not ideal for everyone. It is also inconvenient to connect and disconnect cables between the camera and its power source and the camera and the computer each time you want to import files.

Mounting a storage device

When you connect some cameras or cards to a computer, the computer recognizes them as mounted storage devices and treats them like just another hard drive. You can use the File Browser in Photoshop Elements 2 to view the image files on the card or camera and to open images. You can then save images as PSD files onto your hard drive.

This method, when it works, is more straightforward than the Import method described above. I like using this method with a memory card that I remove from the camera, insert into a PC card mount, and slip into the PC slot in my laptop. This is fast and efficient, and it doesn't involve unwieldy cable connections to the camera.

Using a USB card reader

If you have no camera or other device that mounts as a storage device, you can attach a USB card reader to your computer and feed it memory cards removed from your digital camera. You can copy images onto your computer through the USB card reader and open them in Photoshop Elements 2 for editing. This relatively simple method is reliable and, like the mounted-drive method, avoids connecting and reconnecting the camera.

Importing through other software

Many digital cameras come with their own transfer and file organization software (like Nikon's Nikon View). You can use this software to import files from a recognized card reader, storage device, or camera, and then open the files in Photoshop Elements 2 for editing. Mac users can use Apple's iPhoto for the same purpose.

Software like iPhoto is also useful for organizing and managing your digital photographs. Alternatively, you can use the File Browser built into Photoshop Elements for file management tasks, as you learn in the next tutorial.

Tutorial
» Managing Digital Photographs with the File Browser

Do any of the following situations sound familiar? You search for a particular image in your collection that you would recognize by sight, but you can't remember its filename. Or you import 700 photographs into your system, all with incomprehensible file names like 3502354.jpg. Or you take a mix of horizontal and vertical shots and are dismayed to realize that all the vertical images need to be rotated to be viewed properly. Adobe has come up with a way to solve all these problems and more in the form of the File Browser, which is a multitalented utility that's part image viewer, part file manager, and part batch processor.

<TIP>
You can customize the appearance of the File Browser in several ways. Click and drag the pane borders to change the size of the panes. Click the double-pointed arrow at the bottom of the thumbnail pane to close all but the thumbnail pane. Click the display button at the bottom of the thumbnail pane (which currently reads Large) to change the look of the thumbnails.

1. **Choose Window→File Browser to open the File Browser.**
   Another way to open the File Browser is by choosing File→Browse.

<NOTE>
If you haven't yet installed the tutorial files from the CD-ROM at the back of the book to your hard drive, do so now, following the instructions in Appendix A.

2. **Go to the file hierarchy at the top left of the File Browser, and click the biking folder in the Session 01 folder inside the Tutorial Files folder, on your hard drive.**
   This reveals thumbnails of the files in the selected folder. It may take a minute to see the thumbnails because the file browser is copying them into a cache.

3. **Click on one of the thumbnails on the right side of the File Browser.**
   This displays a larger version of the image and detailed information about the file in the left column. The File Browser can display information that it gleans from the image, as well as information generated by a digital camera about the camera settings and photographic conditions (EXIF data). The button at the bottom left of the File Browser controls which data is displayed.

4. **In the File Browser, click on the center thumbnail (the column of bicycle riders labeled** 326454.jpg**) in order to select that image. If you look closely, you can see that this is a vertical shot that is lying on its side.**

   Digital photographs that are shot vertically often come into your computer with the wrong orientation and must be rotated to be viewed correctly.

5. **To rotate the selected thumbnail 90° so that it is displayed vertically, click the rotate button at the bottom of the File Browser.**

   This generates a prompt explaining that this rotates the thumbnail, but does not rotate the actual image until you open the image file.

6. **To make sure that this prompt doesn't reappear each time you rotate an image, select Don't show again. To dismiss this prompt and invoke the rotation, click OK.**

   The selected thumbnail should now appear right side up in the File Browser. To rotate the image itself, double-click the thumbnail to open the full image. Then close the full image, clicking Yes at the prompt that asks if you want to save changes to the document before closing.

7. **Right-click (Macintosh: Ctrl+click) any of the thumbnails in the File Browser, and choose Select All from the contextual menu that appears. Then right-click (Macintosh: Ctrl+click) any of the selected thumbnails, and choose Batch Rename from the contextual menu.**

   The Batch Rename dialog box opens.

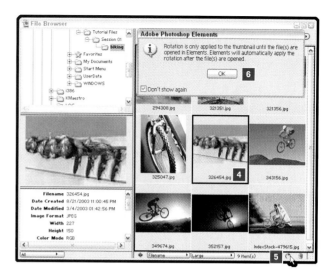

<NOTE>

Because digital photographs often come out of the camera with meaningless strings of numbers as filenames, they need to be renamed. Renaming the files one by one is too time-consuming. You rename all of the files in a folder at once using the Batch Rename command in the File Browser.

<NOTE>

Each click of the File Browser's rotate button turns the thumbnail 90° clockwise. Holding the Alt (Macintosh: Option) key rotates counterclockwise.

8. **Select the Rename in same folder radio button in the Batch Rename dialog box to rename the files in their original folder.**

   The other choice, Move to new folder, moves the files to a new folder and renames them there.

9. **Make sure the File Naming field on the bottom left of the Batch Rename dialog box is set to Document Name, and type** bike **in place of Document Name. Click in the File Naming field on the right and choose 2 Digit Serial Number from that menu. Click OK to close the dialog box and rename all the selected files automatically.**

   This renames each of the files with the prefix bike and a successive two-digit number (e.g., bike01.jpg, bike02.jpg, bike03.jpg). It's important that you at least set one of the naming fields to a changing parameter like serial number or serial letter, rather than a fixed parameter like document name or date. Otherwise, all the renamed files will have the same name.

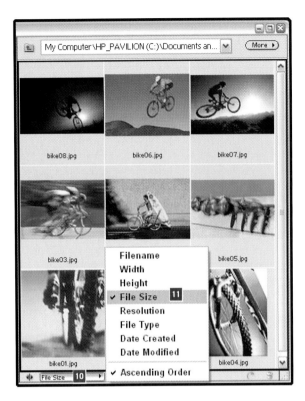

10. **Click the Sort By button at the bottom of the thumbnail pane in the File Browser.**
    A menu opens offering parameters by which you can sort the thumbnails.

11. **Choose File Size from the Sort By menu to reorder the thumbnails by their file size.**
    You can sort based on various image attributes, ranging from the date that images were created to the file format.

<NOTE>
Ascending Order, which is selected by default in the Sort By menu, orders these sorted thumbnails in the File Browser from smallest to largest file size.

12. **Select the Session 01 folder in the file hierarchy on the top left of the File Browser. On the right side of the File Browser, double-click the thumbnail labeled** 01_photo.jpg.
    This opens the corresponding full image file in Photoshop Elements 2. Visually locating and opening files like this is the most common use of the File Browser. The large thumbnails help you to accurately identify a file before opening.

13. **Close the File Browser by clicking the red button on its top-right corner (Macintosh OS X: top-left corner).**

<TIP>
The File Browser has other useful, but hard-to-find features. For example, if you right-click (Macintosh: Ctrl+click) any thumbnail and choose Reveal location in Explorer (Macintosh: Reveal location in Finder), the folder containing that file opens on your screen.

<TIP>
If you want to close the File Browser into the Palette Well, click the More button at the top right of the File Browser and choose Dock to Palette Well.

14. **Choose File→Save As to resave** 01_photo.jpg. **In the Save As dialog box, change the Format field from JPEG to Photoshop to save the file in PSD format as** 01_photo.psd. **Navigate to your ccproject folder, and click Save.**

<NOTE>

Although images acquired from digital cameras are often in JPEG format, it's best not to edit in that format because JPEG is a lossy compression scheme that degrades with each resave, and it does not support transparency, layers, and other useful editing features. PSD is the ideal format for editing in Photoshop Elements 2, so I suggest you save a copy of all your digital photographs in this format and archive the original JPEGs to keep them pristine.

15. **The file** 01_boxing.psd **should be open from an earlier tutorial. If it's not, open it from your ccproject folder.**

Batch Processing

Photoshop Elements 2 has a powerful Batch Processing feature (an alternative to Batch Renaming in the File Browser) that not only renames multiple files, but also resizes files and converts their file formats at the same time. Use the feature as a regular part of your workflow in order to preserve your original files while creating copies in an editable format. To access this feature, choose File→Batch Processing. Just be sure to choose a Destination folder that's different than your Source folder so you don't write over the original images by mistake.

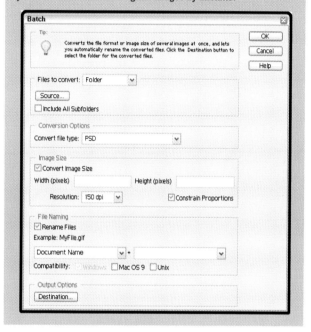

16. **Click the Layers tab in the Palette Well, and drag the Layers palette down into your application window (Macintosh: onto your desktop).**
    This opens the Layers palette so that it stays open. If you had just clicked the Layers palette tab in the Palette Well, the Layers palette would close back up into the Palette Well as soon as you clicked anywhere else on the screen.

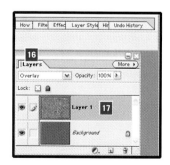

17. **Make sure that** Layer 1, **the layer with the scanned pattern, is highlighted in the Layers palette. If it's not, click the gray (Macintosh: white) area of** Layer 1 **in the Layers palette to select that layer.**
    Selecting **Layer 1** ensures that the new layer you create in the next step is located at the top of the layer stack, directly above **Layer 1**.

18. **Select the Move tool in the Toolbox, and click and drag** 01_photo.psd **into** 01_boxing.psd.
This places the boxing glove photo on a new, separate layer in your greeting card document.

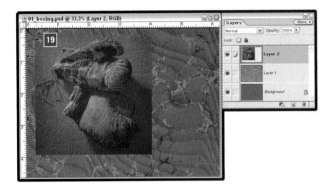

19. **Position the boxing glove photo in** 01_boxing.psd **to match the illustration by making sure its layer—**Layer 2—**is selected in the Layers palette, and clicking and dragging with the Move tool in the document window.**

<TIP>

If you want to be precise about placing the boxing glove photo, choose View→Rulers and position the photo so that its top-left corner is located at the ¼-inch mark on both rulers.

20. **Close** 01_photo.psd **without saving. Choose File→Save to resave** 01_boxing.psd **into your ccproject folder.**
Leave 01_boxing.psd open for the next tutorial.

Tutorial

» Importing Still Frames from Video

A unique feature in Photoshop Elements 2 is the ability to import frames from video footage as still images. In this tutorial, you import a few frames from an old movie into the collage you're creating for your boxing greeting card.

1. **Choose File→Import→Frame From Video from the menu bar.**
   This opens the Frame From Video window.

2. **Click the Browse button in the Frame From Video window to locate the movie file from which you want to import frames. Navigate to Tutorial Files→Session 01→01_boxmovie.mpg, and click Open to open that movie file in the Frame From Video window.**
   You may have to wait a moment for the movie to load. On a Windows machine, the Frame From Video feature works with any file format that is recognized by Windows Media Player, including MPG and AVI. On a Macintosh, the feature works with MPG and MOV (QuickTime format) files.

3. **In the Frame From Video window, click the Play button (the single right-facing arrow under the movie screen) to play the movie.**

4. **As the movie plays, click the Grab Frame button in the Frame From Video window three times to capture three frames of the movie.**
   You can use the controls under the movie screen to stop, rewind, and play the movie if you'd like to see the whole thing before grabbing frames.

5. **Click Done to close the Frame From Video dialog box.**
   You see three small document windows in your application window (Macintosh: on your desktop), each containing one of the frames that you grabbed from the movie.

6. **Your greeting card image—01_boxing.psd—should still be open from the last tutorial. If it's not, open it from your ccproject folder.**

7. **Click the topmost layer in the 01_boxing.psd Layers palette (Layer 2).**
   This ensures that the new layers you create in the next step are located at the top of the layer stack.

8. **With the Move tool, click anywhere inside one of the still movie frames and drag that movie frame into the 01_boxing.psd document window. Repeat this step for each of the other two movie frames.**
   This creates a separate layer in your greeting card image for each of the three movie frames.

< N O T E >

There are replicas of each of three movie frame files in the Session 01 Tutorial Files folder—01_boxmovie1.psd, 01_boxmovie2.psd, and 01_boxmovie3.psd. You can open and use these movie frame files instead of those you grabbed yourself if you prefer.

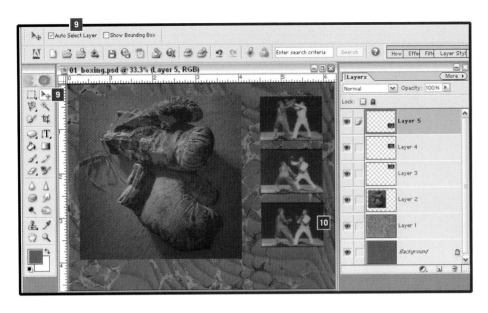

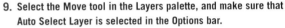

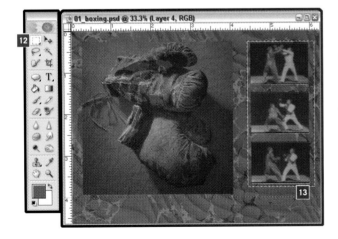

9. **Select the Move tool in the Layers palette, and make sure that Auto Select Layer is selected in the Options bar.**

   The Move tool's Auto Select Layer option is an alternative to manually selecting a layer in the Layers palette. When this option is active, clicking on a piece of artwork in the document window automatically selects the layer on which that artwork is located. You can move the contents of that layer independently of the rest of the image, as you do in the next step.

10. **In the** 01_boxing.psd **document window, click on one of the movie frames (automatically selecting its layer) and drag the frame into position to match the illustration. Repeat this step for each of the other two movie frames.**

    The left edge of each of the movie frames should be at the 4.5-inch mark on the horizontal ruler. The three movie frames can be in any vertical order.

11. **Close each of the three movie frame images without saving by clicking the red button at the top right of its document window (Macintosh: at the top left of the movie frame).**

12. **Select the Rectangular Marquee tool in the toolbox.**

    This is the first tool at the top left of the toolbox. If the Elliptical Marquee tool is showing there, click and hold and then select the Rectangular Marquee from the flyout menu.

13. **Click and drag a rectangular selection around the three movie frames, leaving a small border on all sides of the frames.**

    If you're not pleased with your first try, click anywhere in the document window to deselect and try again.

14. Select Layer 1 **(the pattern layer) in the Layers palette.**

If you don't see that layer, use the scroll bar on the Layers palette to scroll down the layer stack.

15. Choose Edit→Cut.

This cuts a rectangular hole in the pattern layer allowing the solid brown from the layer below to show through. If this is not the result you get, it means you did not have the pattern layer selected; choose Edit→Step Backward and try again.

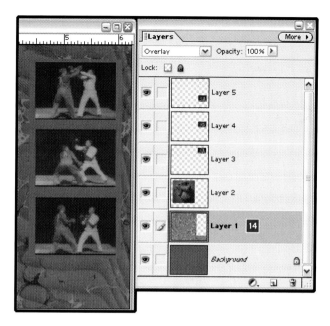

16. In the Layers palette, select Layer 5, **which contains one of the movie frames in the image.**

Don't worry if the corresponding movie frame is one other than the bottom movie frame as in the illustration. Any of the movie frames will do.

17. Click the Blending Mode button (currently labeled Normal) at the top of the Layers palette, and choose Color Dodge from the menu of layer blending modes.

The change in blending mode changes how the colors of the movie frame on this layer blend with the brown color on the *Background* layer below in the layer stack.

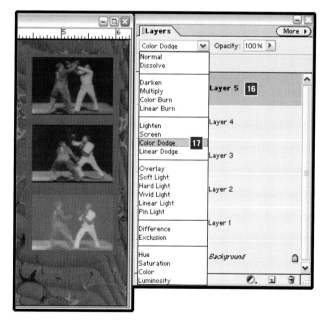

18. **In the Layers palette, select** Layer 4, **which contains another movie frame, and choose Linear Dodge from the Blending Mode menu.**

    This change in blending mode gives a different look to this movie frame by changing the way its colors blend with the brown *Background* layer below.

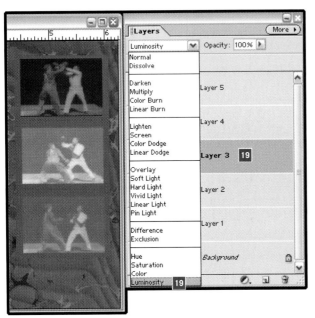

19. **Select** Layer 3, **which contains another movie frame, in the Layers palette, and choose Luminosity from the Blending Mode menu.**

    Applying Luminosity blending mode gives yet another look to this movie frame, changing the way it blends with the brown in the Background layer. As you can see, layer blending modes are a powerful feature. You learn more about them when you study layers in Session 6.

20. **Choose File→Save, and leave** 01_boxer.psd **open for the last tutorial in this session.**

    Your greeting card image now contains images that you imported to Photoshop Elements 2 from a movie file, adding to your repertoire of ways to bring images into the program. You moved these imported movie frames into the greeting card, cut out a frame for them, and blended them into the underlying image layers.

Tutorial
» Harvesting Images from a PDF File

With Photoshop Elements 2, you can harvest images from a PDF file. This feature has great practical potential. It means that if someone sends you a document in PDF format, like the simple calendar in this tutorial or a more complex manuscript with lots of figures, you can take any individual images out of that document for editing, archiving, or combining with other images as you do here.

1. **Choose File→Import→PDF Image. This opens the Select PDF for Image Import dialog box. In that dialog box, navigate to** `01_calendar.pdf` **in the Session 01 folder of your Tutorials folder, and then click Open.**
   This opens the PDF Image Import dialog box, displaying a thumbnail of boxing gloves. This is one of two images contained in this PDF. (The other is a calendar.) You import only the boxing glove image in order to use it in the collage that you build for this session's greeting card.

2. **Scroll up to the boxing glove thumbnail, if it is not already showing, in the PDF Image Import dialog box. Click on that thumbnail to select it, and click OK.**
   After a short delay, a new document window titled `01_calendar0001` opens in Photoshop Elements 2.

3. **Choose File→Save As. In the Save in field of the Save As dialog box, navigate to your ccproject folder. Click Save to save** `01_calendar001.psd`.
   By default, the file is saved in PSD format. That's all there is to taking a graphic image from a PDF file.

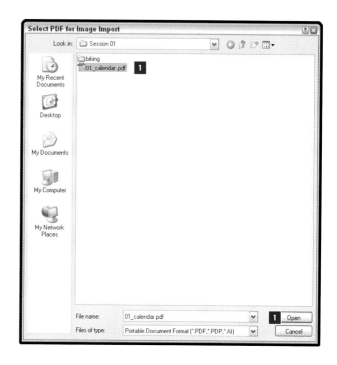

About PDFs

Portable Document Format (PDF) is a file format that can contain multiple pages of text and graphics. It is popular among commercial designers and others who share files because it protects all the formatting in a document, including fonts, vector graphics, bitmap images, layers, and other elements. You can now create PDFs in many programs, ranging from Adobe Acrobat to Microsoft Word. Photoshop Elements 2 can open a PDF so that you can edit each of its pages as a graphic file, or take individual images out of a PDF file for other uses.

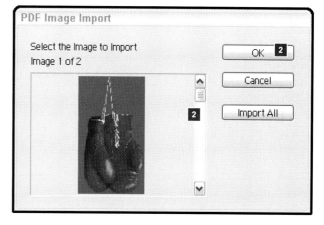

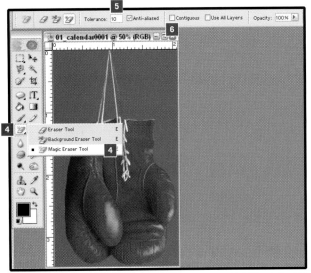

4. **Click and hold the Eraser tool in the toolbox to reveal some additional tools in a flyout menu. Select the Magic Eraser tool (the one with the asterisk).**

   In the next step you use the Magic Eraser tool to eliminate the blue background of the red boxing glove image.

5. **In the Magic Eraser tool Options bar, highlight and delete the number in the Tolerance field and type** 10**.**

   Setting the tolerance at 10 controls the sensitivity of the Magic Eraser tool so that it selects a relatively narrow range of colors to delete from this image.

6. **Remove the check mark from the Contiguous check box in the Options bar. Leave the other options at their defaults.**

   Unchecking Contiguous instructs the tool to select and delete pixels regardless of whether they are next to one another.

7. **Click anywhere in the blue area of the image.**

   The Magic Eraser selects and deletes all of the pixels within a particular color and brightness range of the blue pixel that you happened to click on. Most of the blue pixels should disappear, revealing the checkerboard that identifies transparent pixels in Photoshop Elements 2. There may still be a few blue pixels around the edges of the glove, but you can ignore them because they won't be visible against the patterns on which you place this image.

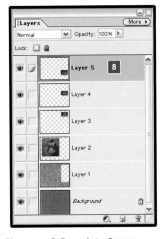

8. **Click on** 01_boxing.psd**, which should still be open from the last tutorial, to make that image active. Open the Layers palette if it is not already open, and select the topmost layer in the layer stack.**

   This determines where the new layer you're about to create is located in the layer stack.

9. **Arrange** 01_boxing.psd **and** 01_calendar0001.psd
   **so that you can see part of both of them on your screen. Select
   the Move tool in the toolbox, click in the**
   01_calendar0001.psd **document window, and drag the
   image of the red boxing glove into** 01_boxing.psd.

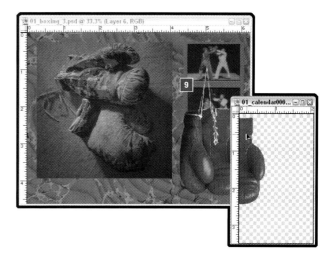

10. **With the Move tool, click and drag the red boxing gloves to posi-
    tion them to match the illustration.**

11. **Click on** 01_calendar0001.psd, **and choose**
    File➔Close.
    You don't need to save because you're finished with this image.

12. **Click on** 01_boxing.psd, **and choose➔Save As. In the Save As
    dialog box, rename this image** 01_boxing_end.psd. **Be sure
    to save it in your ccproject folder.**
    Your completed greeting card now contains an image that you
    extracted from a PDF file. The red boxing gloves join images
    you obtained from a variety of sources, including a background
    image generated in Photoshop Elements 2, a patterned object
    you scanned into the program, a photograph, and frames
    imported from a movie file. Photoshop Elements 2 makes it
    easy to use images from all of these sources.

Discussion
Saving Files

You learned the basics of saving files by experience as you worked through the tutorials in this session. Keep these tips in mind:

» Saving a new file immediately upon its creation, as you did in this session, is wise.

» The first time you save a file, you must use the Save As dialog box, in which you provide basic information about how and where the file is to be saved. Thereafter, you can use the economical Save command to replace the last saved version of the file.

» Memorize the keyboard shortcut for Save, Ctrl+S (Macintosh: ⌘+S). Alternatively, there is a Save button on the Shortcuts bar.

» You can go back to editing states prior to the save by choosing File→Step Backward or pressing Ctrl+Z (Macintosh ⌘+Z).

» To save an extra copy of a file, in either the same or a different format as the one you are working on, choose Save As and select Save: As a Copy in the Save As dialog box. This saves the copy with a modified name in your file structure and leaves the original open in your application window (Macintosh: on your desktop) for further editing.

» You can save a copy of a file in an additional file format by choosing that new format in the format field of the Save As dialog box. However, any changes you made since you last saved in the original format are recorded only in the new format. The new format replaces the original on your desktop, and your only version of the original is the last saved version in your file structure.

» You can optimize (choose compressions settings for) images for display on the Web and save them in Web-appropriate formats, such as JPEG, GIF, and animated GI, simply by choosing File→Save for Web.

Discussion
File Formats

Photoshop Elements 2 offers many formats in which to save files. Those you use most are listed here. You can access these formats from the Save As dialog box, but choose File→Save for Web when you are saving JPEGs or GIFS for a Web site so that you can also optimize them for the Web.

» **PSD (Photoshop Document format):** This is the format in which to do your editing work and in which to save a copy of the final image before flattening layers or saving in another format that might flatten layers. This gives you a full-featured file that you can edit at any time.

» **JPEG (Joint Photographic Experts Group format):** This format offers many colors and handles continuous tones well. It is a common format for digital photographs, but it can be a dangerous one because JPEG is a lossy format. This means that every time you open, change, and resave a JPEG, you lose image information. If your camera saves images as JPEG, I suggest that you run the File→Batch Processing command, converting file type to PSD so that you have a copy of each photo that is not vulnerable to lossy compression. Another downside of JPEG is that it does not support transparency. So any transparent areas of an image are filled with color when you save the image as a photograph. JPEG is one of just a few formats recognized on the Web.

» **GIF (Graphics Interchange Format):** This format uses the Indexed Color Mode, which has a limited number of colors. It is used for animated GIFs and drawings and cartoons made for the Web.

» **TIFF (Tagged Image File Format):** This is a universally recognized format that is one of the few formats other than PSD to retain layers. It offers optional compression (LZW Compression) that reduces the file size.

» **Photoshop PDF (Photoshop Portable Document Format):** Photoshop Elements 2 handles two kinds of PDFs: generic PDFs created in other programs and special Photoshop PDFs. The program opens either kind of PDF, but it allows you to save only in Photoshop PDF format. A Photoshop PDF consists of a single image; unlike generic PDFs, it cannot contain multiple images. However, you can create in Photoshop Elements 2 a PDF slideshow of images that can be opened and played in Adobe Reader (a free download from Adobe's Web site: www.adobe.com).

» Session Review

This session covered creating and acquiring files from a variety of sources for use in Photoshop Elements 2. You generated a background image from scratch while learning about resolution, file size, and color mode. You scanned a three-dimensional object to use as a pattern, while learning how Photoshop Elements 2 handles scanning and interfacing with digital cameras. You converted a digital photograph to PSD format to bring into your project, and you learned how to view, open, and organize digital files with the File Browser in Photoshop Elements 2. You imported frames from video footage and an image from a PDF file to experience how Photoshop Elements 2 handles these more unusual sources of content. And you learned how and in what format to save your files. In doing these things, you generated a compelling piece of digital artwork for the first greeting card in the Complete Course project.

Take a look at the last page of this session for a full-color illustration of the final image. An iteration file of the completed image, `01_boxing_end.psd`, is located in your Tutorial Files➜Session 01 folder. Congratulations on completing the first full session in this course. Aren't you amazed at what you produced after just one session?

1. What is the best image file format in which to edit an image in Photoshop Elements 2? (See Tutorial: Creating a Document from Scratch.)

2. Why might the Save command in the File menu be unavailable, and how can you save a file if it is? (See Tutorial: Creating a Document from Scratch.)

3. Why is RGB Color the ideal color mode for use in an image-editing program like Photoshop Elements 2? (See Tutorial: Creating a Document from Scratch.)

4. How is resolution defined in terms of pixels and inches? (See Discussion: Understanding Resolution.)

5. What is the optimal resolution in pixels per inch of a typical desktop inkjet printer? (See Discussion: Understanding Resolution.)

6. Is it a good idea to increase a file's resolution? (See Discussion: Understanding Resolution.)

7. What is most likely missing if your scanner does not show up in the Import menu in Photoshop Elements 2? (See Tutorial: Scanning into Photoshop Elements 2.)

8. Name three possible methods of getting photographs from a digital camera into Photoshop Elements 2. (See Discussion: Getting Digital Photographs into Photoshop Elements 2.)

9. Name two different features that you can use to rename photographs and other files in Photoshop Elements 2. (See Tutorial: Managing Digital Photographs with the File Browser.)

10. What does the Import Frame from Video feature do? (See Tutorial: Importing Still Frames from Video.)

11. What would you use the Import PDF Images feature for? (See Tutorial: Harvesting Images from a PDF File.)

12. If you save an image, is it impossible to step back to a previous editing state? (See Discussion: Saving Files.)

13. Why is it best not to edit images in JPEG format? (See Discussion: File Formats.)

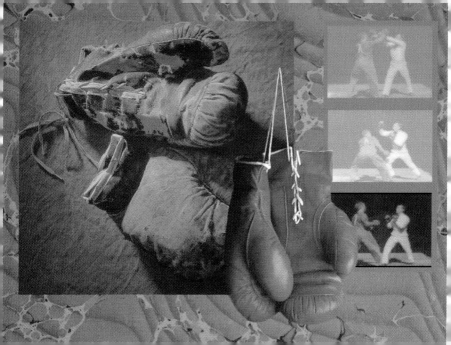

Getting Comfortable with the Interface

Session Introduction

Understanding the interface of Photoshop Elements 2 is the key to getting the most out of the program. In this session, you examine each interface element—the Toolbox, Options bar, Shortcuts bar, and palettes—with emphasis on how these elements work and what they can do for you. You learn how to organize your Photoshop Elements 2 work space. You delve into customizing program preferences and color settings. Then you learn the basics of choosing and applying color. It may be tempting to skip this session and dive right into the heart of the course, but I suggest that you take the time to work through this session first to get the solid foundation that you need to become a power user.

TOOLS YOU'LL USE
Toolbox, Options bar, Shortcuts bar, menu bar, Palettes, Preferences, Color Settings, Hints palette, How To palette, Help system, Color Picker

CD-ROM FILES NEEDED
02_biking.psd, 02_biking_end.psd

TIME REQUIRED
30 minutes

Tutorial
» Making the Most of Tools and Menu Bars

In this tutorial, you explore the main features in the Photoshop Elements 2 interface—the Toolbox, Options bar, menu bar, and Shortcuts bar. You get firsthand experience with these features and pick up some tips about how to use them efficiently.

1. **Reset all your tools to their default options by going to the Options bar at the top of the screen and clicking on the tool icon displayed at the very left of your Options bar.**
   On your screen, this is the icon for whichever tool is selected in your Toolbox.

2. **Choose Reset All Tools from the drop-down menu.**
   This matches your tool options to those you see in this book. Resetting your tools makes sense whenever you begin a new project in Photoshop Elements 2.

<NOTE>
If you just launched Photoshop Elements 2, the Welcome Screen may have appeared. Close it by clicking Exit Welcome Screen on the right side of the Welcome Screen.

3. **Choose File→Browse in the menu bar to open the File Browser.**

4. **Navigate to Tutorial Files→Session 02 in the file tree on the top left of the File Browser; double-click the thumbnail labeled 02_biking.psd on the right side of the File Browser to open that file.**

<NOTE>
If you don't remember how the File Browser works, turn back to Session 1.

5. **Move your mouse over any tool in the Toolbox on the left side of the screen.**

   Notice that the tool icon lights up, and a Tool Tip appears that tells you the name of the tool and its keyboard shortcut.

   Tool Tips also appear when your mouse hovers over controls in palettes and on the Options and Shortcuts bars.

6. **Open the Hints palette, if it is not already open, by choosing Window→Hints from the menu bar. Move your mouse over any tool in the Toolbox.**

   Notice that the Hints palette changes to offer information about that particular tool and links to related topics in the Help system. Hints also appear when you move your mouse over the tab of a palette in the Palette Well.

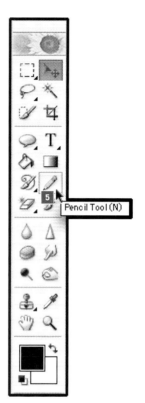

7. **Click on the Eraser tool in the Toolbox to select that tool.**

   You have to select a tool in the Toolbox in order to use it on an image.

<**TIP**>

A quick way to select a tool is to press its keyboard shortcut. For example, pressing B selects the Brush tool. To learn the keyboard shortcut for a tool, move your mouse over the tool and view its Tool Tip or consult the table of tools and their shortcuts in Appendix B.

<**NOTE**>

The separators in the Toolbox group tools by function—selection and moving tools, painting and type tools, darkroom tools, cloning and viewing tools, and color tools.

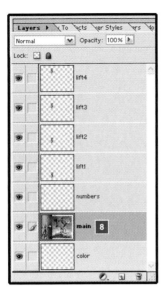

8. **Open the Layers palette by clicking on the Layers tab in the Palette Well on the right side of the Options bar. Click on the gray (Macintosh: white) area of the** main **layer in the Layers palette to select that layer.**
   To use a tool on particular pixels in an image, you have to first select the layer on which those pixels are located.

<**NOTE**>
If you don't see the Layers palette in the Palette Well or in your work area, it is closed. To open it, choose Window→Layers.

9. **To apply the Eraser tool, click and drag in the white background area of the image to delete some of the white pixels as in the illustration.**
   This deletes pixels on the **main** layer. Don't bother erasing all the white pixels now.

10. **Click and hold the black triangle at the bottom right of the Eraser tool to reveal a flyout menu of related tools.**
    This triangle means that more tools are hiding behind the Eraser tool.

<**TIP**>
A quick way to cycle through a group of hidden tools is to hold the Shift key while pressing the keyboard shortcut for that group (which you can find in the Tool Tip). For example, Shift+E cycles through three different eraser tools.

11. **Click on the Magic Eraser tool (the one with the asterisk) in the flyout menu to select that hidden tool.**
    The Magic Eraser tool now appears in place of the Eraser tool in the Toolbox until you choose another tool from this group.

12. **A check mark should appear in the Contiguous check box in the Magic Eraser tool's Options bar at the top of the screen.**
This option is checked as a default and causes the Magic Eraser tool to affect only pixels that are touching one another in the image.

13. **With the** main **layer still selected, click with the Magic Eraser tool anywhere on the white background of the image.**
Presto! All the white pixels are gone. The Magic Eraser tool selects contiguous pixels that are similar in color and brightness and deletes them. It works best on areas of a single contrasting color, like this white background.

14. **Select the Sponge tool in the Toolbox.**
Notice that the Options bar at the top of the screen changes so that it now offers options specific to the Sponge tool.

15. **Click in the Mode field on the Options bar, and choose Saturate from the menu. Leave the other options at their defaults, as in the illustration.**
The Sponge tool has two opposite functions—saturating and desaturating—that change depending on the Mode option you choose. Saturating makes colors more intense, desaturating makes them less intense.

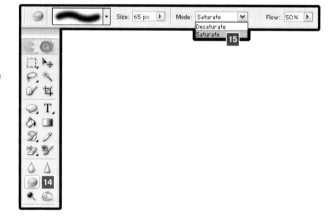

<TIP>
The Saturation tool works best on small areas.

16. **Select the** numbers **layer in the Layers palette. Click and drag over the numbers on the left side of the image to increase their saturation. After the numbers become as intense in color as you want them to be, click and drag one more time.**

<NOTE>
If the numbers in the image aren't becoming more saturated, it's probably because the layer that contains the pixels that you're trying to affect is not selected. This is a common mistake. Repeat Step 16, making sure to select the **numbers** layer in the Layers palette.

17. **In the Shortcuts bar at the top of the screen, click the Step Backward arrow to undo your extra application of the Sponge tool.**

   You can use the Step Backward shortcut up to 20 times in a row.

<NOTE>

The Shortcuts bar contains a number of convenient shortcuts for frequently used commands. It offers an alternative to choosing commands from the menu bar or memorizing key commands in order to use shortcuts.

<TIP>

Tool Tips are available for Shortcuts bar buttons, as well as for tools. To remind yourself of what the other buttons on the Shortcuts bar do, move your mouse over each button to view a Tool Tip, or consult the table of Shortcuts bar buttons in Appendix B.

18. **Choose File→Save As. In the Save As dialog box, navigate to your ccproject folder, and click Save.**

   Leave this image open for the next tutorial. By now you should be getting comfortable with using the Toolbox, the Options bar, and the Shortcuts bar, all of which you experienced as you worked on your greeting card image in this tutorial.

Tutorial
» Using and Organizing Palettes

Palettes contain important controls that you access frequently. Unfortunately, a normal screen doesn't have room to display all the palettes and all their controls simultaneously, so Photoshop Elements 2 contains space-saving features like hidden palette menus, contextual menus, the Palette Well, and multiple ways to combine and arrange palettes. You try out each of these features in this tutorial, as you learn how to use and organize palettes efficiently.

1. **With the** 02_biking.psd **file open from the previous tutorial, reset your palettes to their default locations by choosing Window→Reset Palette Locations from the menu bar.**
   Resetting your palettes is also a fast way to clean up your work area after a crazy work session.

2. **The How To and Hints palettes are open in your work area as freestanding palettes. Double-click the title bar of the How To palette to contract the palette so that just its title bar and tabs are showing.**
   This is a convenient way to keep palettes open as freestanding palettes in your work area without having them take up too much room.

<TIP>
Shift+clicking the title bar of a palette sends it to the nearest horizontal edge of your screen. This is another housekeeping secret to keep palettes out of your way.

<TIP>
The How To palette contains recipes for tasks, like creating Web buttons or adding a beveled edge to type. You can follow a recipe manually, or in some cases the program offers to perform a recipe step for you. This is a useful tool for learning how to approach some specific tasks. From time to time, you can download new recipes by connecting to the Internet, clicking in the Select a Recipe field in the How To palette, and choosing Download New Adobe Recipes.

3. **Click the red button at the top right (Macintosh: top left) of the Hints palette to close it so you have more room to work.**
   Notice that your Hints palette is not gone altogether. Its tab is showing in the Palette Well on the right side of the Shortcuts bar. By default palettes close into the Palette Well.

<NOTE>
In the previous tutorial, you learned that when you move your mouse over a tool or a Palette tab in the Palette Well, the Hints palette offers information about that item. The Hints palette also contains links to related issues in the Photoshop Elements 2 Help system. The Hints palette is very helpful when you're first learning Photoshop Elements 2. After you become familiar with the tools and palettes, close the Hints palette to free up more work space.

4. To consult the Hints palette, choose Window→Hints to reopen the Hints palette.

Notice that it reopens inside the Palette Well.

< N O T E >

You are not able to see the full Palette Well unless your monitor display is set to at least 1024 x 768 pixels. At 800 x 600 pixels, you can see only a truncated Palette Well, and at lower screen resolutions, it does not appear at all. If your monitor is capable of a 1024 x 768 pixel display, I suggest that you change it to at least that resolution by choosing Start→Control Panel→Appearance and Themes→Change the screen resolution, and adjusting Screen resolution in the Settings tab of the Display Properties dialog box (Macintosh OS X: choose Apple→System Preferences→Display; Macintosh OS 9: choose Apple→Control Panels→Monitors).

< N O T E >

If your monitor is at the proper resolution, but you can't see the Palette Well, the Shortcuts bar, in which the Palette Well is located, is probably closed. Choose Window→Shortcuts to open the Shortcuts bar.

5. Click anywhere on the screen outside the Palette Well to close the Hints palette.

Only its tab remains showing in the Palette Well. Palettes automatically close when you click elsewhere, giving you more room to work without having to think about putting the palette away. On the other hand, the automatic closure feature can be frustrating when you work with palettes that you use often, like the Layers palette or the Undo History palette.

6. Click the Layers tab in the Palette Well, and drag the Layers palette from the Palette Well into your work space.

The Layers palette remains open on your work space until you deliberately close it. If you do close the Layers palette, the next time it opens, it appears in the Palette Well again.

7. Click the More button on the right side of the Layers palette to reveal a menu of layers-related commands. Deselect Close Palette to Palette Well in that menu.

From now on, if you close the Layers palette and then open it (by choosing Window→Layers), it appears as a freestanding palette in your work space and does not automatically close into the Palette Well.

< N O T E >

Most palettes have hidden menus of commands related to that palette, similar to the menu that you just used in the Layers palette. When a palette is freestanding, that menu is accessed from the More button on the top right of the palette. When a palette is open inside the Palette Well, the same menu is accessed from a right-facing arrow on the Palette tab.

8. **Right-click (Macintosh: Ctrl+click) on any layer in the Layers palette to reveal another hidden menu of commands.**
   This is called a contextual menu. Many palettes contain contextual menus, as does the document window. If you can't find a command that you know exists, try looking in a hidden contextual menu.

9. **Click and drag the Undo History tab from the Palette Well into the Layers palette. When you see a dark line around the inner border of the Layers palette, release the mouse to create a grouping of these two palettes.**

10. **Click and drag the Undo History palette by its tab away from the Layers palette.**
    This is how you separate grouped palettes.

11. **Click and drag the diagonal lines at the bottom-right corner of the Layers palette until you can see all the layers in the palette.**

<TIP>
When you don't have enough room to expand a palette to its full height, you can use the scroll bars at the side of the palette to view all its contents.

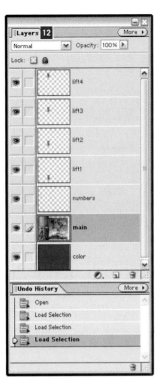

12. **Click and drag the Layers palette by its tab to the top of the Undo History palette. Release the mouse when you see a narrow black band just under the title bar of the Undo History palette.**

    This joins the two palettes so that they move together and both are visible. This is known as *docking*. Docking palettes is a good solution for customizing your work area for particular tasks. Dock the palettes that you use often for a task (like the Layers palette and the Undo History palette when you work on a collage), and undock them when you work on a different task.

13. **Choose File→Save. Leave this file open for the next tutorial.**

    In this tutorial you learned how to use and manage the palettes that are an integral part of this program.

Tutorial
» Selecting Colors

In this tutorial you learn how to use the Color Picker to select colors. Choosing a color is a prerequisite to many operations in Photoshop Elements 2 from filling an area with solid color to creating a color gradient to painting with a brush tool. In this tutorial you select a color with which you fill the background of this greeting card.

1. **With** 02_biking.psd **still open from the last tutorial, select the main layer in the Layers palette. Click the Foreground Color box in the Toolbox to open the Color Picker, where you select a color to fill the image background.**

<TIP>
If Only Web Colors is selected in the Color Picker, deselect it. That command limits the available colors to 216 special colors for the Web.

2. **Type the following numbers into the R, G, and B fields—R:** 54, **G:** 63, **B:** 84. **Click OK to close the Color Picker.**
This loads the selected color into the Foreground Color Box at the bottom of the Toolbox.

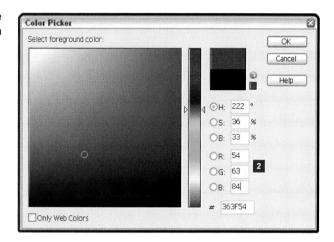

Choosing Colors Visually

It's common not to have specific numeric color values in mind when you're selecting a color for use in Photoshop Elements 2. You can choose a color in the Color Picker visually, rather than numerically, using a combination of the color slider and the color field located in the Color Picker. Start by looking at the vertical color slider in the center of the Color Picker. By default, this color slider displays a range of colors by hue. Click the B radio button to the right of the vertical color slider if you prefer that the slider display colors arranged by brightness, or the S radio button to display colors by saturation. Move the vertical color slider until its arrows point to the color range you seek. Then fine tune your selection by clicking in the large color field on the left side of the Color Picker. The color under the circular marker in the color field is displayed in the top half of the rectangular color box to the right of the vertical color slider. The numeric values of that color appear in the R, G, and B fields. And the value of that color that is used on the Web appears in the hexidecimal field at the bottom of the Color Picker. Click OK to close the Color Picker and to apply the selected color to the Foreground or Background Color box in the Toolbox.

3. Select the color layer in the Layers palette. Choose Edit→Fill from the menu bar.

The Fill dialog box opens.

4. In the Fill dialog box, click the Use field menu and choose Foreground Color.

Leave the other fields at their defaults, as in the illustration.

< N O T E >

Other options in the Use field of the Fill dialog box allow you to fill a selection or a layer with the Background Color (the color in the Background Color Box in the Toolbox), White, Black, 50% Gray, or a Pattern. If you choose Pattern, you can load one of a number of pattern sets that come with Photoshop Elements 2. You can also specify the opacity and blending mode of a fill in the Fill dialog box. If you select the Preserve Transparency check box in the dialog box, only nontransparent pixels on the selected layer are filled, which is a useful technique for changing the color of all the artwork on a layer without doing any selecting.

5. Click OK to close the Fill dialog box.

The **color** layer is filled with dark gray. The **color** layer is at the bottom of the layer stack in the Layers palette, so its gray content is partially obscured in the document window by the artwork on the layers above it. Alt+click (Macintosh: Option+click) the eye icon in the layer visibility field to the left of the **color** layer to hide all the other layers temporarily so that you can see the solid gray with which you filled this layer. Alt+click (Macintosh: Option+click) in that visibility field again to make the other layers visible again.

< N O T E >

Another way to fill all or part of the artwork on a layer is to select the Paint Bucket tool in the Toolbox, set its Fill option on the Options bar to Foreground Color or pattern, and click on a representative pixel with the Paint Bucket tool. The Paint Bucket tool fills all pixels that are similar in color to the pixel on which you click. If you want to fill a larger area, increase the Tolerance value in the Options bar and try filling again. Decrease Tolerance to fill a smaller area.

6. Choose File→Save, and leave 02_biking.psd **open for the next tutorial.**

In this tutorial you learned how easy it is to select a color. You used the color you selected in the Color Picker to fill a layer in your biking greeting card with color. Filling an area isn't the only reason to select a color. For example, you often select a color with which to draw or paint, create shapes, generate a gradient, or provide color for an effect or filter.

Other Ways to Select a Color

There are two other ways, in addition to the Color Picker method, to select a color in Photoshop Elements 2. First, the Eyedropper tool is useful for choosing a color that goes with the other colors in an image. Simply select the Eyedropper tool in the Toolbox and click on a color in an open image to set the Foreground color in the Toolbox. Another way to select a color is by clicking on a color chip in the Color Swatches palette. You can use any of the several color swatches that come with Photoshop Elements 2 or build a custom swatch from which to select colors. To see the Color Swatches palette, choose Window→Show Color Swatches.

< T I P >

If you have any stray white marks in the gray area, it may from some noncontiguous white areas left when you used the Eraser tool early in this session. Select the **main** layer in the Layers palette and the Eraser tool in the Toolbox, and then click and drag over the stray marks to delete them.

Tutorial
» Using Brushes

In this tutorial you create painted elements in your biking greeting card, using the Brush tool in conjunction with the shape dynamics options.

1. With `02_biking.psd` **open from the last tutorial, select the main layer in the Layers palette and choose Layer→New→Layer. The New Layer dialog box opens.**

2. **In the New Layer dialog box, type** grass **as the name of the new layer and click OK.**
   The New Layer dialog box closes.

3. **Select the Brush tool in the Toolbox.**
   The Brush tool is one of several painting tools in Photoshop Elements 2, all of which use brushes from the Brushes palette. The other painting tools are the Pencil tool, which creates a harder line than the Brush tool; the Selection Brush tool, which paints in a selection; and the Red Eye Brush tool, which paints out the red reflection in a subject's eye that is commonly caused by the use of camera flash.

4. **Click in the Brush Sample field in the Options bar.**
   This opens the Brushes palette, where you see the default set of brushes.

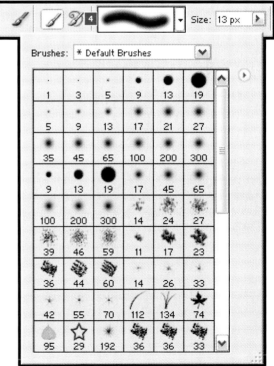

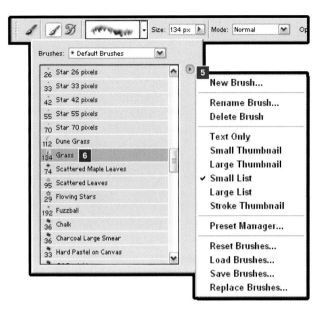

5. **Click the right-facing arrow at the top right of the Brushes palette to open the palette menu, and choose Small List.**

    This changes your view of the brush set so that you can see the name of each brush. There are several ways to view brushes in the Brushes palette—by small or large list, by a sample of each brush stroke, or by a small or large thumbnail of the brush tip.

6. **Click on the scrollbar at the right side of the Brushes palette and drag down until you see the Grass brush. Select the Grass brush.**

    A sample of this brush stroke appears in the Options bar. The Grass brush is one of many preset brushes that comes with Photoshop Elements 2.

7. **In the Options bar, click the More Options button to display the brush dynamics options. Leave the other settings in the Options bar at their defaults — Size: 134 pixels, Mode: normal, Opacity: 100%, Airbrush: deselected.**

    Brush dynamics settings determine whether and by how much a brush stroke changes over the course of the stroke. Brush dynamics often make brush strokes look more natural. For example, you can simulate the appearance of a real brush stroke by setting a brush to dynamically fade as you paint.

8. **In the Brush Dynamics palette, set Color Jitter to 100% and Scatter to 5%. Leave the other brush dynamics settings at their defaults.**

    This high Color Jitter setting causes the brush to use many different colors—variations on the Foreground and Background colors. This low Scatter setting causes your brush strokes to be scattered slightly in the image.

9. **Click in the Foreground Color box to open the Color Picker, and choose a light orange color (R:243, G:155, B:91). Click in the Background Color box and choose a medium brown (R:121, G:70, B:31).**

10. **With the grass layer selected in the Layers palette, paint several brush strokes over the bottom left of the biker image to create some grass in front of the large gray rocks.**

    Your brushstrokes can cross over into the dark gray border. The brush paints randomly with a variety of colors within the range of your Foreground to Background colors as a result of the brush dynamics settings.

11. **Select the Eraser tool from the Toolbox. In the Options bar, set Mode to block to give the eraser tool a straight edge.**

    If the regular Eraser tool is not displayed there, click whichever eraser icon is displayed and choose the Eraser tool from the flyout menu of related tools.

12. **With the** grass **layer still selected, Shift+click and drag along the right and bottom edges of the biker image to clean up the edge of your grass brush strokes.**

13. **Click the Brush menu at the top of the Layers palette and choose Assorted Brushes.**

    Another set of preset brushes appears in the Brushes palette.

14. **In the Brushes palette, scroll down and choose the Crosshatch 4 brush.**

<TIP>

Hovering over any brush in the Brushes palette displays a Tool Tip that identifies the brush by name.

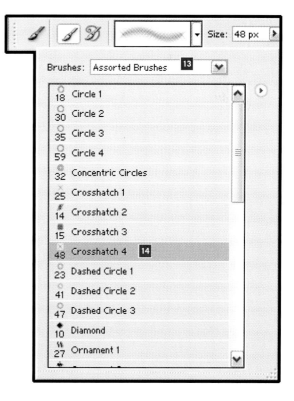

15. **Create a new layer and name it** highlights. **With that layer selected, in the document window click on each shiny, reflective area on the bike to add starburst highlights.**

16. **Choose File→Save As, rename the file** 02_bikers_end.psd, **and click Save to save the greeting card you created in this session into your ccproject folder. Close the file.**

Creating a Custom Brush

The several preset brush sets that ship with Photoshop Elements 2 offer lots of choices of brushes, including calligraphic brushes, brushes with drop shadows, special effects brushes, and more. But you are not limited to those choices. You can create your own custom brush from a graphic or a photograph. A black and white line drawing makes a brush that paints with solid tones; a photograph or a color drawing makes a brush that paints with softer, semi-transparent tones.

To create a custom brush, open the source image of your choice, select the rectangular marquee tool, and draw a selection around the part of the image that you want to use as a brush. The size of this selection determines the size of the brush, so you usually want the selection to be small. Choose Edit→Define Brush. Enter

a name for your brush and click OK. Your new brush appears at the bottom of the currently loaded brush set, ready for use. To save the brush for use another time, resave the current brush set by clicking the right-facing arrow at the top of the Brushes palette and choosing Save. Give the file a name that includes the .abr extension, and save it to the location to which the Save dialog box defaults (the Brushes folder inside the Presets folder in the application).

When you paint with your custom brush, try increasing the Spacing setting in the brush dynamics options to make the brush content more readable. You can click and drag with the brush, or use it like a rubber stamp by dabbing with it.

Tutorial
» Setting Preferences

Preferences are underlying controls that you can use to customize the behavior of Photoshop Elements 2. In this tutorial, you learn how to reset preferences to their default settings and how to change preferences. This is not an exhaustive treatise on preferences. Instead, it provides an overview and identifies those preferences that you might want to customize in your copy of Photoshop Elements 2.

1. **Choose File→Exit (Macintosh: Photoshop Elements→Quit Photoshop Elements) from the menu bar to close Photoshop Elements 2.**

2. **Relaunch the program, holding Ctrl+Alt+Shift (Macintosh: ⌘+Option+Shift) as the program starts up. Click Yes at the prompt that asks whether to Delete the Adobe Photoshop Elements Settings File.**
   Your preferences are now reset to their defaults.

<TIP>

Occasionally, a preferences file becomes corrupted, causing Photoshop Elements 2 to act erratically. If your program is ever behaving oddly, try resetting preferences as you did in Step 2.

3. **Choose Edit→Preferences→General (Macintosh: Photoshop Elements→Preferences→General) to open the Preferences dialog box.**
   This dialog box has seven panes, each with a set of related preferences.

4. **In the General panel, the History States field is set to 20 by default.**
   This is the number of steps available in the Undo History palette and the Step Backward command for fixing mistakes. You can increase this field to up to 100, but you're likely to notice a trade-off in performance and available memory.

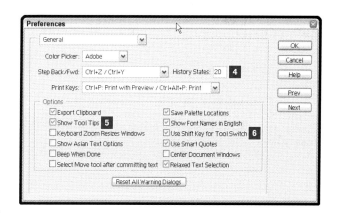

5. **Make sure Show Tool Tips is checked.**
   When you are more familiar with the program, you can turn this option off to reduce clutter, but for now make sure that this option is checked.

6. **Deselect Use Shift Key for Tool Switch.**
   When this option is deselected, you don't have to hold the Shift key when you press a keyboard shortcut to cycle through related tools in the Toolbox.

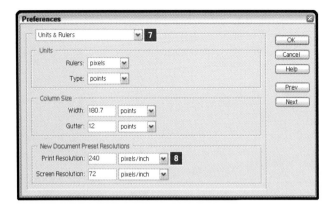

7. Click the topmost button in the Preferences dialog box and choose Units & Rulers from the menu of preference categories that appears.

The Rulers field determines the units of measurement displayed in the Rulers at the top and side of the document window. If you are preparing images for the Web, click the Rulers field and choose pixels from the drop-down menu. Otherwise, leave it set to inches.

<TIP>

You can also set the units of measurement for rulers on the fly by right-clicking (Macintosh: Ctrl+clicking) in a ruler in the document window.

8. Change the Print Resolution field in the Units & Rulers preferences to match your printer's optimum print resolution.

This field controls the resolution of documents created with Preset Sizes in the File➔New dialog box. I set this field to 240 pixels per inch because this is the optimum print resolution for my Epson printer.

<NOTE>

Most desktop inkjet printers print at 240 to 300 pixels per inch with about three dots of ink per pixel. Don't be fooled by the much higher dot per inch resolution often quoted in advertising literature. Read the Discussion on Understanding Resolution in Session 1 to refresh your memory on the subject. Check your printer manufacturer's documentation to determine the resolution of your printer.

9. Choose Plug-Ins & Scratch Disks from the menu of preference categories. If you have an extra hard drive or drive partition, set the First scratch disk to that drive. Otherwise, leave it set to the Startup drive.

The disks designated as scratch disks are what Photoshop uses as virtual memory if it runs out of RAM.

10. Choose Memory & Image Cache from the preference categories menu.

11. In the Memory Usage section, set the Maximum Used by Photoshop Elements to 90% or less.

This puts a cap on the amount of memory that Photoshop Elements uses, ensuring that it leaves some for other open programs.

12. Restart Photoshop Elements 2 so that the changes you made to preferences take effect.

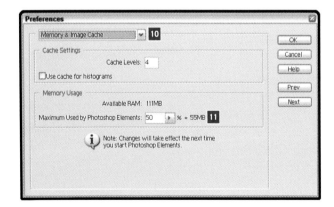

<NOTE>

In Macintosh OS X, as in Windows, memory allocation among applications is now done on the fly. You do not have to manually allocate a set amount of memory to individual programs as was the case in Macintosh OS 9 and earlier operating systems.

Discussion
Color Management in Photoshop Elements 2

Color management is a very complicated subject that Adobe has attempted to simplify in Photoshop Elements 2. I'll try to do the same in this brief discussion.

Color management is an attempt, spearheaded by Adobe and other software and hardware manufacturers, to coordinate the way in which raw color values are interpreted by lots of different devices, including scanners, cameras, computers, printers, and software. This is harder than you might imagine, because every device can interpret color values differently. If you've ever printed the same document on two printers and gotten two different color schemes, you've experienced the problem (or at least the tip of the iceberg). Lots of controversy exists about whether color management is a viable solution to the problem. Theoretically, it makes sense. Practically, it often doesn't work because not every device uses the same color management system and because many people who attempt color management don't really understand how it works.

The process of creating and editing images in Photoshop Elements 2 includes four steps that involve decisions about color management: creating a monitor profile that Photoshop Elements 2 can use to interact with your monitor, choosing color settings in Photoshop Elements 2, embedding a color profile when you save a document in Photoshop Elements 2, and using a printer profile when you print a document from Photoshop Elements 2.

The first step in a color management workflow is to create a monitor profile that tells Photoshop Elements 2 how your particular monitor reproduces color. Calibrating and characterizing your monitor is easy.

In Windows XP, go to Start→Control Panel→Appearance and Themes→Adobe Gamma. Choose the Step-by-Step Wizard to walk you through the process. This generates a monitor profile that is automatically saved in a place that Photoshop Elements 2 can find. In other Windows operating systems, the Adobe Gamma utility is located in Program Files→Common Files→Adobe→Calibration.

In Macintosh systems, you can accomplish the same thing using the Apple Display Calibration utility. In Macintosh OS X, go to System Preferences→Displays, select the Color tab, and click Calibrate. In Macintosh OS 9, go to Control Panels→Monitors, click the Color button, and click Calibrate.

Photoshop Elements 2 offers color settings that are a very simplified version of the color management settings in Photoshop. You are given only three choices in the Edit→Color Settings (Macintosh: Photoshop Elements→Color Settings) dialog box in Photoshop Elements 2:

» No color management

» Limited color management—optimized for Web graphics

» Full color management—optimized for print

Behind the scenes, your choice determines the following:

» How Photoshop Elements 2 interprets and displays color values while you create or edit a document in the program.

» How Photoshop Elements 2 treats documents that you bring in that were created in different color environments.

» Whether Photoshop Elements 2 tags a document with a profile that describes the color environment in which that document was created or edited. Color profiles are the basic currency of color management. The idea is that if a document carries information about its color environment, a printer or another computer can use that information to better reproduce the intended colors in that document.

You can choose to ignore Photoshop Elements 2 color settings altogether, as many people do. That is the same as opening the Color Settings dialog box and choosing No color management. If you work in a closed setting (for example, a scanner, computer, and inkjet printer in a home office), and you have a good feel for how your devices work together, you probably can get along fine without going near color settings in Photoshop Elements 2. If you share documents with other computers or outside printers, you may want to choose one of the other two settings in the Edit→Color Settings (Macintosh: Photoshop Elements→Color Settings) dialog box.

Table 2-1 explains briefly what each of the color settings in Photoshop Elements 2 does.

In addition to characterizing your monitor, choosing a color setting, and embedding a profile upon saving, you can decide whether to use a printer profile when you are printing a document. If you have a profile that describes your particular printer and you use that profile when you print, the colors in the image are temporarily converted to the device-specific color space that your printer uses. This option is buried deep in Photoshop Elements 2, but it is there nonetheless. When you're ready to print, go to File→Print Preview. In the Print Preview dialog box, select the Show More Options check box. Click the Output field, and choose Color Management from the menu. The Document Source Profile reports whether the document is Untagged or has an embedded profile. Choose your printer's profile from the Profile menu in the Print Space area.

With this basic information under your belt, it's up to you to decide whether and at what level you want to attempt color management. The files provided with this course are not tagged with a color profile, so you can experiment with them and decide for yourself whether and how to apply color settings. I suggest that you try changing the color settings and seeing how that affects a single image as it appears on screen. Then experiment with embedding color profiles when you save the image, and see how that affects the image on the screen and in print. Or, if you'd rather spend your time learning other things, ignore color management altogether. It's your call.

Table 2-1: Color Management Settings Overview

Color Setting	Effect on RGB Working Environment (the way documents look on screen in your copy of Photoshop Elements 2)	Treatment of Documents from Other Color Environments	Profile Embedding Choices
Edit (Macintosh: Photoshop Elements)→Color Settings→No color management	Uses your computer display system's native RGB environment. If you work in Windows, this probably is close to sRGB, which is a typical Windows color environment.	If you open a document that is tagged with a color profile, that profile is honored. The software does not attempt to convert a tagged document to the working color environment (your monitor's native working space).	In the File→Save As dialog box, you have the option to embed the color profile of your monitor (the profile that you created when you characterized your monitor as discussed previously).
Edit (Macintosh: Photoshop Elements)→Color Settings→Limited color management	Sets the RGB environment to sRGB, a typical Windows color environment with a narrower range of colors than Adobe RGB. This choice is advertised as the best environment for creating Web graphics, although I recommend no color management as the best choice for Web graphics because Web browsers can't read color profiles anyway. So, you don't need to make a document look different in Photoshop Elements 2 than it would in a Web browser or other non-color managed application on your computer.	If you open a document that has a color profile, it converts to the sRGB working environment.	In the File→Save As dialog box, you have the option to embed the sRGB color profile. This tells a printer or another computer about the sRGB environment in which you created the document. Theoretically, this should help the output device to reproduce colors as you saw them when you were working on the document in Photoshop Elements 2.

Color Setting	Effect on RGB Working Environment (the way documents look on screen in your copy of Photoshop Elements 2)	Treatment of Documents from Other Color Environments	Profile Embedding Choices
Edit (Macintosh: Photoshop Elements)→Color Settings→Full color management	Sets the RGB environment to Adobe RGB (1998), a widely recognized color space for images destined for print. Adobe RGB has a wide range of reproducible colors (its color gamut), so colors generally look richer and brighter than sRGB.	If you open a document that has no color profile, it converts to the Adobe RGB working environment. If you open a document that has a different color profile, that profile is respected.	In the File→Save As dialog box, you have the option to embed the Adobe RGB color profile if the document was originally untagged. If the document was tagged with another profile, you have the option to retain that profile. Theoretically, this should help the output device to reproduce colors as you saw them when you were working on the document in Photoshop Elements 2.

Discussion
Help System Summary

Adobe went out of its way to include an extensive Help system in Photoshop Elements 2, in order to make the program accessible to a wide audience. You had the opportunity to use parts of the Help system in this session. You used Tool Tips to identify tools, buttons, and controls. You worked with the Hints palette, which offers information about tools and palettes and links to online Help screens. You saw the How To palette, which contains recipes for performing specific tasks in Photoshop Elements 2. The Help menu on the menu bar also offers a number of options:

» **Photoshop Elements Help** takes you to Help, which includes explanations of all the programs' features and a special section of Tutorials. You do not need Internet access to view this HTML-based Help.

» **About Plug-Ins** displays a list of filters, effects, and other installed plug-ins.

» **Glossary of Terms** takes you to a glossary in Help.

» **Photoshop Elements Tutorials** takes you to the Tutorials in Help.

» **System Info** shows you all kinds of information about your system and how it uses Photoshop Elements 2.

» If you're connected to the Internet, **Support** takes you to customer support pages on the Adobe Web site, www.adobe.com.

» **Common Issues** opens the How To palette, offering access to its Recipes.

Clicking the flower icon at the top of the Toolbox opens Adobe Online, which offers program updates from time to time.

Features like the Welcome Screen and the Quick Fix window collect and organize related features making them easier to access and to understand.

» Session Review

In this session, you learned how the program interface functions. You worked with the Toolbox and its tools, the Options bar, the Shortcuts bar, and the menu bar. You learned about the Palette Well, using and organizing palettes, and finding hidden menus in palettes. You studied some of the program's preferences, considering which preferences you might change to customize your copy of Photoshop Elements 2. You tackled the complex subject of color management, and reviewed the many help features in Photoshop Elements 2. All of these activities led to the creation of another greeting card for your collection.

On the last page of this session, you see a final illustration of the biking image that you worked with in this session. A copy of the completed image, 02_biking_end.psd, is located in your Tutorial Files➜Session 02 folder.

1. How do you reset all tools to their default options? (See Tutorial: Making the Most of Tools and Menu Bars.)

2. What is a Tool Tip? (See Tutorial: Making the Most of Tools and Menu Bars.)

3. What information does the Hints palette offer? (See Tutorial: Making the Most of Tools and Menu Bars.)

4. What does a triangle at the bottom-right corner of a tool indicate? (See Tutorial: Making the Most of Tools and Menu Bars.)

5. What does it mean to say that the Options bar is context sensitive? (See Tutorial: Making the Most of Tools and Menu Bars.)

6. How do you reset palettes to their default locations? (See Tutorial: Using and Organizing Palettes.)

7. Where is the Palette Well located? (See Tutorial: Using and Organizing Palettes.)

8. Why might it be frustrating to dock a frequently used palette, like the Layers palette, in the Palette Well? (See Tutorial: Using and Organizing Palettes.)

9. How do you dock one palette to another? (See Tutorial: Using and Organizing Palettes.)

10. Name three ways to choose a color in Photoshop Elements 2. (See Tutorial: Selecting Colors.)

11. What are brush dynamics options? (See Tutorial: Using Brushes.)

12. When would it make sense to change the preference for units of measurement on the rulers from inches to pixels? (See Tutorial: Setting Preferences.)

13. When might it help to reset all preferences to the default settings? (See Tutorial: Setting Preferences.)

14. At what four points in the image creation and editing process do color management issues come into play? (See Discussion: Color Management in Photoshop Elements 2.)

15. What three choices are offered in the Color Settings dialog box? (See Discussion: Color Management in Photoshop Elements 2.)

16. In what palette will you find recipes for performing common tasks? (See Discussion: Help System Summary.)

Session 3

Handling Documents

Session Introduction

This session covers functions and features related to the document window, where you create and edit images in Photoshop Elements 2. In the pages that follow, you practice controlling the magnification of images in the document window, opening a single image in multiple document windows, navigating in the document window, using rulers and grids, and seeking out sources of information about documents in Photoshop Elements 2. Most importantly, this session teaches you how to resize a document by modifying image size and resolution, changing canvas size, and cropping—all as you work toward the creation of another greeting card.

TOOLS YOU'LL USE
Document window, File Browser, Status bar, File Info dialog box, Info palette, Rulers, Grid, Zoom tool, Hand tool, Navigator palette, Image Size dialog box, Canvas Size dialog box, Crop tool

CD-ROM FILES NEEDED
03_stopwatch.psd, 03_stopwatch_end.psd

TIME REQUIRED
45 minutes

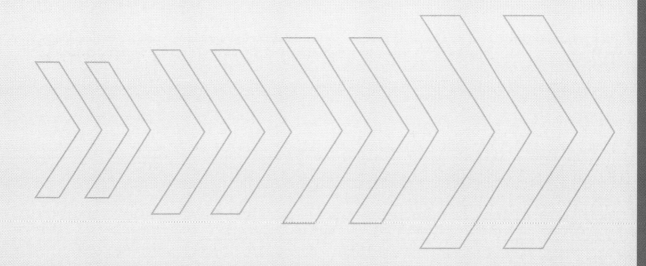

Tutorial

» Viewing Document Information

Photoshop Elements 2 offers multiple sources of information about image files. In this tutorial, you learn where those sources are located and what they offer. You review the information area in the File Browser and are introduced to the status bar, Info Palette, and File Info dialog box. You learn not only where to get document information, but also how to add information, such as copyright notices and captions, to an image.

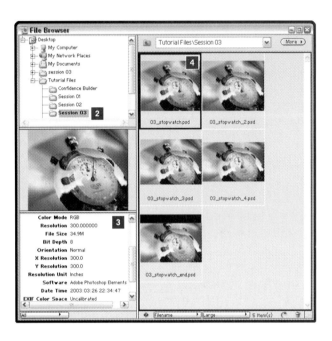

1. **Choose File→Browse to open the File Browser.**

2. **Navigate to the Tutorial Files→Session 03 folder on your hard drive in the file tree on the top left of the File Browser. Click once on the** 03_stopwatch.psd **thumbnail on the right side of the File Browser to select that file.**

3. **Look at the file information section at the bottom left of the File Browser.**

   This area contains information about the selected file, including its orientation, resolution, color space, dimensions, and the date and time it was created. You can view all the information by using the scroll bars to the right of the information section, or by clicking on the top border of the section and dragging up.

EXIF Data

You see even more information in the file information area of the File Browser when the files you work with are photographs imported from a digital camera. Many digital cameras embed detailed camera setting and file information, called EXIF data, in the images that they produce. Photoshop Elements 2 can read EXIF data and display it in both the File Browser and in the File Info dialog box. EXIF data includes all kinds of useful information about a digital photograph, including f-stop, shutter speed, lens size, white balance, date and time of exposure, format, and even whether a flash fired.

The way some digital cameras record a file's color space in EXIF data can cause photographs from those cameras to be treated incorrectly by the color management system in Photoshop Elements 2.0. Adobe offers a free plug-in for Photoshop Elements 2.0 to address this problem. You can download the Ignore EXIF Color Space plug-in from the Adobe Web site by going to www.adobe.com/support/downloads and following the link to Photoshop Elements 2.0 for Windows or Macintosh. The download page contains a more detailed explanation of the issue and instructions for installing the plug-in.

4. **Double-click the** `03_stopwatch.psd` **thumbnail in the File Browser to open the corresponding image in the document window.**

   The File Browser closes on its own by default. If it doesn't, click the red button on the top right (Macintosh: top left) of the File Browser to close it.

5. **In the status bar at the bottom of the application window (Macintosh: at the bottom of the document window), click the right-facing arrow to display a menu of information about the open document. Select Document Dimensions.**

   This displays the width and height of `03_stopwatch.psd` in the status bar. See the sidebar "Document Information Menu Items" for a description of each item in this menu.

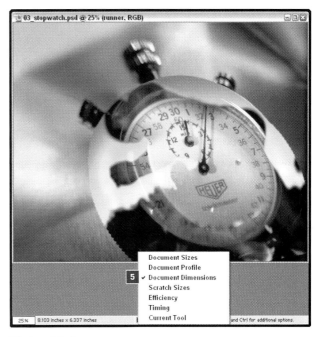

Windows interface

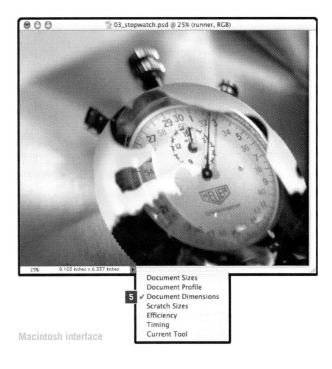

Macintosh interface

Document Information Menu Items

The menu of document information in the status bar contains the following items. Select any one of them to display that information in the status bar.

» **Document Sizes** displays two approximations of a document's file size. The number on the left is the approximate file size if all the document's layers were flattened into one. The number on the right is the file size with layers intact.

» **Document Profile** offers color management information about a document. It identifies the color mode of a document and whether a color profile has been embedded in the file. The Untagged notation indicates that this file does not carry a color profile. For more information on color profiles, be sure to read the discussion of Color Management in Session 2.

» **Document Dimensions** displays the height and width of a document.

» **Scratch Sizes** shows two measurements of RAM (random access memory), which is the memory that your computer uses to process operations. On the left, you see how much RAM is being used for currently open images. On the right, you see how much total RAM is available to Photoshop Elements 2. The program works most efficiently if the number on the left is smaller than the number on the right. Otherwise, Photoshop Elements 2 resorts to virtual memory (swapping files between RAM and your scratch disks).

» **Efficiency** indicates the percentage of time that Photoshop Elements 2 is using RAM, as opposed to virtual memory, for file processing. A value of 100% indicates that the program is running at its most efficient.

» **Timing** tells you the amount of time in seconds that Photoshop Elements 2 took to perform its last operation. You probably won't use this feature much, unless you're comparing one computer against another.

» **Current Tool** indicates which tool is selected in the toolbox. You may find this display handy if you're still learning the program's tools.

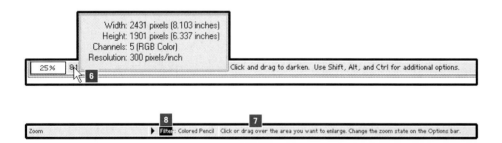

6. **Click and hold inside the information display in the status bar to reveal another menu with useful information about file size—document dimensions in both inches and pixels, color mode, the number of channels in the document, and resolution.**

7. **Windows users only: Select any tool in the toolbox.**
   The information about the selected tool is displayed on the right side of the status bar. The Macintosh status bar does not offer this feature.

8. **Windows users only: Choose Filter→Artistic→Colored Pencil from the menu bar.**
   The status bar tracks the progress of the filter as it's applied to the image. If you press Ctrl+Z, you stop the progress of the filter or undo the filter when it's finished. Filter progress on the Macintosh is displayed in a separate pop-up window, rather than in the status bar.

9. **Choose File→File Info from the menu bar to open the File Info dialog box. Click in the Section field and choose EXIF to switch to the EXIF pane.**
This is another place, in addition to the File Browser, to view detailed EXIF exposure information about a digital photograph.

10. **Click in the Section field of the File Info dialog box again, and choose General to switch back to the General pane.**

11. **In the General pane, type** Stopwatch Montage **in the Title field,** Kabili **in the Author field,** Photo Montage **in the Caption field, and** 2003 **in the Copyright Notice field, as shown in the illustration.**

12. **Click in the Copyright Status field in the File Info dialog box, and choose Copyrighted Work from the menu.**
This creates a copyright symbol (©) in both the title bar at the top of the document window, and in the status bar.

<TIP>
If you had a Web site that offered further copyright information, you could type the full Web address in the Owner URL field of the File Info dialog box. Viewers could go directly to that site on the Internet by clicking the Go To URL button in the File Info dialog box.

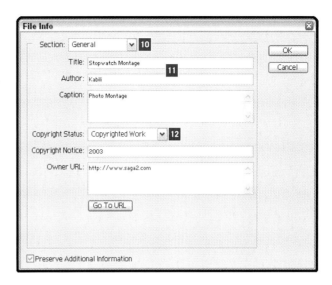

Uses for File Info

The information that you enter into the File Info dialog box can be used in several ways:

» The information is saved with the file and can be viewed in the File Info dialog box in Photoshop Elements 2 and in Photoshop.

» If you create a Picture Package (File→Print Layout→Picture Package), you can instruct the program to use one of these items as an image label. For example, you could print the author's name or the copyright notice across the center of proof prints in a Picture Package.

» If you create a Web Photo Gallery (File→Create Web Photo Gallery), you can tell the program to use this information as titles for the images and thumbnails in the resulting Web site.

» If you print an image, you can instruct the program to include the information that you entered in the Caption field as a caption under the printed image (File→Print Preview→Show More Options→Caption). Unfortunately, you have no control over the appearance of this caption, which always prints in the same font and size at the bottom center of the page. A more flexible way to create a caption is to increase the canvas size at the bottom of the document, as you learn to do later in this session, and then use the Type tool to create a caption in the font and size of your choosing. Use the Move tool to position the caption.

You revisit these techniques in the last session in this book.

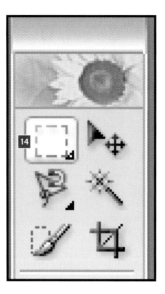

13. **Open the Info palette by choosing Window→Info.**
    The Info palette offers dynamic information about color and position as you work on an image in the document window.

14. **Click the Rectangular Marquee tool in the toolbox to select it.**

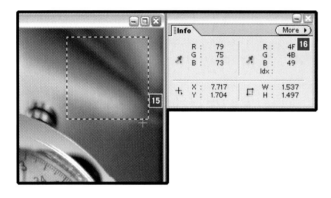

15. **Click and drag to draw a small rectangular selection in the image, keeping your eye on the changing values in the Info palette.**
    The color and location numbers in the Info palette change as you move your cursor in the document window.

< N O T E >

The Info palette is divided into four quadrants. The upper-left quadrant describes the color beneath the cursor using the actual color values of the document (RGB color for most images that you handle in Photoshop Elements 2). The upper-right quadrant identifies the same color using the special hexadecimal numbering system that describes color for the Web. The bottom-left quadrant tells you the X and Y coordinates of the location of the cursor, measured from the top-left corner of the document window. The bottom-right quadrant tells you the height and width of any selection that you drag out with a Selection or Crop tool.

16. **Click the More button at the top right of the Info palette. Choose Palette Options from the More menu to open the Info Options dialog box.**

17. **In the Info Options dialog box, click the Ruler Units field and choose Pixels from the menu.**

    Use the Info Options dialog box when you want to change the default units of measurement or color mode displays in the Info palette. You can see the effect of this change on Rulers in the next tutorial.

18. **Click OK to close the Info Options dialog box.**

19. **Choose Select→Deselect from the menu bar at the top of the screen to eliminate the selection you made in the image.**

20. **Choose File→Save As. In the Save As window, navigate to the ccproject folder on your hard drive.**

    Make sure that the format is set to Photoshop and that a check mark appears next to Layers.

21. **Click Save. Leave** 03_stopwatch.psd **open for the next tutorial.**

Associating Image File Formats with Photoshop Elements 2

If Photoshop Elements 2 is your main image editor, you may want to associate PSDs, JPEGs, GIFs, or other file formats with this program. When you double-click an image file whose format has been associated with Photoshop Elements 2, the file opens in this program rather than in Windows Picture and Fax Viewer, Macintosh Preview, Adobe Photoshop, or some other application.

If you installed Photoshop Elements 2 on Windows, you were asked at the time of installation which file formats you wanted to open with this program. Don't worry if you weren't sure what that meant at the time. It was just one way to associate files with Photoshop Elements 2. You can change or add to those associations after installation of Photoshop Elements 2. In Windows, one alternative is to set up file associations through the operating system. Right-click any image file of the desired format on your hard drive, and choose Properties from the menu. In the Properties dialog box, click the Change button in the General tab. In the Open With dialog box, choose Adobe Photoshop Elements. Make sure that a check mark appears next to *Always use the selected program to open this kind of file*, and click OK. Back in the Properties dialog box, click Apply and OK.

A second option for Windows users is the File Association Manager located inside Photoshop Elements 2 for Windows. In the program, choose Edit→File Association from the menu bar. In the File Association Manager dialog box, put a check mark next to all the file formats that you want to associate with Photoshop Elements 2, and click OK. Note that this has no effect on a file format that you have previously associated with a different program through the operating system, as described in the preceding paragraph. You have to go back to the Windows Properties dialog box to modify an association made there.

Macintosh users have no File Association Manager in Photoshop Elements 2. Changes to file associations can be made only through the Macintosh operating system. Click once on a file of the desired format on your hard drive to select that file, and choose Get Info from the File menu in the Finder. In the Info window, click the right-facing arrow next to Open with. Choose Adobe Photoshop Elements 2 from the menu. Click the Change All button to apply the association to all files of the selected format (with the exception of files created in the full version of Photoshop). Click continue at the prompt.

After you make these changes, it's quick and easy to open a file in Photoshop Elements 2 by double-clicking its filename on your hard drive.

Tutorial
» Using Rulers and Grids

Sometimes, you want to align items to one another or position items or selections in particular locations in the document window. Rulers and Grids can help you do that. In this tutorial, you explore how these features work.

1. Use the copy of 03_stopwatch.psd **that you left open at the end of the last tutorial, or reopen** 03_stopwatch.psd **from the Session 03 Tutorial Files folder on your hard drive.**

2. **Choose View→Rulers from the menu bar at the top of the screen.** This opens a horizontal ruler at the top and a vertical ruler at the left side of the document window.

<CAUTION>

You changed Ruler Units to pixels in the Info Options dialog box in the last tutorial. The program assumes that you want to use pixels in your rulers as well as in the Info palette. This is a hidden feature that could catch you off-guard.

3. **Right-click (Macintosh: Ctrl+click) inside a ruler to display a contextual menu, and choose Inches from that menu.** This changes the unit of measurement in both rulers back to inches.

4. **Move your cursor around in the document window, and notice that small dotted lines in both rulers identify the location of the cursor at all times.**

5. **Click and hold inside the small square intersection of the two rulers at the top left of the document window, and drag diagonally down and to the right toward the stopwatch in the image.**
A horizontal guide and a vertical guide indicate your location as you drag.

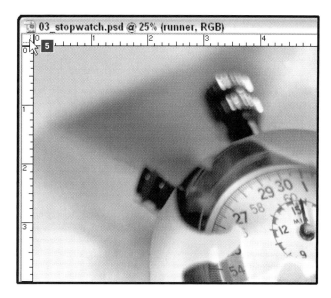

6. **Release the mouse anywhere inside the image.**
The 0 point on each ruler relocates to the point at which you released the mouse. Relocating the 0 points on the rulers can help you measure from a particular point in the image.

03_stopwatch.psd @ 25% (runner, RGB)

7

<CAUTION>

If you have trouble drawing selections or crops or positioning items where you want them, it's probably because the Snap to Grid feature is on. Snap to Grid magnetizes the grid so that objects and selections snap to its intersections. Choose View→Snap to Grid to deselect this feature.

7. **Double-click in the small square at the top left of the document window to return the 0 point of both rulers to their original location at the top left of the document window.**

8. **Choose View→Grid from the menu bar at the top of the screen to open a grid that spans the document window.**
   The grid is not part of the image and does not print or save with the image. It just acts as a reference against which you can position, rotate, or align artwork or selections in the document window.

<TIP>

Choose Edit→Preferences→Grid (Macintosh: Photoshop Elements→Preferences→Grid) to open a Preferences panel in which you can change the style of the grid. If the grid is difficult to see, click in the Color field to choose a brighter color. If you want the grid to be less prominent, click in the Style field and choose Dots as the grid style. If you want to change the location of the grid lines, make changes in the Gridline spacing or Subdivisions fields in this Preference panel.

9. **Choose View→Grid again to close the Grid.**

10. **Leave** 03_stopwatch.psd **open for the next tutorial.**
    You don't need to save now because you made no changes to the image in this tutorial. It simply walked you through how to use rulers and grids to your benefit when working on your project.

Tutorial
» Zooming In and Out

This tutorial covers increasing and decreasing the magnification at which you view an image in the document window. As you work through this tutorial, keep in mind that changing image magnification has no effect on the actual size of the image; it affects only how you see an image on your screen.

1. Use the copy of 03_stopwatch.psd **that you left open at the end of the last tutorial, or reopen** 03_stopwatch.psd **from the Session 03 Tutorial Files folder on your hard drive.**

< N O T E >

When you first open an image, it appears at the highest of the program's preset magnification levels that can display the entire image on your screen. This depends on the size and display resolution of your monitor. On a 17-inch monitor set to 1024x768 pixels, this image opens at 25 percent. Your settings may be different.

2. Click the Zoom tool in the toolbox to select it.
   The Options bar changes to display options specific to the Zoom tool.

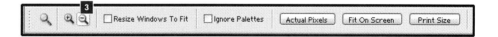

3. Select the Zoom Out button (the one with the minus symbol) in the Options bar.

4. Click inside the document window until the magnification percentage in the title bar of the document window reads 16.7%.
   Zooming out decreases the magnification at which you see an image, making the image appear smaller on your screen (although the actual image size has not changed). The gray area around the image is empty space in the document window that is not part of the image.

< T I P >

Zooming out is useful when you are working on an image that is larger than your screen and you want to see the whole image, or when you want to fit more than one image on your screen at the same time.

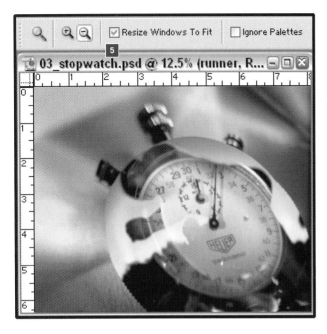

<NOTE>

The magnification percentage of an image is displayed in two places—in the title bar of the document window and at the far left of the status bar at the bottom of the application window (Macintosh: bottom of the document window).

5. In the Options bar, select Resize Windows to Fit. Then click inside the image to zoom out again to 12.5%.

The gray area in the document window disappears as the document window resizes to match the new image magnification. Leave this option checked to automatically resize the document window as you zoom in or out.

<NOTE>

You can resize the document window manually. Move your mouse over the bottom-right corner of the document window until the cursor becomes a diagonal double-pointed arrow. (Macintosh: Move your mouse over the diagonal lines at the bottom-right corner of the document window.) Then click and drag to resize the document window. In Windows only, you can also click and drag any edge of the document window to resize the corresponding dimension separately.

6. Switch to the Zoom In button (the one with the plus symbol) in the Options bar, and click twice in the document window to zoom in to 25%.

Zooming in magnifies your view of the image, making it appear larger on your screen.

<TIP>

Zooming in is useful when you want to do close work, like selecting a tight area with the Selection brush or covering unwanted pixels with the Clone tool. However, giving your work a final review at 100% magnification is always wise, because that's how your audience usually sees the work.

7. With the Zoom tool selected in the toolbox and the Zoom In button still selected in the Options bar, click and drag around the center of the watch in the image.

You now see the selected area magnified to the highest percentage (up to a maximum of 1600%) at which it fits on your screen.

<TIP>

While you select an area to magnify, you can move the selection boundary so that you can zero in on a desired spot. With the Zoom tool, click and begin dragging out a selection. Then, without releasing the mouse, click and hold the spacebar and drag the selection to a new place in the image. Release the spacebar, but not the mouse, and continue to drag out a selection boundary. Don't worry if you find this difficult. It's a relatively advanced technique.

8. **Click the Fit On Screen button in the Zoom tool Options bar.**
   This displays the image at the largest magnification at which the entire image fits on your screen.

<TIP>
The downside of using the Fit On Screen button is that it usually results in fractional magnification levels, which can cause an image to look degraded. Instead, use the Zoom tool to zoom to a round numbered preset (25%, 50%, or 100%) at which your entire image fits on screen. These particular presets often make an image look smoother on screen, particularly if the image includes text.

9. **Click the Actual Pixels button in the Zoom tool Options bar.**
   This displays the image at 100% magnification. You can't see the entire image in the document window because at 100% this image is 2431 pixels wide and 1901 pixels high (according to the pop-up information box in the status bar), and the document window is smaller than that (according to a right-click [Macintosh: Ctrl+click] in the rulers to temporarily change them to pixels). Notice that the document window resized when you clicked the Actual Pixels button, but it stopped short of the space occupied by your palettes.

10. **Select the Zoom Out button in the Options bar, and click in the image to zoom back to any magnification lower than 100%.**

Multiple Ways to Zoom In and Out

You can increase or reduce image magnification in Photoshop Elements 2 in many ways, as summarized here. Pick a couple of favorites and stick with them to keep things simple.

» Click with the Zoom tool: Select the Zoom In or Zoom Out button in the Options bar, and click with the Zoom tool in the document window to use preset magnification levels. The view centers on the spot you click.

» Click and drag with the Zoom tool: Select the Zoom Out button in the Options bar, and click and drag around an area that you want to magnify. The program chooses the highest image magnification that will display all of the selected area on your screen.

» Use the scroll wheel on your mouse: If your mouse has a scroll wheel, click and hold the Alt key (Macintosh: Option key) while you use the scroll wheel to zoom in and out. This works only if the image is smaller than the document window. If you zoom in so that the image is larger than the document window, the mouse scroll wheel acts like a scroll bar, moving the image in the document window.

» Enter a custom magnification level: Type a percentage between .04% and 1600% in the Image Magnification field at the far left of the status bar.

» Toggle between zoom options: With the Zoom tool set to zoom out mode, Alt+click (Macintosh: Option+click) in the document window to zoom in. When you release the mouse, the Zoom tool returns to zoom-out mode. The opposite is true when the Zoom tool is set to zoom-in mode; this shortcut temporarily changes it to zoom-out mode.

» Choose View→Zoom In or View→Zoom Out from the menu bar.

» Use the Navigator palette: In the Navigator palette, move the Zoom Slider, enter a custom percentage, or click the Zoom In or Zoom Out buttons.

» View the image at 100% magnification: Double-click the Zoom tool, click the Actual Pixels button in the Options bar, or choose View→Actual Pixels in the menu bar to magnify an image to 100%.

» View the image at the largest magnification that fits on your screen: Double-click the Hand tool, click the Fit On Screen button in the Zoom tool's Options bar, or choose View→ Fit on Screen to display an image at the largest magnification at which the entire image fits on your screen.

11. **With the Zoom tool still selected, put a check mark next to Ignore Palettes in the Options bar. Then click the Actual Pixels button again.**

    The document window expands beneath your open palettes, displaying even more of the image at 100% magnification.

12. **Leave** 03_stopwatch.psd **open at 100% magnification for the next tutorial.**

    You don't need to save because no substantive changes were made.

Tutorial

» Opening Multiple Document Windows

In this short tutorial, you learn how to display a single image in multiple document windows. This comes in handy when you have to zoom in close to an image to do detail work, but you want to keep an eye on the big picture at the same time.

<NOTE>

Photoshop Elements 2 has two preset window arrangements that you can try. Choose Window→Images→Tile to place multiple windows next to one another, or choose Window→Images→Cascade to overlap multiple windows. Determine the best arrangement for multiple windows on a case-by-case basis. One arrangement may be better than another depending on the image involved and your monitor setup.

1. Use the copy of 03_stopwatch.psd that you left open at the end of the last tutorial, or reopen 03_stopwatch.psd from the Session 03 Tutorial Files folder on your hard drive.

2. Select View→New View from the menu bar to open another document window containing the same image.
   The availability of multiple document windows allows you to do close up work at a high magnification, and also see the results in a low-magnification view of the entire image. Changes made in either document window appear simultaneously in the other view.

3. Click on the smaller document window with the Zoom Out option selected to reduce that view to 12.5%.
   This is a comfortable working arrangement that gives you access to both windows.

4. Close the smaller document window by clicking the red button at its top right (Macintosh: top left). Leave the document window with the 100% view open for the next tutorial.

Tutorial
» Navigating in the Document Window

When you work on an image that's larger than the document window, knowing how to move the image around in the document window so that you can access all parts of the image is important. In this tutorial, you use scroll bars, the Hand tool, and the Navigator palette to navigate in the Document Window.

1. **Continue using** 03_stopwatch.psd **from the last tutorial. If you closed it, open the original document from the Session 03 Tutorial Files folder on your hard drive.**

2. **If no scroll bars appear at both the bottom and right sides of the document window, select the Zoom tool in the toolbox and the Zoom In button on the Options bar, and click in the document window until you see scroll bars.**
   Scroll bars indicate that the image has been magnified to a point at which it is larger than the document window.

3. **Click and drag either of the scroll bars to see a different area of the document in the document window.**
   You can access all areas of a large document with the scroll bars, but it can be awkward.

4. **Click on the Hand tool in the toolbox to select that tool.**
   The Hand tool offers a more flexible way to access all areas of a document on screen.

5. **Click anywhere in the document window with the Hand tool, and drag to move the image around in the document window.**

<CAUTION>
A common mistake is to try to use the Move tool to navigate in the document window. If you do that, you end up moving just the selected layer of artwork, destroying the composition. The Hand tool is the proper tool for this purpose.

6. **Select any tool in the toolbox, press the spacebar to switch the cursor temporarily to the Hand tool, and drag to move the image in the document window.**
   When you release the spacebar, the cursor changes back to the selected tool. This allows you to navigate around the image regardless of the tool selected.

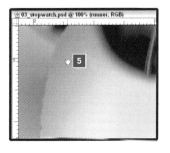

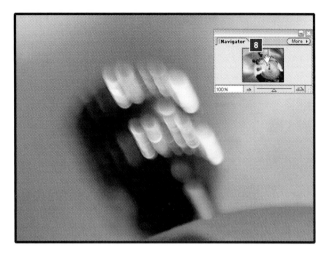

7. **Choose Window→Navigator to open the Navigator palette.**

   The Navigator palette usually opens in the Palette Well.

< T I P >

You can drag the Navigator palette by its tab out of the Palette Well if you prefer that it stay open while you work. Otherwise, the Navigator palette closes back into the Palette Well every time you click elsewhere on the screen.

8. **Click inside the red box in the Navigator palette and drag.**

   This moves the image inside the document window. You see the same area in the document window that is defined by the red box in the Navigator palette. The red box acts like a remote control to help you navigate to a particular area that you want to access in the document window.

9. **Move the Zoom Slider at the bottom of the Navigator palette to the left.**

   This causes the image in the document window to zoom out, and the larger area defined by the red box in the Navigator palette is visible in the document window. You can also use the mountain icons to the left and right of the Zoom Slider in the Navigator palette to zoom in or out by preset percentages, or you can type a zoom percentage into the field at the bottom left of the Navigator palette.

10. **Close** 03_stopwatch.psd **without saving.**

    In this tutorial you learned several different ways to move around a large image in the document window, using scroll bars, the Hand tool, and the Navigator palette.

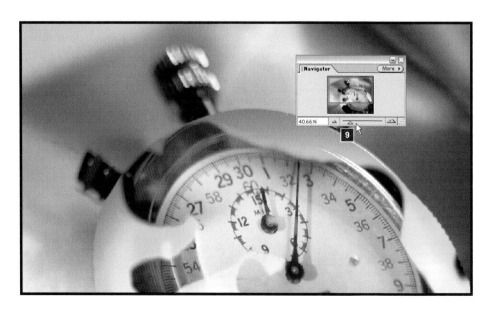

Tutorial
» Changing Image Size and Resolution

This tutorial addresses the important topic of how and when to change image size and resolution. You learn to size an image in two ways. You use the nondestructive method, which trades off physical dimensions for resolution, leaving the total file size of the image the same. Then you permanently change the total file size by resampling the information in the image. It's okay to resample down, but not to resample up. It's important to understand the distinctions between changing image size, cropping, and changing canvas size. I suggest that you treat this and the next two tutorials as a group, working through all of them in one sitting.

1. **Open** `03_stopwatch.psd` **from the Session 03 Tutorial Files folder on your hard drive.**
   Start again with the original file in case you inadvertently changed the copy you were working on in the preceding tutorials.

2. **Choose Image→Resize→Image Size from the menu bar to open the Image Size dialog box.**
   The Document Size section of this dialog box indicates that this image is 8.103 inches wide by 6.337 inches high, with a resolution of 300 pixels per inch (ppi). This results in a total file size, reported at the top of the dialog box, of 13.2 megabytes (M). For purposes of this example, assume that your printer, like many current ink jet printers, needs only 240 ppi to make an optimal print.

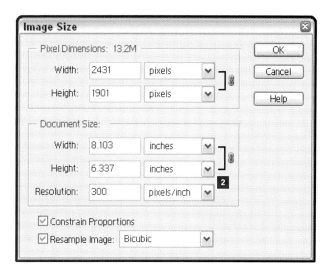

<NOTE>
Reread the Discussion called "Understanding Resolution" in Session 1 if you want to refresh your memory about inkjet printer resolution.

3. **In the Image Size dialog box, uncheck Resample Image if a check mark appears in that box.**
   This tells the program not to recalculate the total file size of the image.

4. **Click in the Resolution field, and type** 240 **in place of 300.**
   This instructs the program to reduce the number of pixels in each inch of the image. When you decrease the number of pixels per inch from 300 to 240, the Width and Height fields in the Image Size dialog box automatically increase to 10.129 inches and 7.921 inches respectively to compensate. The overall file size displayed at the top of the dialog box (13.2M) remains constant.

5. **Click OK to close the Image Size dialog box.**
   The physical dimensions of the image are resized.

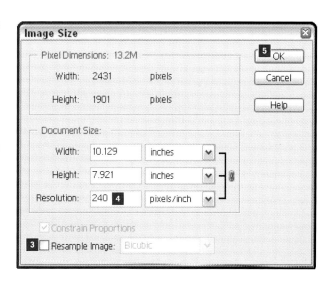

03_stopwatch.psd @ 25% (runner, RGB)

<NOTE>

Understanding why the width and height automatically increase when you change resolution with Resample unchecked is important. The overall file size is a function of the physical dimensions of the image (the width and height in inches) and the resolution (the number of pixels per inch). When you uncheck Resample Image, you tell Photoshop Elements 2 to keep the overall file size the same. When you type **240** in the resolution field, you tell the program to decrease resolution. Simple math tells you that the trade-off has to be an increase in the physical dimensions of the image, which the program calculates for you and reports in the Width and Height fields.

6. **Take a look at the rulers in the document window to confirm that the physical dimensions of the document have increased to around 10 inches by 8 inches.**

   In the next steps you use resampling to reduce the physical dimensions and overall file size of the image while retaining its 240 ppi resolution so that it prints well.

<NOTE>

The current dimensions are larger than the greeting card that you are creating.

<NOTE>

If you make an error when you fill in the Image Size dialog box and want to start over, press the Alt (Macintosh: Option) key to temporarily change the Cancel button in the dialog box to a Reset button. Without releasing the mouse, click the Reset button to put all values in the dialog box back to their last settings.

7. **Choose Image➞Resize➞Image Size from the menu bar to open the Image Size dialog box again.**

Using Images from Digital Cameras

If you shoot photos with a digital camera that exports images to your computer at 72 ppi, the images look blurry and pixelated when you print them. As you learned in Session 1, most inkjet printers need a resolution of more than 72 ppi. Optimal print quality on a desktop inkjet printer requires around 240 to 300 ppi.

To ensure optimal print quality, you must increase the resolution of photos that come into your computer at 72 ppi. If you increase

resolution in the Image Size dialog box, leave Resample Image unchecked to avoid resampling up. Change the value in the Resolution field to between 240 and 300, and expect a significant reduction in width and height as a trade-off. If you're unhappy with the smaller physical dimensions of the photographs, the solution is to shoot with a camera capable of producing more file information.

8. **In the Image Size dialog box, select Resample Image Size so that a check mark appears in that box.**
   This instructs the program to recalculate the total file size of the image.

9. **Place a check mark next to Constrain Proportions if it isn't already checked.**
   This instructs the program to maintain the proportional ratio of height to width when it resizes the image.

10. **Make sure that the Width and Height fields are set to inches. Then type** 7.5 **in the Width field.**
    The Height field changes automatically to around 5.86 inches. Photoshop Elements 2 reduces image height so that it's proportional to the width you enter because you selected Constrain Proportions. Otherwise, the resized image would be disproportionately tall. Also notice that the Resolution field remains set to 240 pixels per inch. There is no trade-off of resolution for physical dimensions as there was the last time you resized (in Steps 2 through 5), because this time you instruct the program to resample (which means recalculate) the total file size.

11. **Notice that the total file size reported at the top of the Image Size dialog box decreases from 13.2M to 7.25M.**
    The total file size is smaller because you're instructing the program to resample the file information down, reducing one component of the equation (physical dimensions) without increasing the other (resolution).

12. **Click OK to close the Image Size dialog box and resize the image.**

13. **Choose File➜Save As, navigate to the ccproject folder on your hard drive, and click Save.**

14. **Leave this file open for the next tutorial.**

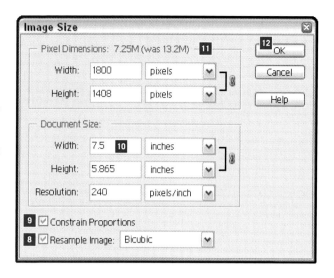

<NOTE>
In most cases, you don't harm your image by resampling down. However, resampling up usually degrades the appearance of an image because the program has to manufacture information to fill in the gaps. This means that you should always try to start your work in Photoshop Elements 2 with photographs, scans, and other source images that have sufficient file size to cover the resolution and physical dimensions of your largest planned output.

Tutorial

» Cropping an Image

In this tutorial, you use the Crop tool in two ways. First, you manually create a crop marquee to define the boundaries of a crop. Second, you apply the fixed-size crop option to resize the image as you crop away unwanted portions.

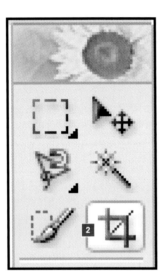

1. **Continue with** `03_stopwatch.psd` **open from the previous tutorial. If you closed that file, reopen it from your ccproject folder.**
   As a reminder, the file you start this tutorial with is 7.5 inches wide and around 5.86 inches high at 240 ppi.

2. **Select the Crop tool in the toolbox.**

3. **Click Clear in the Options bar to make sure that no fixed-size height, width, or resolution settings remain from a previous use of the Crop tool.**

<TIP>

If you ever have trouble dragging out a crop selection boundary, it's probably because some fixed-size settings are left over from the last time you used the Crop tool.

4. **Click on the bottom-right corner of the document window, and drag to expose some gray area in the document window.**
   Dragging a selection outline to the edge of an image is easier if you start and end in the gray area of the document window.

5. **Move your mouse into the gray area of the document window just to the left of the image at around the 5 5/8-inch mark on the vertical ruler.**

   Use the small dotted line on the ruler to identify the location of your cursor.

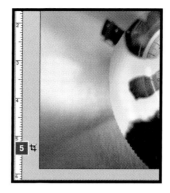

6. **Drag a selection boundary up and to the right. Release the cursor when the boundary encompasses all of the upper part of the image, as in the illustration.**

   The area outside the selection boundary is the portion that is cropped away. It is darker than the rest of the image by default. You can remove the dark shield over this area for a clearer view of the area to be cropped by deselecting Shield in the Options bar.

   < T I P >
   If you need to adjust your selection, with the Crop tool still selected, click on any of the selection boundaries or anchor points and drag. You can move the entire selection by clicking inside it and dragging. You can rotate the selection by clicking just outside one of the corners of the selection and dragging.

7. **When you're satisfied with your selection, click the large check mark at the top right of the Options bar.**

   The crop is performed, and the result resembles the illustration.

   < T I P >
   Press the Esc key to cancel the crop at any time before you perform it. Even after you perform a crop, you can undo it by choosing Edit→Step Backward.

8. **Choose File→Save As. In the Save As dialog box, navigate to your ccproject folder and click Save to protect your work.**

9. **With the Crop tool still selected in the toolbox, in the Options bar, click in the Width box and type** 6.25 in**, click in the Height box and type** 3.8 in**, and then click in the Resolution box and type** 240**.**

Don't forget to type the abbreviation **in** after the measurements, or you may get a selection boundary measured in pixels.

10. **Click in the gray area of the document window just outside the bottom left of the image, and drag up and to the right to create a selection boundary.**

Don't stop along the way, or your selection will be smaller than you intended. If your selection doesn't look like that in the illustration, press the Esc key and perform this step again.

11. **Click the large check mark on the Options bar to perform the crop.**

You can see your results in the illustration.

12. **Click in the information area on the left side of the status bar to see image details.**

The image is now 6.25 inches wide by 3.8 inches tall at a resolution of 240 ppi. When the Crop tool is set to a fixed size, as it was here, it not only selects and removes part of the image, it also resizes the remaining portion of the image to your settings.

13. **Choose File→Save As, navigate to your ccprojects folder, and click Save. Leave this file open for the next tutorial.**

In the previous two tutorials you changed the size of the image several ways: by resizing with and without resampling, by manually cropping, and by cropping and resizing at the same time. You now have an image that is slightly smaller than the greeting card you're creating.

Tutorial
» Changing Canvas Size

Every Photoshop image has a backdrop called the canvas that can be increased separately from the image. This feature comes in handy when you want to add to the area of an image without resizing or scaling the original image. You use this feature in this tutorial to make some space at the top of your collage for adding more imagery.

1. **Continue with the file left open in the last tutorial—**
   `03_stopwatch.psd`. **If you closed that file, reopen it from your ccproject folder.**
   As a reminder, the file is now 6.25 inches wide by 3.8 inches high at a resolution of 240 ppi.

2. **Click the default color icon (the tiny black and white squares) at the bottom of the toolbox to set the Foreground Color box in the toolbox to black and the Background Color box to white.**

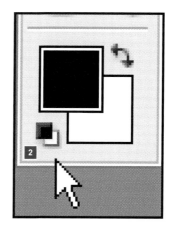

3. **Click the double-pointed arrow above and to the right of the Color Boxes in the toolbox to switch the default colors.**
   The Background Color box in the toolbox changes to black.

4. **Choose Image→Resize→Canvas Size to open the Canvas Size dialog box.**

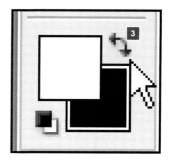

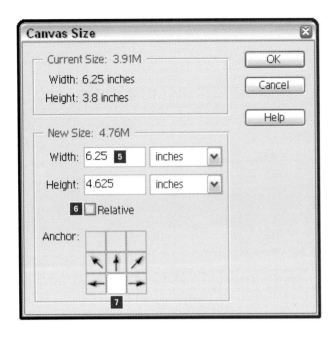

5. **Set the Width and Height fields to inches in the Canvas Size dialog box. Leave the Width field set to 6.25 and type** 4.625 **in the Height field in place of 3.8.**

6. **Uncheck the Relative check box in the Canvas Size dialog box.**
   If the Relative box is checked, the program adds 6.25 inches to the existing height of the canvas and 4.625 inches to the existing width of the canvas, creating a canvas that's much bigger than the 6.25-inch by 4.625-inch greeting card that you're making.

< TIP >
The Relative box is useful, for example, if you want to add 1 inch to the bottom of an image for a caption. You would type **1** in the Height field, leave the Width field blank, and click the center square in the top row of the anchor icon to add an extra inch to the bottom of the canvas.

7. **Click the center square in the bottom row of the anchor icon so that the extra canvas is added to the top of the image.**
   The square in which you click represents the existing canvas. The arrows indicate the directions in which new canvas is added. The trick is to click on a square that is opposite the intended location of the additional canvas.

8. **Click OK to close the Canvas Size dialog box and increase the Canvas size, adding canvas to the top of the image.**
   The extra canvas automatically fills with black, the color you set in the Background Color box, as you see in the illustration.

9. **Choose File→Save As. In the Save As dialog box, name this file** 03_stopwatch_end, **and navigate to your ccproject folder. Make sure that Format is set to Photoshop, and Layers is checked. Click Save.**
   You complete this greeting card in the next session. You increased the canvas size in this tutorial, without affecting the size of the stopwatch image. You now have additional space to add more imagery to this greeting card, which you do in the next session.

» Session Review

You used some fundamental document handling features in this session. You learned how to change image size, resolution, and canvas size. You cropped a document manually and with fixed-size measurements. You learned about changing the magnification at which you view documents. You practiced navigating around a document, and you opened a single document in multiple windows. You learned about using rulers and grids in the document window and where to find information about documents in Photoshop Elements 2.

1. Where can you find EXIF data imported from a digital camera in Photoshop Elements 2? (See Tutorial: Viewing Document Information.)

2. What information is found in the Info palette? (See Tutorial: Viewing Document Information.)

3. How do you change rulers from displaying pixels to displaying inches? (See Tutorial: Using Rulers and Grids.)

4. What does the Snap to Grid feature do? (See Tutorial: Using Rulers and Grids.)

5. List two ways to zoom in to and out of an image. (See Tutorial: Zooming In and Out.)

6. What is the result of putting a check mark next to Resize Windows to Fit in the Zoom tool Options bar? (See Tutorial: Zooming In and Out.)

7. What is the result of putting a check mark next to Ignore Palettes in the Zoom tool Options bar? (See Tutorial: Zooming In and Out.)

8. In what situation might it be helpful to view a single image in multiple document windows? (See Tutorial: Opening Multiple Document Windows.)

9. Which tool should you use to move an image around in the document window—the Zoom tool, the Move tool, or the Hand tool? (See Tutorial: Navigating in the Document Window.)

10. How do you zoom in close to a particular area of a document? (See Tutorial: Navigating in the Document Window.)

11. What are you asking the program to do if you put a check mark next to Resample Image in the Image Size dialog box? (See Tutorial: Changing Image Size and Resolution.)

12. In the Image Size dialog box, what happens to the Width and Height measurements if you uncheck Resample Image and increase the value in the Resolution field? (See Tutorial: Changing Image Size and Resolution.)

13. How do you remove part of the image and resize the portion that remains at the same time using the Crop tool? (See Tutorial: Cropping an Image.)

14. When you're increasing canvas size, how do you make sure that the additional canvas appears at the top of the image? (See Tutorial: Changing Canvas Size.)

15. What is the function of the Relative check box in the Canvas Size dialog box? (See Tutorial: Changing Canvas Size.)

Fixing Mistakes

Session Introduction

This session covers the indispensable features in Photoshop Elements 2 that allow you to move backward and forward in time. You use these features often to fix mistakes; however, that's not their only value. The undo commands, the Undo History palette, the Revert command, and the eraser tools also give you the freedom to experiment and to exercise the prerogative to change your mind as you create. In this session, you learn how and when to use each eraser tool—the Eraser, the Background Eraser, and the Magic Eraser tools. You see how easy it is to reverse actions you take by using the Undo and Step Backward commands and their shortcuts. Then you learn a more controlled way to retrace your steps in the Undo History palette. Finally, you apply the wholesale Revert command to return to the last saved version of a file. The product of these tutorials is a piece of artwork with transparent pixels, which you combine with the image that you worked on in the last session to complete another in your line of greeting cards.

TOOLS YOU'LL USE
Eraser tool, Magic Eraser tool, Background Eraser tool, Undo command,
Step Backward button, Undo History palette, Revert command

CD-ROM FILES NEEDED
04_runners.psd, 04_stopwatch_.psd,
04_stopwatch_end.psd

TIME REQUIRED
30 minutes

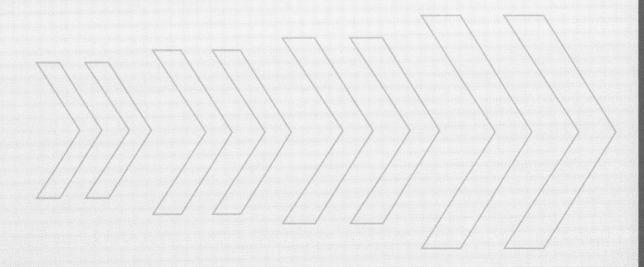

Tutorial
» Using the Eraser Tools and the Undo Commands

When you make a mistake, your first reaction might be to reach for the Eraser tool. However, there are other tools in the eraser group—the Background Eraser and the Magic Eraser tools—that are sometimes more useful. You get a chance to try out and compare all three of the eraser tools in this tutorial. At the same time, you take a look at the undo commands.

1. **Open** 04_runners.psd **from the Tutorial Files→Session 04 folder on your hard drive.**

<NOTE>
Resetting your tools at the beginning of each session is a good idea, so that your tool options match those in the illustrations. Click on whichever tool icon is displayed at the top left of the Options bar, and choose Reset All Tools.

2. **Choose File→Save As from the Photoshop Elements 2 menu bar. In the Save As dialog box, select the As a Copy check box, navigate to the ccproject folder on your hard drive, and click Save.**
The Save As dialog box closes. This preserves an untouched, closed copy of this file named 04_runners copy.psd. This copy offers the ultimate undo because you can always come back to it to begin again. 04_runners.psd remains open for you to work on in this tutorial.

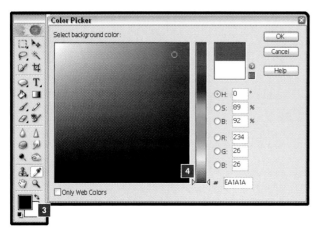

3. **Click in the Background Color box at the bottom of the toolbox to open the Color Picker.**

4. **Move the vertical color slider in the Color Picker to red. Click in the bright red area on the left side of the Color Picker to select a bright red. Click OK to close the Color Picker.**
This fills the toolbox's Background Color box with red, defining the background color to be used by the Eraser tool in the next steps.

5. **Click the Eraser tool, represented by a plain eraser icon in the toolbox, to select that tool.**

The Eraser tool is stored in a tool group with the Background Eraser and Magic Eraser tools. If one of these other eraser tools was last selected, its icon, rather than the Eraser tool icon, is displayed in the toolbox. In that case, click and hold whichever tool is displayed in place of the Eraser tool and choose the Eraser tool from the flyout menu that appears.

6. **Click the Mode button in the Eraser tool's Options bar and choose Block.**

You have the option to erase in the shape of a block, a preset brush, or a preset hard-edged pencil. The block is particularly useful for erasing along a straight, hard edge.

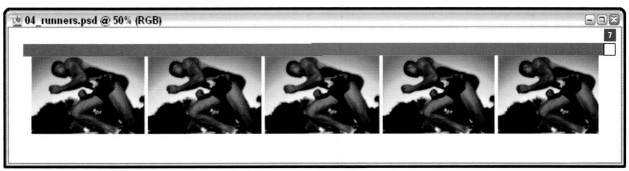

7. **Shift+click in the white area just above and to the left of the small images of the runner. Then Shift+click in the white area just above and to the right of those images to erase in a straight line.**

The Eraser tool erases to the red background color. You may be surprised by the behavior of the Eraser tool. When it's used on a *Background* layer, the Eraser tool reveals the color in the Background Color box in the toolbox, rather than the transparent pixels that you might expect. Your red erasure is not the transparent result you're after.

< N O T E >

A ***Background*** layer is a layer with special properties that differentiate it from a regular layer. Open the Layers palette (Window→Layers) to confirm that you have been working on a layer labeled ***Background***. If this were a regular layer, the Eraser tool would have revealed transparent pixels, because there's nothing beneath this layer. The upcoming session on layers contains more information on ***Background*** layers.

< T I P >

Shift+clicking with the Eraser tool constrains the erasure to a 90° line. Alternatively, you can click and drag to use the Eraser tool in a freehand manner.

8. **Choose Edit→Undo Eraser from the menu bar at the top of the screen.**

   This reverses the last operation you performed, removing most of the red erasure mark from the image. Notice that one red block is still left in the image. That's because it took more than one operation to create the erasure.

<N O T E>

After you undo a step, you can change your mind and redo that step. Click on the Edit menu again, and notice that the first item in the menu now reads Redo Eraser. You can toggle back and forth between Redo Eraser and Undo Eraser until you perform another operation.

9. **Choose Edit→Step Backward to undo another step, removing the red block.**

   The first item in the Edit menu now reads Undo State Change. This command, which appears when you've undone all your preceding operations, gives you the opportunity to undo one more thing—your last step backward. Continue without clicking Undo State Change.

<N O T E>

You can step backward up to 20 states by default. This number can be increased up to 100 states in the General pane of the Preferences dialog box, but only at the expense of available memory. States are steps that are listed in the History palette.

10. **Click and hold the Eraser tool in the toolbox, and choose the Background Eraser tool from the flyout menu.**

    The Background Eraser is a combination selection tool and eraser tool. It selects pixels by their color and deletes those pixels.

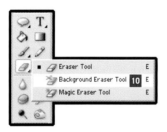

11. **In the Background Eraser tool's Options bar, click the arrow on the Size field. Move the Size slider to around 80 pixels to set the diameter of the Background Eraser.**

    Leave the other options at their defaults as in the illustration. Limits→Contiguous tells the Background Eraser to erase only pixels that are touching one another. This avoids inadvertently erasing any white pixels in the small images of the runner. Tolerance describes how close in color pixels must be to the pixel under the Background Eraser's crosshair in order to be affected by the Background Eraser tool.

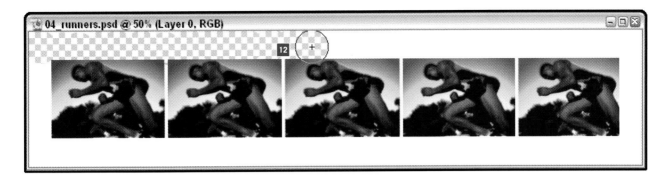

12. **Click and drag with the crosshair of the Background Eraser in the white area around the images of the runner. As you move the cursor, the Background Eraser deletes pixels inside the circle that are similar in color to the pixel currently under the crosshair.**

    The trick to using the Background Eraser is to keep the crosshair over the background color (white), and not to move it over the foreground images. If you inadvertently erase parts of a foreground image, choose Edit→Step Backward to restore the foreground image.

<NOTE>

The gray checkerboard pattern that you see after erasing represents transparent pixels. Unlike the Eraser tool, the Background Eraser erases to transparency even on a ***Background*** layer or on a layer with locked transparent pixels.

13. **Press the left bracket ([) key on your keyboard six times to reduce the diameter of the Background Eraser tool to 20 pixels, as reported in the Size field of the Options bar.**

    The left bracket key reduces the diameter of the Background Eraser by 10 pixels at a time. The right bracket key increases the diameter by the same increment. These are useful shortcuts for modifying the size of the Background Eraser tool on the fly.

14. **Shift+click at the top and then at the bottom of one of the narrow white areas between the images to erase the white background there without affecting the images.**

    This constrains the erasure to a 90-degree line, which comes in handy in a tight space like this.

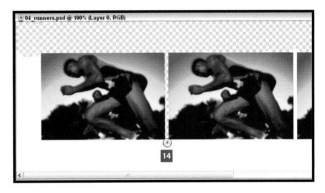

<NOTE>

The Background Eraser is particularly useful for deleting backgrounds, as its name implies. It usually doesn't leave a fringe of background pixels around the foreground image. The main advantage of the Background Eraser tool is that you can change its parameters (size, limits, and tolerance) as you work to get good results on different areas of an image. The downside of using this tool is that it can be relatively time-consuming to apply.

Background Eraser Tool Options

The Background Eraser tool offers the following options in the Options bar:

Size—sets the size of the brush tip within which pixels are erased;

Limits—determines whether the Background Eraser will erase pixels that are Contiguous (adjacent to) or Discontiguous (not adjacent to) the tool's crosshairs;

Tolerance—describes the range of colors to be erased, based on their similarity to the color under the Background Eraser's crosshairs. The higher the Tolerance, the more pixels are erased.

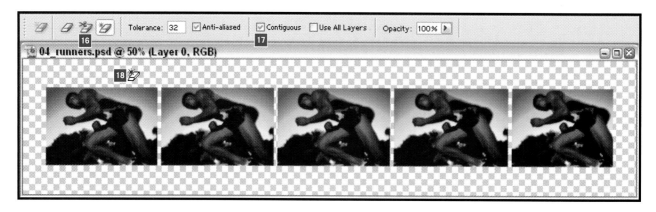

<NOTE>

The Magic Eraser tool offers a quick way to eliminate the background in images like this one, which have a single color background that contrasts sharply with the foreground detail. But the Magic Eraser tool does not always work this flawlessly. In some cases, keeping the foreground images intact when the Magic Eraser is applied to the background is more difficult. This tool also may leave a residue of background pixels around the foreground image.

Magic Eraser Tool Options

The Magic Eraser tool offers the following options in the Options bar:

Tolerance—Describes the range of colors to be erased, based on their similarity to the color on which you click with the Magic Eraser tool; the higher the tolerance, the more pixels are erased.

Anti-aliased—Softens the image edges that remain after erasing.

Contiguous—Erases only pixels that are adjacent to the pixel on which you click with the Magic Eraser tool.

Use All Layers—Samples from the artwork on all layers to determine the color to be erased, but still erases only on the selected layer.

Opacity—Determines whether the tool erases completely or only partially—to transparency on a regular layer or to the background color on a locked layer.

15. **Click the Step Backward button on the Shortcuts bar repeatedly until all of the white background reappears in the image.**
This button shortcut is an alternative to choosing Edit➜Step Backward from the menu bar. The default number of states you can undo—20—is the same for this shortcut as it is for the Step Backward command. Notice that the Step Forward button on the Shortcuts bar becomes available as soon as you click the Step Backward button, giving you a chance to change your mind.

16. **Click the Magic Eraser tool icon on the Options bar.**
This is another way to switch between tools in a tool group. Alternatively, you can click on the Background Eraser tool in the toolbox, and choose the Magic Eraser tool from the flyout menu.

17. **Leave the settings in the Magic Eraser tool Options bar at their defaults: Tolerance 32, Anti-aliased checked, Contiguous checked, Use All Layers unchecked, and Opacity 100%.**

18. **Click anywhere in the white background area of the image with the Magic Eraser tool.**
This deletes the entire white background, but leaves the foreground images intact.

19. **Choose File➜Save As, navigate to your ccproject folder, and click Save to save** 04_runners.psd. **Leave this file open for the next tutorial.**
You now have a series of small images of the runner set against a transparent background. In this tutorial you used the three Eraser tools—the Eraser, Background Eraser, and Magic Eraser tools. You also used the Undo and Step Backward commands to move back in time.

Tutorial
» Retracing Your Steps in the Undo History Palette

When you rely on the undo or step commands that you used in the last tutorial, you have to work blind, relying on your memory and clues from the image about where you are in the editing sequence. By contrast, the Undo History palette offers a measured, informed way to trace your steps backward and forward and directly restore your image to a particular state. You work with the Undo History palette in this tutorial.

1. **Use the copy of** 04_runners.psd **that you left open at the end of the last tutorial. If you closed the document, reopen it from your ccproject folder.**

2. **Click on the Undo History tab in the Palette Well, and drag the Undo History palette out of the Palette Well and onto your desktop.**
   This keeps the Undo History palette open in your workspace until you deliberately close it. If the Undo History tab is not available in the Palette Well, choose Window→Undo History to open the palette.

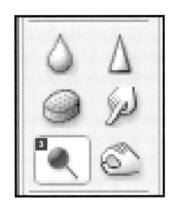

3. **Select the Dodge tool in the toolbox, and leave the tool options at their defaults.**
   The Dodge tool is used to lighten areas of an image.

4. **Click and drag in one sweep across all the images of the runner to lighten them slightly. Release your mouse.**

5. **Repeat the preceding step several times until your image looks a little too light.**

Each time you do this, a new state labeled Dodge Tool appears in the Undo History palette.

< N O T E >

The Undo History palette displays a list of the last 20 major operations performed on an open image. Each item in the list represents the state of the image at the time that operation was performed. Each new history state appears at the bottom of the palette, and older states roll off the top of the palette.

6. **Click the arrow on the left side of the Undo History palette, and drag up to slide the arrow up the list of history states. As you move from state to state, evaluate the exposure of the image in the document window. When you're satisfied with the appearance of the image, release the arrow to restore the image to the selected state.**

Releasing the arrow returns the image to the way it looked at the time of a particular application of the Dodge tool. Notice that all later states are grayed-out in the Undo History palette. You can move forward through these grayed-out states, as long as you don't perform another action on the image. As soon as you perform another action, the grayed-out states disappear, because you change the linear course of this history.

< T I P >

An alternative to using the arrow on the left of the Undo History palette is simply clicking from state to state in the Undo History palette.

< N O T E >

One advantage of using the Undo History palette, rather than an undo or step command, to move backward and forward in time is that the Undo History palette gives you a preview of each image state in the document window so that you can choose the optimal state visually.

7. **Choose File→Save As, navigate to the ccproject folder on your hard drive, and click Save to save** 04_runners.psd **with these changes. Leave this image open for the next short tutorial.**

Move right on to the last short tutorial in this session. Don't skip this step, or the last tutorial won't work as planned. In this tutorial you learned how the Undo History palette works. In the course of doing that, you applied the Dodge tools to your set of small images of the runner. This caused the images to look slightly bleached out.

Tutorial
» Reverting to the Last Saved Version

The Revert command is a wholesale method of moving backward. It returns you directly to the last saved version of your document.

1. **In the copy of** `04_runners.psd` **that you saved and left open at the end of the last tutorial, double-click the Zoom tool in the toolbox to zoom in to 100%.**

2. **Select the Background Eraser tool in the toolbox. Set the Size field in the Options bar to around 15 px.**

3. **Click anywhere in the blue sky inside one of the small runner images, and drag around the runner to try to isolate his figure from the rest of the image. Keep the crosshair of the Background Eraser tool just outside the figure as you drag.**
   The Background Eraser tool doesn't work very well when you get to the bottom of the image where the contrast between the runner and the dark trees is not very evident. At this point, you can use the Undo History palette or the Step Backward command to undo your failed attempts to isolate the figure.

4. **Choose File→Revert from the menu bar at the top of the screen.**
   This restores the image to its last saved state, which is the way it was at the end of the last tutorial and the way you want it now.

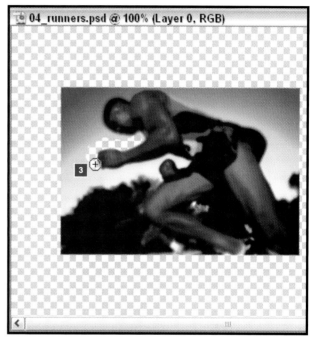

<NOTE>
Don't be fooled into thinking that the Revert command restores an image to its original state. This command restores an image only to its last saved state. This reinforces the importance of saving an untouched copy of the original. If you wanted to return to the original state of this image, you would have to open the copy file, `04_runners copy.psd`, which you saved to your ccproject folder at the very beginning of this session.

5. **Open** `04_stopwatch.psd` **from the Session 04 Tutorial Files folder on your hard drive.**
   This file is a replica of the completed image from the last session, `03_stopwatch_end.psd`.

6. **Select the Move tool in the toolbox.**

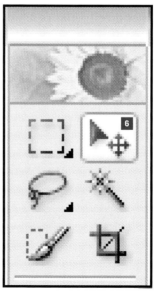

7. **Make sure that Auto Select layer is selected in the Options bar, and then click on the image of the runner reflected in the watch in** 04_stopwatch.psd.

This selects the layer on which the image of the runner is located—the top-most **runner** layer.

<CAUTION>

When Auto Select layer is selected and you click with the Move tool on a particular spot in an image, the program automatically activates the top-most layer on which there are nontransparent pixels. This can have unexpected consequences, such as causing you to work on a layer that you don't realize is activated or preventing you from performing actions that are disallowed on special kinds of layers. I suggest that you usually leave Auto Select layer unchecked, turning it on only when you specifically need it.

8. **Click anywhere in** 04_runners.psd, **and drag that image into** 04_stopwatch.psd.

This creates a new **Layer 1** in 04_stopwatch.psd above the **runner** layer in the Layers palette. **Layer 1** contains the small images of the runner surrounded by transparent pixels through which you can see the other artwork in 04_stopwatch.psd.

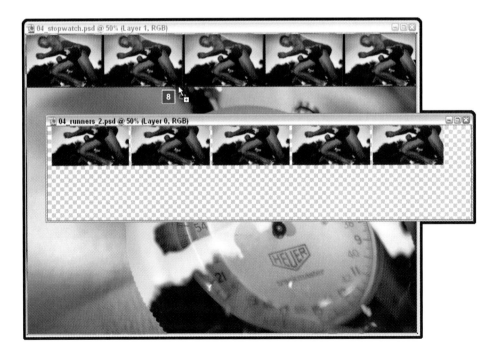

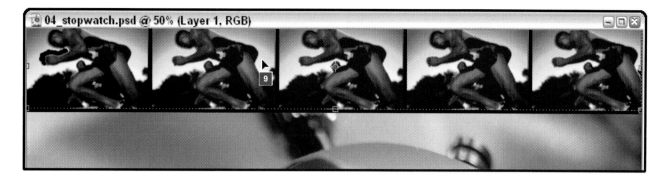

9. **With the Move tool still selected, click on the band of runner images in** 04_stopwatch.psd **and drag to move that artwork into position over the black strip at the top of the image.**

10. **Choose File→Save As, navigate to the ccproject folder on your hard drive, name this completed collage** 04_stopwatch_end.psd**, and click Save.**

    There's a copy of 04_stopwatch_end.psd in the Session 04 Tutorial Files folder. In this tutorial you put the finishing touches on an image for another greeting card. You combined two images you've been working on, as you learned about the Revert command. Congratulations. You finished another image for your greeting card collection.

» Session Review

In this session, you learned about the features in Photoshop Elements 2 that allow you to retrace your steps to correct a mistake or to try a different editing approach. You practiced using all three Eraser tools—the Eraser, the Background Eraser, and the Magic Eraser to isolate images against a transparent background. You applied the Undo and Step Backward commands and learned some shortcuts for these commands. You used the Undo History palette to move backward at a measured pace, and the Revert command to move all the way back to the last saved version of an image. Along the way, you moved one image into the other to create an intriguing digital collage.

1. How can you constrain the Eraser tool to erase in a straight line? (See Tutorial: Using the Eraser Tools and the Undo Commands.)

2. Does the Eraser tool erase to transparent pixels or to the background color when you're working on a **Background** layer? (See Tutorial: Using the Eraser Tools and the Undo Commands.)

3. Describe what the Background Eraser tool does. (See Tutorial: Using the Eraser Tools and the Undo Commands.)

4. How many times can you use the Step Backward command by default? (See Tutorial: Using the Eraser Tools and the Undo Commands.)

5. Describe what the Magic Eraser tool does. (See Tutorial: Using the Eraser Tools and the Undo Commands.)

6. What is the effect of unchecking Contiguous in the Options bar when you use the Magic Eraser tool? (See Tutorial: Using the Eraser Tools and the Undo Commands.)

7. How many steps can you move back in the Undo History palette by default? (See Tutorial: Retracing Your Steps in the Undo History Palette.)

8. Name one advantage of using the Undo History palette to move back to previous states of an image. (See Tutorial: Retracing Your Steps in the Undo History Palette.)

9. When can you not move forward through states in the Undo History palette? (See Tutorial: Retracing Your Steps in the Undo History Palette.)

10. To what state does an image return when you use the Revert command? (See Tutorial: Reverting to the Last Saved Version.)

Part III
Mastering Selections and Layers

Making Selections

Session Introduction

Selecting is a crucial skill to master, because selections are so fundamental to image editing in Photoshop Elements 2. A selection defines which parts of an image are affected by your edits. When part or all of an image is selected, only the selected pixels can be filled, painted, copied, moved, adjusted, transformed, or filtered. This session teaches how to make and use selections. You learn how and when to apply various selection tools, how to make anti-aliased and feathered selections, and how to modify and move selections, as you work on another greeting card.

TOOLS YOU'LL USE
Elliptical Marquee tool, Magnetic Lasso tool, Selection Brush tool,
Magic Wand tool, Move tool

CD-ROM FILES NEEDED
05_graffiti.psd, 05_skateboarder.psd,
05_grafitti_end.psd

TIME REQUIRED
60 minutes

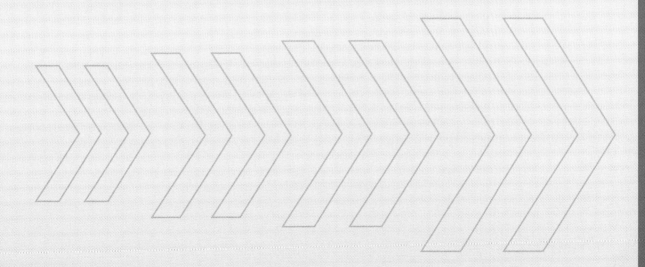

Tutorial

» Selecting with the Magnetic Lasso Tool

In this tutorial, you use the Magnetic Lasso tool to select the edge of a foreground image against a contrasting background. The Magnetic Lasso tool is often the tool to start with when you try to separate an image from its background. It works best when contrast between the foreground and background images is significant. This is also the first of a series of tutorials in which you use multiple tools in combination to select an image of a skateboarder. In a later tutorial, you move the selected skateboarder from the original background to a more vibrant background to create an original greeting card.

1. **Choose File➔Open, navigate to the Session 05 Tutorial Files folder on your hard drive, and open** `05_skateboarder.psd`. **Click the tool icon at the far left of the Options bar, and choose Reset All Tools to start with a clean slate.**

2. **Click and hold the Lasso tool that is currently displayed in the toolbox, and choose the Magnetic Lasso tool from the flyout menu.**

<NOTE>

The Magnetic Lasso tool works best if you customize its Frequency, Edge Contrast, and Width settings.

3. **In the Options bar, decrease the Frequency setting to** 30.
   This determines the rate at which the Magnetic Lasso tool generates points to fasten the selection boundary to the image edge. Higher rates (more points) are necessary to fit a selection to a rough edge. Lower rates work fine on a relatively smooth edge like this one.

4. **Increase the Edge Contrast setting in the Options bar to** 70%.
   Edge Contrast controls which edges the Magnetic Lasso tool detects, based on the degree of contrast between an edge and its surroundings. When you have high-contrast edges, as in this image, set the Edge Contrast relatively high (on a scale of 1% to 100%). This causes the tool to detect only the high-contrast edges and ignore extraneous non-edge pixels. When you work on an image with low-contrast edges, lower the Edge Contrast setting to cause the tool to be more sensitive to image edges.

5. **Increase the Width setting in the Options bar to** 35 px.
   The Width setting determines the range of pixels within which an edge is detected, as measured from the cursor. The larger the number, the more leeway you have as you move the cursor around the edge. When you have high-contrast edges with lots of empty space around them, as in this image, increase the Width setting. Lower-contrast, tighter edges require a lower Width setting and more precise tracing of the edges.

<NOTE>

You can change the Width setting on the fly as you create a selection. The left bracket key reduces width, letting you get into tight places, and the right bracket key increases width. If you use a graphics tablet and pen and have the Pen Pressure option selected in the Options bar, pressing on the pen reduces the Width setting temporarily.

6. **Click the Caps Lock key on the keyboard to change the cursor into a circle that represents the Width Setting you chose.**
   The crosshair is the location of the cursor; the circle represents the area within which the tool detects edge pixels.

7. **Position the crosshair on the edge of the skateboarder's right hand (the hand on your left), with the circle overlapping his hand. Click, release the mouse, and move your cursor to the right around the edge of the skateboarder until you get to the back edge of the skateboard. Do not hold down the mouse as you move the cursor.**
   You don't have to trace the edge very precisely, as long as the circle stays just over the edge of the image to detect the edge. The selection automatically fastens itself to the image edge with anchor points as you move around the edge.

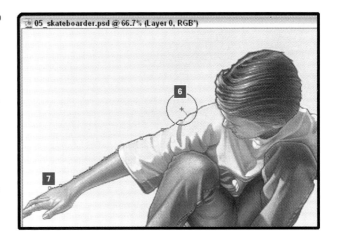

<NOTE>

As you move around the skateboarder, the Magnetic Lasso may deposit an anchor point away from the figure's edge. This is most likely to happen in small areas like the skateboarder's shoelace. If if does occur, click the Backspace (Macintosh: Delete) key, causing your selection boundary to shrink back, until you reach the anchor point that you want to change. Click Backspace (Macintosh: Delete) one more time to delete that anchor point. Click in the correct spot along the edge of the skateboarder to reset the anchor point manually. Then continue moving the cursor in the original direction without holding down the mouse, allowing the Magnetic Lasso tool to set more anchor points automatically.

8. **When you reach the back edge of the skateboard, click and hold the Alt (Macintosh: Option) key. This changes the Magnetic Lasso tool to the Lasso tool temporarily.**

9. **With the Lasso tool, click and drag a freehand selection around the underside of the skateboard and the back wheels.**
   The Lasso tool works better than the Magnetic Lasso tool in dark areas like this, where the edge contrast is too low to support the Magnetic Lasso tool.

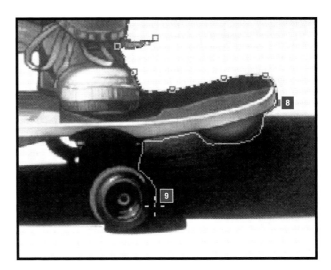

10. **Release the Alt (Macintosh: Option) key to switch back to the Magnetic Lasso tool when you reach the bottom of the back wheels. Release the mouse, and continue to move the cursor around the outside edge of the skateboard and the skateboarder to the starting point.**

11. **When you reach the starting point, click the small circle to close the selection.**

    The small circle indicates that you have reached the beginning of the selection. You now have an initial selection of the skateboarder and the skateboard. You refine this selection using other selection tools in the tutorials that follow. In the next step, you save the selection that you just made so you don't lose it.

    <NOTE>
    The selection boundary appears as a series of animated dashes, which are known as marching ants.

12. **Choose Select→Save Selection from the menu bar at the top of the screen.**

    The Save Selection dialog box opens.

13. **Make sure that the Selection field reads New. In the Name field, name the selection** magnetic lasso. **Click OK.**

    You can bring back this selection at any time by choosing Select→Load Selection and choosing magnetic lasso from the Selection menu in the Load Selection dialog box.

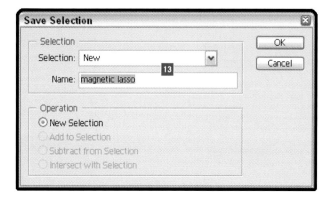

14. **Choose File→Save As, navigate to the ccproject folder on your hard drive, and click Save.**

    Leave the image open for the tutorial that follows the discussion of anti-aliasing. In this tutorial you learned the nuances of using the magnetic lasso tool and saving a selection, as you began the process of selecting a figure in preparation for moving it into the greeting card you're creating in this session.

Discussion
Anti-aliased versus Aliased Selections

All the selection tools have the Anti-aliased option checked by default in the Options bar. This causes selections to have soft, blended edges, which is often desirable when you're compositing selected artwork with other images. The terms anti-aliased and aliased may sound complicated, but the important point to remember is simply that an anti-aliased edge appears smooth and an aliased edge looks jagged.

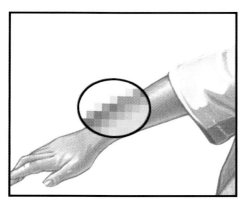

An anti-aliased edge looks soft and smooth because it contains some partially selected pixels. When you fill an anti-aliased selection with color, or copy or delete an anti-aliased selection, the edge pixels become only partially filled, creating a gradual transition between the colors in the selected artwork and whatever colors are in the background. For example, this illustration shows an anti-aliased selection of the skateboarder cut out and placed against a white background. You can see in the magnified insert that some of the edge pixels are only partially filled, allowing the white background to show through. When the image is viewed at normal magnification, this creates the illusion of a smooth edge.

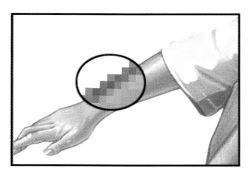

An aliased edge, by contrast, is composed of fully selected pixels that are completely filled with the selected artwork. In this illustration of an aliased selection of the skateboarder against a white background, the edge pixels are completely filled. They do not allow the white background to show through. This creates a hard, jagged edge that you can see even at normal magnification.

Before you fill, copy, or delete a selection, you cannot see whether the selection has been anti-aliased. A selection boundary looks the same—a series of marching ants like those in this illustration—whether it is anti-aliased or aliased. If you're curious about whether a selection boundary is anti-aliased or aliased, you must turn on a mask to see the difference. To do that, zoom in close, choose the Selection Brush tool in the toolbox, click in the Mode field in the Options bar, and choose Mask.

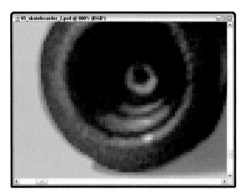

This illustration is a magnified view of the soft edge of an anti-aliased selection boundary seen through the red mask of the Selection Brush tool. Notice that the red mask changes color gradually along the soft edge of the selection.

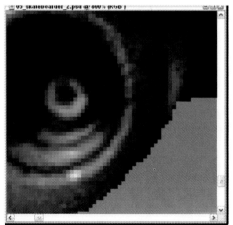

This illustration, by way of contrast, shows the hard, jagged edge of an aliased selection boundary seen through the red Selection Brush tool mask.

Tools other than the selection tools allow you the choice of a soft anti-aliased edge or a hard aliased edge as you create parts of an image. The painting tools (Brush, Eraser, and Pencil tools) and the darkroom tools (Blur, Sharpen, Sponge, Smudge, Dodge, Burn, and Clone tools) do so by offering soft and hard brushes. The type tools have an Anti-aliased button in the Options bar.

Tutorial
» Selecting with the Magic Wand Tool

The Magic Wand tool selects pixels based on similarity of color value. It works best on areas of solid color that differ in color brightness from the object to be selected. The downside of the Magic Wand tool is that its results are not very predictable and are difficult to adjust with precision. In this tutorial, you use the Magic Wand to subtract from the initial selection that you made with the Magnetic Lasso tool, as you continue to create a selection around the figure to be included in this session's greeting card.

1. **Make sure that** 05_skateboard.psd **is still open with the selection that you made in the first tutorial.**
   If it's not, reopen 05_skateboard.psd from your ccproject folder, and bring back the selection you made earlier by choosing Select➔Load Selection from the menu bar, choosing magnetic lasso in the Selection field of the Load Selection dialog box, and clicking OK.

2. **Select the Magic Wand tool in the toolbox.**

3. **In the Options bar, click the Subtract from Selection button.**
   This causes the selection you make to be deleted from the existing selection. Leave the other Magic Wand options at their defaults—Tolerance: 32, Anti-aliased checked, Contiguous checked, and Use All Layers unchecked.

<NOTE>
The other selection combination buttons in the Options bar can be used respectively to create a new selection (which deletes the existing selection), add to an existing selection, or create a selection that intersects with the existing selection.

4. **Click in the area between the skateboarder's legs to subtract that area from the selection that you previously made with the Magnetic Lasso tool.**
   The Magic Wand tool selects pixels that are similar in color value to the sampled pixel on which you click and within the tolerance range and other parameters that you can set in the Options bar.

5. **If you take a break now, save your selection again so you don't lose it. Choose Save➔Save Selection from the menu bar. In the Save Selection dialog box, set Selection to New, type** magic wand **in the Name field, and click OK.**

6. **Choose File➔Save.**
   Leave the file open for the next tutorial, and move right on to refine your selection.

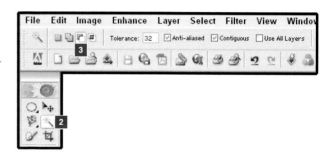

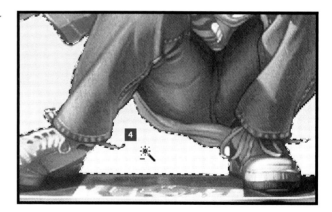

<TIP>
If the Magic Wand tool selects fewer pixels than you want, try undoing and increasing the Tolerance setting in the Options bar. If the Magic Wand selects pixels that you don't mean to select, try reducing the Tolerance setting.

<NOTE>
To increase a selection made with the Magic Wand tool (or any other selection tool), you can try Select➔Grow to add neighboring pixels that are similar in color value to those already selected, or Select➔Similar to include pixels anywhere in the image that are similar in color value to those already selected.

Tutorial

» Selecting with the Selection Brush Tool

The Selection Brush tool is unique to Photoshop Elements 2 and is one of its most useful features. This tool offers an intuitive, easily controlled way to make a selection—by painting the selection into place with a brush. In Selection mode, you generate marching ants as you paint in a selection. In Mask mode, as you paint you change the shape of a visible mask that defines non-selected areas. In this tutorial, you use the Selection Brush in both its Selection mode and its Mask mode to refine the initial selection that you made with other selection tools, as you continue to build a selection around the figure to be used in your greeting card.

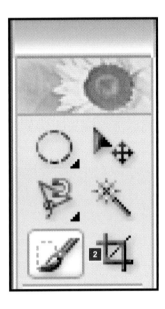

1. **Make sure that** 05_skateboarder.psd **is still open from the preceding tutorial, with the selection still showing.**

   If it's not, open the file from your ccproject folder and choose Select→Load Selection to load the magic wand selection that you saved at the end of the preceding tutorial.

2. **Select the Selection Brush tool in the toolbox.**

   Don't confuse this tool with the regular Brush tool.

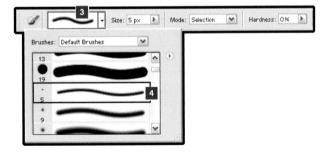

3. **Click the brush sample in the Options bar to open the Brush Presets palette.**

   The Selection Brush gives you access to the preset brushes and brush options available with other brush tools. This palette displays a sample stroke made with each brush in the Default group of preset brushes.

4. **Use the scroll bar on the Brush Presets palette to move down until you see the 5-pixel soft round brush. Click on that brush to select it.**

   Holding your mouse over a sample stroke reveals the name of that brush in a Tool Tip.

   <TIP>

   The Brush Presets palette shows the last set of brushes that you loaded. If your palette does not say Default Brushes at the top, click the arrow at the top right of the Brush Presets palette and choose Reset Brushes to bring back the Default set of brushes.

5. **Click the arrow to the right of the Size field in the Options bar. Drag the Size slider slightly to the right to increase the brush size to 7 px (pixels).**

   Leave the other fields in the Options bar at their defaults for now.

6. **Press and hold the Alt (Macintosh: Option) key as you paint inside the bows of the sneakers.**

   This subtracts those background areas from the existing selection.

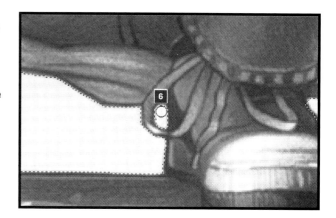

7. **With the Alt (Macintosh: Option) key still depressed, paint inside the light blue area to the left of the back wheel to remove it from the existing selection.**

<NOTE>

To add to a selection, just paint with the Selection Brush tool. You don't have to use any modifier keys or combination buttons as you do to add to a selection with other selection tools. To subtract from a selection, hold the Alt (Macintosh: Option) key as you paint with the Selection Brush tool.

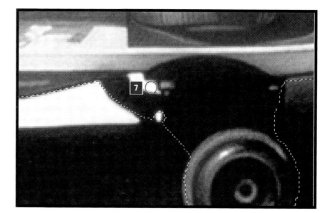

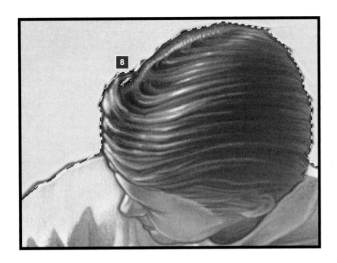

8. **Reduce the brush size to 3 px in the Size field on the Options bar. Hold the Alt (Macintosh: Option) key and paint in the tiny blue area in the curl of the skateboarder's hair.**
   This subtracts that background area from the selection. This also illustrates the high degree of control over a selection that the Selection Brush tool offers.

9. **In the Options bar, click on the arrow to the right of the Mode field and choose Mask from the menu.**
   The nonselected areas of the image are displayed under a translucent red mask. With the mask activated you can see that the selection boundary does not perfectly trace the edge of the skateboarder. In some places, the red mask crosses over that edge slightly, and in others, it arches away from edge.

10. **Select the Zoom tool in the toolbox and zoom in close to an area where the mask strays from the image edge. Paint in the unmasked area to add to the red mask.**
    The area you paint is subtracted from the selection.

11. **Press and hold the spacebar to temporarily change the Selection Brush tool to a Hand tool. Click and drag to move to an area where the red mask crosses the edge to cover part of the skateboarder image. Release the spacebar to return to the Selection Brush tool.**
This is a shortcut for moving a magnified image in the document window so you can see different areas of the image.

12. **Press and Hold the Alt (Macintosh: Option) key and paint where the red mask covers part of the skateboarder image.**
This removes part of the red mask (adding to the selection).

13. **Press and hold the spacebar to switch to the Hand tool again, click and drag until you see the back of the skateboard (where you drew a freehand selection with the Lasso tool).**
In Mask mode your freehand selection may look as jagged as in this illustration. If so, use the Selection Brush tool to smooth it out. Mask mode reveals selection detail that you can't otherwise see, like this jagged edge or the effect of anti-aliasing that you observed in an earlier discussion. This makes it useful for evaluating the detail of a selection.

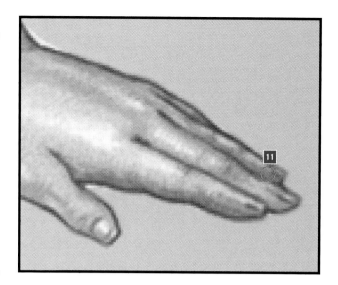

<TIP>

If the red of the mask makes it difficult to see the edge of the artwork, click the arrow on the Overlay Opacity field in the Options bar and drag the Opacity slider to the left until you can see through the mask. You can also change the color of the mask by clicking in the Overlay Color field in the Options bar to open the Color Picker, choosing a color there, and clicking OK.

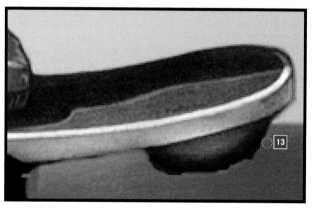

14. **Continue to paint in refinements to the selection in Mask mode, changing brush Size and Hardness in the Options bar as necessary. When you're done, switch back to Selection mode in the Options bar.**

<NOTE>

After you make a complex selection, you may want to save the selection boundary. This ensures that you are able to bring the selection back if you accidentally deselect it. It also creates the possibility of reloading a selection to use on another layer.

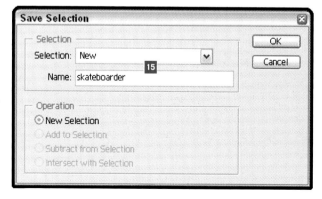

15. **Choose Select→Save Selection. In the Save Selection dialog box, set the Selection field to New. Type** skateboarder **in the Name field to identify this selection, and click OK to save the selection.**

16. **Choose File→Save.**
In this series of tutorials, you created and refined a selection around the edge of the skateboarder using three of the most useful selection tools—the Magnetic Lasso tool, the Magic Wand tool, and the Selection Brush tool. In the next tutorial, you learn how to contract and feather a selection boundary to prepare the selected image for compositing with another image for your greeting card project.

<TIP>

If you inadvertently paint a mask where you don't want it, fix the mistake by holding the Alt (Macintosh: Option) key and painting over that area again to remove the mask.

Tutorial
» Modifying a Selection

You can modify a selection in a number of ways. In this short tutorial, you contract and feather the selection boundary around the skateboarder to prepare the selected image to blend in with a new background in your greeting card.

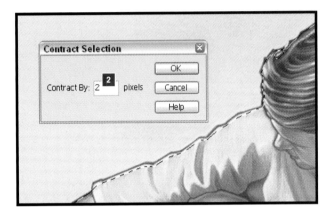

<TIP>
The Border command in the Select→Modify menu creates a feathered double selection that you can fill with color or pattern to create a frame around a selected area. Don't confuse the Border command with the Stroke command (Edit→Stroke), which adds a flat stroke of pixels around a selection or around all the artwork on a layer.

1. **Make sure that** 05_skateboarder.psd **is open from the previous tutorial, with the selection that you saved at the end of the preceding tutorial still showing.**
   If it's not, open 05_skateboarder.psd from your ccproject folder, choose Select→Load Selection, choose the skateboarder selection, and click OK.

2. **Choose Select→Modify→Contract to open the Contract Selection dialog box. Click in the Contract By field, enter** 2**, and click OK.**
   The selection around the skateboarder contracts by 2 pixels. This ensures that the selection has a clean edge without any lingering background pixels.

<TIP>
You can expand a selection by choosing Select→Modify→Expand, or smooth out a selection by choosing Select→Modify→Smooth. These commands are also useful when you're trying to isolate an image from a background and want to avoid any background pixels hanging around the edges of the foreground image.

3. **Choose Select→Feather. In the Feather dialog box, enter** 1 **in the Feather Radius field and click OK.**

   This slightly softens the edges of the selection so that the selected image blends more smoothly with a new background. You should use this technique routinely when you prepare an image for compositing with other images.

< N O T E >

Feathering blurs the pixels on the inside and outside of a selection boundary. Don't confuse feathering with anti-aliasing. Both techniques soften the edge of a selection, but they work differently and each technique creates a slightly different look.

< N O T E >

To see the effect of feathering, you can select the Selection Brush tool and choose the Mask option in the Options bar.

4. **Choose Select→Save Selection, choose New in the Selection field, and type** modified **in the Name field. Click OK to close the Save Selection dialog box.**

5. **Choose File→Save to resave the file to your ccproject folder.**

   Leave this file open for the next tutorial, in which you move the selected skateboarder into a new image. In this tutorial, you contracted the selection boundary and added a feather so the selection blends smoothly when placed on a new background in your greeting card.

< T I P >

You can include feathering when you create a selection by typing the number of pixels by which you want to feather in the Feather option that is located in the Options bar for some of the selection tools (the marquee tools and the lasso tools).

Tutorial
» Moving a Selection

One important reason to create a selection is so that you can move or copy a selected area to another document. In this tutorial, you move the skateboarder that you selected from its background to a more exciting background image.

<TIP>

If you want to paste a selection into a particular spot in another image, make a selection around that spot in the receiving image. Click back on the first image, and choose Edit→Copy. Then choose Edit→Paste Into. This pastes the copied pixels into the receiving selection boundary. The pasted pixels can be moved around inside the receiving selection boundary for optimum placement until the selection boundary is deselected. You might use this technique, for example, to select and replace a drab sky with copied pixels from a more exciting sky.

<NOTE>

Distinguishing between moving a selected area and moving a selection boundary is important. To move just a selection boundary, select one of the lasso tools or marquee tools and drag. You can move a selection boundary within an image or between images.

1. **Make sure that** 05_skateboarder.psd **is still open from the previous tutorial, with its selection active.**
   If it's not, open 05_skateboarder.psd from your ccproject folder, choose Select→Load Selection, choose modified in the Selection field, and click OK.

2. **Choose File→Open, navigate to the Session 05 Tutorial Files folder on your hard drive, choose** 05_graffiti.psd, **and click Open.**
   Make sure that you can see both images on your screen. You may have to use the Zoom tool to reduce the magnification of both images.

3. **Select the Move tool in the toolbox.**

4. **Click in the skateboarder image, and drag the selected area into the graffiti image.**
   Alternatively, click in the skateboarder image, and choose Edit→Copy in the menu bar. Then click in the graffiti image, and choose Edit→Paste. This pastes the selected image into the middle of the graffiti image.

5. **With the Move tool, drag the skateboarder image into place to match this illustration.**

    You can move the skateboarder image separately because it is on its own layer. A new layer was created when you moved the image into this document.

6. **Double-click the** Layer 1 **name in the Layers palette, and type** skateboarder **to give this layer a more meaningful name.**

7. **Click in the** 05_skateboarder.psd **document window to make that image active, and choose File→Close.**

    You don't need to save the file again.

8. **Click in the** 05_graffiti.psd **document window. Choose File→Save As, navigate to your ccproject folder, and click Save.**

    Leave this file open for the next tutorial. In this tutorial, you added your selection to a new background to make your greeting card more visually interesting.

Tutorial
» Editing Selected Artwork

In previous tutorials, you selected an image in order to move it into another document. Another reason to select an area is so you can edit its content without affecting the rest of the artwork on the same layer, as you do in this tutorial. You select the skateboarder's hands so that you can add a motion blur filter to just the selected area to incorporate a sense of movement. You also get a chance to use another selection tool—the Elliptical Marquee tool.

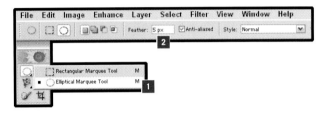

1. **With** 05_graffiti.psd **open from the previous tutorial, select the Elliptical Marquee tool in the toolbox.**
   If it's not showing, click the Rectangular Marquee tool to display a flyout menu of marquee tools and select the Elliptical Marquee from there. If you closed 05_graffiti.psd, open that file from your ccproject folder.

<NOTE>
The Elliptical Marquee tool creates elliptical selections. You can constrain it to create a circular selection by holding the Shift key as you drag out a selection. Similarly, the Rectangular Marquee tool is used to make rectangular selections, but can be constrained to a square selection by holding the Shift key as you draw.

2. **In the Options bar, enter** 5 px **in the Feather field.**
   This allows you to create a feathered edge as you draw the selection. Feathering the edge of this selection is necessary so that the demarcation between the filtered and unfiltered part of the skateboarder's arm are not apparent.

3. **Click and drag an elliptical selection around the skateboarder's right hand (the hand on your left) to match the illustration.**

4. **Click the Add to Selection button in the Options bar.**
   This allows you to add another area to the selection without eliminating the original selection.

5. **Click and drag another elliptical selection around the skate-boarder's left hand (the hand on your right) to match the illustration on the preceding page.**

6. **Select Filter→Blur→Motion Blur from the menu bar at the top of the screen.**
   This opens the Motion Blur dialog box where you can choose settings for this filter.

<NOTE>
You can find lots more useful information on filters in Bonus Session 1, Using Filters, on the CD-ROM at the back of the book.

7. **In the Motion Blur dialog box, move the Distance slider to 10 and click OK.**
   The Distance slider controls the amount of blur.

<TIP>
If you want to preview the effect of the blur before you apply the Motion Blur filter, move the cursor over the preview area in the Motion Blur dialog box so that the cursor changes to a hand. Click and drag to bring one of the skateboarder's hands into view.

8. **Choose Select→Deselect from the menu bar.**
   This eliminates the selection. Alternatively, use Ctrl+D (Macintosh: ⌘+D).

9. **Notice the directional blur that you added to the skateboarder's hands.**
   It gives the entire image the illusion of motion.

10. **Choose File→Save As, navigate to your ccproject folder, rename the file** 05_graffiti_end.psd**, and click Save.**
    You finished this session on selections and completed another greeting card. As you created this card, you learned funda-mental skills about working with the many selection tools and features in Photoshop Elements 2.

» Session Review

This session was all about selections. You selected the skateboarder image using a combination of three powerful selection tools—the Magnetic Lasso tool (which is useful for selecting high-contrast edges), the Magic Wand tool (which comes in handy for selecting areas of a single color), and the Selection Brush tool (which is great for cleaning up selections). You moved a selected image from one document to another to add a more dynamic background. And you used the Elliptical Marquee tool to select parts of the new image for further editing with a filter. Along the way, you learned about anti-aliasing, modifying a selection, and feathering a selection.

1. Does the Magnetic Lasso tool work best when the contrast between an image you select and the background is great or small? (See Tutorial: Selecting with the Magnetic Lasso Tool.)

2. What does the Width setting do to customize the Magnetic Lasso tool? (See Tutorial: Selecting with the Magnetic Lasso Tool.)

3. Should you hold down the mouse when applying the Magnetic Lasso tool? (See Tutorial: Selecting with the Magnetic Lasso Tool.)

4. How do you switch temporarily between the Magnetic Lasso tool and the regular Lasso tool to make a freeform selection? (See Tutorial: Selecting with the Magnetic Lasso Tool.)

5. What does the term "marching ants" refer to? (See Tutorial: Selecting with the Magnetic Lasso Tool.)

6. Does an anti-aliased edge look soft or jagged? (See Discussion: Anti-aliased versus Aliased Selections.)

7. Do you usually want to make an anti-aliased or aliased selection when you select an image to be combined with other images? (See Discussion: Anti-aliased versus Aliased Selections.)

8. Can you see the difference between an aliased and anti-aliased selection by examining just the selection boundary? (See Discussion: Anti-aliased versus Aliased Selections.)

9. What does the Subtract from Selection button do? (See Tutorial: Selecting with the Magic Wand Tool.)

10. If the Magic Wand tool selects fewer pixels than you want to select, what setting in the Options bar should you consider increasing? (See Tutorial: Selecting with the Magic Wand Tool.)

11. What tool would you use if you wanted to paint a selection into place? (See Tutorial: Selecting with the Selection Brush Tool.)

12. What modifier key do you press if you want to use the Selection Brush tool to subtract from a selection? (See Tutorial: Selecting with the Selection Brush Tool.)

13. When might switching to the Mask mode of the Selection Brush tool be useful? (See Tutorial: Selecting with the Selection Brush Tool.)

14. What does the Contract command do? (See Tutorial: Modifying a Selection.)

15. Is feathering the same as anti-aliasing? (See Tutorial: Modifying a Selection.)

16. Describe one situation in which feathering a selection is useful. (See Tutorial: Modifying a Selection.)

17. What tool would you use to move a selected area from one image to another? (See Tutorial: Moving a Selection.)

18. What tool would you use to move a selection boundary, as opposed to a selected area? (See Tutorial: Moving a Selection.)

19. Can you edit just a selected area of artwork without affecting the other artwork on the same layer? (See Tutorial: Editing Selected Artwork.)

20. What tool would you use to draw an elliptical selection? (See Tutorial: Editing Selected Artwork.)

Session 6

Working with Layers

Session Introduction

Layers are the basic building blocks of images and are at the top of the list of important features in Photoshop Elements 2. In this session, you learn how to use layers to build a flexible, visually interesting image from multiple pieces of artwork. The session begins by teaching you several ways to create layers—starting a new image with a Background layer, generating a new layer, copying layers from other documents, turning a selection into a layer, and duplicating an existing layer. In the process, you learn fundamental layer-handling skills, including how to name, select, and move layers. Then you manage layers in the Layers palette—linking, locking, hiding, reordering, and deleting layers. You move on to more advanced techniques for using adjustment layers and fill layers to edit nondestructively. You learn techniques for blending and compositing layer content, including a workaround for the lack of layer masking features in Photoshop Elements 2. You apply layer styles, and you learn how and why to merge layers together. No matter what your skill level, you'll find useful information about editing and compositing with layers in this important session.

TOOLS YOU'LL USE
Layers palette, Move tool, Adjustment layers, Fill layers

CD-ROM FILES NEEDED
06_baseball.psd, 06_boy.psd, 06_batter.psd,
06_cards.psd, 06_baseball_end.psd

TIME REQUIRED
90 minutes

Discussion
Layer Basics

Every document you open in Photoshop Elements 2 has at least one layer, and you often add more layers as you build or edit an image. Each layer is a container for part of the artwork that makes up the image. The great advantage of layers is that they are a way of isolating individual pieces of artwork from one another. When you place a piece of art on a separate layer, you can edit and move that item freely without affecting the content of other layers.

You might think of a layer as a flat pane of glass. Like glass, a layer is transparent by nature. As you add artwork to a layer, you replace the layer's transparent pixels with pixels of color. Transparent areas of layers are represented by a gray checkerboard pattern on your screen.

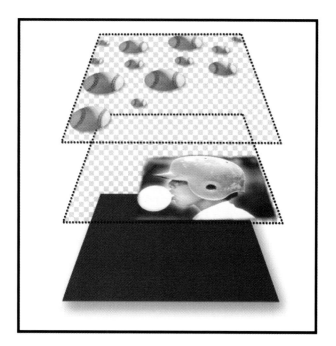

A document with multiple layers is like a stack of glass panes, each containing some artwork. Viewing a layered document on your monitor is like looking down through the stack of glass panes from the top. Where layers are transparent or contain semi-opaque artwork, you can see through them to the contents of the layers below.

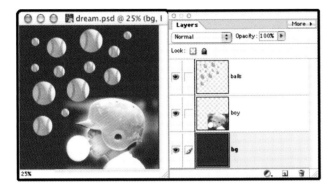

The Layers palette represents the stack of layers in a document and offers many controls for managing layers. You can change the stacking order of layers by moving them up or down in this palette. You can delete a layer by dragging it to the Trash icon at the bottom of the Layers palette. The Layers palette is where you select a layer, so that editing changes affect only that layer. In this palette, you can link layers to move their contents as one or lock a layer to protect its contents from change. You can make a layer temporarily invisible so that you can see what's on the layers below. You can also change the way a layer interacts with underlying layers by varying layer opacity, changing blending mode, or grouping layers.

There are several kinds of layers—regular layers that contain pixel-based artwork, adjustment and fill layers that adjust the look of an image without directly changing any artwork, and type layers and shape layers that contain vector-based elements. This session contains general information that applies to all kinds of layers, although the focus here is on pixel-based layers. You learn more specifics about shape layers and type layers in Sessions 9 and 10 respectively.

Tutorial
» Creating and Converting a Background Layer

The first five tutorials in this session address ways to create layers. This tutorial, the first of the group, covers creating an initial *Background* layer by starting a new document. You also learn why and how to convert a *Background* layer to a regular layer.

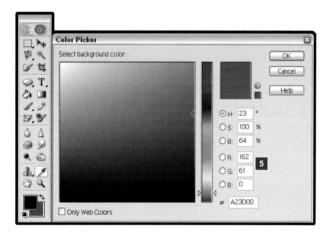

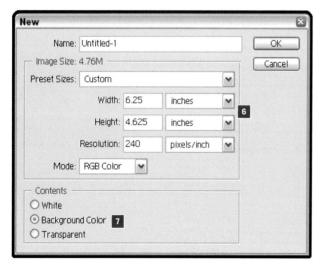

1. **Reset all tools to their default settings by clicking the Tool icon at the far left of the Options bar, choosing Reset All Tools, and clicking OK at the query.**

2. **Reset palettes to their default locations by choosing Window→ Reset Palette Locations. Close the Hints and How To palettes.**

3. **Click the Layers tab in the Palette Well, and drag the Layers palette onto your desktop to keep it open as you work.**
   This assures that the Layers palette stays open. Otherwise it closes back into the Palette Well each time you click elsewhere.

4. **Click in the Background Color box in the toolbox.**
   The color picker opens.

5. **In the Color Picker, enter R:**162 **G:**61 **B:**0 **to choose a medium brown as the Background color for the image you are about to create. Click OK.**
   The Background Color box fills with that color.

6. **Choose File→New to open the New dialog box. Set the parameters of your new document: Width:** 6.25 **inches, Height:** 4.625 **inches, Resolution:** 240 **pixels/inch, and Mode: RGB Color.**

7. **Select the Background Color radio button in the Contents section of the New dialog box. Click OK.**
   A new document is created with a *Background* layer filled with medium brown pixels. In the Layers palette, a single layer labeled *Background* appears. A *Background* layer has special restrictive properties, as described in the nearby sidebar.

<N O T E >
The only option in the New dialog box that does not generate a special *Background* layer is Transparent. The Transparent option creates a regular layer that is composed entirely of transparent pixels. Use this option if you're creating images with transparent areas for the Web, for video, or for a page layout program that recognizes transparency. (Check your page layout program to make sure it supports transparency. If it doesn't, it converts your transparent pixels to solid colors.)

Do You Need a *Background* Layer?

You don't have to have a *Background* Layer in a document, unless you want to use it to store an untouched original of an image while you work on a copy layer. The *Background* layer has some significant restrictions that make it less flexible than a regular layer:

>> The *Background* layer must remain at the bottom of the layer stack; it can't be moved above other layers in the Layers palette.

>> The *Background* layer is always locked; its content cannot be moved in the Document window.

>> The *Background* layer is opaque; its opacity can't be lowered, its blending mode can't be changed, and none of its pixels can be made transparent.

These restrictions can make it difficult to work with a *Background* layer. Many users, as a matter of course, change the *Background* layer into a regular layer as you do in Steps 8 and 9 of this tutorial.

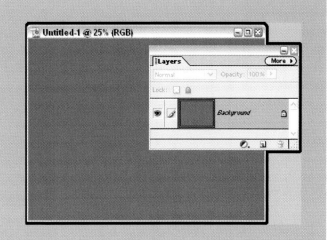

8. In the Layers palette, double-click anywhere on the bar that represents the *Background* layer to open the New Layer dialog box.

9. Enter bg as the new name of this layer, and click OK.
   This converts your ***Background*** layer to a regular layer. Renaming a ***Background*** layer with any name other than *Background* changes it to a regular layer.

10. Choose File➜Save to open the Save As dialog box. Name this file 06_baseball.psd, make sure Layers is checked, navigate to your ccproject folder, and click Save.
   Leave the file open for the next session. You just created a new project greeting card, added a ***Background*** layer, and then converted that layer to a regular layer that does not have the restrictive properties of a ***Background*** layer. A copy of 06_baseball.psd as it should look at this point is in the Session 06 tutorial files folder.

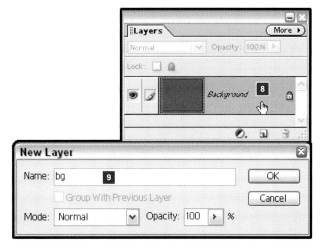

< T I P >

In the rare event that you have reason to convert a regular layer into a ***Background*** layer, choose Layer➜New➜Background from Layer from the menu bar at the top of the screen. If the regular layer contains transparent pixels, they are filled with the color in the Background Color box in the toolbox. There can be only one ***Background*** layer in an image, so first convert any existing ***Background*** layer to a regular layer.

Tutorial

» Generating a New Layer

In this tutorial, you add a new, empty layer to an existing document, give the layer a meaningful name, and populate the layer with artwork.

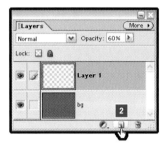

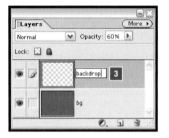

1. **Make sure that** `06_baseball.psd` **is still open from the last tutorial.**
   If you closed the file at the end of the previous tutorial, you can open it from your ccproject folder or use the prebuilt version of the file in the Session 06 folder of the Tutorial Files on your hard drive.

2. **Click the Create New Layer button at the bottom of the Layers palette to generate a new layer.**
   An empty layer labeled **Layer 1** appears above the selected layer in the Layers palette.

< T I P >
Alternatively, Alt+click (Macintosh: Option+click) on the Create New Layer icon to open the New Layer dialog box, where you can give the layer a name and pre-assign layer properties (grouping, opacity level, and blending mode) at the same time you create the layer.

3. **Double-click directly on the** Layer 1 **label in the Layers palette to unlock the naming area on that layer. Type the name** backdrop **in place of the generic label.**
   It's good practice to give each layer a meaningful name that makes the layer easy to identify. This is particularly important if the final document will have lots of layers. Choose layer names that mean something to you, and get in the habit of naming layers as you create them.

< N O T E >
Alternatively, you can rename a layer in the Layer Properties dialog box. Right-click (Macintosh: Ctrl+click) on a layer in the Layers palette, and choose Rename Layer from the contextual menu. Type the new layer name in the Layer Properties dialog box, and click OK.

4. **Choose View→Rulers from the menu bar at the top of the screen.**
   If the rulers are not displaying inches, right-click (Macintosh: Ctrl+click) inside a ruler and choose Inches from the contextual menu.

5. **Click on the Foreground Color box in the toolbox to open the Color Picker. Enter these settings to choose a dark brown:**
   R: 97, **G:** 36, **B:** 0. **Click OK.**
   The Color Picker closes, and the Foreground color is set to dark brown.

< T I P >
When you create a new layer, it is automatically located directly above the layer that is selected in the Layers palette. If you want a new layer to be positioned directly below the selected layer, Ctrl+click (Macintosh: ⌘+click) the Create New Layer button.

< T I P >
The thumbnail on each pixel-based layer displays a miniature version of the layer's contents, including a gray checkerboard to indicate any transparent areas on a layer. If you prefer thumbnails that are larger than the default size, click the More button on the Layers palette to open the Palette menu and choose Palette Options. In the Layers Palette Options dialog box, select the large thumbnail and click OK. The downside of using large layer thumbnails is a longer Layers palette, which can be unwieldy if you have lots of layers and a small monitor.

6. **Select the Rectangular Marquee tool in the toolbox.**

7. **Click and drag in the image to create a large rectangular selection about ¼ inch from the edges of the image.**
   Use the rulers to help draw the selection to size, but don't worry about being too precise.

8. **Make sure that the** backdrop **layer is highlighted in the Layers palette.**
   If the **backdrop** layer is not selected, click on the bar in the Layers palette that represents that layer. That's all there is to selecting a layer so that its contents are affected by an edit. Although this seems easy, forgetting to select a layer or selecting the wrong layer are common errors.

9. **Choose Edit→Fill in the menu bar at the top of the screen to open the Fill dialog box. Set the Use field to Foreground Color, and click OK.**
   The selection fills with dark brown.

<TIP>
The keyboard shortcut for filling with the Foreground Color is Alt+Backspace (Macintosh: Option+Delete).

10. **Choose Select→Deselect to deselect the rectangular selection.**
    Or just click elsewhere in the image to deselect.

11. **Select File→Save, and leave the file open for the next tutorial.**
    Your greeting card now has two layers, one generated when you created the file and one generated as a new layer.

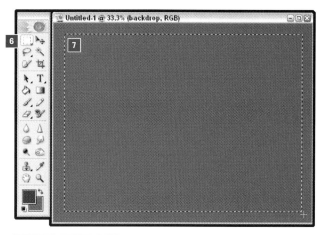

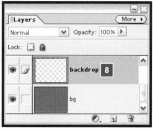

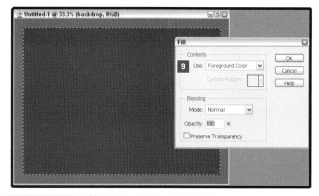

Automatically Selecting Layers

Selecting a layer by hand can be challenging if you have lots of layers in a document. So Adobe built in two features to help you select layers—Auto Select Layer and a contextual layer menu. Auto Select Layer, which you encountered in earlier sessions, is a default option for the Move tool. When it is on, clicking anywhere in a document selects the topmost layer that contains opaque artwork at the spot you clicked. Auto Select Layer sounds like a good idea, but in practice it often seems to have a mind of its own. It doesn't recognize pixels that are partially transparent nor adjustment layers. And

it always selects the topmost layer that has content at a designated spot. So I suggest that you deactivate this feature by selecting the Move tool and unchecking Auto Select Layer in the Options bar.

There's another somewhat automatic selection feature that is more user friendly. Right-click (Macintosh: Ctrl+click) anywhere in a document to see a contextual menu that lists the layers that contain artwork at the spot you clicked, including adjustment and fill layers. Choose one of those layer names in the contextual menu to jump to the corresponding layer in the Layers palette.

Tutorial

» Copying Layers between Documents

Another way to create a new layer in a document is to copy a layer from another document, as you do in this tutorial. The techniques you learn here you use often when you composite images.

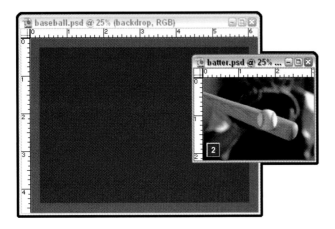

<NOTE>

If you closed the 06_baseball.psd file at the end of the previous tutorial, you can open it from your ccproject folder.

1. **With** 06_baseball.psd **open from the last tutorial, make sure that the** backdrop **layer is selected in the Layers palette.**
   This ensures that the new layer you're about to create in 06_baseball.psd is located directly above the **backdrop** layer.

2. **Open a second document—**batter.psd**—from the Session 06 Tutorial Files folder on your hard drive.**
   This is the source file for the layer you're about to copy. Position it so you can see both images on your screen.

3. **Take a look at the** 06_batter.psd **Layers palette.**
   The **slugger** layer is highlighted there by default because it's the only layer in the document. If you were working with a source file that had multiple layers, you would have to manually select the layer that you planned to copy.

4. **Select the Move tool in the toolbox, and deselect Auto Select Layer in the Options bar.**
   The Auto Select Layer option was reactivated when you reset all tools at the beginning of this session.

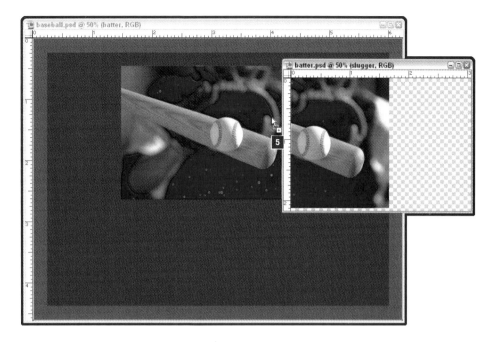

5. **Hold down the Shift key. Click in the** 06_batter.psd **document window, and drag into the** 06_baseball.psd **document window. Release the mouse when you see a blue outline around the** 06_baseball.psd **image.**

This copies the **slugger** layer from one document to the other. The **slugger** image is positioned in the center of the destination document. If you had not held the Shift key while dragging, the image would have been positioned wherever you released the mouse in the destination document.

< T I P >

If you hold the Shift key while dragging between two documents that are the same size, the image is positioned in exactly the same place in the destination document that it occupied in the source document.

6. Notice the new slugger **layer in the Layers palette of the destination document** 06_baseball.psd.

Copying a layer from one document to another automatically creates a new layer in the destination document. You don't have to rename this new layer because it automatically takes its name from the copied layer in the source document.

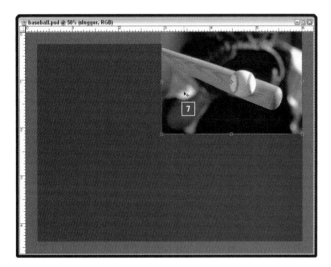

7. Check that the slugger **layer is selected in the** 06_baseball.psd **Layers palette. With the Move tool, click on the slugger image in the** 06_baseball.psd **document window and drag that image into place to match the illustration.**

The ability to move the artwork on a layer independently of the content of other layers is a major advantage of placing artwork on separate layers.

8. Open 06_boy.psd **from the Session 06 Tutorial Files folder on your hard drive.**

The single **Layer 0** layer in this file is selected by default.

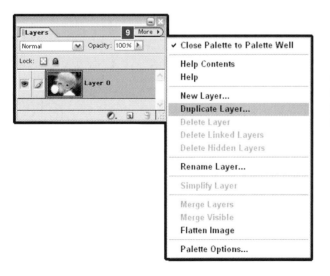

9. Click the More button on the top right of the 06_boy.psd **Layers palette. Choose Duplicate Layer from the Palette menu.**

The Duplicate Layer dialog box opens.

< N O T E >

When the Layers palette is open in the Palette Well, rather than on your desktop, the More button has no label. It is just a right-facing arrow located on the palette's tab.

10. **In the Duplicate Layer dialog box, change the name in the As field to** bubble.
    This field determines the layer name of the duplicate layer.

11. **Click in the Document field to display a list of potential destination documents for your duplicate layer. Choose** 06_baseball.psd **from this list.**
    The Document list includes all files that are currently open in Photoshop Elements 2.

12. **Click OK to copy the selected** bubble **layer from** 06_boy.psd **to** 06_baseball.psd.

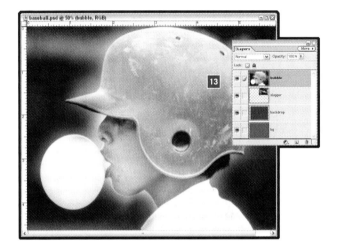

13. **Click on the** 06_baseball.psd **document window to activate that document.**
    A large bubble image occupies the entire 06_baseball.psd document window, and a new **bubble** layer appears in the 06_baseball.psd Layers palette. The two documents, 06_baseball.psd and 06_boy.psd, were not resized to match before the **bubble** layer was copied between these documents. So the imported bubble image, which comes from the larger document, fills too large an area in 06_baseball.psd. You often run into this situation when you combine layers from different images.

14. **Check that the Move tool is selected in the Tools palette and that the** bubble **layer is selected in the** 06_baseball.psd **Layers palette.**

15. **Click Ctrl+O (zero) (Macintosh: ⌘+O).**
    This expands the document window and adjusts the zoom just enough that you can see the bounding box that surrounds the bubble layer and reach its resizing handles. The bounding box is used to resize, rotate, and perform other image transformations. It appears around the artwork on a selected layer when the Move tool is selected and the Show Bounding Box option is activated in the Options bar.

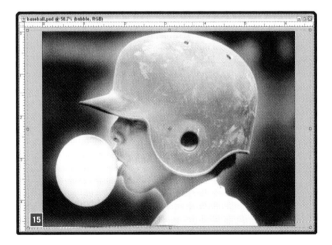

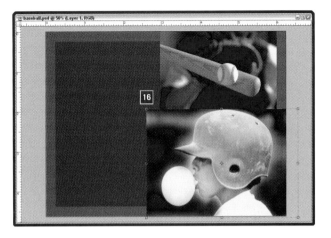

16. Hold down the Shift key to maintain proportions as you resize the image. Move your cursor over the top-left corner handle of the bounding box so that it becomes a double-pointed arrow. Click and drag down and to the right to reduce the size of the image on the bubble **layer. Release the mouse when the tiny dotted line in the top ruler (which tracks your cursor) reaches the 3-inch mark. Then release the Shift key.**

If you release the Shift key before releasing the mouse, the cursor may jump a little.

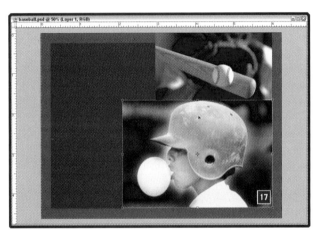

17. **Click inside the bounding box, and drag to move the bubble image into place.**

The bottom-right corner of the bubble image should be snug against the bottom-right corner of the dark brown backdrop, as in the illustration.

18. **Click again on the top-left corner handle, hold the Shift key, and drag down and to the right until the top of the bubble image is flush to the bottom of the slugger image, as in this illustration. Click the large check mark on the right side of the Options bar to commit the transformation.**

The transformation is completed, and the slugger image is now sized and positioned to fit your greeting card.

<NOTE>

Beginners tend to use the standard copy and paste method to copy a layer between documents (select a layer in the source document, choose Edit→Select All, choose Edit→Copy, activate the destination document, click Edit→Paste, and move the copied layer into position). Copy and paste is not as efficient as the methods you used in this tutorial, because it requires so many separate operations and it uses the clipboard to transfer data.

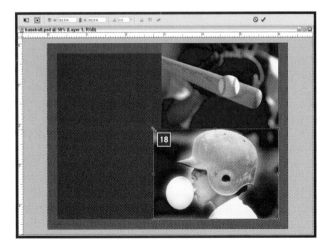

19. **Choose File→Save to save** 06_baseball.psd **to your ccproject folder, and leave that file open. Close** 06_batter.psd **and** 06_boy.psd **by clicking the red button on the top right (Macintosh: top left) of each document window.**

Tutorial
» Creating a Layer from a Selection

Copying a selection is yet another way to create a new layer. In this tutorial, you use the Layer via Copy command to create a new layer from a selection of the baseball in your greeting card. The copied baseball, located on a separate layer, further embellishes this card.

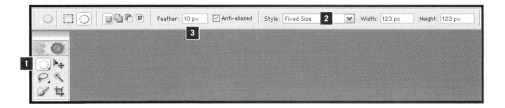

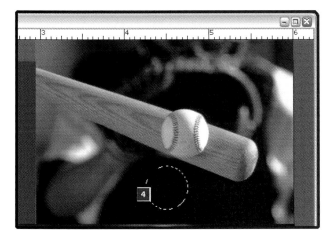

1. **With** 06_baseball.psd **open from the last tutorial, select the Elliptical Marquee tool in the toolbox.**
   Open 06_baseball.psd from your ccproject folder if it's not already open.

2. **In the Options bar, click the arrow on the Style field and choose Fixed Size. Type** 123 px **in both the Width and Height fields.**
   This is a shortcut for creating a circular selection with a diameter that is slightly smaller than the baseball in the slugger image. Alternatively, you could leave the Style field set to Normal and drag out a selection.

3. **Enter** 10 px **in the Feather field in the Options bar.**
   This adds a blurry edge to your selection.

4. **Click once in the** 06_baseball.psd **document window.**
   A circular selection of the fixed size that you entered in the Options bar is created.

5. **With the Elliptical Marquee tool still selected, click inside the circular selection and drag it on top of the baseball in the image.**
   Dragging with a selection tool moves a selection outline, as opposed to the contents of a selection.

6. **Select the** slugger **layer in the** 06_baseball.psd
   Layers palette.
   This is the layer to be copied.

7. **Choose Layer→New→Layer via Copy from the menu bar.**
   This copies the selected content (the baseball) from the
   slugger layer and automatically creates another layer, **Layer 1**,
   with that content. The new **Layer 1** appears above the **slugger**
   layer in the Layers palette. You won't notice the copied baseball in the document window yet because it's located directly
   on top of the original baseball.

   <TIP>
   Another way to access the Layer via Copy command is to right-click
   (Macintosh: Ctrl+click) on a layer in the Layers palette to bring up
   a contextual menu.

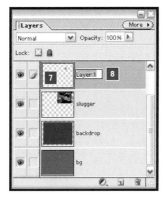

8. **Double-click the** Layer 1 **name in the Layers palette, and type** ball
   to give that layer a more descriptive name.

9. **Select the Move tool, and click and drag to position the contents**
   of the new ball **layer to match the illustration.**
   The highly feathered edges of the copied baseball give it a
   different look than the original baseball.

   <TIP>
   Repurposing selected content from one layer by copying it to other
   layers, where you can change its appearance and position, is a
   useful technique for creating a collage of elements that work
   well together.

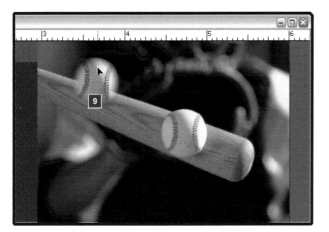

10. **Select the Elliptical Marquee tool, click on the Tool icon at the**
    far left of the Options bar, and choose Reset Tool.
    This is a housekeeping task to eliminate sticky Fixed
    Size settings.

11. **Choose File→Save. Leave the file open for the next tutorial.**
    Your greeting card is now embellished with a feathered base-
    ball, which you copied from the slugger image using Layer
    via Copy.

Tutorial
» Creating a Layer by Duplication

Another way to create a new layer is to duplicate an existing layer. In this short tutorial, you duplicate the **ball** layer in your greeting card to create a series of baseballs.

1. **With** 06_baseball.psd **open from the last tutorial, click on the** ball **layer in the Layers palette and drag the layer to the Create New Layer button at the bottom of the Layers palette.**

<**NOTE**>
If you closed 06_baseball.psd at the end of the previous tutorial, you can open it from your ccproject folder.

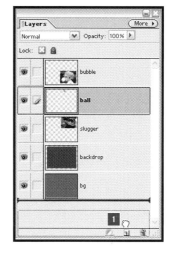

2. **Release the mouse to create a duplicate layer labeled** ball copy **above the** ball **layer.**
The duplicate ball is not yet visible in the document window because it's positioned right on top of the original ball.

<**NOTE**>
Using the Create New Layer icon is the fastest way to duplicate a layer. Alternatively, right-click (Macintosh: Ctrl+click) on a layer in the Layers palette, choose Duplicate Layer from the contextual menu, and click OK to accept the default settings in the Duplicate Layer dialog box.

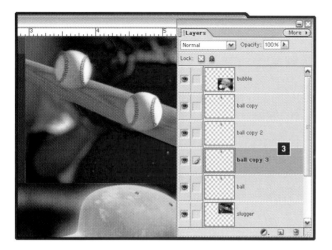

3. **Repeat Steps 1 and 2 two more times, creating** ball copy 2 **and** ball copy 3 **layers in the Layers palette.**
   You won't see these copies in the document window until you move them.

4. **Select the Move tool in the toolbox.**

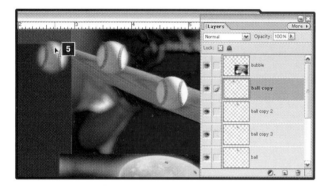

5. **Select the** ball copy **layer in the Layers palette. In the document window, click on the stack of baseballs that have a feathered edge. Press and hold the Shift key, and drag to the left. The baseball on the** ball copy **layer comes into view as you drag. Position that baseball to match the illustration.**
   Holding the Shift key as you drag, restrains movement to a straight line.

6. **Repeat Step 5 two more times, selecting the** ball copy 2 **layer and then the** ball copy 3 **layer. Pull each baseball further to the left to match this illustration.**

7. **Choose File→Save. Leave the file open for the next tutorial.**
   Your greeting card now includes a series of baseballs, each on a separate layer duplicated from the original.

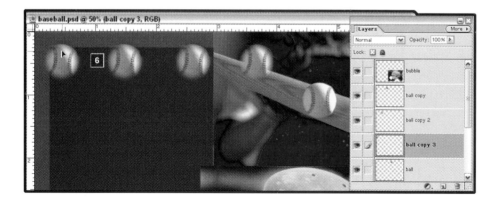

Tutorial
» Managing Layers in the Layers Palette

The Layers palette offers a variety of controls for managing the layers in a document, many of which you use in this tutorial. You link layers together in order to transform them all at once. You see how easy it is to delete a layer, which removes all of its content from the image. You learn to lock layers to avoid moving them out of position. You reorder layers in the Layers palette. And you turn layer visibility off and on to see the content of underlying layers. This is an important tutorial that teaches fundamental layer management skills. In the process, you transform the content of the ball layers in your greeting card so that the baseballs appear to move into the distance, and you add a layer containing baseball cards to the project.

1. **With** `06_baseball.psd` **open from the last tutorial (or reopened from your ccproject folder if necessary), select the** ball **layer in the Layers palette.**
   Your next task is to link the ball layers to one another so that you can rotate them as one unit.

2. **Click inside the link field to the left of the layer thumbnail on each of the other ball layers (**ball copy, ball copy 2, **and** ball copy 3**) to link these layers to the selected** ball **layer.**

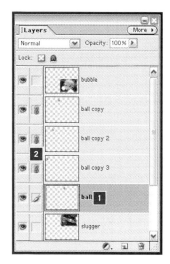

<NOTE>
Moving or transforming any one of a group of linked layers affects all the linked layers.

3. **Select the Move tool in the toolbox.**
   Notice that the Move tool's bounding box surrounds the art-work on all the linked layers.

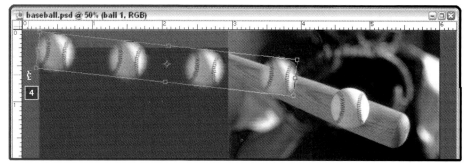

4. **Move the cursor outside the bottom-left corner of the bounding box so that it becomes a curved, double-pointed arrow. Click and drag up to rotate the balls on all four linked layers.**
   Try to match the illustration as you apply this transformation.

<TIP>
You can cancel a transformation before it's committed by clicking the large Cancel icon on the far right of the Options bar. To undo a transformation after it's committed, choose an earlier state in the Undo History palette.

Layer Transformations

There are several ways to transform the contents of a layer. You can accomplish some layer transformations with just the Move tool bounding box:

» To scale, click in a bounding box handle and drag.

» To rotate, move the cursor outside a handle until it becomes a double-pointed arrow and drag, as you did in this tutorial.

» To distort, Ctrl+click (Macintosh: ⌘+click) in a handle and drag.

» To skew (slant), Ctrl+Shift+click (Macintosh: ⌘+Shift+click) in a side handle and drag.

» To apply perspective, Ctrl+Alt+Shift+click (Macintosh: ⌘+Option+Shift+click) on a corner handle and drag.

Alternatively, you can use the Free Transform, Rotate, Distort, Skew, and Perspective commands in the Image→Transform menu. And there are specific layer-based commands in the middle section of the Image→Rotate menu. For example, you can flip the contents of a layer by choosing Image→Rotate→Flip Layer Horizontal.

In addition to transforming layers, you can transform selections, as you learned in Session 5, or shapes, as you learn in Session 9. Some transformations even apply to a whole image, like the rotate, flip, and straighten commands in the Image→Rotate menu.

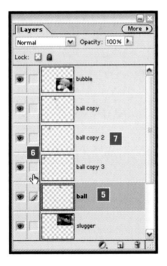

5. **In the Layers palette, select one of the ball layers.**

6. **Click in the link field of each of the other three ball layers to remove the link symbols.**

   Your next task is to size each ball differently to create the illusion that they recede into the distance. This required unlinking the ball layers.

< T I P >

A quick way to unlink neighboring layers is to click on the lowest link symbol and run your mouse up the column of link fields in the Layers palette.

7. **In the Layers palette, select the** ball copy 2 **layer, which contains the second ball from the left.**

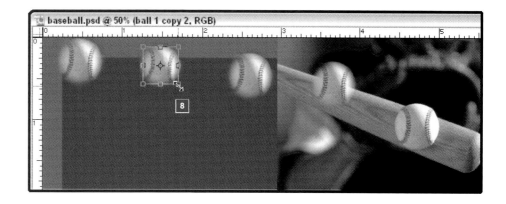

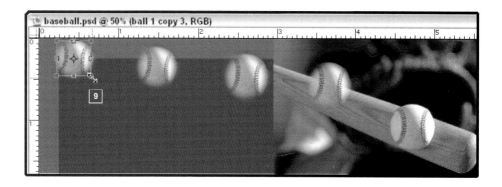

8. **With the Move tool still selected and the Show Bounding Box option on, Shift+click on a corner handle of the bounding box around the second ball from the left and drag toward the center of the ball.**

   This makes the ball slightly smaller while retaining its circular proportions.

9. **Repeat Steps 7 and 8 on the** ball copy 3 **layer (the ball at the far left).**

   Make this ball even smaller than its neighbor to make it look farther away.

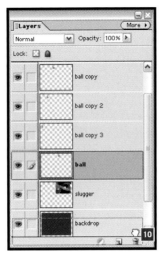

10. **Click on the** ball **layer, and drag it to the Trash icon at the bottom of the Layers palette.**

    That's how easy it is to delete a layer along with all its contents. If you accidentally delete a layer, the only way to get it back is with an Undo. You cannot open the Layers palette Trash to retrieve its contents.

< N O T E >

One of the advantages of isolating artwork on a separate layer is that you can delete it at any time without disturbing the rest of the composition.

< T I P >

Another way to delete a layer is to select it, click on the Trash icon at the bottom of the Layers palette, and choose Yes at the confirmation prompt. Or you can right-click (Macintosh: Ctrl+click) on a layer in the Layers palette and choose Delete Layer from the contextual menu.

11. **Select the** ball copy **layer, and click the Lock All button on the top of the Layers palette. Repeat this with the** ball copy 2 **and** ball copy 3 **layers.**

    Notice that a black lock icon appears on each of the locked layers. This lock prevents you from doing almost anything to the locked layers, including deleting, moving, or editing the layer.

< T I P >

To unlock a layer at any time, select the layer and click the Lock All icon at the top of the Layers palette.

< T I P >

Another lock button (the small checkerboard square) at the top of the Layers palette protects only the transparent pixels on a layer, leaving pixels of existing artwork free for editing. You can use this Lock Transparency feature along with the Fill command to quickly change the color of artwork on a layer, because filling a protected layer with color affects only the artwork and not the surrounding transparent areas. You activate and deactivate Lock Transparency the same way as Lock All. Lock Transparency displays a white lock icon on the affected layer.

< N O T E >

In the next section of this tutorial, you learn how to change layer visibility and reorder layers in the Layers palette.

12. **Select the** bg **layer at the bottom of the Layers palette.**

13. **Open** 06_cards.psd **from the Session 06 Tutorial Files folder on your hard drive.**

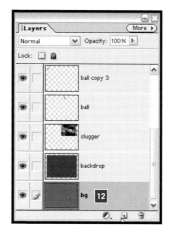

14. **Click in the** 06_cards.psd **document window, and drag into the** 06_baseball.psd **document window to import the baseball card image into your project.**

    This creates a new **cards** layer in the Layers palette just above the selected **bg** layer. You can't see the baseball card image in the 06_baseball.psd document window because it is hidden by the large rectangle of brown pixels in the **backdrop** layer. The **backdrop** layer is located above the **cards** layer in the Layers palette, illustrating the importance of layer stacking order in the Layers palette.

15. **Click the Eye icon located in the Visibility field to the left of the** backdrop **layer.**

    This makes the contents of the **backdrop** layer invisible in the document window, even though that layer remains part of the file. Now you can see that the baseball card image is indeed there, although it may be partially obscured by the contents of other overlying layers.

<TIP>

The ability to make layers invisible means that you can store extra layers—such as different versions of a logo, various type treatments, or graphics with different color schemes—in a file, as long as you have enough RAM and storage space to handle the inflated file size.

<TIP>

Making any layer temporarily invisible is a good way to figure out what artwork is located on that layer. You can deconstruct an entire file by making all layers except one invisible (by Alt+clicking [Macintosh: Option+clicking] the Eye icon on that layer), and then making the other layers visible one by one so that you can see what content each adds to the image.

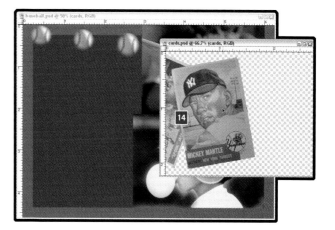

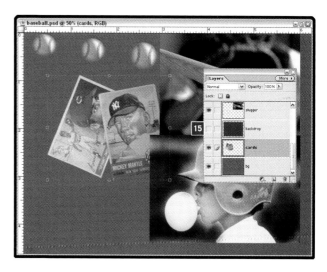

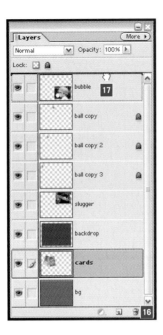

16. **Click and drag down on the bottom-right corner of the Layers palette.**

    This expands the height of the palette so that you can see all the layers.

17. **Click and drag the cards layer up to the top of the layer stack. When you see a dark line above the top bubble layer, release the mouse.**

    The layers are reordered. The **cards** layer now occupies the top spot in the layer stack.

18. **Click in the Visibility field to the left of the backdrop layer to add an Eye icon.**

    The brown backdrop is again visible in the document window. The baseball card image remains visible too, because the **cards** layer has been moved above the other layers in the layer stack.

19. **With the Move tool, click on the baseball card image in the document window and move it into place to match the illustration.**

Now that all the elements of this card are in place, you can turn off the Rulers at your discretion by choosing View➔Rulers.

20. **Choose File➔Save to resave** 06_baseball.psd **with these changes, and leave it open for the next tutorial. Close** 06_cards.psd **without resaving.**

Your greeting card now consists of numerous layers, each containing one of the pieces of artwork that are included in the final piece. In this tutorial, you transformed the ball layers to add an illusion of depth, and varied layer stacking order and layer visibility as you created a new cards layer.

Discussion
Demystifying Blending Modes

Layer blending modes are formulas that determine how colors in a layer interact with colors in the layers below. Blending modes are very useful for artists and designers, because they significantly impact the look and feel of an image. Unfortunately, some users shy away from blending modes because they find them unpredictable. That's a mistake, because this is a feature that you have to use to understand. Read this discussion, work through the tutorial that follows, and try some of these techniques on your own images. No doubt you'll become hooked on blending modes like the pros.

What are blending modes?

Blending modes work by mathematically combining each pixel of color in the layer that's selected (called the blending color) with the color directly below (the base color). If the layer below the selected layer has opaque artwork, it provides the base color. If the layer below is not completely opaque or has its own blending mode, the base color comes from a combination of underlying layers. If you're looking for a practical way to choose blending modes, this discussion offers some useful information and some practical approaches to consider. A more technical explanation of how each mode combines blending colors and base colors can be found in the Photoshop Elements 2 Help files.

Layer blending modes are organized by category in the Blending Modes menu on the Layers palette. Within each of these categories are some basic modes that are used most often and some variations on those modes. Here is a practical look at the most popular, basic modes in each category:

Normal and Dissolve modes have specific, very predictable effects.

>> Normal is the default blending mode. In Normal mode, the blending color is completely opaque and there is no interaction between it and any base color.

>> Dissolve mode affects only semi-opaque pixels—those whose opacity has been lowered or that are located along a feathered edge of an image. It has no effect on pixels that are completely opaque. This mode takes its name from the look it creates—a random stippled pattern made up of some pixels of the blending color and some pixels of the base color.

Multiply and Darken are among the modes that darken color.

» Multiply is a popular basic blending mode. It works, as its name implies, by multiplying blending colors by base colors, which results in darker color overall. The result is what a traditional photographer would get by sandwiching two color slides together. The sandwich is darker than either slide on its own, and it reveals image elements from both slides. A practical use of this blending mode is to darken an underexposed (too light) image, by duplicating its layer one or more times and applying Multiply mode to the duplicates. This mode is also useful for artists who want to blend a scan of a dark sketch on white paper into other artwork. Set the scan layer to multiply, and the white paper disappears because multiplying an underlying color by white eliminates the white blending color with no effect on the underlying color.

» Darken compares the brightness of each pixel on a selected layer with the pixel below. The colors in the selected layer are displayed only where they are darker than the colors below. To complicate matters, the brightness comparison is done on each color channel separately, so this mode can cause significant color changes.

Screen and Lighten are among the modes that always lighten color.

» Screen mode is the opposite of Multiply mode. It brightens all colors, mimicking the look that you get if you project two photographic slides onto a white screen (hence the name Screen mode). Where the projected slides overlap, all colors look significantly brighter. A practical use of this mode is to lighten an underexposed (too dark) image by duplicating its layer one or more times and applying Screen mode to the duplicates. This mode can also be used to brighten selected areas of an image, like reflective highlights or a glowing light source, by selecting and copying those areas to an overlaying layer set to Screen mode.

» Lighten is the opposite of Darken. It displays only those colors in the selected layer that are lighter than those below. Like Darken, it works on the basis of individual color channels, so it can cause color changes.

Overlay, Soft Light, and Hard Light, are among the modes that brighten or darken, depending on the colors involved.

» Overlay mode brightens some pixels as in Screen mode and darkens others as in Multiply mode. Which pixels get which effect depends on the brightness of the underlying base color. This makes Overlay mode a good choice for blending a pattern (like a texture or even a tattoo) with an underlying photograph, because the overlaying pattern appears to pick up the tonal values of the photograph. This is also the mode to try first when you want to blend two images but retain the detail in both. If the blended images compete too strongly, try reducing opacity of the selected layer or applying the milder Soft Light mode.

» Soft Light mode also brightens some colors and darkens others, but it offers a softer, more diffused effect than Overlay mode.

» Hard light mode brightens and darkens various colors too, producing an effect that's similar to but more contrasty than Overlay mode.

Difference and Exclusion modes produce some extreme color changes.

» Difference mode inverts the base color (color on underlying layers) where there are bright colors on the selected layer above. The base color stays the same where there is black on the selected layer and changes the most where there is white on the selected layer.

» Exclusion mode is a less contrasty version of Difference mode.

Color, Hue, Saturation, and Luminosity modes work by combining color properties of images.

» Color mode is the most popular of this group. It's used to give a monochromatic, colorized look to an image. Color mode combines the hue and saturation of color on the selected layer with the brightness values (luminosity) of the underlying colors. Like the other modes in this category, Color mode works only where there is color, as opposed to a grayscale image, on the selected layer.

» Hue, Saturation, and Luminosity modes work the same way as Color mode, but each uses a different color property from each layer. For example, Luminosity mode combines the luminosity of color on the selected layer with the hue and saturation of the base color.

Choosing a mode

How do you choose which blending mode to apply, other than hit and miss experimentation? You can use what you now know about blending modes and their categories to focus your search. Start with a general idea of the effect that you want to create. For example, you may know that you want to lighten or darken an image, maintain or replace its colors, or create a subtle or extreme look. Start by applying a blending mode in the appropriate category, and then methodically cycle through the related blending modes that follow in the menu until you find the one you like. If none fit the bill, analyze what you don't like and try another category. For example, if you want a darkening effect, start by applying the Darken blending mode. Then move down the menu list applying the related modes that follow—multiply, color burn, and linear burn—until you find the one that provides the effect that you want. (If you're a Windows user, you can use the arrow keys on your keyboard to cycle through the menu of blending modes immediately after making one blending mode change.) If the effect of all these modes is too dark, move to the category of modes that darkens some pixels and lightens others and try each of those modes—overlay, soft light, etc. As you become more familiar with the effect of blending modes, you'll be able to zero right in on the one that can accomplish a particular task for you.

Another way to choose a blending mode is to consult a visual reference. You can use the accompanying illustration to compare the effect on the same image of each of the layer blending modes in Photoshop Elements 2. This test image contains two layers—a black and white photograph on the top layer to which blending modes have been applied, and a light to dark color gradient on the bottom layer. Use it only as a point of comparison, keeping in mind that not all images react the same way to particular blending modes. (For example, dissolve mode shows little effect on this image because the photograph is opaque. If the opacity of the photograph had been lowered, dissolve would cause a stippled effect. And Color mode shows no effect on the black and white photograph in this image, as it would on a color photograph.)

Keep in mind that you can reduce the effect of a blending mode change by reducing the opacity of the layer to which the mode was applied. One more thing that you should know about blending modes is that you can paint with them. Many of the painting tools have blending mode options on their Options bars. These work the same way as layer blending modes, except that the blend color is the color with which you paint and the base color is the color of the existing artwork under the paint. The painting tools have two additional blending modes—Behind, which paints behind artwork on a transparent layer, and Clear, which makes pixels transparent.

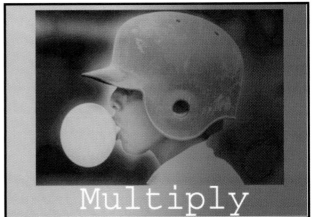

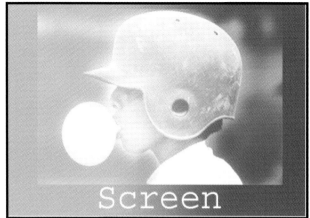

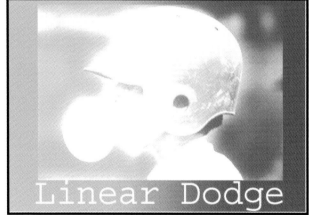

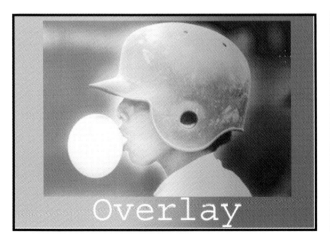

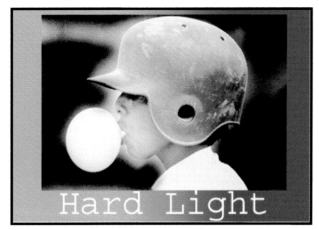

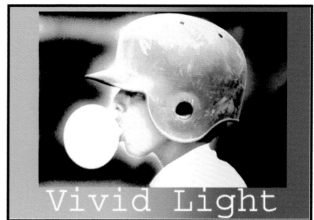

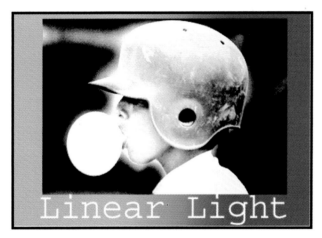

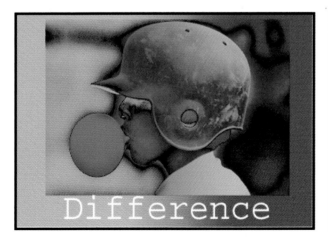

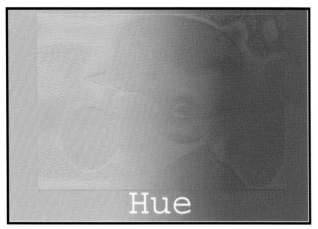

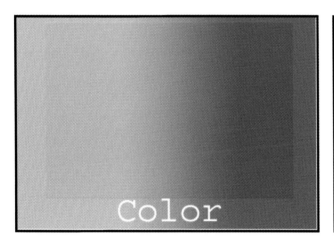

Tutorial
» Changing Layer Blending Mode and Opacity

In this tutorial, you change the blending mode and opacity of layers to alter the way they interact with layers below. These powerful features can significantly change the appearance of layered artwork. This helps blend the layers of imagery in the greeting card you're building.

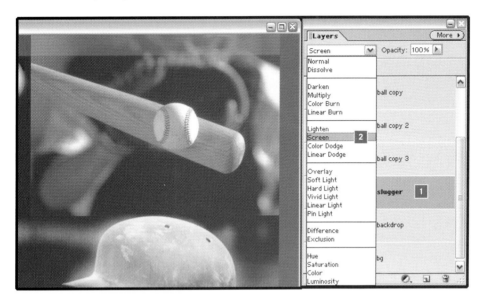

1. **With** `06_baseball.psd` **open from the previous tutorial (or opened from your ccproject folder), select the** slugger **layer in the Layers palette.**

2. **Click the arrow to the right of the Blending Modes field. Choose Screen from the Blending Modes menu.**
   Screen mode brightens all the colors in the slugger image by combining each of the pixels of color on the **slugger** layer with the pixel directly below it on the **backdrop** or **bg** layer using a mathematical formula that brightens, but retains, photographic detail. Notice that the effect is different where the slugger image overlays the brighter **bg** layer at the top of the screen.

3. **Click on any selection tool, such as the Rectangular Marquee tool, in the toolbox. Type** 9 **to automatically reduce the percentage in the layer Opacity field in the Layers palette to 90%.**
   Lowering the opacity of a layer to which you applied a layer blending mode reduces the intensity of the blending mode. In this case, it reduces the brightness generated by the Screen blending mode, particularly in the brightest areas like the baseball. This method of changing opacity varies the opacity of a layer by multiples of 10%. You can type 0 (for 100%), 1 (for 10%), and so on up to 9 (for 90%).

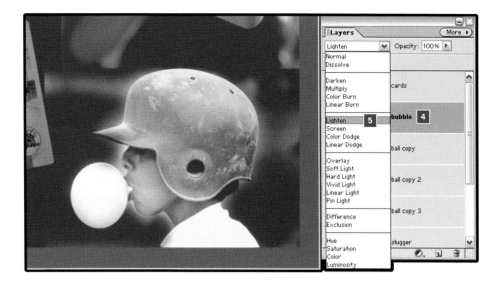

<NOTE>

Choosing a selection tool and typing a number to change opacity works when you select any selection or navigation tool. However, it does not work when a painting tool (like the Brush tool, Selection Brush tool, etc.) or an editing tool (like the Dodge tool, Burn tool, etc.) is selected. In that case, you can type a number directly into the Opacity field or use the slider on that field to vary layer opacity.

<NOTE>

Opacity also controls the transparency of a layer. Lowering a layer's opacity increases the degree to which you can see through the artwork on that layer to the layers below.

4. **Select the** bubble **layer in the Layers palette.**

5. **Change the blending mode of the** bubble **layer by choosing Lighten from the Blending Mode menu.**
   Lighten mode brightens the bubble image by looking for pixels on the **bubble** layer that are darker than the pixels directly below on the **backdrop** layer—like the dark areas in the background of the bubble image. Those pixels are replaced by the brighter pixels from the underlying **backdrop** layer. As a result, the background of the bubble image fades into the collage.

6. **Click the arrow to the right of the Opacity field, and use the Opacity slider to lower the opacity of the selected** bubble **layer to 95%.**
   This is another way to change opacity to a number other than a multiple of 10%. Alternatively, you can type a number into the Opacity field.

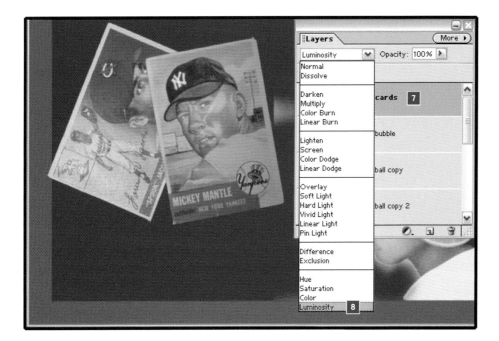

<**NOTE**>

Notice the small sliver of lavender on the bottom right of the baseball card? This is where the baseball cards overlap the slugger image, to which a different blending mode has been applied. In this area, the Luminosity blending mode combines artwork on the **cards** layer with a composite of artwork on the **slugger** layer and the **backdrop** layer, which in turn are combined with a Lighten blending mode. This gives you just a glimpse of the complexities the program must handle when blending modes are applied to many layers.

7. **Select the** cards **layer in the Layers palette.**

8. **Change the blending mode of the** cards **layer by choosing Luminosity from the Blending Mode menu on the Layers palette.**
   This mode combines the luminosity of each pixel on the **cards** layer (which provides the tonal detail) with the hue and saturation of the pixel directly below. The result is a brown color tint that does not overpower the details of the baseball cards. This simple change integrates the baseball cards with the emerging dominant color of the collage.

9. **Choose File→Save, and leave** 06_baseball.psd **open for the next tutorial.**
   Changing the blending modes and opacities of various layers in your greeting card helped blend the various images in the card with one another, giving the final product a more sophisticated look.

Tutorial
» Using Fill and Adjustment Layers

Fill layers and adjustment layers are special layer types that give you the power to edit images with maximum flexibility. They are invaluable because they change the look of underlying layers without touching the original artwork and because they remain editable. In this tutorial, you change the appearance of this greeting card by applying a Solid Color fill layer to tint the entire image, a Pattern fill layer to add a subtle texture to portions of the image, and a Brightness and Contrast adjustment layer to pump up image contrast.

1. **With** 06_baseball.psd **open from the last tutorial, select the cards layer (the top layer in the Layers palette).**
   This ensures that the fill layer you're about to create is located at the top of the layer stack.

2. **Click the Add New Adjustment or Fill Layer button at the bottom of the Layers palette, and choose Solid Color from the menu.**
   This creates a Solid Color fill layer in the Layers palette that's automatically named **Color Fill 1** and opens the Color Picker.

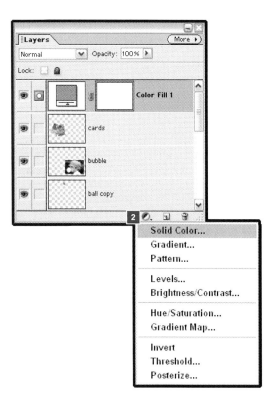

3. **In the Color Picker, choose a light brown color by entering R: 204, B: 153, C: 102, and click OK.**
   This sets the color of the Solid Color fill layer. The Color Picker closes, and the opaque color of this layer fills the document window.

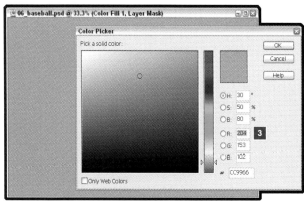

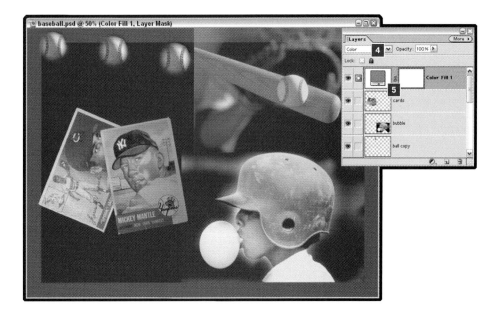

Why Use a Fill Layer?

You may be wondering why I suggested that you use a Solid Color fill layer rather than a regular layer filled with color. Either would have the same tinting effect when set to Color blending mode, but the significant advantage of the fill layer is that it remains editable. You can replace the color of the fill layer at any time by clicking its left thumbnail to open the Color Picker and choosing a new color. You can even change the nature of the fill layer by choosing Layer→Change Layer Content from the menu bar and selecting one of the other types of fill or adjustment layers from the resulting menu. All types of fill and adjustment layers share this advantage over regular layers.

4. **Click the arrow to the right of the Blending Mode field, and choose Color from the Blending Modes menu.**

This causes the fill layer to interact with all of the layers below it, generating a brown tint that unifies the elements in this collage.

5. **Notice that the new** Color Fill 1 **layer in the Layers palette displays two thumbnails.**

The thumbnail on the left represents the color fill. The thumbnail on the right represents an empty layer mask. (The layer mask can be used to limit the color fill to a selected area of the image, as you do later in this tutorial.) The icon between the two thumbnails links the two components of the layer together. (Clicking this icon disables the link, allowing the content of the layer to be moved independently of the layer mask.) And the circle-in-a-square icon to the left of the layer identifies the layer as a special fill or adjustment layer.

<NOTE>

All the different types of fill layers and adjustment layers are constructed the same way. They differ only in the content represented by the thumbnail on the left. There are three kinds of fill layers: Solid Color, Pattern, and Gradient Fill. There are six kinds of adjustment layers: Levels, Brightness/Contrast, Hue/Saturation, Gradient Map, Inversion, Threshold, and Posterize.

<TIP>

A fill or adjustment layer affects an entire image, unless you specifically limit its effect. One way to do that is to have a selection active at the time you create the fill/adjustment layer.

<NOTE>

A fill or adjustment layer affects the artwork on all the layers below it in the Layers palette unless you group the fill or adjustment layer with the underlying layer. In the Layers palette, hold the Alt key (Macintosh: Option key) and move the cursor over the line between the fill/adjustment layer and the layer below. When the cursor changes to a double circle, click to group the two layers. The grouped fill/adjustment layer is indented and displays a down-pointing arrow. The fill/adjustment now affects only the artwork on the grouped layer. To ungroup these layers, repeat this operation.

6. **In the Layers palette, Ctrl+Shift+click (Macintosh: ⌘+Shift+click) on the** ball copy 2 **and the** ball copy 3 **layers to select the solid part of the two baseballs on the left.**

   Holding the Ctrl key (Macintosh: ⌘ key) while you click on a layer selects all the solid artwork on that layer. Adding the Shift key while you click on multiple layers adds to the selection.

7. **Choose Select→Modify→Expand, enter** 10 **pixels in the Expand Selection dialog box, and click OK.**

   This expands the selection to include the feathered edges of the baseballs.

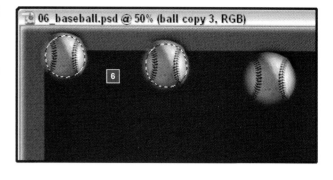

8. **Choose Select→Invert to invert the selection so that it includes everything except the two baseballs.**

   This selection restricts the effect of the pattern fill layer you're about to create to everything except these baseballs.

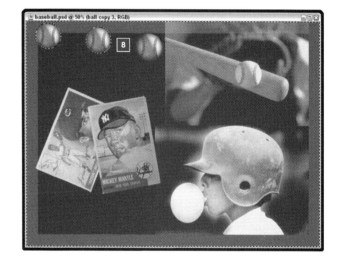

9. **Select the** Color Fill 1 **layer in the Layers palette. Click the Create New Adjustment or Fill Layer button at the bottom of the Layers palette, and choose Pattern.**

   This adds a **Pattern Fill 1** layer in the Layers palette, fills the document window with a default pattern, and opens the Pattern Fill dialog box. The default pattern fills only the selected area of the image, which doesn't include the baseballs.

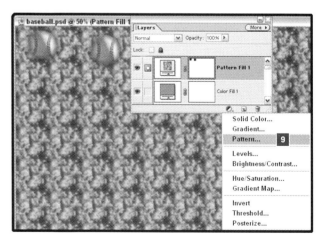

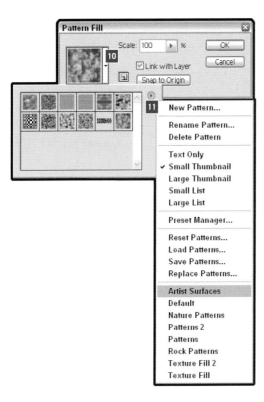

10. **In the Pattern Fill dialog box, click the arrow to the right of the Pattern Sample to open the Pattern Picker.**

11. **Click the arrow on the top right of the Pattern Picker to open a Palette menu. Choose Artist Surfaces from the list of additional pattern sets at the bottom of the Palette menu.**
    This loads that pattern set into the Pattern Picker. This is one of several extra sets of prebuilt patterns that ship with Photoshop Elements 2.

12. **Click on the Stone pattern thumbnail to apply that pattern, and then click OK to close the Pattern Fill dialog box.**
    If you hold your mouse over any thumbnail in the Pattern Picker, you see a tool tip that identifies that pattern by name.

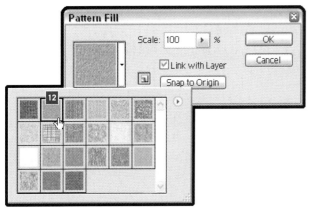

Creating Your Own Patterns

You are not limited to using the prebuilt patterns that ship with Photoshop Elements 2. You can create your own pattern from any image by selecting a small area of the image with the Rectangular Marquee tool, and choosing Edit→Define Pattern from the menu bar. In the Pattern Name dialog box, give the pattern a meaningful name and click OK. The next time you open the Pattern Picker, you'll see your new pattern at the end of the current pattern set.

It's important that you save this pattern set to retain your new pattern. Click the arrow at the top right of the Pattern Picker, and choose Save Patterns from the Palette menu. In the Save dialog box, enter a name for the pattern set and click Save. This saves a pattern format file into the Presets→Patterns folder inside the Photoshop Elements 2 application folder on your hard drive. (Placing a .pat format pattern file that you download or acquire from a third party into this folder is another way to expand your library of available patterns.)

Your new pattern is now available whenever you load this pattern set into the Pattern Picker, whether you work with a **Pattern Fill** layer, fill a regular layer with a pattern using the **Edit→Fill** command or the **Paint Bucket** tool, or use the **Pattern Stamp** tool to paint with a pattern.

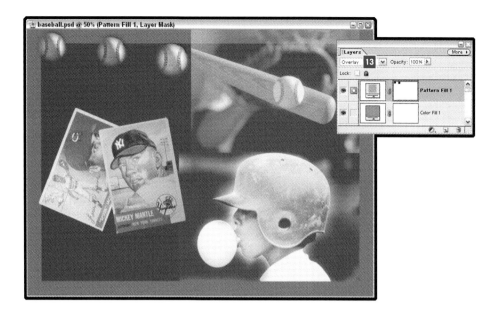

13. **With the new** Pattern Fill 1 **layer selected in the Layers palette, choose Overlay from the Blending Modes menu at the top of the Layers palette.**

This changes the Stone pattern into a subtle texture that blends with all the layers below within the selected area. Overlay is a useful mode for blending a pattern into underlying images, as mentioned in the preceding discussion.

<NOTE>

You can change the pattern at any time by clicking the left thumbnail in the **Pattern Fill 1** layer to open the Pattern Fill dialog box and repeating Steps 10 through 12. This editability makes using a Pattern Fill layer preferable to creating a regular layer filled with a pattern.

Restricting the Effect of a Fill or Adjustment Layer with a Layer Mask

A layer mask is a grayscale element that is automatically generated when you create a fill or adjustment layer of any kind. The layer mask controls the area affected by the fill/adjustment, which is effective only on that part of the image that lies beneath white areas of the mask. The fill/adjustment has no effect on parts of the image that lie beneath black areas of the mask and only partial effect under gray areas of the mask.

The layer mask starts out white, so that the entire image is affected by the fill/adjustment. There are two ways to generate dark areas on the mask that restrict the fill/adjustment:

» Make a selection just before you create the fill/adjustment layer as you did in this tutorial. (You can see the dark areas of the mask that were not included in that selection on the layer mask thumbnail on the Pattern Fill 1 layer in the Layers palette.)

» Paint or fill directly on the layer mask with black or gray.

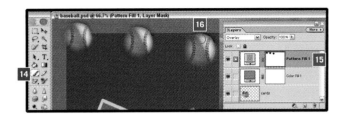

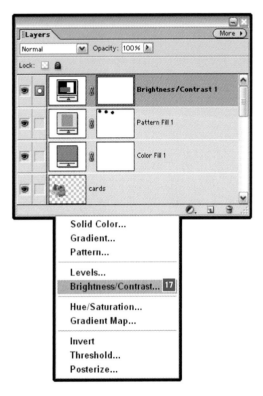

14. **Select the Brush tool in the toolbox. Type** 50 **px in the Size field in the Options bar to set the brush size.**

15. **Make sure that the** Pattern Fill 1 **layer is selected in the Layers palette.**

    This actually selects the layer mask on this layer (as you can see by the double border around the layer mask thumbnail), and changes the Foreground and Background colors in the toolbox to black and white respectively. Selecting a layer mask automatically sets the Foreground and Background colors to black and white because a layer mask is a grayscale element.

16. **In the document window, paint over the third baseball from the left.**

    The pattern disappears from the baseball as you paint. You actually paint on the layer mask rather than directly on the image. Notice that there's now a third black spot on the **Pattern Fill 1** layer mask in the Layers palette, which protects this baseball from the pattern fill. If you paint outside the third baseball by mistake, click the double-pointed arrow above the color boxes in the toolbox to switch the Foreground color to white, and paint over the mistake to redisplay the pattern fill.

17. **Make sure that the** Pattern Fill 1 **layer is selected in the Layers palette. Click the Create New Adjustment or Fill Layer button at the bottom of the Layers palette, and choose Brightness/Contrast.**

    This opens the Brightness/Contrast dialog box, and adds a **Brightness/Contrast 1** layer to the Layers palette.

<TIP>

If you want a closer look at the layer mask, Atl+click (Macintosh: Option+click) on the layer mask thumbnail on the **Pattern Fill 1** layer in the Layers palette to display just the layer mask in the document window. Alt+click (Macintosh: Option+click) again to switch back to the image.

<NOTE>

An adjustment layer is very similar to a fill layer. Like a fill layer, an adjustment layer displays a content thumbnail and a layer mask thumbnail in the Layers palette. It remains editable, it affects all the layers below unless it's grouped with another layer, and its scope can be limited by painting in its layer mask. The difference is that it affects the layers below it with an image adjustment (like Brightness/Contrast, Levels, or Hue/Saturation) rather than a fill.

<TIP>

A layer mask remains editable. You can always change your mind and paint over its black areas with white to eliminate a masked area. Or you can add a masked area by painting with black or gray.

18. **In the Brightness/Contrast dialog box, move the Brightness slider to the left to -20 to darken the image and the Contrast slider to the right to +25 to increase its contrast. Leave the Preview box in the dialog box checked to see a live preview of this change. Click OK to apply the adjustment.**

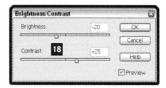

Adding contrast increases the difference between the darkest shadows and brightest highlights in an image, making the image look less flat.

19. **Choose File→Save, and leave** 06_baseball.psd **open for the next tutorial.**

Adding a Solid Color fill layer, a Pattern fill layer, and a Brightness/Contrast adjustment layer to your greeting card in this tutorial enhanced the appearance of the image without harming the original pixels.

<CAUTION>

Don't confuse an adjustment layer with a regular image adjustment (which is accessible from the Enhance menu and Image→ Adjustments submenu). The difference is that a regular adjustment is applied directly to a selected layer, permanently altering the artwork on that layer. The beauty of an adjustment layer is that it allows you to edit nondestructively, without disturbing any pixels of artwork. For this reason, applying an adjustment layer is almost always preferable to using a regular image adjustment.

<NOTE>

After you apply one adjustment layer to an image, additional adjustment layers do not add to file size in a significant way. This advantage—in addition to the nondestructive nature of adjustment layers, their constant editability, and the ability to limit their effect to specific areas and layers—makes them among the most useful features in your Photoshop Elements 2 toolbox. In the next tutorial you learn a special use for an adjustment layer—as a work-around for the lack of layer mask controls in this program. In the next part of the course you learn more about using adjustment layers to correct tone and color in photographs.

Tutorial
» Combining Images with a Layer Mask

You can make images appear to blend into one another using a layer mask with a black to white gradient. Unfortunately, there is no direct way to add a layer mask to a regular layer in Photoshop Elements 2. This tutorial offers a workaround, using features with which you're already familiar—adjustment layers and layer grouping. You use this work-around to gradually blend the slugger image with the backdrop of the greeting card.

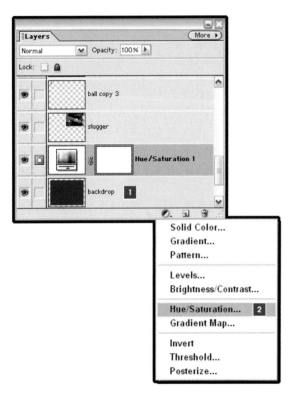

1. **With** 06_baseball.psd **open from the previous tutorial, select the** backdrop **layer in the Layers palette. If this image is no longer open, open it from your ccproject folder.**
   In the steps that follow, you fade the edges of the **slugger** layer into this **backdrop** layer. The ability to combine images with a seamless look is a fundamental compositing skill.

2. **Click the Create New Adjustment or Fill Layer button at the bottom of the Layers palette, and choose Hue/Saturation from the menu.**
   This adds a new **Hue/Saturation 1** adjustment layer to the Layers palette and opens the Hue/Saturation dialog box. Notice that a layer mask thumbnail appears to the right of the content thumbnail on the **Hue/Saturation 1** layer in the Layers palette.

3. **Leave the Hue/Saturation settings at their defaults of 0, and click OK to close the Hue/Saturation dialog box.**
   A Hue/Saturation adjustment layer is normally used to modify the color, saturation, and brightness of the layers below it, but in this case adjusting layers is not your main goal. You're more interested in using the layer mask that comes with the adjustment layer. The Levels or Brightness/Contrast adjustment layers would also work for this purpose.

4. **In the Layers palette, move the cursor over the border between the** Hue/Saturation 1 **adjustment layer and the** slugger **layer above it. Click when the cursor changes to a double circle icon to group these two layers together.**

Grouping the layers is the essential step in this workaround. In effect, it borrows the layer mask from the adjustment layer and uses it as if it were located on the image layer (the **slugger** layer) with which the adjustment layer is grouped.

<NOTE>

The most difficult part of this workaround is remembering which layers to group together and in what order. The trick is to place the layer with an image to be blended (the **slugger** image in this case) above the layer into which you want to blend (the **backdrop** layer). The adjustment layer with the mask goes between those two layers and is grouped with the layer above.

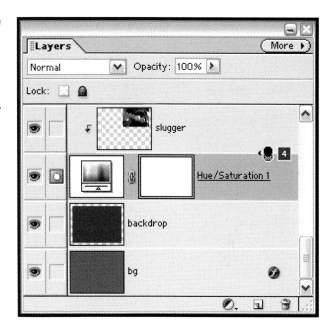

5. **Make sure that the** Hue/Saturation 1 **layer is selected in the Layers palette. Press X on your keyboard to switch the colors in the Foreground and Background Color boxes in the toolbox so that white becomes the Foreground color.**

Selecting an adjustment layer originally sets the Foreground and Background colors to black and white, respectively.

6. **Select the Gradient tool in the toolbox.**

7. **In the Options bar, make sure that the Gradient field is set to a white to black gradient.**

This is the default gradient. If it's not set to this, click in the Gradient field to open the Gradient Editor, choose the Foreground to Background gradient thumbnail in the Presets area of the Gradient Editor, and click OK.

8. **Click the Radial Gradient button in the Options bar.**

This sets the Gradient tool to draw a gradient that radiates out from the center of a circle. Leave the other settings on the Options bar at their defaults.

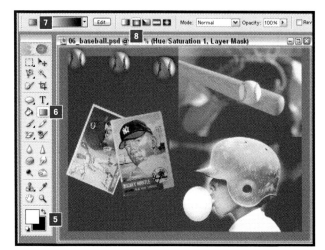

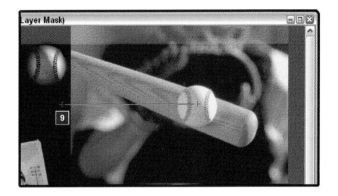

9. **Click on the baseball in the slugger image, and drag straight to the left, just beyond the left edge of the slugger image.**
   This creates a white-to-black radial gradient on the layer mask on the **Hue/Saturation 1** layer. The mask applies to the grouped **slugger** layer, gradually fading the edges of the slugger image into the background. This is the same effect that you'd get if you could apply a layer mask directly to the **slugger** layer.

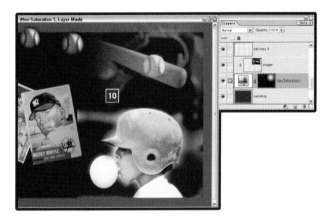

10. **Notice the radial gradient on the layer mask on the Hue/Saturation layer in the Layers palette and the corresponding gradual blend of the slugger image into the backdrop of the image.**
    If your fade doesn't look just right, you don't have to undo the gradient. Just draw another gradient, which replaces the first. Do this until you're happy with the result. The exact shape of the gradient depends on the length and direction of the line you draw.

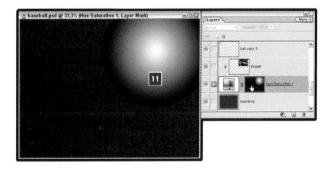

11. **Alt+click (Macintosh: Option+click) on the** Hue/Saturation 1 **layer mask in the Layers palette to look at the layer mask gradient in the document window.**
    Notice the white area, which reveals the slugger image, and the gray area fading to black, which causes the slugger image to fade from view.

12. **Alt+click (Macintosh: Option+click) again on the** Hue/Saturation 1 **layer mask to close the layer mask view.**

< T I P >

You can temporarily disable the effect of a layer mask by holding the Shift key as you click on the layer mask thumbnail in the Layers palette. A red X appears across the layer mask thumbnail in the Layers palette. Shift+click on the layer mask thumbnail again to reactivate the layer mask.

13. **To use the** Hue/Saturation 1 **layer for its normal purpose—adjusting the look of an image—click the thumbnail on the left side of** Hue/Saturation 1 **layer to open the Hue/Saturation dialog box for editing. Move the Lightness slider to the right to about +15 to lighten the slugger image.**

Recall from the last tutorial that an adjustment layer remains editable. Notice that the adjustment affects only the layer with which the adjustment layer is grouped (the **slugger** layer).

<NOTE>

This tutorial deliberately does not instruct you to mask the **bubble** layer, so that you can see the difference between the sharp edges of the **bubble** layer and the faded edges of the **slugger** layer. If you'd like, you can try applying the same technique you learned in this tutorial to the bubble image for extra practice.

14. **Choose File→Save to save** 06_baseball.psd **again. Leave it open for the next tutorial.**

In this tutorial you performed a workaround for the lack of a direct layer mask feature in Photoshop Elements 2. You used the layer mask that comes with an adjustment layer, grouped it with the **slugger** layer, and applied a gradient to the layer mask to blend the edges of the slugger image with the backdrop of your greeting card. This is a relatively complicated technique that is worth the hard work. Congratulations!

Tutorial
» Applying Layer Styles

Layer styles are special effects, ranging from drop shadows to complex image effects, that affect an entire layer. In this tutorial, you apply an Inner Glow layer style to a layer in your greeting card.

1. With `06_baseball.psd` **open from the previous tutorial (or reopened from your ccproject folder if you just took a break), select the** bg **layer in the Layers palette.**

2. **Click the Layer Styles tab in the Palette Well to open the Layer Styles palette. Drag the Layer Styles palette out of the Palette Well to keep it from closing prematurely.**
   If you don't see the Layer Styles tab in the Palette Well, choose Window→Layer Styles from the menu bar to open the Layer Styles palette.

3. **Click the Category button at the top of the Layer Styles palette to see a menu of layer style categories. Choose Inner Glows.**
   This displays a set of inner glow styles in the Layer Styles palette. The thumbnail view of layer styles in the palette offers a small preview of each layer style. An alternative list view is available by clicking the More button at the top right of the Layer Styles palette and choosing List View.

4. **Click the Simple inner glow thumbnail on the Layer Styles palette to apply that style to the selected** bg **layer.**
   A thin glow appears around the edge of the solid brown fill on the **bg** layer that you intensify in the next step.

<NOTE>
Another way to apply a layer style to a layer is to drag the style from the Layer Styles palette onto a piece of artwork in an image. This avoids the extra step of selecting a layer. However, when you work with a multi-layered document like this one, it can be difficult to attach the layer style to the right artwork using this method.

<NOTE>
You can choose from a variety of Layer Style categories ranging from traditional effects, such as bevels, drop shadows, and inner glows, to photographic effects, glass buttons, and more. Try out some styles from each category to get a sense of what they offer. Some of the more interesting ones are the Simple Noisy inner glow, the Fire outer glow, the Ghosted look from the Visibility category, the Puzzle style from the Image Effects category, the Salt style from the Complex category, the Smoke effect from the Patterns category, and the Wow-Neon styles.

<TIP>
A Layer Style applies to all the artwork on a layer. So plan ahead when you create artwork, and place each item on a separate layer if you may want to give it a drop shadow, a bevel, or any other layer style later. For example, if you create a button by filling an oval selection on a *Background* layer, you'll be disappointed if you later try to put a drop shadow behind that button.

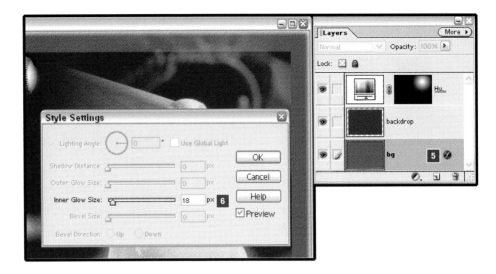

5. **Double-click the *f* symbol on the** bg **layer to open the Style Settings dialog box to settings specific to this layer style.**

   The *f* symbol on the **bg** layer in the Layers palette indicates that a layer style is applied to this layer.

6. **In the Style Settings dialog box, set the Inner Glow Size slider to around** 18 **to make the style more visible in your image.**

   Not all settings are active in the Style Settings dialog box. The inactive settings apply to other kinds of layer styles. The Size setting is the only setting available.

7. **Save** 06_baseball.psd, **and keep it open for the next tutorial.**

   Your card now has a three dimensional look attributable to the layer style you added in this tutorial.

< C A U T I O N >

The danger of using prebuilt effects is that they can make your work look like everyone else's. Modifying Style Settings is one way to customize a layer style. You can also apply multiple layer styles to a single layer to get a cumulative effect. For more variety, apply Filters and Effects along with Layer Styles for unique combination effects. Above all, use Layer Styles with prudence.

The Layer Style Menu

The Layer Style submenu is easy to overlook because it's accessible only from the Layer menu at the top of the screen. This menu is worth remembering; it contains some useful layer style commands that you won't find elsewhere.

» **Clear Layer Style:** This important command is the one you need when you want to remove a layer style from a layer. It's unfortunate that it's buried here.

» **Copy Layer Style; Paste Layer Style:** Use these commands to apply the same layer style to multiple layers. These commands come in handy when you've fashioned a unique style and want to apply it to multiple buttons, icons, or other pieces of artwork.

» **Scale Effects:** Use this command to change the size of a layer style without affecting the size of the artwork to which it's applied.

» **Hide Effects:** Use this command to make a layer style temporarily invisible so you can see behind it without deleting it from the layer.

Tutorial
» Merging and Saving Layers

This is the last tutorial in this session. Here, you learn to merge and flatten layers to save file size, and review how to save a file with its layers intact, putting the finishing touches on this greeting card.

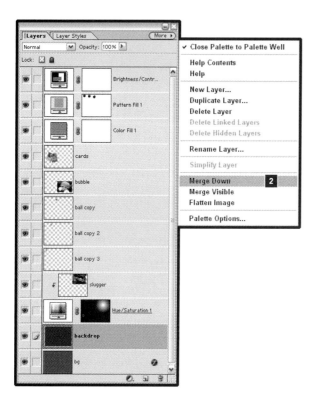

1. **With** 06_baseball.psd **open from the previous tutorial, click the arrow on the Status bar at the bottom of the screen (Macintosh: at the bottom of the document window), and choose the Document Sizes information display.**
   Notice that this file weighs in at around a hefty 13Mb, accounting for all its layers, but if the file were flattened into a single layer, it would be only 4.76Mb. Flattening all layers or merging selected layers is a strategy for reducing file size. Don't worry if your file size is not exactly the same as the numbers mentioned here.

   <CAUTION>
   I can't urge too strongly that you should always save a copy of your working file with all its layers intact before merging or flattening a file, so that you can do further editing if necessary.

2. **Select the** backdrop **layer in the Layers palette. Click the More button on the top of the Layers palette, and choose Merge Down.**
   This merges the **backdrop** layer with the **bg** layer. Specifically, this command merges a selected layer with the layer immediately below it. The Document Sizes information display indicates that merging just these two layers saved around 2Mb.

3. **Select the** ball copy **layer in the Layers palette. Click in the Link field to the left of the** ball copy 2 **and** ball copy 3 **layers to add links to each of those layers. Click the More button in the Layers palette, and choose Merge Linked.**

   Notice that the Merge Down command is no longer in the Palette menu. It changes to a Merge Linked command when the selected layer is linked to other layers.

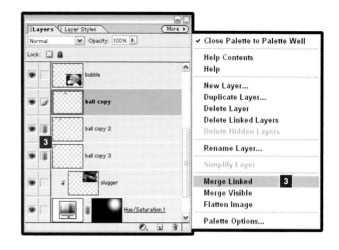

< N O T E >

Other file slimming commands in the Palette menu include Merge Visible, which merges all layers that contain an Eye icon in the Layers palette, and Flatten Image, which discards all layers that do not have an Eye icon and merges all visible layers into a single layer.

< C A U T I O N >

There are only a handful of file formats that save a file with its layers intact—PSD/PDD, PDF, and TIFF. If you save an image in any other format (JPEG, GIF, EPS, etc.), the file is automatically flattened. So remember to save a layered version before saving in any non-layered format.

4. **Choose File→Save As. With the Format field set to Photoshop (PSD/PDD) and the Layers option checked, name the file** 06_baseball_end, **and choose Save.**

   This saves the final version of the greeting card that you created in this session. The Layers check box must be checked to save a document with layers intact. The 06 Tutorial Files folder contains a copy of 06_baseball_end.psd.

< N O T E >

If you deselect the Layers check box and try to save in one of the formats that does support layers (PSD, PDD, PDF, or TIFF), you see a yellow warning that the file must be saved as a copy. This is a built-in safeguard against saving over a layered file.

» Session Review

In this session, you learned about the many features associated with layers. You created layers in several different ways, while learning about naming, moving, and selecting layers. You worked with the management features of the Layers palette, locking, linking, and reordering layers, and changing their visibility and opacity. You delved into some more advanced features too, including blending modes, grouping layers, layer masks, adjustment and fill layers, and layer styles. And you touched on merging, flattening, and saving layered documents. In the process you created a complex, multi-layered greeting card that benefits from the flexibility and style offered by the many layers features.

1. What is the main advantage of putting individual pieces of artwork on separate layers? (See Discussion: Layer Basics.)

2. Name at least one restrictive property of a *Background* layer. (See Tutorial: Creating and Converting a Background Layer.)

3. Must you keep a *Background* layer in every document? (See Tutorial: Creating and Converting a Background Layer.)

4. Where is the button that you click to create a new layer from scratch? (See Tutorial: Generating a New Layer.)

5. How can you copy a layer between documents other than by clicking and dragging? (See Tutorial: Copying Layers between Documents.)

6. What keyboard shortcut makes the resizing handles of a bounding box visible when you bring a large image into a smaller one? (See Tutorial: Copying Layers between Documents.)

7. For what purpose might you use the Layer via Copy command? (See Tutorial: Creating a Layer from a Selection.)

8. How do you duplicate a layer in the same document? (See Tutorial: Creating a Layer by Duplication.)

9. Why might you link layers together? (See Tutorial: Managing Layers in the Layers Palette.)

10. What can't you do to a layer after you apply the Lock All button to that layer? (See Tutorial: Managing Layers in the Layers Palette.)

11. What can't you do to a layer after you apply the Lock Transparency button to that layer? (See Tutorial: Managing Layers in the Layers Palette.)

12. What happens to a layer if you remove the Eye icon from its visibility field? (See Tutorial: Managing Layers in the Layers Palette.)

13. What is a blending mode? (See Discussion: Demystifying Blending Modes.)

14. How do you reduce the intensity of a blending mode after it's applied? (See Discussion: Changing Layer Blending Mode and Opacity.)

15. What are the two components of a fill or adjustment layer? (See Tutorial: Using Fill and Adjustment Layers.)

16. What is the advantage of using an adjustment layer over a regular layer adjustment? (See Tutorial: Using Fill and Adjustment Layers.)

17. Describe one way to restrict the effect of a fill or adjustment layer with a layer mask. (See Tutorial: Using Fill and Adjustment Layers.)

18. Describe a workaround for blending images together, given the lack of direct layer mask controls in Photoshop Elements 2. (See Tutorial: Combining Images with a Layer Mask.)

19. What danger does overusing layer styles hold? (See Tutorial: Applying Layer Styles.)

20. What should you always do before merging or flattening layers in the Layers palette? (See Tutorial: Merging and Saving Layers.)

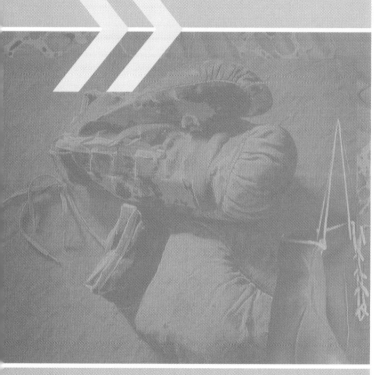

Part IV
Fixing Photographs

Retouching and Adjusting Photographs

Session Introduction

In this session, you learn how to make a photograph look better. You start with a scanned photograph and work through a retouching process that addresses everything except color correction, which is covered in the following session. This session teaches a semi-professional method of retouching that emphasizes manual over automatic adjustments. You start by straightening and cropping a scan. Then you remove dust and fix damage using the Dust & Scratches filter and the Clone Stamp tool. You learn how to apply Levels adjustments to improve contrast and brightness. You use selections and adjustment layer masks to limit the reach of Levels adjustments, and you try out Auto Levels. Next, you learn some tricks for fixing exposure, using blending modes and a special dodge/burn layer. You learn how to remove content from an image using the Clone Stamp tool and feathered patches. Finally, you sharpen the image using the Unsharp Mask filter. This session uses vintage black and white images, because old photographs are often candidates for retouching and because understanding tonal adjustments is easier in black and white without the added element of color. Most of the skills you learn here, however, are just as applicable to modern, color photographs.

TOOLS YOU'LL USE
Crop tool, Dust & Scratches filter, Clone Stamp tool, Histogram, Levels
Adjustment layer, Auto Levels, blending modes, Unsharp Mask filter

CD-ROM FILES NEEDED
07_racecars.psd, 07_wheelie.psd,
07_wheeliespotted.psd, 07_car20.psd, 07_car28.psd,
07_twocars.psd, 07_race.psd, 07_racecars_layered.psd,
07_racecars_end.psd

TIME REQUIRED
60 minutes

Discussion

The Quick Fix Approach

Retouching and adjusting photographs can involve a series of detailed procedures. If you find this process daunting, or if you're working on snapshots or less serious photo projects, you may appreciate the Quick Fix dialog box in Photoshop Elements 2. It offers one-stop access to the program's simpler photo adjustment features. The Quick Fix dialog box does not include all the retouching and adjustment features that you learn about in this session. It focuses on the one-button, automatic features. For example, you can apply Auto Levels from the Quick Fix interface, but you can't access the Levels dialog box or create a Levels Adjustment layer from here.

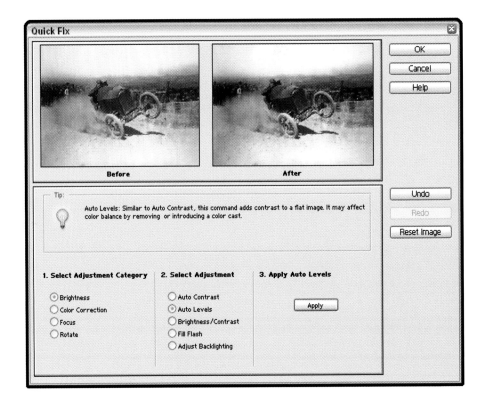

To open the Quick Fix dialog box, open an image and choose Enhance→Quick Fix or click the Quick Fix button on the Shortcuts bar. Select one of the adjustment categories in column 1—Brightness, Color Correction, Focus, or Rotate—to view a collection of related adjustment features in column 2. If you're not sure what a particular feature does, select it and read the brief explanation in the Tip section of the Quick Fix dialog box.

To apply an adjustment to an image preview, select the adjustment in column 2, and in column 3 click the Apply button or manipulate the controls that accompany a few of the adjustments. The Before and After thumbnails at the top of the Quick Fix interface offer a small, comparative preview of the adjustment. You also can see a live preview in the regular document window.

Adjustments are cumulative; you can apply more than one at a time. Click the Undo button in the dialog box one or more times to undo successive adjustment previews, or click the Reset Image button to remove all adjustment previews at once. After you're satisfied with the adjustments you've made, click the OK button to apply the adjustments to the image. Quick Fix adjustments affect only the selected layer in an image. If a selection boundary is present in the document window when you open the Quick Fix dialog box, adjustments apply only to the selected area of the targeted layer.

Although the Quick Fix dialog box does offer convenient access to multiple commands, it is not designed for the serious photographer. Most of the features it includes are automatic commands that don't account for a photographer's judgment or personal interpretation. In addition, the simple Quick Fix commands directly impact the original image; they don't make use of more advanced features like adjustment layers, masks, layer grouping, and blending modes, which allow for nondestructive, reversible editing. And although the Before and After adjustment previews in the Quick Fix dialog box are a good idea, their small size makes judging the effect of a slight adjustment hard, and you can't zoom in for a closer look. In the tutorials that follow, you learn how to retouch and adjust a photograph manually using methods that offer more control, editability, and personalization than the Quick Fix route.

Tutorial
» Straightening and Cropping a Scanned Photograph

When you scan a photograph, more often than not it comes in crooked and includes areas that you don't want in your final image. In this tutorial, you learn to straighten, crop, and resize a scanned photograph all at once. This is the first step in creating this session's greeting card from some prescanned vintage photographs.

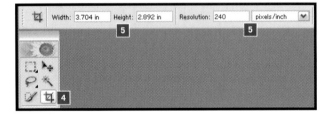

1. **Reset all tools to their default settings by clicking the Tool icon at the far left of the Options bar, choosing Reset All Tools, and clicking OK at the query.**

2. **Reset palettes to their default locations by choosing Window➞Reset Palette Locations. Close the Hints and How To palettes.**

3. **Choose File➞Open, navigate to the** `07_wheelie.psd` **file in your Session 07 Tutorial Files folder, and click Open.**
   The `07_wheelie.psd` file opens. This image suffers from flaws that you often find in a scanned photograph. It is slightly crooked as a result of improper alignment on the scanner bed. It contains unnecessary elements (the numbers on the far right). Its composition could be improved by eliminating some of the surrounding area to focus attention on the car. And the size of the image does not match the greeting card that you are creating in this session. Fortunately, you can fix all of these problems with a single application of the Crop tool.

4. **Select the Crop tool in the toolbox.**

5. **In the Options bar, type** 3.704 in **in the Width field and** 2.892 in **in the Height field, making sure to include the** in **for inches. Type** 240 **in the Resolution field, which should be set to pixels/inch.**
   Entering figures in these fields causes the Crop tool to resize the portion of the image inside the crop boundary at the same time as it removes the area outside the boundary. These particular specifications make this image just the right size to fit into the greeting card that you create in this session.

<NOTE>
Cropping the image early in the retouching process assures that the removed areas won't influence the Levels or Histogram features that you use later to make tonal adjustments. And reducing an image to its final size now prevents you from wasting time fixing small imperfections that aren't noticeable at the reduced file size.

6. **Click in the top left of the image, and drag down and to the right to create a crop boundary.**

   Include the following landmarks inside the crop boundary: the plume of dust on the left side of the image and the vertical scratch in the sky on the right side of the image. If your crop boundary doesn't match the illustration, click on any of the corner handles to adjust the boundary, or click inside the boundary and drag to reposition the whole boundary. If necessary, click the Cancel button on the right side of the Options bar to delete the boundary, and try again.

7. **Move the cursor outside any of the corner handles of the crop boundary to change the cursor to a curved, double-pointed arrow. Click and drag to rotate the crop boundary until it parallels an edge of the image.**

   This straightens the portion of the image that remains after the crop.

8. **Click the large check mark on the right side of the Options bar to apply the crop, and then examine the remaining portion of the image.**

   You accomplished several things with one application of the Crop tool: deleting the extraneous white numbers at the edge of the image, tightening up the composition, straightening the image, and resizing it to fit your design.

9. **Choose File→Save As. In the Save As window, navigate to your ccproject folder and click Save. Leave this image open for the next tutorial.**

   This image is now cropped and straightened for inclusion in the greeting card you create in this session.

Automatic Image Straightening

Applying the Crop tool as you did in this tutorial is the most efficient way to straighten and crop an image. It kills two birds (straightening and cropping) with one stone; and it works in every situation. Alternatively, you should be familiar with two automatic straighten commands.

then have to apply the Crop tool separately to eliminate the border. Cropping and rotating all at once, as you do in the tutorial, is more efficient.

The Straighten Image command (Image→Rotate→Straighten) may come in handy if you find manually rotating the crop boundary to line up with the image edge difficult. This command does a good job of straightening most images, but it leaves the canvas at its original size, resulting in a border of background pixels and transparent pixels around the straightened image, as in the figure. You

The Straighten and Crop Image command (Image→Rotate→Straighten and Crop Image) attempts to straighten an image and remove the resulting border at the same time. Unfortunately, this command doesn't work well on a crooked image that comes close to or extends beyond the edge of its canvas. If the command doesn't succeed in straightening an image or cropping away all the border pixels, as in the illustration above, try undoing the crop (Ctrl+Z [Macintosh: ⌘+Z]) and enlarging the canvas (Image→Resize→Canvas Size). In the Canvas Size dialog box, select the Relative check box and enter additional inches of width and height sufficient to allow the image to rotate without encountering the edge of the canvas. Then reapply the Straighten and Crop command.

Tutorial
» Fixing Discoloration

Black and white photographs are often scanned in color mode rather than grayscale mode to take advantage of the wider range of tonal values. A color scan can pick up stains or overall yellowing that's common in old or improperly developed black and white prints. In this short tutorial, you learn how to eliminate discoloration from a black and white photograph so that it looks good in your greeting card.

1. **With** 07_wheelie.psd **open from the previous tutorial, choose Enhance➡Adjust Color➡Remove Color.**
   The color mode of this image is RGB, indicated by the check mark in the Image➡Mode menu at the top of the screen. This command eliminates all color from a selected layer other than shades of gray, but leaves the image in RGB color mode.

<N O T E>
Another way to remove color is to create a Hue/Saturation adjust-ment layer and move the Saturation slider in the Hue/Saturation dialog box to the left. This method has some advantages: The adjustment affects all underlying layers by default. The change is editable. And you can control how much color is removed with the Saturation slider. The disadvantage is that removing spots doesn't always work as expected on an image with a Hue/Saturation adjust-ment layer.

2. **Choose File➡Save to resave** 07_wheelie.psd **to your ccproject folder.**
   In this tutorial you eliminated the yellow color cast from this RGB image.

<T I P>
Another way to eliminate stains or discolorations from a black and white image is to change its mode from RGB Color to Grayscale by choosing Image➡Mode➡Grayscale. But this eliminates the possi-bility of adding color to any part of the image.

Tutorial
» Removing Dust and Damage

A digitized photograph is subject to damage from a variety of sources. The original print or film may have had physical damage. The scanning process invariably contributes dust spots. And a digital camera or scanner may add damage in the form of digital noise. In this tutorial, you learn several ways to remove common imperfections. You use the Dust & Scratches filter to obscure imperfections in nondetailed areas of an image. You use a layer mask to paint this filter effect onto specific areas of an image. And you use the Clone Stamp tool to remove individual dust spots and scratches. These techniques clean up dust and damage visible in the vintage photograph you're readying for this session's greeting card.

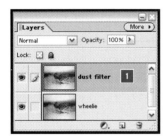

1. **With the version of** 07_wheelie.psd **open from the previous tutorial, copy the wheelie layer by dragging it to the Create New Layer icon at the bottom of the Layers palette. Double-click the new layer name, and rename the layer dust filter.**
   The dust filter layer is the layer to which you apply the Dust & Scratches filter. You then apply a layer mask to reveal only parts of this filtered layer.

2. **With the** dust filter **layer selected, choose Filter→Noise→ Dust & Scratches.**
   The Dust & Scratches dialog box opens.

3. **Move the Radius to 2 pixels and the Threshold slider to 2 levels. Click OK.**
   The filter is applied to the selected layer, and the dialog box closes. The image you now see in the document window is the opaque, filtered copy of the photo on the **dust filter** layer. The Dust & Scratches filter reduced the dust spots, but it also threw the image out of focus. This is acceptable in nondetailed areas of the photo like the sky and landscape, but not in detailed areas like the car and driver. So you limit the area affected by this filter in the following steps.

< T I P >
If you're working on an image with multiple layers of damaged content, you can create a composite of those layers and apply the Dust & Scratches filter to the composite layer. To create a composite layer, make a new empty layer above the layers to be included in the composite. With the new layer selected, click in the Link field of each of the layers to be included. Click the More button at the top right of the Layers palette to open the palette menu. Hold the Alt (Macintosh: Option) key and choose Merge Linked. The program merges and copies the content of the linked layers and places that composite copy in the new layer.

Choosing Dust & Scratches Filter Settings

The Dust & Scratches filter is most useful for obscuring small dust spots scattered across a wide area. It works by blurring the area around pixels that differ from their neighbors in color or brightness. The Radius setting determines which pixels get this treatment. This setting should be just big enough to hide the spots that you want to eliminate; a higher Radius causes unnecessary blurring. To choose a Radius setting on your own, click the plus symbol beneath the preview pane in the Dust & Scratches dialog box to magnify the preview to 200%. Start with the Radius slider set to 0. Move the slider slowly to the right until the spots are no longer visible in the preview pane. Click and drag in the preview pane to move the image around so you can see all relevant areas.

Alternatively, check the Preview box in the Dust & Scratches dialog box to see a live filter preview in the document window.

The blurring action of the Dust & Scratches filter hides film grain, making a photo look unaturally smooth. The Threshold setting puts grain back into the image. To choose a Threshold setting on your own, start with the Threshold slider at 0. Move the slider to the right until some imperfections reappear in the preview pane. Then move the slider back to the left just a bit until those imperfections disappear again.

4. **Select the** wheelie **layer in the Layers palette. Click the Create New Fill or Adjustment Layer button at the bottom of the Layers palette, and choose Hue/Saturation.**
   The Hue/Saturation dialog box opens.

5. **Leave all the settings in the Hue/Saturation dialog box at their defaults (0) and click OK.**
   A Hue/Saturation adjustment layer is created between the **wheelie** layer and the **dust filter** layer and automatically selected. You use the automatically generated layer mask on this adjustment layer to hide the blurring effect of the Dust & Scratches filter in areas of the photo that need sharpness and detail.

< N O T E >

Notice that the **Hue/Saturation 1** adjustment layer, like all new adjustment and fill layers, contains a white layer mask. When a layer mask is white, it reveals everything (i.e., hides nothing) on the layers it affects.

< T I P >

You can use any kind of adjustment or fill layer (except a Gradient fill layer with transparent pixels) when you're performing this layer mask workaround. The layer mask that comes with any adjustment or fill layer is what you're really after. The nature of the adjustment or fill layer is irrelevant.

< N O T E >

You can limit the effect of the Dust & Scratches filter to nondetailed areas of the image that won't suffer much from the filter's blurring effect by hiding the filter effect with a layer mask, and then "painting" the filter back into specific areas. Photoshop Elements 2 does not offer a way to directly apply a layer mask to a regular layer, so you borrow a layer mask by grouping the **dust filter** layer with an adjustment layer that has its own layer mask. Don't worry if you find this complicated. Layer masking is a relatively advanced concept to start with, and the layer grouping workaround further complicates the subject. However, these techniques are so useful that it's worth stretching a little to understand them.

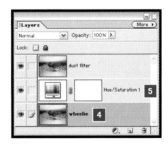

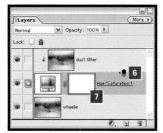

6. **Hold the Alt (Macintosh: Option) key, and move your cursor over the line between the** dust filter **layer and the** Hue/Saturation 1 **adjustment layer in the Layers palette. When the cursor changes to a double circle, click to group these layers together.**
   The **dust filter** layer is slightly indented and displays a down-facing arrow, indicating that it is grouped with the **Hue/Saturation 1** layer below.

< N O T E >
An alternative way to group these two layers together is to select the **dust filter** layer in the Layers palette, and choose Layer➜ Group with Previous.

7. **Select the** Hue/Saturation 1 **layer in the Layers palette if it isn't already selected.**
   A dark frame appears around the layer mask thumbnail on the **Hue/Saturation 1** layer, indicating that the layer mask is selected.

< N O T E >
The reason you no longer see the filter effect in the document window is that the now black mask on the **Hue/Saturation 1** layer hides the content of the **dust filter** layer, allowing you to see the unfiltered content of the **wheelie** layer below. A black mask always hides the content of the layers to which it applies. The black mask on the **Hue/Saturation 1** layer also applies to the **dust filter** layer because you grouped those two layers together.

8. **Choose Edit➜Fill. In the Fill dialog box, click in the Use field and choose Black. Click OK.**
   The selected layer mask is filled. The layer mask thumbnail on the **Hue/Saturation 1** adjustment layer is now black, and the image in the document window no longer shows the filter effect (all the spots are visible, and the image is not blurred).

9. **Select the Brush tool in the Layers palette, and choose a large soft brush in the Options bar (the Soft Round 100 pixel brush is used here, but any similar brush will do).**

   Check that the **Hue/Saturation 1** adjustment layer and its mask are still selected.

10. **Click the tiny white and black square icon at the bottom of the toolbox.**

    This ensures that the Foreground Color box is set to its default of white. The default colors for the Foreground and Background color boxes are white and black respectively when you work in a layer mask.

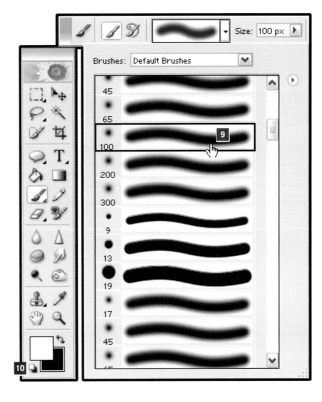

11. **Zoom in to at least 100%, and paint over the entire sky and the background landscape in the document window.**

    As you paint, it looks like you are painting with the Dust & Scratches filter, hiding the dust particles and blurring the image as you go. In fact, you are painting with white in the black layer mask, which reveals the dust filter layer wherever you paint.

<TIP>

If you make a mistake and paint over the driver or the car, click the double-pointed curved arrow at the bottom of the toolbox to switch the Foreground Color to black and paint back over those areas to remove the filter effect again.

<TIP>
The technique that you just used to paint away dust spots with the Dust & Scratches filter has other uses, too. Try using it in a portrait to paint away wrinkles or puffy skin under a subject's eyes.

12. **Click the Foreground Color box in the toolbox to open the Color Picker. Select a light gray (R: 204, G: 204, B: 204), and click OK.**

13. **Click and drag over the dust plume to the left of the car, and dab at any spots you see in the road around the car.**
    You are now painting with gray in the layer mask. The gray paint only partially reveals the **dust filter** layer, hiding some of the spots and showing some of the blur. Some scratches survived the Dust & Scratches filter, and some dust particles remain in the detailed areas of the photo. In the next steps, you eliminate them with the Clone Stamp tool.

<TIP>
You can see where you painted with white and gray by opening the layer mask in the document window. Alt+click (Macintosh: Option+click) on the **Hue/Saturation 1** layer mask thumbnail in the Layers palette to switch to a view of the mask. While the mask is open in the document window, you can paint directly on it with white or gray. Alt+click (Macintosh: Option+click) on the thumbnail again to close the layer mask.

14. **Select the Zoom tool, make sure that the Zoom In button (the plus symbol) is selected in the Options bar, and click near the steering wheel to zoom in to that area to 300% magnification.**
    Magnification should be high enough so you can see individual pixels in the area that needs repair.

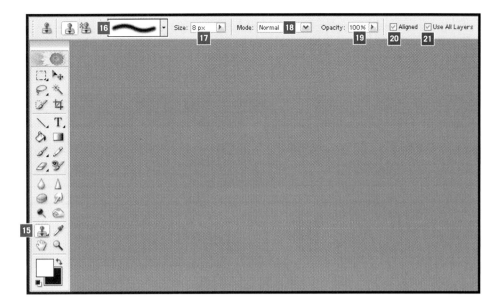

15. Select the Clone Stamp tool in the toolbox.

The Clone Stamp tool samples or copies pixels from one area and uses them to cover pixels elsewhere. In the next steps, you clone healthy pixels and use them to cover nearby scratches and spots.

16. In the Options bar, click in the Brush Presets field and choose a soft round brush.

The soft edges of the brush help blend cloned pixels with pixels at their destination.

17. Enter 8 px **(pixels) in the Size field to set the brush size.**

The brush size should be a little larger than the item you plan to cover.

18. Leave the Blending Mode set to Normal.

The pixels deposited by the Clone Stamp tool blend with destination pixels according to blending mode formulae. The blending modes associated with this and other brush tools are similar to the layer blending modes that you studied in the last session. The Clone Stamp tool's Normal blending mode works fine when you clone pixels between areas of similar brightness.

<TIP>

If you clone from a dark area to a lighter area, try the Lighten blend mode so as not to affect the surrounding light pixels. Similarly, try the Darken blending mode if you're cloning from a lighter area to a darker area.

19. Leave Opacity at 100% in order to completely cover the pixels you want to eliminate.

20. Leave Aligned selected.

This aligns the spot from which pixels are first sampled (the source point) to the brush tip that applies them, so that each time you release the mouse and resample, you copy pixels from a new source point. If you deselect Aligned, the source point jumps back to its original location each time you release the mouse and resample.

21. Leave Use All Layers selected.

This instructs the Clone Stamp tool to include the content of all layers when it samples pixels. If this option is deselected, the tool samples from and clones to the same layer. This is an important option because you clone to a new empty layer in the next step.

22. **Select the** dust filter **layer in the Layers palette. Click the Create New Layer button at the bottom of the Layers palette to make a new layer. Double-click the new layer name, and rename it** cloning.

This is the layer that holds all the pixels you clone from non-damaged areas of the photograph to cover dust spots and scratches in this photograph. You could clone directly onto a layer of artwork, but cloning onto a separate layer makes cloning reversible and editable. As mentioned above, you must select the Use All Layers option when cloning to a separate layer.

23. **Hold the Alt (Macintosh: Option) key over an area of nondamaged pixels close to one of the white dust spots on the car. When the cursor changes to a target symbol, indicating that it is in sampling mode, click to sample the pixels under the target cursor.**

This sets the starting point for sampling clean pixels to cover the dust spots on the car.

24. **Release the mouse and the Alt (Macintosh: Option) key. Click on the neighboring white spot with the regular brush cursor to cover that spot with the pixels that you sampled in the preceding step.**

The plus symbol you see near the cursor when you press down on the mouse indicates the spot from which you sampled those pixels.

25. **Repeat Steps 23 and 24 as many times as necessary to cover all the dust spots on the car and driver. Move the image around in the document window to check for dust spots by holding the Alt (Macintosh: Option) key while clicking and dragging.**

The car and driver should now appear dust-free.

26. **Use the same technique you learned in Steps 23 and 24 to clone over the long scratch across the grill of the car.**

You may be tempted to click and drag. Avoid that temptation because it creates a repeating pattern. Instead, dab at the scratch, Alt+clicking (Macintosh: Option+clicking) on a new source point every few clicks to match the pattern and tone of each source point to its destination point and to avoid a repeating pattern.

27. **Increase the brush size to around 12 px in the Size field of the options bar. Alt+click (Macintosh: Option+click) next to the scratch on the far right of the image. Release the mouse, and drag down the length of the scratch to clone over this scratch.**
Dragging does not create a repeating pattern here because this is an area of relatively solid tone.

28. **Continue moving around the image, cloning over all the scratches.**
Use your judgment about whether to dab or drag over various scratches, depending on whether the area contains imagery (which usually requires dabbing) or solid tone (where dragging may be adequate). You can undo any mistakes by clicking the Undo button on the Shortcuts bar, or by dragging over an area on the cloning layer with the Eraser tool. The Clone tool takes a little practice to get used to. By the time you finish cleaning up the scratches and dust on this image, you should have a good feel for how to use the tool to cover damage without creating repeating patterns.

<TIP>
A quick way to change brush size as you work is to click the left bracket key on your keyboard to reduce brush size and the right bracket key to increase brush size. As you do this, you see changes in the brush fields in the Options bar.

<NOTE>
Be careful not to Alt+click (Macintosh: Option+click) on a source point that touches the edge of the document window or you replicate that edge in the cloned pixels.

<TIP>
To get a sense of how much you improved the image so far, Alt+click (Macintosh: Option+click) on the Eye icon on the **wheelie** layer in the Layers palette to see a Before view. Repeat this step to return to the After view.

29. **Choose File→Save, and leave the file open for the next tutorial.**
Your vintage photograph is now free of dust spots, scratches, and other signs of damage. In this tutorial you retouched the photo to eliminate flaws using the Dust & Scratches filter limited by a layer mask, and the Clone Stamp tool. As a bonus, all of the retouching was done on added layers so that it is reversible and did not destroy the original image pixels.

Tutorial

» Adjusting Tones with Levels

Improving the appearance of a photograph is largely a matter of adjusting the tonal value of its highlights, shadows, and mid-tones. The best way to do this in Photoshop Elements 2 is with a Levels adjustment layer. In this tutorial, you apply a Levels adjustment layer to the wheelies photo you're preparing for your greeting card to redistribute its tones across the tonal range, improving the contrast and brightness of the photograph. These principles are easiest to understand when you work with a black and white photograph, as in this tutorial, but they apply to color images as well.

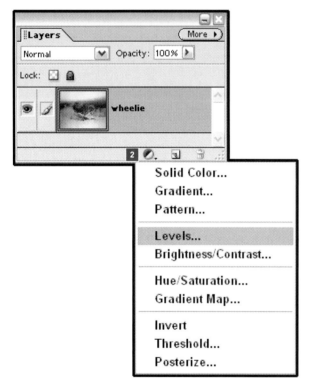

1. **With** `07_wheelie.psd` **open from the previous tutorial, select the** wheelie **layer in the Layers palette. Click the More button at the top right of the Layers palette, and choose Merge Visible.**
   This merges all the layers, flattening the image to a single layer. You do not have to flatten an image before applying a Levels adjustment layer. A Levels adjustment layer affects all the layers below it by default. The reason you flatten this image now is just to simplify it.

   < N O T E >
   If you closed the `07_wheelie.psd` file, you can open the last saved version from your ccproject folder.

   < N O T E >
   Make sure that you saved a layered copy before you flatten a file, in case you want to go back to make further changes. You can feel comfortable flattening this image because the CD-ROM at the back of the book contains a layered version of this image with all the changes to this point. If you ever want to revisit what you've done to this image so far, open `07_wheeliespotted.psd` from the Session 07 Tutorial Files folder.

2. **Click the Create New Fill or Adjustment Layer button at the bottom of the Layers palette, and choose Levels from the menu of adjustment and fill layers.**
   This creates a Levels adjustment layer in the Layers palette and opens the Levels dialog box.

   < N O T E >
   I strongly recommend that you use a Levels adjustment layer rather than a direct Levels adjustment (Enhance➔Adjust Brightness/Contrast➔Levels) whenever possible. A Levels adjustment layer offers all the benefits associated with adjustment layers, which include preserving the original image, editability, built-in layer masks, and opacity and blending mode controls.

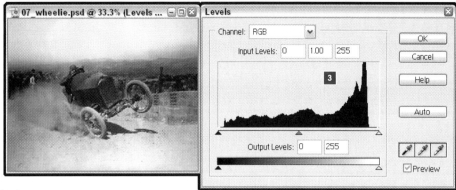

3. **Look at the chart in the Levels dialog box.**

   This chart, called a histogram, represents the tones in this image. It is made up of tightly packed vertical bars, each of which represents the relative number of pixels in the image of a particular tone (the tone directly below that vertical bar in the black to white gradient at the bottom of the dialog box). The taller the bar, the more pixels of that tone are in the image. For example, this image has lots of light tones (in the sky and foreground). The tall bars on the right side of the histogram represent these tones.

<NOTE>

Notice that the histogram for this image has almost no pixels at either end of the scale—in the dark shadow and bright highlight areas. This means that you have room to increase the contrast of the image making the shadow tones darker and the highlight tones brighter.

Reading a Histogram

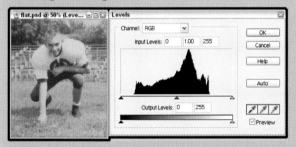

Knowing how to read a histogram can help you understand the tonal values in an image and consider how to correct them. For example, you may not realize from looking at this photograph of a football player that the image is rather flat and would benefit from increased contrast. The histogram tells you that there is no image data in the shadow and highlight portions of the tonal scale, confirming that the image needs more contrast.

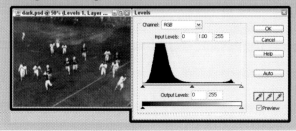

A histogram reflects not only the contrast of an image, but also whether it is a high-key (bright) image or a low-key (dark) image. This underexposed photograph is an extreme example of a dark image. Notice that most of the pixels are spiked in the dark area on the left side of the histogram. You might try to correct an image like this by moving the midtone slider to the left. However, not all low-key or high-key images need correcting. Sometimes, a dark or light look is exactly what you're after.

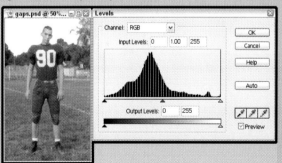

Gaps in a histogram represent a lack of image data. They indicate that the image has already been corrected, as this one has, or perhaps has been damaged in the scanning or exposure process. If gaps are too pronounced, the image may not be a good candidate for further correction.

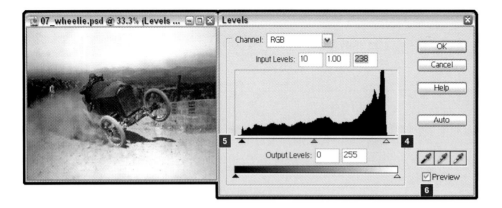

4. **Click on the white slider on the right side of the histogram, and pull it to the left until it reaches the first of the solid pixels in the histogram.**

   This forces all pixels at and to the right of that point to become pure white, so that they have no detail or texture and print with no dot. This change is reflected numerically in the Input Levels and Output Levels fields in the Levels dialog box. If your rightmost Input field now reads 238, all pixels that were of a value equal to or greater than 238 have been remapped to the value in the right-hand Output field—255.

5. **Click on the black slider on the left of the histogram, and pull it to the right until it is under the first of the solid pixels on this side of the histogram.**

   This forces all pixels at and to the left of this slider to become pure black, so they print without any detail. This change is reflected in the leftmost Input Levels and Output Levels fields. All pixels of a value of around 10 or less are remapped to 0.

   < N O T E >
   Moving the Input Levels sliders not only resets the darkest and lightest tones in the image. It also remaps all the tones in the photograph, spreading them out so they cover the full range of 256 tones available in a black and white photograph. You can see this if you view the standalone histogram that is accessible by choosing Image→Histogram. (This histogram is similar to the one in the Levels dialog box for black and white images.) Notice that the tones are spread out across the entire tonal range. Spreading the image tones caused the gaps you see in this histogram.

< N O T E >
If you move the black and white sliders in beyond the beginning of the solid parts of the histogram, you increase contrast even more, but you sacrifice detail in the light and dark areas of the photograph—a result that normally is not desirable.

6. **Deselect and then reselect the Preview check box in the Levels dialog box to see the effect of these changes on the image in the document window. Leave Preview selected.**

   When Preview is selected, you see increased contrast in the image.

Dealing with Histogram Tails

You ignored some narrow tails of black on both sides of the solid pixels in this histogram when moving the sliders in toward the solid pixels. This turned the pixels represented in those tails to black or white respectively. Tails like these often represent scattered dark or light pixels that are too insignificant to take into account when modifying levels. However, some images may have long tails, and you may be unsure whether to move the sliders past them or not. You can base this decision on a threshold view of the actual pixels represented by the tails.

Hold the Alt (Macintosh: Option) key, and click on the white slider as you move it. The image in the document window is temporarily replaced by a black and white threshold view. The image pixels behind the white spots in this view are those represented by the tail to the right of the white slider in the histogram. If you want these pixels to retain image detail and not turn pure white, move the slider slightly to the right until the white pixels disppear. Release the Alt (Macintosh: Option) key to return the document window to its normal view. Repeat with the black slider.

Setting Black and White Points with the Levels Eyedroppers

An alternative to using the Levels sliders to reset black and white points in an image is to use the Black and White Eyedroppers in the Levels dialog box. Use the threshold view described in the last sidebar to find the brightest tone in which you want some texture or detail. Alt+click (Macintosh: Option+click) the right Input Levels slider as you drag it all the way to the right and then slowly back to the left. When you see a small group of white pixels in the threshold view, release the Alt (Macintosh: Option) key to return to normal view. Make a mental note of the image location that corresponds to those white pixels. (If this location is a specular highlight, like a shiny reflection, ignore it and try again, pulling the

slider in further. Specular highlights should be pure white.) Select the White Eyedropper in the Levels dialog box, and click on that location in the image. This forces all brighter pixels to pure white. Repeat this exercise pulling the left Input Levels slider to the right to find the darkest shadow in which you want detail. Click there with the Black Eyedropper to force all darker pixels to black. Finally, if you're creating an image to be printed at a service bureau, ask the service bureau for the best black and white point values for their output device. You can set the White and Black Eyedroppers accordingly by double-clicking each eyedropper to open the Color Picker and entering the values there.

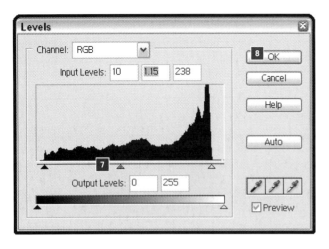

7. **Click on the gray slider in the image, and drag it slightly to the left until the middle Input Levels field reads around 1.15.**
   This brightens the midtones in the image (between approximately the one-quarter to three-quarter tones), but leaves the black and white points as you set them in previous steps. The gray slider represents the gray tones in the image. It starts out at the midpoint and moves to try to stay at the midpoint as you adjust the black and white sliders. Adjusting the gray slider separately, as you did here, allows you to control brightness directly.

<NOTE>

Sometimes, a tweak of the gray slider is the only adjustment a black and white image needs. If the histogram displays tones across the tonal range, but the image is too dark, you may be able to forgo resetting the black and white points, and just move the gray slider to the left to lighten the midtones.

8. **Click OK.**
   The changes are applied, and the Levels dialog box closes. Leave 07_wheelies.psd open.

<CAUTION>

Don't be tempted to use a Brightness/Contrast adjustment rather than a Levels adjustment to improve brightness or contrast. The Brightness/Contrast adjustment suffers in comparison to levels because it adjusts all tones in an image to the same degree, which can result in too much or too little overall contrast, and lack of detail in highlights or shadows. Levels is the better feature because it can adjust highlights, shadows, and midtones separately.

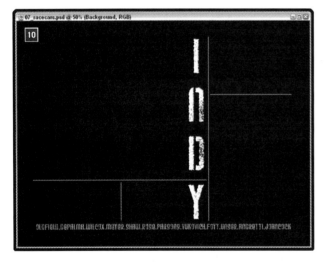

9. **Choose File→Open, navigate to** 07_racecars.psd **in the Session 07 Tutorial Files folder on your hard drive, and click Open.**
   This is the background of the greeting card that you create in this session.

10. **In** 07_racecars.psd**, select the** *Background* **layer.**

11. **Prepare** 07_wheelie.psd **to become part of the greeting card by doing the following in the** 07_wheelie.psd **Layers palette.**
    You use a similar procedure on each of the photographs that you add to the greeting card as this session goes on:

    » **Double-click the** Levels 1 **label, and rename that layer** wheelie levels**.**

    » **Select the** wheelie **layer, and click in the Link field on the** wheelie levels **layer.**
    Linking these layers allows you to copy them together into the greeting card document.

    » **Hold the Alt (Macintosh: Option) key, move your cursor over the line between the** wheelie **layer and the** wheelie levels **layer, and click to group these two layers.**
    Alternatively, select the wheelie levels layer and choose Layer➔Group with previous. Grouping these layers limits the effect of the **wheelie levels** layer to the **wheelie layer** when it becomes part of the greeting card image.

12. **Select the Move tool. Click in the** 07_wheelie.psd **document window, and drag the image and its linked adjustment layer into the** 07_racecars.psd **document window.**

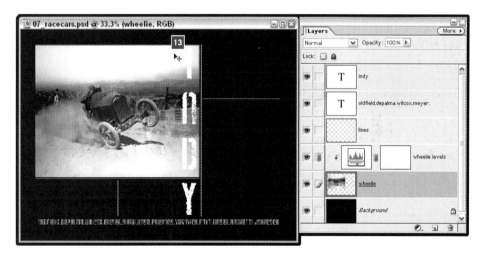

13. **With the Move tool, position the wheelie image in the top-left section of** 07_racecars.psd**.**
    If you want to be precise, line up the top edge of the wheelie image with the top of the vertical line to its right and the right edge of the wheelie image with the right edge of the horizontal line below it.

14. **With** 07_racecars.psd **active, choose File➔Save As, navigate to your ccproject folder, and click Save.**
    Leave this file open for the next tutorial.

15. **Click in the** 07_wheelie.psd **document window to make that image active. Choose File➔Close, and click Yes at the prompt that asks if you want to save changes before closing.**
    In this tutorial, you adjusted the shadow, highlight, and mid-tone values in the wheelie image using a Levels adjustment layer, and combined that image with the background of your racecars greeting card.

Tutorial
» Limiting Levels Adjustments

This tutorial expands on the basics of using levels that you learned in the preceding tutorial. Here, you apply multiple Levels adjustment layers to another image that becomes part of the racecars greeting card, limiting the area affected by each adjustment. In this tutorial, you learn two ways to limit the reach of a Levels adjustment—by drawing selections and by painting on the adjustment layer's mask. These skills come in handy when some parts of an image require different Levels adjustments than others.

1. **Choose File→Open, navigate to the Session 07 Tutorial Files folder on your hard drive, and open** 07_car28.psd.
   Parts of this image lack brightness and contrast to varying degrees. In the next steps, you create a selection to limit a tonal correction to the street area.

2. **Select the rectangular marquee tool in the toolbox, and set the Feather field in the Options bar to** 1 **to soften the edge of the selection. Click and drag a rectangular selection around the street.**
   Alternatively, you can load the prebuilt, feathered selection of the street that I saved with this file by choosing Select→ Load Selection, choosing street in the Selection field of the Load Selection dialog box, and clicking OK.

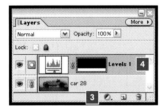

3. **Click the Create New Fill or Adjustment Layer button at the bottom of the Layers palette, and choose Levels to create an adjustment layer labeled** Levels 1.
   The Levels dialog box opens.

4. **Look at the layer mask thumbnail on the** Levels 1 **layer.**
   Notice that only the area inside the street selection boundary is white. This is the only area that is affected by this adjustment layer. Recall that if you create an adjustment layer when a selection is active, only the selected area is affected by the adjustment. White areas of a layer mask reveal the adjustment on an adjustment layer; black areas hide it.

5. **In the Levels dialog box, drag the white slider to the left until the right Input Levels field is about 125. The gray slider moves to the left along with the white slider. Click OK to close the Levels dialog box.**
   This opens up highlights and midtones in the selected area. No single formula exists for adjusting tones in all images. In this case, moving the white slider all the way to the solid part of the histogram would create too much contrast in the street. Moving the shadow slider to the right would make the street too dark.

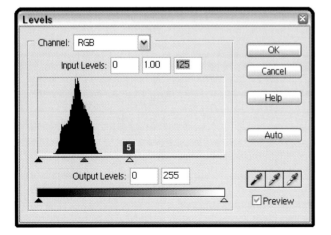

6. **Choose Select→Reselect to redisplay the street selection. Choose Select→Inverse to select everything but the street.**
   If the Reselect command is grayed out because you performed another operation after deselecting, choose Select→Load Selection and choose street to load a prebuilt selection. Then invert the selection.

7. **Click the Create New Adustment or Fill Layer button at the bottom of the Layers palette, and choose Levels to create another adjustment layer labeled** Levels 2**.**
   The Levels dialog box opens. Notice that the white and black areas of this layer mask thumbnail are the opposite of those on the **Levels 1** layer, corresponding to the inverted selection. This **Levels 2** adjustment layer applies only to the area above the street, which is covered by the white area of this layer mask.

8. **In the Levels dialog box, drag the white slider to the left until it touches the solid area of the histogram (at about 196 in the right-hand Input Levels field). Click OK to close the dialog box.**
   This brightens the highlights and midtones in the selected area above the street.

<NOTE>

Another way to limit the area affected by a Levels adjustment is by painting directly on the adjustment layer mask, as you do in the next steps.

9. **Click the Create New Adjustment or Fill Layer button on the bottom of the Layers palette, and choose Levels to create a third adjustment layer labeled** Levels 3**.**
   The Levels dialog box opens again.

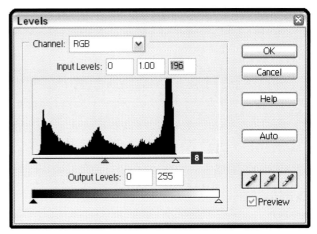

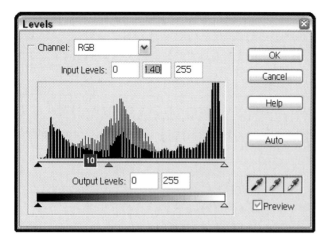

10. In the Levels dialog box, move the gray slider to the left (to about 1.40 in the middle Input Levels field), and click OK.

The dialog box closes, and the entire image is brightened.

< N O T E >

The gaps you see in this histogram are caused by the other two Levels adjustments.

11. Choose Edit→Fill to open the Fill dialog box. Select Black in the Use field of that dialog box. Click OK to close the Fill dialog box.

This fills the layer mask on the **Levels 3** layer with black, hiding the brightening adjustment on that layer across the entire image.

12. Select the Brush tool in the toolbox and a soft brush in the Options bar. Make sure that the Foreground Color box in the toolbox is set to white.

13. In the document window, click and drag over just the body of the car (not including the undercarriage of the car) to paint in just that portion of the Levels 3 adjustment.

This brightens the body of the car.

14. **Notice the white area in the layers mask thumbnail on the** Levels 3 **layer.**
It represents the limited portion of the image affected by the **Levels 3** adjustment layer.

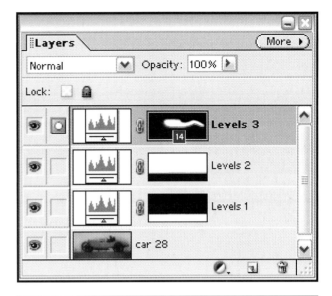

15. **Prepare the car 28 image for inclusion in the greeting card document by doing the following:**

   » **Double-click the** Levels 1 **label, and rename that layer** car28 Levels 1. **Rename the other levels layers** car28 Levels 2 **and** car28 Levels 3.

   » **Select the** car28 **layer, and click in the Link fields on the three levels layers.**

   » **Hold the Alt (Macintosh: Option) key, move your cursor over the line between the** car28 **layer and the** car28 Levels 1 **layer, and click to group these two layers. Repeat this with each of the other two levels layers so that all four layers in this image are grouped together.**
   Alternatively, use the Layer→Group with Previous command three times.

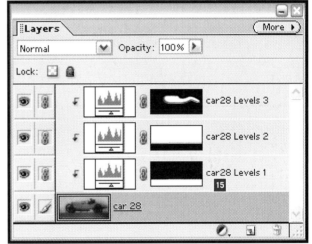

16. **With** 07_racecars.psd **still open from the previous tutorial, select the** wheelie levels **layer.**

< N O T E >
If you closed 07_racecars.psd, reopen it from your ccproject folder.

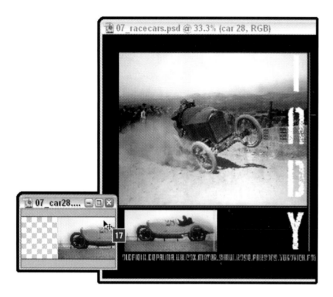

17. **Select the Move tool. Click in the** `07_car28.psd` **document window, and drag the car 28 image and its three linked adjustment layers into the** `07_racecars.psd` **document window.**
The adjusted car 28 image becomes part of your racecars greeting card.

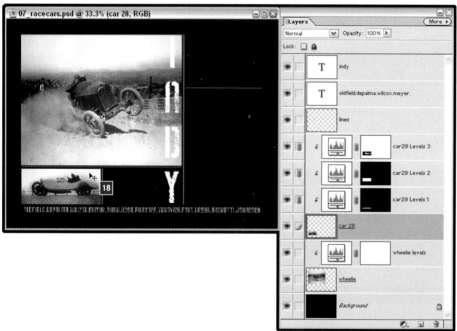

18. **With the Move tool, position the car 28 image in** `07_racecars.psd` **as shown in the illustration, using the lines in the image as guides.**

19. **With** `07_racecars.psd` **active, choose File→Save to resave the greeting card image to your ccproject folder.**
Leave this file open for the next tutorial.

20. **Click in the** `07_car28.psd` **document window to make that image active. Choose File→Save As, navigate to your ccproject folder, and click Save. Choose File→Close.**
In this tutorial you created multiple Levels adjustment layers to adjust tones separately in different areas of the car 28 image. You then brought the car 28 image, with its adjustment layer, into your racecars greeting card.

Tutorial
» Applying Auto Levels

Before you leave the subject of levels, work through this short tutorial on adjusting tones with Auto Levels. Although manual commands are usually preferable to auto commands because they give you more control and input, sometimes Auto Levels is all you need.

1. **Choose File→Open, navigate to your Session 07 Tutorial Files folder, choose** 07_twocars.psd, **and click Open.**
   The 07_twocars.psd file opens.

2. **Click the Create New Adjustment or Fill Layer button at the bottom of the Layers palette, and choose Levels to create a Levels adjustment layer,** Levels 1.
   The Levels dialog box opens.

3. **In the Levels dialog box, click the Auto button to invoke Auto Levels in the adjustment layer.**
   This has the same effect as a direct Auto Levels adjustment, which is accessible from the Quick Fix dialog box or the Enhance menu at the top of the screen. But it is preferable to apply Auto Levels in an adjustment layer, as you do here, to take advantage of the benefits of this nondestructive, editable layer.

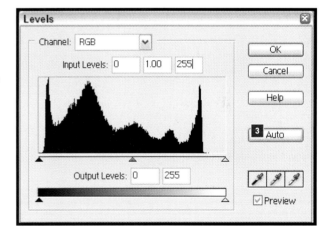

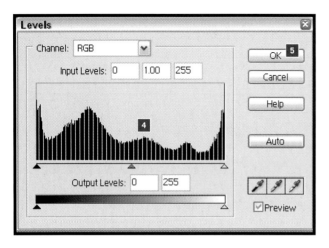

4. **Look at the Levels histogram.**

   The adjusted tones are spread out across the Levels histogram, causing some gaps because there is less image data than necessary to stretch across the graph. Small gaps won't have much effect on an image. If gaps are too wide, they can cause posterization or banding in an image.

5. **Click OK to apply the Auto Levels adjustment.**

   The Auto Levels feature resets the black and white points to the darkest and lightest pixels in the image, increasing image contrast. This sometimes results in overly dense shadows or blown-out highlights, like some of the highlights in this adjusted image.

< N O T E >

Another automatic tonal adjustment, Auto Contrast, has a similar effect on a black and white image. (The difference between Auto Levels and Auto Contrast is more apparent on a color image.) Auto Contrast is less useful than Auto Levels for a black and white image because Auto Contrast can only be applied directly, not in an adjustment layer.

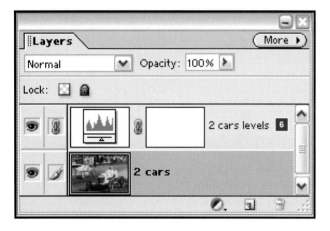

6. **Prepare the the two cars image for inclusion in the greeting card:**

   » **Double-click the** Levels 1 **label, and rename that layer** 2 cars levels**.**

   » **Select the** 2 cars **layer, and click in the Link field on the** 2 cars levels **layer.**

   » **Hold the Alt (Macintosh: Option) key, move your cursor over the line between the** 2 cars **layer and the** 2 cars levels **layer, and click to group these two layers.**
   Alternatively, select the 2 cars levels layer and select Layer→Group with Previous from the menu bar.

7. 07_racecars.psd **should still be open from the previous tutorial. If it's not, open it from your ccproject folder. In** 07_racecars.psd, **select the** car28 Levels 3 **layer, so that new layers you create are located above this layer.**

8. **Select the Move tool. Click in the** 07_twocars.psd **document window, and drag the two cars image and its linked adjustment layer into the** 07_racecars.psd **document window.**

9. With the Move tool, position the two cars image in
   07_racecars.psd in the upper-right corner of the
   greeting card, using the lines in the image as guides.

10. With 07_racecars.psd active, choose File→Save.
    Leave this file open for the next tutorial.

11. Click in the 07_twocars.psd document window to make that
    image active. Choose File→Save As, navigate to your ccproject
    folder, and click Save. Choose File→Close.
    In this tutorial you adjusted tones in the two cars image
    using the Auto Level command, and moved that adjusted
    image into your racecars greeting card, which now contains
    multiple images.

Tutorial
» Adjusting Exposure

In this tutorial, you learn a quick way to adjust the exposure of an image that is too dark or too light using layer blending modes, and a nondestructive way of adjusting the exposure of small areas with a dodge/burn layer. This adjusts the exposure in another image that becomes part of your racecars greeting card.

1. **Choose File→Open, navigate to the O7 Tutorial Files folder on your hard drive, choose** 07_race.psd, **and click Open.**

   This image is underexposed (too dark). You lighten it with a blending mode change in the next steps.

2. **Click on the** race **layer in the Layers palette, and drag to the Create New Layer icon at the bottom of the Layers palette.**
   This creates a duplicate layer labeled **race copy**.

3. **Select the** race copy **layer in the Layers palette. Click in the Blending Mode field in the Layers palette, and choose Screen.**
   This brightens the image considerably.

<TIP>
If you wanted the image to be even brighter, you could create multiple copies of the **race** layer, setting each consecutive copy to Screen blending mode.

<TIP>
The Darken blending mode has the opposite effect. If an image is overexposed (too light), duplicate the layer and apply the Darken blending mode to the duplicate layer. You can do this more than once if necessary.

4. **Select the Eraser tool. Select a large soft brush (around 100 px) from the Brush Presets palette and set the Opacity of the Eraser tool in the Options bar to 40%.**

5. **Stroke over the top third of the image to reduce the brightening effect there.**
   This focuses attention on the brighter areas in the foreground.

6. **Prepare the race image to be moved into the greeting card by selecting the race layer and clicking in the Link field on the** race copy **layer.**

7. **With** 07_racecars.psd **open from the previous tutorial, select the** 2 cars levels **layer, to ensure that new layers you create are located above this layer.**

<NOTE>
If you closed 07_racecars.psd at the end of the previous tutorial, you can open it from your ccproject folder.

8. **Select the Move tool. Click in the** 07_race.psd **document window, and drag the** race **layer and its linked** race copy **layer into the** 07_racecars.psd **document window.**

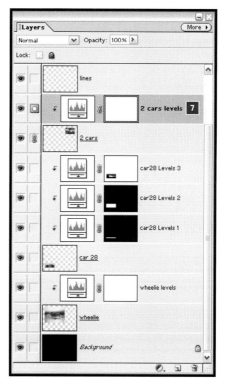

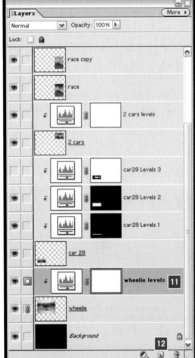

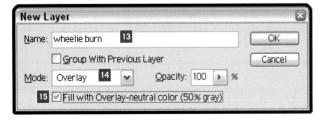

9. **With the Move tool, position the race image in** `07_racecars.psd` **in the lower-right corner of the greeting card, using the lines in the image as guides.**

10. **Click in the** `07_race.psd` **document window to make that image active. Choose File→Save As, navigate to your ccproject folder, and click Save. Choose File→Close.**
    Leave the greeting card image, `07_racecars.psd`, open for the next steps.

<NOTE>

The blending mode technique is useful for changing the exposure of an entire layer, as you did in the race image. When you want to improve the exposure of smaller areas, dodging (making lighter) and burning (making darker) are appropriate techniques. You could use the Dodge tool and Burn tools in the toolbox for this purpose. However, the changes they make are permanent ones that affect the original image. In the next steps you learn a nondestructive method of dodging and burning on a special invisible layer, as you put some final touches on your racecars greeting card.

11. **In the greeting card image,** `07_racecars.psd`, **select the** wheelie levels **layer.**

12. **Alt+click (Macintosh: Option+click) the Create New Layer button at the bottom of the Layers palette.**
    The Layers Properties dialog box opens.

13. **In the New Layer dialog box, name the new layer** wheelie burn**.**

14. **Click in the Mode field, and choose Overlay from the menu of layer blending modes.**
    This causes the Fill with Overlay-neutral color (50% gray) check box to become active.

15. **Select the Fill with Overlay-neutral check box, and click OK.**
    The dialog box closes. The 50% gray with which the new layer is filled is invisible in the document window when the layer is in Overlay mode, although you can see the gray thumbnail in the Layers palette.

<NOTE>

Quite a few blending modes have an invisible "neutral" color. For example, the neutral color for the Lighten blending mode is black, and the neutral color for the Darken blending mode is white.

16. **Press D on your keyboard to set the Foreground Color box in the toolbox to black.**
    This is a shortcut for clicking the small black and white squares icon at the bottom of the toolbox.

17. **Select the Brush tool in the toolbox, and choose a large soft brush (around 100 px) in the Options bar.**

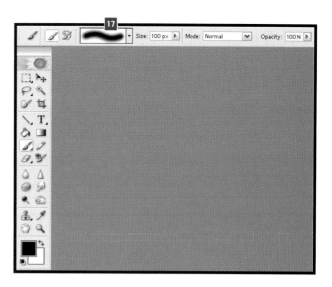

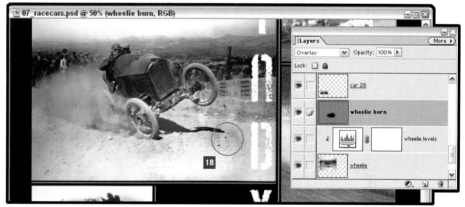

18. **In the document window, navigate to the wheelies image in the greeting card. Paint some strokes in the foreground of the wheelies image.**

    The Brush tool works like a burn tool, darkening the image pixels below the neutral **wheelie burn** layer. Notice in the Layers palette that your black strokes show up on the gray thumbnail on the **wheelie burn** layer.

19. **Choose File→Save to resave the greeting card, 07_racecars.psd, to your ccproject folder.**

    Leave the file open for the next tutorial. In this tutorial you learned two methods of modifying exposure using layer blending modes, and added another image to your racecars greeting card.

<NOTE>

If you switch the Foreground Color to white, the Brush tool acts like a dodge tool, lightening pixels as you paint.

<NOTE>

Neutral layers like this one are very useful for nondestructive editing. They can be moved, deleted, or otherwise edited without affecting the image on the layer below.

<TIP>

Another use for a neutral layer is as a location for a filter that affects the layer below.

Tutorial
» Manipulating Content

The ability to add or remove content from an image is the ultimate editing tool. You can use these skills to change the story that a photograph tells, to amaze your friends, or simply to improve a composition by eliminating extraneous elements as you do here. In this tutorial, you use the Clone Stamp tool and a patch to cover items that you want to remove from a photograph. In this tutorial you manipulate the content of another image for your greeting card, covering an unsightly antenna and eliminating an entire building.

1. **Choose File→Open. Navigate to the Session 07 Tutorial Files folder on your hard drive, and open** 07_car20.psd.
   In the next steps you eliminate the antenna from the car in this image to enhance the composition and remove an unsightly detail.

<NOTE>
You can remove or add content with the Clone Stamp tool, using it just as you did in an earlier tutorial in which you applied the Clone Stamp to fix dust and scratches.

2. **Click the Create New Layer button at the bottom of the Layers palette. Double-click the** Layer 1 **label on the layer, and rename it** cloning.

3. **Select the Zoom tool, and zoom in to at least 200%.**

4. **Select the Clone Stamp tool in the toolbox. In the Options bar, select a Soft Round brush of about 9 pixels. Make sure Aligned and Use All Layers is selected.**

5. **Alt+click (Macintosh: Option+click) next to the antenna to select the source point for cloning.**

6. **Click and drag the length of the antenna to cover it with the source pixels.**
   It's gone! That's how easy it is to change the content of a photograph. Another way to eliminate content from a photograph is to cover it with a patch from another part of the image, as you do in the next steps.

<TIP>
The Clone Stamp tool can also be used to add an item to a photo. Alt+click (Macintosh: Option+click) on the item to set it as the source point, and click and drag elsewhere in the image to copy it there. You can even use another photograph as the source point.

7. **Select the cloning layer, click the More button on the top right of the Layers palette, and choose Merge Down to merge the cloned pixels and the image.**

8. **Select the Lasso tool in the toolbox. In the Options bar, make sure that Anti-aliased is checked, and enter** 2 px **in the Feather field to soften the edges of the patch.**

   The Lasso tool is useful for drawing irregular selections that help hide the edges of a patch. Anti-aliasing and feathering are also important for hiding patch edges. If you don't add the feather in the Options bar, you can do so after you create a selection by choosing Select→Feather from the menu bar.

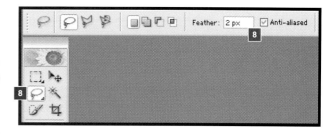

9. **Select the** car 20 **layer in the Layers palette.**

10. **Click and drag a selection in the sky next to the building.**

11. **Choose Layer→New→Layer via Copy.**

    This creates a new **Layer 1** with the contents of the selection.

12. **Click the Move tool, and drag the contents of** Layer 1 **on top of the building on the right side of the image to start eliminating the building from the photograph.**

13. **Repeat Steps 9 through 12 as many times as necessary to cover the building.**

    Alternatively, after you get a good patch layer, duplicate that layer by dragging it to the Create New Layer button at the bottom of the Layers palette. Then move the new layer over a bit with the Move tool. Repeat until the building is covered. Don't worry if the bottom of the patches cover part of the grass. You fix that next.

14. **Select one of the patch layers, and click in the Link field of all the other patch layers to link them all together. Click the More button on the Layers palette, and choose Merge Linked.**

    You now have just one patch layer.

15. **With the patch layer selected, drag the Opacity slider in the Layers palette to around 90% so you can see through the patch.**

    Reducing the opacity of the patch makes it easier to clean up its edge in the next step.

16. **Select the Eraser tool in the toolbox, and choose a soft round brush (around 13 pixels) in the Options bar. In the document window, click and drag over the bottom of the patch, erasing its edge to match the edge of the grass. Move the Opacity slider back to 100%.**

    If you're not satisfied with the bottom of the patch, use the Clone Stamp tool to smooth it out, using the plain sky as the source pixels.

17. **Select the Smudge tool in the toolbox and a small brush (try 8 pixels) in the Options bar. Move the Smudge tool slightly back and forth along the left edge of the patch to further blend that edge with the sky.**

    Continue to do this until you are satisfied with the patch.

18. **Click the More button on the Layers palette, and choose Merge Down. Choose Select→All and then Image→Crop from the menu bar.**

    If you placed some of the patch over the edge of the image, it is still there outside the boundaries of the image. The Crop command crops away everything outside the selection so you have a clean edge on the image that you move into your greeting card.

19. **Your greeting card, 07_racecars.psd, should still be open. If it's not, open it from your ccproject folder. Select the** race copy **layer in that image.**

20. **Select the Move tool, click in 07_car20.psd, and drag the car 20 image into the greeting card. Position the car 20 image in the greeting card to match the illustration, using the lines in the image as a guide.**

21. **Make sure that the greeting card image (07_racecars.psd) is active. Choose File→Save As. In the Save As dialog box, rename the file 07_racecars_layered.psd and save it to your ccproject folder.**

    Leave this image open for the last tutorial in this session. In the next tutorial, you flatten this file, so it's important to save a layered version if you want to make changes later.

<NOTE>

A copy of this layered file as it should look at this point is also in the Session 07 Tutorial Files folder on your hard drive.

22. **Click in 07_car20.psd, choose File→Save As, navigate to your ccproject folder, and click Save. Choose File→Close to close 07_car20.psd.**

    In this tutorial you cleaned up the background of a vintage photograph, eliminating distracting objects using the Clone Stamp tool and a patch. Then you moved that photograph into your racecars greeting card.

Tutorial
» Sharpening

Digital cameras and scanners almost always produce a soft image that looks more crisp and focused after proper sharpening. Sharpening is the last step in a photo retouching workflow and is the subject of the last tutorial in this session. In this tutorial, you learn to use the Unsharp Mask filter.

1. **Your greeting card,** `07_racecars_layered.psd`, **should still be open from the last tutorial. If it's not, open it from your ccprojects folder. Click the More button at the top right of the Layers palette and choose Flatten Image.**
   Don't worry about losing all your layers. You saved a layered copy of this file at the end of the last tutorial. And a copy of the layered file is in your Session 07 Tutorial Files folder called `07_racecars_layered.psd`.

<TIP>
I strongly suggest that when you work on your own images, you make a master copy of your final file before sharpening. This prevents you from permanently damaging the original by inadvertently oversharpening. It also allows you to repurpose the image at different sizes, sharpening as appropriate for a particular image size and medium. (Larger images usually need more sharpening than smaller ones, and images for print usually need more sharpening than images for the screen.)

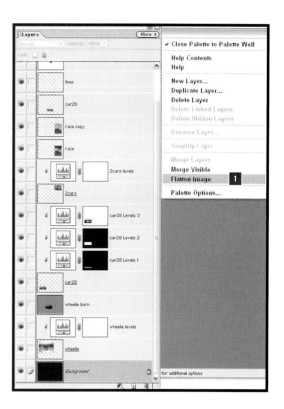

2. **Double-click the Zoom tool to magnify the greeting card to 100%.**
   You should always view an image at 100% when you're sharpening because other views are not as accurate. Use the Hand tool if necessary to move around a large image.

3. **Choose Filter→Sharpen→Unsharp Mask from the menu bar at the top of the screen.**
   The Unsharp Mask dialog box opens. Unsharp Mask works by looking for image edges (actually edges between tones) and increasing the contrast along those edges so they look sharper.

<NOTE>
The Unsharp Mask filter is the only choice in the Sharpen menu that offers the controls you need to do a good job of sharpening. You can forget about the other choices you see there. The odd name, unsharp mask, comes from a traditional graphic arts sharpening technique that combined pieces of film, one of which was blurry or "unsharp."

4. **Set the Amount slider to** 85%, **the Radius slider to** 1.0, **and the Threshold slider to** 10.

   The Amount slider controls the amount by which the filter increases contrast in image edges; the Radius slider controls the width of the sharpening effect around an edge. The Threshold slider determines whether a pixel is different enough from its neighbors to be viewed as an edge that should be sharpened. It tries to distinguish between real image edges and film grain or noise. The lower the Threshold setting, the more likely it is that a pixel is sharpened and the more intense the overall effect appears.

5. **Make sure that the Preview box is checked in the Unsharp Mask dialog box.**

   This ensures that you have a live preview in the document window. A preview is also available in the Unsharp Mask dialog box.

<TIP>
If you need to sharpen local areas—for example, a subject's eyes in a portrait—use the Sharpen tool in the toolbox.

6. **Choose File→Save As, rename this file** 07_racecars_end.psd, **navigate to your ccproject folder, and click Save.**

   In this tutorial you completed the racecars greeting card, adding focus and clarity to the final image by applying the Unsharp Mask filter.

Choosing Unsharp Mask Settings

When you choose Unsharp Mask settings for your own images, your goal should be to maximize sharpness while minimizing exagerrated halos or noise. No one formula works with each and every image. The ideal combination of settings depends on lots of factors, including image size, resolution, and content. You might start with the settings in Step 4. Move the Amount slider up if you see little or no sharpening effect, or move it down if sharpening causes halos in the image. You usually have no reason to increase the Radius setting above 2; too high a radius can have an extreme effect. Move the Threshold setting down for more sharpening or up for less sharpening, staying between about 2 and 20. And keep in mind that sharpening is more obvious on screen than in print. So if you're creating an image for print, make it a little sharper than you otherwise would.

» Session Review

In this session, you mastered a workflow for retouching and adjusting tonal values in a photograph. You took a quick look at the Quick Fix dialog box, and moved on to learn how to adjust a photograph manually. You straightened and cropped a scan, removed discoloration from an old photo, and got rid of dust and scratches on a photograph. Then you turned to the important subject of adjusting tonal values in a photograph. You covered the fundamentals of adjusting tones with Levels and applied multiple Levels adjustment layers to an image, limiting the effect of each. You tried out Auto Levels. Next, you improved the exposure of an image, using blending modes and a special dodge/burn layer. You changed the content of an image. And you sharpened the final image with the Unsharp Mask filter. The result is a composite image of retouched vintage photographs that now shine as if they were new.

1. What kind of commands do you find in the Quick Fix dialog box? (See Discussion: The Quick Fix Approach.)

2. What is the most efficient way to straighten and crop an image? (See Tutorial: Straightening and Cropping a Scanned Photograph.)

3. Describe one way to eliminate stains and discoloration from a black and white image in RGB color mode? (See Tutorial: Fixing Discoloration.)

4. What does the Dust & Scratches filter do to the appearance of a photo? (See Tutorial: Removing Dust and Damage.)

5. What technique would you use to make a layer mask on an adjustment layer affect the content of another layer? (See Tutorial: Removing Dust and Damage.)

6. Name two uses for the Clone Stamp tool. (See Tutorial: Removing Dust and Damage and Tutorial: Manipulating Content.)

7. Can you clone from multiple layers to a separate layer? (See Tutorial: Removing Dust and Damage.)

8. Sometimes clicking and dragging with the Clone tool produces what unwanted result? (See Tutorial: Removing Dust and Damage.)

9. What are some advantages of using a Levels Adjustment layer over a direct Levels adjustment? (See Tutorial: Adjusting Tones with Levels.)

10. Describe what the Levels histogram shows. (See Tutorial: Adjusting Tones with Levels.)

11. What is the effect of moving the white Input Levels slider so that it touches the solid pixels in the Levels histogram? (See Tutorial: Adjusting Tones with Levels.)

12. What is the effect of resetting the black and white points in the Levels histogram on the other tones in an image? (See Tutorial: Adjusting Tones with Levels.)

13. What is the effect of moving the gray Input Levels slider in the Levels histogram? (See Tutorial: Adjusting Tones with Levels.)

14. What feature in the Levels dialog box other than the Input Levels sliders could you use to reset the black and white points in an image? (See Tutorial: Adjusting Tones with Levels.)

15. Name two ways to limit the reach of a Levels adjustment layer. (See Tutorial: Limiting Levels Adjustments.)

16. What does the Auto Levels command do? (See Tutorial: Applying Auto Levels.)

17. Describe how to lighten an overexposed image using a layer blending mode. (See Tutorial: Adjusting Exposure.)

18. Name at least one selection feature that helps blend a patch into an image. (See Tutorial: Manipulating Content.)

19. What is the advantage of using a special neutral dodge/burn layer to adjust image exposure instead of the Dodge and Burn tools. (See Tutorial: Adjusting Exposure.)

20. What is the name of the sharpen filter that is recommended for sharpening an image? (See Tutorial: Sharpening.)

OLDFIELD.DEPALMA.WILCOX.MEYER.SHAW.ROSE.PARSONS.VUKOVICH.FOYT.UNSER.ANDRETTI.JOHNCOCK

Color Correcting Photographs

Session Introduction

This session covers how to correct color in a photograph. You can use the same workflow that you stepped through in the previous session to approach a color photograph, except that when you get to the stage of adjusting tonal values, you have another powerful variable to deal with—color. Photoshop Elements 2 simplifies color correction, making it something that you can and should do to make your photographs look better. Here, you learn step-by-step how to apply the Levels feature to adjust color along with tone. You try out some automatic color correction features in Photoshop Elements 2: Auto Color Correction, Color Cast, and Color Variations. You apply automatic Backlighting and Fill Flash adjustments and the Red Eye brush to deal with lighting problems in a color photograph. And you learn a couple of ways to replace one color with another, using the Replace Color feature and the Hue/Saturation adjustment. The result is a collage of corrected color images that adorns the face of another greeting card.

TOOLS YOU'LL USE
Levels, Auto Color Correction, Color Cast, Color Variations, Fill Flash, Adjust Backlighting, Replace Color, Hue/Saturation, Red Eye brush

CD-ROM FILES NEEDED
08_ride.psd, 08_mountain.psd, 08_stretch.psd, 08_trek.psd, 08_field.psd, 08_rider.psd, 08_beach.psd, 08_child.psd, 08_ride_end.psd

TIME REQUIRED
90 minutes

Tutorial
» Correcting Color with Levels

In the previous session, you learned how to use Levels to adjust tonal values. Here, you use Levels to correct color as well as to adjust tonal values in a color photograph. You apply the Black, White, and Gray Eyedroppers in a Levels adjustment layer to remove color casts from shadows, highlights, and midtones. The result is a photograph for your greeting card that has more accurate color and expanded dynamic range.

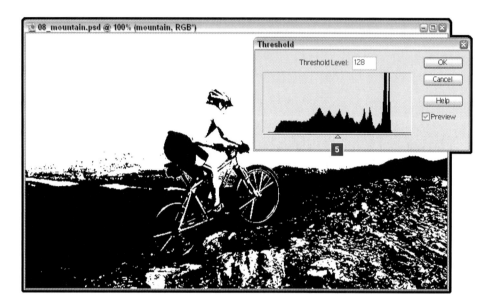

1. **Reset all tools to their default settings by clicking the tool icon at the far left of the Options bar, choosing Reset All Tools, and clicking OK at the query.**

2. **Reset palettes to their default locations by choosing Window→Reset Palette Locations. Close the Hints and How To palettes.**

<TIP>
If you did not work through the tutorials on Levels in the last session, turn back and read through those now. They contain information about levels and the histogram in the Levels dialog box that makes this tutorial a more valuable learning experience for you.

3. **Choose Window→Info to open the Info palette. Drag the Layers palette out of the Palette Well.**
It's useful to have these two palettes open on your desktop when you correct color.

4. **Choose File→Open, navigate to the** 08_mountain.psd **file in your Session 08 Tutorial Files folder, and click Open.**
A photograph of a mountain biker opens.

<NOTE>
The tutorial files for this session are tagged with the Adobe RGB (1998) color profile so that they have consistent color values.

5. **Choose Image→Adjustments→Threshold to view the photograph in the document window as a high-contrast black and white image.**
The Threshold dialog box opens. The Threshold command displays all pixels as if they were black or white, depending on their brightness values. All pixels darker than the value at the location of the slider in the Threshold dialog box appear black, and all pixels lighter than the location of the slider appear white.

6. **Drag the slider in the Threshold dialog box all the way to the left and then slowly back to the right until you see a small clump of black pixels. Turn the Preview check box off and then on to see where these pixels are in the image (the back of the biker's shorts).**

Remember this location; you use it later in this tutorial for resetting the black point in the photograph. This is the darkest area in the photograph other than some scattered pixels.

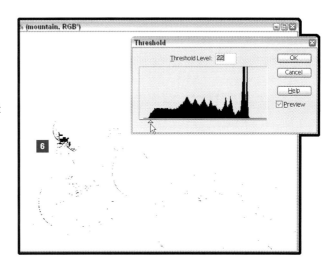

< N O T E >

In the previous session, you produced a threshold view by Alt+clicking (Option+clicking) on the Input Levels sliders in a Levels dialog box. If you try that with a color image, you see color as well as black and white pixels, representing brightness values in each color channel. The Image→Adjustments→Threshold command is easier to use here, because it displays only black and white.

7. **Click and drag the Threshold slider all the way to the right and then slowly back to the left until you see some clumps of white pixels in the foreground. Turn the Preview check box off and then on to take note of where these pixels are located in the picture (the light parts of the rocks). You use this information later in this tutorial when you reset the white point in the photograph. Click cancel.**

The Threshold dialog box closes. These pixels are the brightest pixels in the photograph (other than specular highlights in the helmet and bicycle, which are not representative of highlight areas with content).

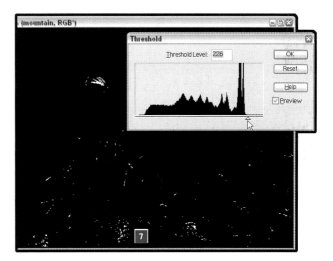

8. Alt+click (Macintosh: Option+click) on the Create New Fill or Adjustment Layer button at the bottom of the Layers palette, and choose Levels.

The New Layer dialog box opens.

9. **Name the new layer** mountain levels**, and select Group With Previous Layer in the New Layer dialog box. Click OK.**

The Levels dialog box opens. Grouping the **mountain levels** layer with the **mountain** layer ensures that when you move the mountain biker's image into your greeting card later in this tutorial, other layers in the greeting card won't be affected by this levels adjustment.

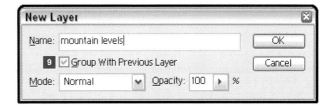

< N O T E >

Applying Levels in an adjustment layer is preferable to making a direct Levels adjustment, because adjustment layers are nondestructive and editable.

10. **If the Levels dialog box is covering your Info palette, click on the title bar of the Levels dialog box and drag the dialog box out of the way so you can see both items.**

    You may have to move the Info palette, too. If so, close the Levels dialog box by clicking OK, move the Info palette, and reopen the Levels dialog box by double-clicking the thumbnail on the left side of the **mountain levels** layer.

<NOTE>

In this tutorial, you use the Eyedroppers in the Levels dialog box to remap the tonal values of representative shadows, highlights, and midtones. The Input Levels sliders in the Levels dialog box could be used instead, but the Eyedroppers offer more control over which pixels are affected.

11. **Select the Black Eyedropper in the Levels dialog box, and click on the dark area of the biker's shorts that you identified in Step 6.**

    This forces all pixels that are as dark as or darker than the one on which you clicked to pure black. Leave your mouse where it is for the next step.

<TIP>

You may find it helpful to zoom in to see where you are clicking with the Levels Eyedroppers. To zoom in to the image with the Levels dialog box open, press Ctrl+spacebar (Macintosh: ⌘+spacebar) and click in the image. To move a magnified image in the document window, press the spacebar and drag. To zoom back out, press Ctrl+Alt+spacebar (Macintosh: ⌘+Option+spacebar) and click in the image.

12. **In the Info palette, look at the RGB readout in the top-left quadrant.**

    The numbers to the left of the slash are the RGB values of the selected pixel before this adjustment. They will be different than those in the illustration depending on exactly where you clicked in the last step. The relative values of these numbers reflect the pre-adjustment color cast in the shadow areas. For example, a higher value in the B field than in the R and G fields tells you that there was a blue color cast in the shadow areas represented by the selected pixel. The numbers to the right of the slash are the post-adjustment values of the selected pixel—0, 0, 0—which is pure black with no color cast.

13. **Select the White Eyedropper in the Levels dialog box and click on the white area in the foreground rocks that you identified in Step 7.** This forces all pixels as bright as or brighter than the one on which you clicked to pure white. Notice in the Info palette that the RGB values of the pixel that you selected in the preceding step are now 255, 255, 255, which is pure white.

< N O T E >

The important point is that resetting representative shadows and highlights to pure black and white removes color cast in the shadows and highlights of the photograph.

14. **Deselect and reselect the Preview check box in the Levels dialog box to see that your adjustments of the black and white points also increased the contrast in the image.** This photograph still has a bluish color cast in the midtones. You neutralize that color cast in the next steps using the Gray Eyedropper in the Levels dialog box.

< N O T E >

You can change the target value of a Levels Eyedropper to other than pure black, white, or gray by double-clicking that Eyedropper to open the Color Picker and choosing a different color. The target values of the Black and White Eyedroppers are commonly changed to compensate for the inability of commercial printing presses to print pure black or white. A less traditional use for this feature might be to introduce an intentional color cast to an image.

< N O T E >

Resetting the black and white points to the darkest shadows and brightest nonspecular highlights expands the tonal range of the image, increasing its overall contrast. This adjustment not only remaps the dark and light pixels; it also redistributes all the in-between pixels. The pixels are now stretched out across the entire tonal range, as you can see in the histogram in the Levels dialog box.

15. **Select the Gray Eyedropper in the Levels dialog box.**
    If you already closed the Levels dialog box, double-click the left thumbnail on the **mountain levels** adjustment layer in the Layers palette. The Levels dialog box reopens for further editing.

16. **Click on an area of the rocks that you think should be gray.**
    This shifts the value of the pixel on which you click to a neutral gray and redistributes the other midtone pixels without affecting the darkest and brightest pixels that you already adjusted. This should neutralize the color cast in the midtones, although the result can be very different depending on where you click. Leave your cursor where it is for the next step.

< T I P >
If you don't like the result, choose Edit➔Undo Color Sample and try again, clicking on another pixel that should be gray.

< T I P >
Alt+clicking (Macintosh: Option+clicking) on the Cancel button in the Levels dialog box changes the button to Reset and undoes all Levels adjustments you made to this layer. So use it with caution.

17. **Notice in the Info palette that the RGB values of the pixel that you selected in the preceding step are now equal to one another. (Equal R, G, and B values represent a neutral shade of gray.) Click OK.**
    The Levels dialog box closes and applies all your Levels adjustments.

< T I P >
Photographers sometimes include a gray card (available at many camera stores) in a photograph. Clicking with the Gray Levels Eyedropper on a gray card in the photograph is an easy way to set the midtones to a neutral gray.

< N O T E >
Levels adjustments affect all channels of a color image individually. If you check the image histogram (Image➔Histogram) before and after adjusting Levels, you see the values change in each of the Red, Green, and Blue channels.

< N O T E >
For the record, the method used in this tutorial is not the only way to use Levels to adjust color. You can also make Levels adjustments to individual color channels. To do so, click on the Channel field in the Levels dialog box and choose the Red channel. The Levels histogram displays the distribution of tonal values in the Red channel only. Pull the black and white sliders to the beginning of the solid area of pixels in the Red channel to expand the tonal range and increase contrast in that channel. Repeat these operations in the Green channel and in the Blue channel. Return to the RGB composite channel, and move the gray Levels slider as necessary to brighten or darken the entire image. This method sometimes improves the color of an image, but it also can introduce new color casts, because clipping the highlights and shadows differently in the three channels changes the mix of color.

18. **Choose File→Save As. In the Save As dialog box, navigate to your ccproject folder, make sure that Layers and ICC Profile: Adobe RGB (1998) (Macintosh: Embed Color Profile (Adobe RGB 1998)) are selected, and click Save.**
Checking Layers ensures that the saved file is not flattened, but retains its layers. Checking ICC Profile tags the file with the indicated color management profile.

<NOTE>
Your color corrections with the Levels Eyedroppers improved the color cast and contrast of the mountain biker image in preparation for including this photograph in a new greeting card.

19. **Open the original version of the greeting card that you complete in this session by navigating to your Session 08 Tutorial Files folder and choosing 08_ride.psd.**
The 08_ride.psd file opens in a new window.

20. **In 08_mountain.psd, select the mountain layer and click in the Link field of the mountain levels layer. Select the Move tool, click inside the 08_mountain.psd document window, and drag the mountain biker image into the 08_ride.psd document window.**
This moves both layers of the mountain biker image, which are grouped together, into the greeting card.

21. **Press Ctrl+spacebar (Macintosh: ⌘+spacebar) and click in 08_ride.psd to zoom in until you can see the thin colored lines in the image. Position the mountain biker image in the greeting card to match the illustration, moving it up against the left and bottom lines in the top-left corner of the greeting card.**
Don't confuse the lines in this greeting card with official Guides. These are actual graphics that I drew with the Pencil tool.

22. **In the greeting card image, 08_ride.psd, choose File→ Save As, navigate to your ccproject folder, make sure that Layers and ICC Profile: Adobe RGB (1998) (Macintosh: Embed Color Profile (Adobe RGB 1998)) are selected, and click Save. Close 08_mountain.psd. Leave 08_ride.psd open for the next tutorial.**
In this tutorial you added a Levels adjustment layer to the mountain biker photograph, used the Levels Eyedroppers to remove color cast and improve contrast in that photograph, and moved the corrected photograph into your greeting card.

Tutorial
» Correcting Color with the Auto Color Correction Command

Adobe has tried to make the task of correcting color as easy as possible by including a number of automatic features that attempt to do the job for you. One in particular—the Auto Color Correction command—stands out. It works much like the Levels adjustment that you made in the last tutorial to reset black and white points and reduce color cast in midtones, as you see in this tutorial. You apply the Auto Color Correction command to improve the color of another photograph that becomes part of your greeting card.

1. **Choose File→Open, navigate to your Session 08 Tutorial Files folder, and choose** 08_stretch.psd. **Click Open.**
   You can see a blue color cast in this image of a biker stretching. In the next step, you confirm this color cast in the Info palette.

2. **Select the Eyedropper tool from the toolbox. Keeping an eye on the RGB values in the Info palette, move the cursor over the mountain and logs in the image.**
   Although these areas should be neutral gray, they do not have equal Red, Green, and Blue values. Instead, the Blue value is significantly higher than the other two values.

3. **Choose Enhance→Auto Color Correction from the menu bar at the top of the screen.**
   Auto Color Correction works in a manner similar to the Levels method described in the previous tutorial. It identifies the darkest and lightest points in the composite color channel, resets them to black and white, and attempts to make the midtones more neutral.

< N O T E >
This command is also accessible from the Quick Fix dialog box by selecting the Color Correction Adjustment Category and choosing Auto Color in that dialog box.

4. **Click the Step Backward button and then the Step Forward button on the Shortcuts bar to compare the before and after state, so you can judge how well the command reduced the color cast in this image.**

5. **Choose File→Save As, navigate to your ccproject folder, make sure that ICC Profile: Adobe RGB (1998) (Macintosh: Embed Color Profile (Adobe RGB 1998)) is selected, and click Save to save** 08_stretch.psd **with these changes.**

6. **Select the** mountain levels **layer in the greeting card image** 08_ride.psd **that is still open from the previous tutorial.**
   If this document is not open, reopen it from your ccproject folder.

7. **Select the Move tool in the toolbox. Click inside the** 08_stretch.psd **document window, and drag the stretch image into the** 08_ride.psd **document window.**

8. **Position the stretch image to match the illustration, moving it up against the right and top guide lines in the bottom-right corner of the greeting card.**

9. **Close** 08_stretch.psd **without saving again. Click in the** 08_ride.psd **document window, and choose File→Save. Leave** 08_ride.psd **open for the next tutorial.**

In this tutorial, you used the best of the auto correction methods—the Auto Color Correction command—to correct a color cast in the stretch image before bringing that photograph into your greeting card.

Should You Use Auto Color Correction?

I usually recommend avoiding automatic adjustments in favor of methods that are more flexible and allow room for personal interpretation. However, if you're in the market for fast and easy color correction, Auto Color Correction is the command to try first. It is a time-saver and often does a decent job of correcting color cast in shadows, highlights, and midtones. Auto Color Correction doesn't add a color cast, like Auto Levels sometimes does, because it does not adjust each color channel individually. Rather, it identifies the dark, light, and midtone points in the composite image.

Although Auto Color Correction is the most attractive of the auto adjustment methods, I urge you to use the Levels techniques that you learned in the previous tutorial rather than Auto Color Correction on any serious photographic project. I have three reasons for this recommendation:

» Auto Color Correction is not available as an adjustment layer. It is a direct adjustment that changes the original pixels in the image and cannot be edited as a Levels adjustment layer can.

» Auto Color Correction, like all auto adjustment tools, makes the decisions for you. It does not allow for subjective judgment or artistic interpretation.

» Auto Color Correction does not offer the option to go into individual R, G, and B color channels to make adjustments there if necessary. It works only on the composite channel.

Should You Use Other Automatic Commands to Correct Color?

You may be tempted to use one of three other automatic commands when correcting color—Auto Levels, Auto Contrast, and Color Cast. None of these is a preferred method of correcting color, but each has an effect on color balance that you should know about:

>> Auto Levels adjusts each color channel by remapping its darkest and lightest pixels and redistributing the pixels in between, increasing contrast in each channel. The problem with Auto Levels is that it often adds a color cast because it adjusts each color channel independently. Auto Levels is accessible from the Enhance menu (Enhance→Auto Levels), the Brightness category in the Quick Fix dialog box, and the Auto button in the Levels dialog box. Avoid activating Auto Levels from the first two locations because they operate on the original image. If you must use Auto Levels, you should create a Levels adjustment layer and click the Auto button to apply the feature.

>> Auto Contrast remaps the darkest and lightest pixels in the composite image, redistributing the pixels in between. It does not adjust each color channel individually like Auto Levels. This increases contrast without removing or adding a color cast. So Auto Contrast can come in handy to pop the contrast on an image with a color cast that you want to retain, such as a sunset glow. For example, if you apply Auto Contrast to 08_trek.psd, the sunset-lit photograph that you use in the tutorial on correcting with the Color Cast command, you slightly increase image contrast without removing the red glow of sunset. A downside of Auto Contrast is that it is a direct correction that is not available as an adjustment layer.

>> Color Cast is a somewhat automatic method of removing color cast that allows you to choose which value to neutralize. It too is a direct correction, rather than an adjustment layer.

>> Color Variations is a visual means of correcting color by choosing from a series of thumbnails. Unfortunately, this feature has some limitations that make it difficult to use for serious color correction: It offers no measurable way to evaluate a color cast, its thumbnails are too small to be of serious use, and it is another direct correction, unavailable as an adjustment layer.

Tutorial
» Correcting Color Cast with the Color Cast Command

The Color Cast Command is another way to fix a color cast in an image. This method automatically neutralizes a color value you select in an image. In this tutorial, you use the Color Cast command to reduce a late afternoon red cast from an image. Another important point to take from this tutorial is that you can combine color correction methods.

1. **Open** 08_trek.psd **from your Session 08 Tutorial Files folder.**

2. **Select the Eyedropper tool from the toolbox, and make sure that the Info palette is still open. Move your cursor around the image, keeping your eye on the RGB values in the Info palette.**
   Notice that the Red value is significantly higher than the Green and Blue values almost everywhere in the photograph.

<NOTE>
This photograph has a strong red color cast because it was taken at sunset. You may want to retain the general red glow that speaks of that time of day, but reduce the strength of the color cast. If you apply the Auto Color Correction command to this image, the background automatically becomes neutral gray with no hint of red. (Give it a try as a point of comparison, and then click the Step Backward button on the Shortcuts bar to undo Auto Color Correction.) The Color Cast command offers more control than the Auto Color Correction command over removal of the color cast.

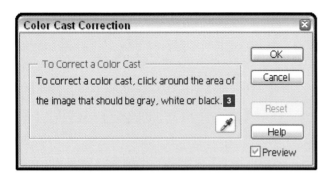

3. **Choose Enhance→Adjust Color→Color Cast.**

   This opens the Color Cast Correction dialog box that tells you to "click around the area of the image that should be gray, white or black" to remove a color cast. This is similar to the way you used the Gray Eyedropper in the Levels dialog box to remove a color cast.

4. **Click on the patch of snow on the mountain behind the riders, which is an area that should be light gray.**

   The pixel on which you click turns a light neutral gray (as evidenced by the equal amounts of Red, Green, and Blue reported to the right of the slash in the Info palette). Other pixel values adjust accordingly, removing the extreme color cast but leaving some red in the image.

5. **Deselect and reselect Preview in the Color Cast Correction dialog box to see a before and after view from which you can judge the impact of the correction.**

   In the figure, you see both the before view on the left and the after view on the right. The difference should be even more obvious on your screen than here in the book.

< T I P >

If you are not satisfied with the resulting color, click the Reset button in the Color Cast Correction dialog box and try clicking on a different part of the snow patch.

6. **When you like the result, click OK in the Color Cast Correction dialog box.**

   This accepts the correction and closes the dialog box.

< N O T E >

Notice that the Color Cast command works on the original image, rather than on an adjustment layer, which is a major disadvantage. To get the flexibility of an adjustment layer with the effect of the Color Cast command, you could apply a Levels adjustment layer and use only the Gray Eyedropper in the Levels dialog box.

< N O T E >

Automatic commands don't have to be used in isolation. You can use them to do a partial correction, and then also apply a manual correction. For example, the models in this image are still quite dark following the Color Cast correction. In the next steps you apply a Levels adjustment layer on top of the Color Cast correction to make their skin tones lighter.

7. **Alt+click (Macintosh: Option+click) the Create New Fill or Adjustment Layer button at the bottom of the Layers palette, and choose Levels.**

   The New Layer dialog box opens.

8. **Name this layer** trek levels**, select Group With Previous Layer, and click OK in the New Layer dialog box.**

   This creates a new Levels adjustment layer grouped with the **trek** layer and opens the Levels dialog box where you set the parameters of the adjustment layer.

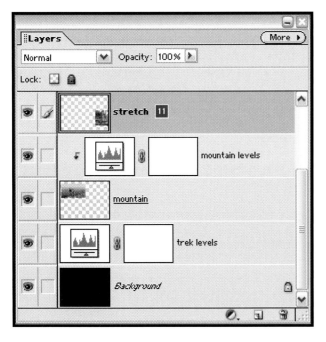

9. **In the Levels dialog box, click on the gray slider and drag it slowly to the left to lighten the image. Stop when the models' skin is a lighter, more natural shade. Click OK.**
   The Levels dialog box closes.

10. **Choose File→Save As. In the Save As dialog box, navigate to your ccproject folder, make sure that ICC Profile: Adobe RGB (1998) (Macintosh: Embed Color Profile (Adobe RGB 1998)) is selected, and click Save to save** 08_trek.psd **with these changes.**
    The color cast in this photograph has been neutralized using the Auto Color Correction command in conjunction with a Levels adjustment layer.

11. **Select the** stretch **layer in the greeting card image** 08_ride.psd **that is still open from the previous tutorial so that the new layer you are about to create is located above the** stretch **layer.**
    If 08_ride.psd is not open, reopen it from your ccproject folder.

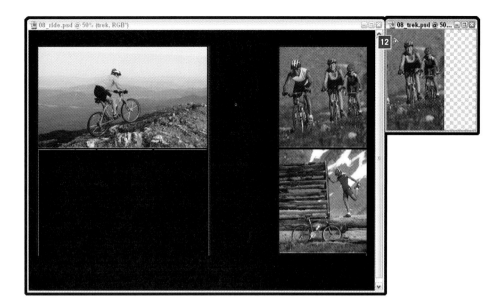

12. **In** 08_trek.psd**, select the** trek **layer and click in the Link field of the** trek levels **layer. Move both layers into the greeting card by selecting the Move tool, clicking inside the** 08_trek.psd **document window, and dragging into the** 08_ride.psd **document window.**

13. **Position the trek image to match the illustration, moving it up against the right and bottom guide lines in the top-right corner of the greeting card.**

14. **Click in the** 08_ride.psd **document window, choose File➞Save, and leave** 08_ride.psd **open for the next tutorial. Close** 08_trek.psd **without saving again.**

In this tutorial you removed a color cast from the trek photograph using the Auto Color Correction command and a Levels Adjustment layer, in preparation for including that corrected photograph into your greeting card.

Tutorial
» Applying Color Variations

Color Variations is a visual means of correcting a color cast. This method is useful for quick color fixes, but it is not a tool that's often used for professional color correction. You learn how to use its features in this tutorial as you tweak the color of another photograph for this session's greeting card.

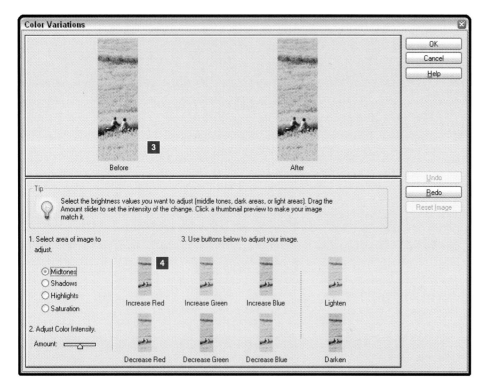

1. **Open** 08_field.psd **from your Session 08 Tutorial Files folder.**

2. **Choose Enhance→Adjust Color→Color Variations to open the Color Variations dialog box.**

3. **Look at the Before thumbnail, which represents the unadjusted image, and try to determine its color cast.**
   Although it's difficult to tell from this thumbnail, this image has a preponderance of red and a lack of blue.

4. **Compare the Before thumbnail to the six adjustment thumbnails in the lower, central part of the dialog box to determine which of the three colors—Red, Green, or Blue—you might add or subtract to improve the color cast.**
   Don't worry if you find it difficult to make this determination. The small thumbnails and the slight differences between them make it difficult to make a rational choice. Trial and error is often the only viable approach in this dialog box.

   <NOTE>
   You already encountered two of the problems that limit the utility of the Color Variations feature and keep it from being a professional color correction tool: The only way to determine the nature of a color cast in the original image is by visual inspection of the Before thumbnail; and the adjustment thumbnails in the dialog box are too small to be of much value. Even so, you may find Color Variations useful as a way to preview an image with various color changes.

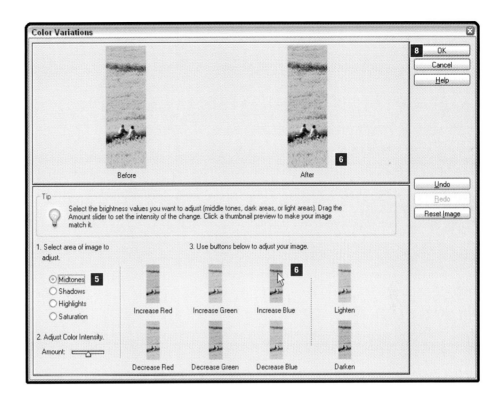

5. **Select Midtones from the portion of the Color Variations dialog box labeled Select area of the image to adjust so that you can correct the color of the middle tones of the image.**
   You can adjust generic Midtones, Shadows, and Highlights separately in this dialog box. However, you don't know which values correspond to these labels so you can't be as precise here as you could with a manual Levels adjustment.

6. **Select the thumbnail for Increase Blue to add to the amount of blue in the midtones of this photograph. Then look at the After thumbnail at the top right of the dialog box to preview this adjustment.**

7. **Repeat Steps 5 and 6, selecting Shadows and then Highlights in the Select Area portion of the dialog box.**

8. **Click OK to close the Color Variations dialog box and apply the changes you made there.**

<NOTE>
Adjustments made with the Color Variations feature are permanent, so you may want to apply them to a duplicate layer rather than to the original artwork.

<NOTE>
If you change your mind about the last adjustment you made, click the Undo button on the right side of the Color Variations dialog box. To undo multiple adjustments and start again, click the Reset Image button.

<NOTE>
The Color Variations dialog box also includes generic brightness (Lighten and Darken), Saturation, and Color Intensity controls. Applying these settings is a hit-or-miss process of experimentation. The only way to measure the effect of these settings is to visually inspect the small After thumbnail. So I suggest that you use other tools, like the Levels or Hue/Saturation features, to adjust these parameters.

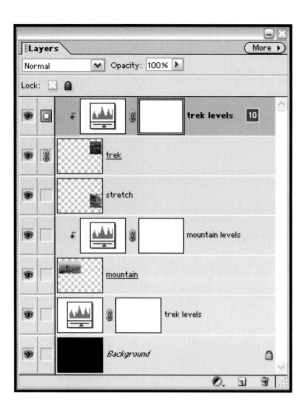

9. **Choose File➔Save As. In the Save As dialog box, navigate to your ccproject folder, make sure that ICC Profile: Adobe RGB (1998) (Macintosh: Embed Color Profile (Adobe RGB 1998)) is selected, and click Save to save** 08_field.psd **with the color changes you made.**

10. **Select the** trek levels **layer in the greeting card image** 08_ride.psd **that is still open from the previous tutorial.**
    If this file isn't open, reopen it from your ccproject folder.

11. **Select the Move tool in the toolbox. Click inside the** 08_field.psd **document window, and drag the field image into the** 08_ride.psd **document window.**

12. **Position the field image to match the illustration, moving it up against the left guide line in the middle of the greeting card.**

13. **Click in the** 08_ride.psd **document window, choose File➔Save, and leave** 08_ride.psd **open for the next tutorial. Close** 08_field.psd **without saving again.**
    In this tutorial you used the Color Variations feature to modify the color cast in the field photograph before bringing that image into your greeting card.

Tutorial
» Adjusting Backlighting

Lighting, tone, and color are closely connected. Adobe included some unique tools in Photoshop Elements 2 to help you fix common lighting problems automatically. In this tutorial, you apply the Adjust Backlighting command to darken an overexposed background in another photo that becomes part of your greeting card.

1. **Open** 08_beach.psd **from your Session 08 Tutorial Files folder.**
   The light source in this image is coming from behind the subject, resulting in overexposed (excessively bright) sky and water in the background. In the next steps, you darken the background, bringing out image detail.

2. **Choose Enhance→Adjust Lighting→Adjust Backlighting to open the Adjust Backlighting dialog box.**
   This feature is also accessible from the the Brightness category in the Quick Fix dialog box.

3. **Click the Darker slider in the Adjust Backlighting dialog box, and move it to the right to darken the image to suit your taste.**
   I stopped at +35. The biker in the foreground doesn't change, but the background becomes darker, displaying richer color and additional detail.

4. **Deselect and reselect the Preview check box in the Adjust Backlighting dialog box to compare the before and after views. After you're satisfied with the result, click the OK button to close the dialog box and apply the adjustment.**
   This is a direct adjustment that changes the original pixels.

5. **Choose File→Save As. In the Save As dialog box, navigate to your ccproject folder, make sure that ICC Profile: Adobe RGB (1998) (Macintosh: Embed Color Profile (Adobe RGB 1998)) is selected, and click Save to save** 08_beach.psd **with these changes.**

6. **Select the field layer in the greeting card image** 08_ride.psd **that is still open from the previous tutorial.**
   If 08_ride.psd is not open, reopen it from your ccproject folder.

7. **Select the Move tool in the toolbox. Click inside the** 08_beach.psd **document window, and drag the beach image into the** 08_ride.psd **document window.**

8. **Position the beach image to match the illustration, moving it up against the top guide line at the bottom of the greeting card.**

9. **Click in the** 08_ride.psd **document window, choose File→Save, and leave** 08_ride.psd **open for the next tutorial. Close** 08_beach.psd **without saving again.**
   The beach image that you brought into your greeting card no longer suffers from an overly bright background, thanks to the automatic Adjust Backlighting feature.

Tutorial
» Remedying Flash Problems

In this tutorial, you use two features designed to automatically correct problems associated with photographic flash. You use the Fill Flash command to add light to a badly underexposed (dark) image of a bicycle racer. You also apply the Red Eye Brush tool to remove a red reflection in a young biker's eye caused by direct flash. And you bring both of these corrected images into your greeting card collage.

1. **Open** 08_rider.psd **from your Session 08 Tutorial Files folder.**
   Images like this one would have benefited from a flash on the camera. From now on, you don't have to throw out images that are too dark. Just apply Fill Flash.

2. **Choose Enhance→Adjust Lighting→Fill Flash to open the Fill Flash dialog box.**
   This feature is also accessible from the the Brightness category in the Quick Fix dialog box.

3. **In the Adjust Fill Flash dialog box, move the Lighter slider to the left to lighten the image. Click OK to close the dialog box and apply the adjustment.**
   I stopped at 40. Lightening the image left it looking dull. You could saturate the whole image by moving the Saturation slider to the right, but adding the amount of saturation needed for the yellow vest makes the subject's nose and cheeks too red. Wait till the next tutorial to add saturation to specific areas using a Hue/Saturation adjustment layer with a layer mask.

<TIP>
Some images benefit from applying both the Fill Flash adjustment to brighten the foreground and an Adjust Backlighting adjustment to darken the background.

< N O T E >
Adjust Fill Flash is another adjustment that affects the original pixels and is noneditable. You can apply it to a duplicate layer in order to preserve the source image.

4. **Choose File→Save As. In the Save As dialog box, navigate to your ccproject folder, make sure that ICC Profile: Adobe RGB (1998) (Macintosh: Embed Color Profile (Adobe RGB 1998)) is selected, and click Save to save** 08_rider.psd **with the changes that you just made.**

5. **Select the** beach **layer in the greeting card image** 08_ride.psd **that is still open from the previous tutorial.**
If this image is not open, open it from your ccproject folder.

6. **Select the Move tool in the toolbox. Click inside the** 08_rider.psd **document window, and drag the rider image into the** 08_ride.psd **document window.**

7. **Position the rider image to match the illustration, moving it up against the top guide line at the bottom of the greeting card.**

8. **Click in the** 08_ride.psd **document window, choose File→Save, and leave** 08_ride.psd **open for the next tutorial. Close** 08_rider.psd **without saving again.**
You applied the Adjust Fill Flash feature to simulate flash in the photograph of a bicycle racer before moving that picture into your greeting card. Next, you fix another frequent flash problem—red eye.

9. **Choose File→Open, navigate to your Session 08 Tutorial Files folder, and open** 08_child.psd.

   This model suffers from red eye—a common result of camera flash bouncing off the back of a subject's eye. In the next steps you eliminate this problem with the Red Eye Brush tool.

10. **Select the Zoom tool, and click on the subject's eye to zoom in to 200%.**

    Clearly seeing the area that you are working is important.

11. **Select the Red Eye Brush tool in the toolbox.**

12. **In the Options bar, select a brush a little smaller than the subject's eye.**

    A brush 5 pixels wide works fine.

13. **Click the Default Colors button on the Options bar.**

    This sets the Current and Replacement colors to their defaults.

14. **Make sure that First Click is selected in the Sampling field.**

    This determines the sampling method. The First Click method samples the red color under the brush crosshairs when you first click. The Current Color method is more difficult to use because it requires you to choose the red color to be replaced from the Color Picker, rather than sample it from the image.

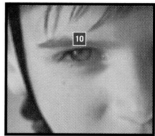

15. **Leave the Tolerance set to its default of 30% for now.**

    If you find that not all of the red is replaced, you can increase the Tolerance to broaden the color range subject to replacement.

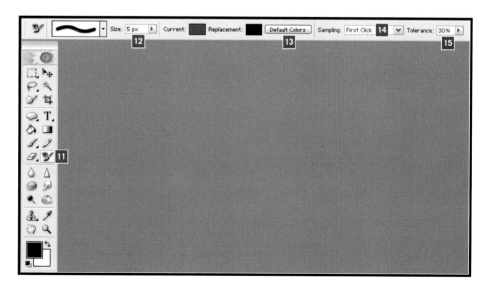

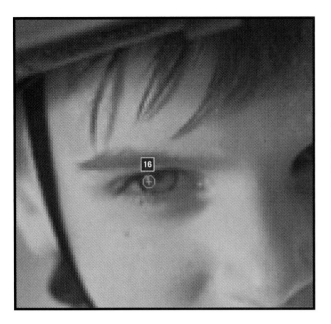

16. **Place the crosshairs over the red part of the subject's right eye. Click to sample the red color, keep the mouse held down, and move it over the rest of the red reflection.**
    As you drag, the red color is replaced with a tint of the color in the Replacement field. The tinted black in the Replacement field appears as dark gray in the subject's eye.

< T I P >
As you paint away the red eye effect, try not to stray over neighboring pinkish pixels that might fall within the Tolerance limits, or they too are replaced with dark gray.

17. **Choose File➜Save As. In the Save As dialog box, navigate to your ccproject folder, make sure that ICC Profile: Adobe RGB (1998) (Macintosh: Embed Color Profile (Adobe RGB 1998)) is selected, and click Save to save** 08_child.psd **with these changes.**

18. **Select the** rider **layer in the greeting card image** 08_ride.psd **that is still open.**

19. **Select the Move tool in the toolbox. Click inside the** 08_child.psd **document window, and drag the child image into the** 08_ride.psd **document window.**

20. **Position the child image to match the illustration, moving it up against the top and left guide lines at the bottom left of the greeting card.**

21. **Click in the** 08_ride.psd **document window, choose File→Save, and leave** 08_ride.psd **open for the next tutorial. Close** 08_child.psd **without saving again.**
    In this tutorial, you added fill flash to an image of a bicycle rider and applied the Red Eye Brush tool to remove red eye in a photograph of a young bicyclist. You moved both these images into your session greeting card, which is now almost complete.

Tutorial
» Adjusting Color Saturation

In this tutorial, you use a Hue/Saturation layer to modify the saturation of the bicycle racer photograph that you lightened with Fill Flash earlier. The layer mask that comes with the adjustment layer allows you to limit this adjustment to specific portions of the image.

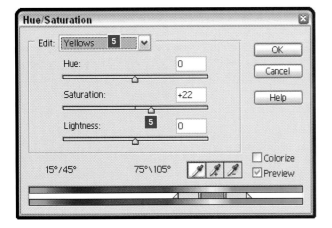

1. **Select the** rider **layer in the Layers palette of** 08_ride.psd.
   The 08_ride.psd file should be open from the preceding tutorial. If it's not, open it from your ccproject folder.

2. **Hold the Alt key (Macintosh: Option key), click the Create New Fill or Adjustment Layer button at the bottom of the Layers palette, and choose Hue/Saturation.**
   This opens the New Layer dialog box.

3. **In the New Layer dialog box, enter** rider hue/sat **as the name of the new adjustment layer, select Group with Previous Layer, and click OK to open the Hue/Saturation dialog box.**
   This creates a Hue/Saturation adjustment layer that's grouped with the **rider** layer so that the adjustment affects only the **rider** layer and not all the layers beneath it.

< N O T E >
You can also apply a Hue/Saturation adjustment from the Color Correction category of the Quick Fix dialog box. But that method does not use an adjustment layer; it applies the correction directly to the image.

4. **In the Hue/Saturation dialog box, leave the Edit field set to Master and drag the Saturation slider to the right to about +22. Move the Lightness slider to about +5.**
   Moving the Saturation slider increases the intensity of color in the **rider** layer. Adjusting the Lightness slider brightens the layer.

5. **Click in the Edit field of the Hue/Saturation dialog box, and choose Yellows. Drag the Saturation slider to about +22 to increase the saturation further in only the yellow pixels in the image. Click OK to close the Hue/Saturation dialog box and apply this adjustment.**
   This saturates the model's yellow vest without affecting other areas of the photograph. The colors that are affected by this adjustment are those that fall between the sliders at the bottom of the Hue/Saturation dialog box. Colors above the dark gray bar are affected most intensely; colors above the light gray bars are partially affected.

6. **Select the** rider hue/sat **layer in the Layers palette. Notice that a double line appears around the white layer mask on that layer, indicating that the layer mask is selected.**
   The adjustments from Step 5 oversaturated a few red areas on the model's skin. So you block the adjustments from those areas by painting on the layer mask on the Hue/Saturation adjustment layer.

7. **Press D (for default colors) and then X (for switch colors) to change the Foreground Color box in the toolbox to black.**

8. **Select the Brush tool in the toolbox, and choose a small brush size (around 13 px) in the Options palette.**

9. **In the document window, paint over the sunburned red spots on the model's face and legs.**
   This blocks the effect of the Hue/Saturation adjustments from these areas so that they don't look too saturated.

< N O T E >
Adjusting saturation with a Hue/Saturation adjustment layer is preferable to using the simple Saturation slider in the Fill Flash dialog box. The effect of the Hue/Saturation adjustment layer can be limited to a specific area, it does not destroy original pixels, and it remains editable.

10. **Choose File→Save As. In the Save As dialog box, navigate to your ccproject folder and click Save to save the greeting card** 08_ride.psd **with these changes. Leave** 08_ride.psd **open for the next tutorial.**
    In this tutorial you adjusted color saturation in a limited area of the bicycle racer photograph in your greeting card by applying a Hue/Saturation adjustment layer and painting on its layer mask.

Tutorial
» Replacing Color

In this tutorial, you learn two methods for replacing one color with another, using a Hue/Saturation adjustment layer and the Replace Color command. You apply the first method to change a bike helmet in your greeting card from red to yellow, and the second to change the color of the mountain biker's shirt.

1. **Select the** stretch **layer of** 08_ride.psd **in the Layers palette.**
   It should still be open from the previous tutorial. If it's not, reopen it from your ccproject folder.

2. **Hold the Alt key (Macintosh: Option key), click the Create New Fill or Adjustment Layer button at the bottom of the Layers palette, and choose Hue/Saturation.**
   This opens the New Layer dialog box.

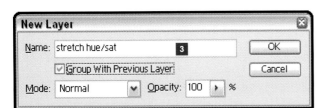

3. **In the New Layer dialog box, enter** stretch hue/sat **as the name of the new adjustment layer, select Group with Previous Layer, and click OK to open the Hue/Saturation dialog box.**
   This creates a Hue/Saturation adjustment layer that's grouped with the **stretch** layer so that the adjustment affects only the **stretch** layer, rather than all the layers beneath it.

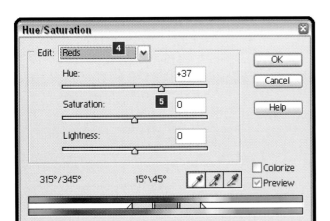

4. **In the Hue/Saturation dialog box, click in the Edit field and choose Reds.**
   This ensures that the hue change you make affects only red colors in the image.

5. **Drag the Hue slider to about +37 to change the reds in the image to yellows. Click OK.**
   You want to turn the bicycle and helmet yellow, but not other areas that contained red pixels, like the skin tones. In the next step, you fix that problem by blocking the effect from all but the desired areas of the **stretch** layer.

6. **Choose Edit→Fill to open the Fill dialog box, and set the Use field to Black. Click OK.**

   The selected layer mask on the **stretch hue/sat** layer fills with black. Black blocks the hue adjustment that you just made from the entire **stretch** layer. Recall that grouping an adjustment layer with a content layer applies the adjustment layer's mask to the content layer.

7. **Select the Brush tool in the toolbox. Press X to switch the Foreground Color to white.**

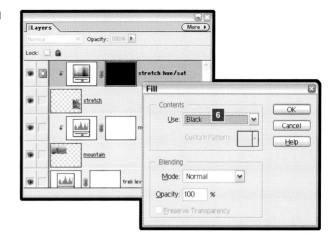

8. **Zoom in to about 300%, and paint over the helmet and bicycle parts in the document window to turn them yellow.**

   You're actually painting with white in the **stretch hue/sat** layer mask, which removes the blockage of the hue adjustment from the painted areas. You don't have to paint very carefully over the bicycle parts because nothing else in that area (other than the cap of the water bottle) was affected by the hue adjustment that you made to reds only.

9. **Choose File→Save. Leave** 08_ride.psd **open for the next steps.**

   You changed the hue of part of the stretch image in your greeting card with a Hue/Saturation adjustment layer limited by a layer mask. In the next steps you explore another way of changing hue—with the Replace Color command.

10. **Select the** mountain **layer in the Layers palette.**

11. **Select the Magnetic Lasso tool in the toolbox.**

12. **Click on the edge of the mountain biker's shirt in the top left of the greeting card. Move (you don't have to drag) the cursor around the shirt to select the shirt with the Magnetic Lasso tool.** There is quite of bit of edge contrast, so you have to click only a couple of times to set a point that the tool may not make for you.

<TIP>
If the Magnetic Lasso sets a point you don't like, press the Delete (Macintosh: Backspace) key on your keyboard and move (don't drag) the cursor back to the previous point. If you forgot how the Magnetic Lasso tool works, flip back to Session 5.

13. **Select the Add to Selection button in the Options bar, and make an additional selection around the orange label on the mountain biker's pants.**

<NOTE>
You can use the Replace Color command without a selection. But in this case, the shirt and logo are similar in color to the biker's skin color. So a selection is necessary to keep the color replacement from affecting the skin tones.

14. **Choose Enhance→Adjust Color→Replace Color.** The Replace Color dialog box opens.

15. **In the Replace Color dialog box, click the leftmost Eyedropper, and choose the Selection radio button.** Leave the other options at their defaults for now. Fuzziness determines the range of colors selected by the Eyedropper. Increase Fuzziness if the Eyedropper does not select enough of the orange area. Selection sets the dialog box to display a black and white mask of the areas that you select with the Eyedropper.

16. **Click on the orange shirt in the image.** Notice that the dialog box preview displays an area of white. This area represents the range of orange pixels that you just selected. You add to this area in the next step.

17. **Select the middle Eyedropper with the plus symbol in the Replace Color dialog box. Click on other shades in the mountain biker's shirt and in the logo on his pants to expand the area selected.**

<NOTE>

If you select an area that you do not want to replace, select the Eyedropper with the minus symbol and, in the dialog box preview, click on the unwanted area to delete it from the selection.

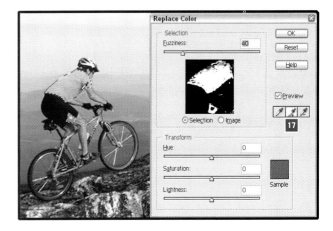

18. **After you're satisfied with your selection, drag the Hue slider in the dialog box to the right to about +22 and click OK.**

The dialog box closes, and the color of the selected areas changes from orange to yellow.

<NOTE>

You can also change the saturation and lightness of selected areas in the Replace Color dialog box.

<NOTE>

The Replace Color command accomplishes the same thing as a Hue/Saturation adjustment. However, unlike a Hue/Saturation adjustment layer, the Replace Color command makes permanent, noneditable changes to the original image pixels. This factor may impact your choice of features when you work on your own images.

19. **Choose Select→Deselect to delete the selection.**

20. **Choose File→Save As, rename the file** 08_ride_end.psd, **and save it with its final changes to your ccproject folder.**

In this tutorial you changed the color of items in your greeting card using a Hue/Saturation adjustment layer with layer mask, and the Replace Color feature. The greeting card for this session is now complete, and you've learned about the many ways to correct color photographs in Photoshop Elements 2!

» Session Review

This session covered techniques for correcting color to add to the photo retouching workflow that you initiated in the preceding session. First, you learned the preferred way to correct color in a color photograph—manually using a Levels adjustment layer. You applied some auto color corrections using the Auto Color Correction command and the Color Cast command. You used some special features—including the Adjust Backlighting command, the Fill Flash command, and the Red Eye Brush tool—to automatically correct lighting problems. You adjusted color saturation with a Hue/Saturation adjustment layer. And you replaced color in two ways—with a Hue/Saturation adjustment layer and the Replace Color command. All of this work resulted in a collage of corrected color photographs for another greeting card.

1. What does a Threshold view show? (See Tutorial: Correcting Color with Levels.)

2. What is the function of the Black and White Eyedroppers in the Levels dialog box? (See Tutorial: Correcting Color with Levels.)

3. What is the function of the Gray Eyedropper in the Levels dialog box? (See Tutorial: Correcting Color with Levels.)

4. Name one advantage of correcting color with a Levels adjustment layer over an automatic method. (See Tutorial: Correcting Color with the Auto Color Correction Command.)

5. Why is Auto Levels not a preferred method of correcting color? (See Tutorial: Correcting Color with the Auto Color Correction Command.)

6. How do you correct a color cast with the Color Cast command? (See Tutorial: Correcting Color Cast with the Color Cast Command.)

7. Can you apply more than one color correction method to the same photograph? (See Tutorial: Correcting Color Cast with the Color Cast Command.)

8. Describe two limitations that make the Color Variations feature difficult to use. (See Tutorial: Applying Color Variations.)

9. Describe a lighting problem that the Adjust Backlighting command is designed to correct. (See Tutorial: Adjusting Backlighting.)

10. Describe a lighting problem that the Fill Flash command can correct. (See Tutorial: Remedying Flash Problems.)

11. What causes a subject to have red eye in a color photograph? (See Tutorial: Remedying Flash Problems.)

12. Which sampling method is best to use with the Red Eye brush tool? (See Tutorial: Remedying Flash Problems.)

13. What feature would you use to increase the saturation in a photograph? (See Tutorial: Adjusting Color Saturation.)

14. Name two ways to replace one color with another. (See Tutorial: Replacing Color.)

Part V

Using Text and Shapes

Adding Shapes

Session Introduction

The shape tools in Photoshop Elements 2 offer an easy way to add graphic elements to your artwork. Shape outlines are vector-based, which means that shapes have crisp edges and can be resized at will. Shapes are useful for making logos, icons, and web page buttons, and for embellishing other artwork. In this session, you use Shape tools to create both geometric shapes and pictorial custom shapes in a project greeting card that contains graphic shapes. You learn how to move and transform shapes, and join shapes into unique combinations. You'll quickly realize that the Shape tools can make you look like a seasoned artist even if drawing by hand is not your forte.

TOOLS YOU'LL USE
Ellipse tool, Custom Shape tool, shape layers, Move tool

CD-ROM FILES NEEDED
09_snow.psd, 09_snow_end.psd

TIME REQUIRED
40 minutes

Discussion

The Anatomy of a Shape

The images you worked with in previous sessions were created entirely from pixels. Pixels are ideal for displaying continuous tone photographs and artwork with soft edges. However, as you learned in Session 1, pixel-based art is resolution-dependent, so increasing its size usually degrades its appearance.

The shape tools—the Rectangle, Rounded Rectangle, Ellipse, Polygon, Line, and Custom Shape—create another kind of art, called a shape, that can be resized up or down without degradation. This makes shapes ideal for creating logos, Web graphics, and other objects that you may want to use at different sizes. Shapes also have crisp edges when printed on a postscript printer, making them useful for creating commerical graphics. These qualities are a result of the vector-based component of shapes.

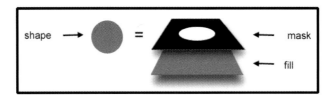

Shapes are hybrid objects that consist of vector outlines (which are generated by mathematical instructions) as well as pixels. Drawing with any of the shape tools creates a special shape layer made up of a fill of colored pixels covered by a grayscale mask. The white areas of the mask reveal the color fill below; the black areas of the mask hide the color fill. The boundary between the white and black areas of the mask is a vector outline of the shape. This vector outline, because it is mathematically generated, is sharp-edged and can be resized and reshaped at will. Transforming a shape does not affect any pixels; it simply modifies the vector outline so that more or fewer of the underlying pixels show through the mask.

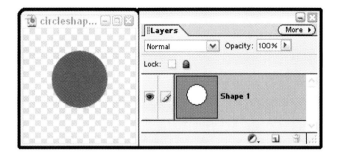

If you look closely at the thumbnail icon on a shape layer in the Layers palette, you can see a representation of the mask and the vector outline of the shape. The white area inside the outline reveals the shape color in the image. The black area outside the outline masks the shape color. Apart from its hybrid nature, a shape layer is similar to any other layer. It can be reordered, linked, and locked. Its opacity and blending mode can be changed. And it can be treated with a Layer Style.

All this flexibility, along with the ease of creating shapes, make the Shape tools among the most useful features in Photoshop Elements 2.

Tutorial
» Creating Geometric Shapes

Making shapes in geometric forms is a snap, using the geometric shape tools (the Ellipse tool, Rectangle tool, Rounded Rectangle tool, Polygon tool, and Line tool). In this tutorial, you learn how easy it is to create a geometric shape that fills automatically with a color and layer style of your choice. You're also introduced to shape geometry options that you can use to draw specific geometric shapes, like perfect circles, stars, and arrowheads.

1. **Open** 09_snow.psd **from the Tutorial Files→Session 09 folder on your hard drive.**

2. **Prepare your workspace by choosing Window→Reset Palette Locations, closing the Hints and How To palettes, and choosing Reset All Tools from the menu that appears when you click the Tool icon on the far left of the Options bar.**

3. **Click the Layers tab in the Palette Well on the Shortcuts bar, and drag the Layers palette out of the Palette Well so that it remains open on your desktop.**

4. **Select the** snowboarder **layer in the Layers palette.**
   This ensures that the next layer you create is located directly above the **snowboarder** layer.

5. **Click and hold the Rectangle tool, or whichever shape tool is currently displayed in your toolbox, to display a flyout menu of shape tools. Choose the Ellipse tool from the flyout menu.**
   A quick way to locate a particular shape tool is to click Shift+U to cycle through the shape tools until you see the one you want.

<NOTE>
Don't confuse the Ellipse tool, which creates shapes, with the Elliptical Marquee tool, which draws selections. You can make an ellipse by drawing a selection with the Elliptical Marquee tool and filling or stroking that selection with color. However, the result is static, pixel-based artwork, rather than a flexible shape.

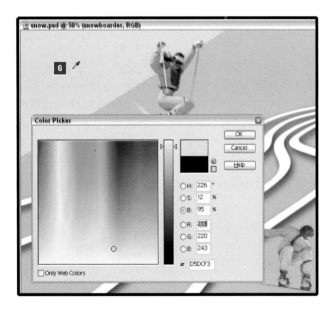

6. **Click in the Color field in the Options bar to open the Color Picker. Move over the open image to change the cursor to an Eyedropper, and click on the light blue background at the top left of the image. Click OK to close the Color Picker.**
   This sets the Color field in the Ellipse tool Options bar to light blue, determining the color that automatically fills the shape you draw.

<TIP>
To select a shape color other than one in the image, click in the Color field on the Options bar to open the Color Picker, click on the desired color in the large color field on the left side of the Color Picker, and click OK.

<TIP>
A shortcut for selecting a shape color from an open image is to click and hold the Alt (Macintosh: Option) key while a shape tool is selected to temporarily change the cursor to an eyedropper. Click in any open image to select the color under the cursor.

7. **Click in the Style field on the Options bar to open the Style picker.**

   The Style picker displays all the styles in the currently loaded style set.

8. **Click the right-facing arrow on the Style Picker to open its palette menu, and choose Drop Shadows.**

   This replaces the current style set with the Drop Shadows style set, one of several style sets that ship with Photoshop Elements 2.

9. **Click on the Low drop shadow style in the Style Picker.**

   This selects the layer style that automatically applies to the shape you draw.

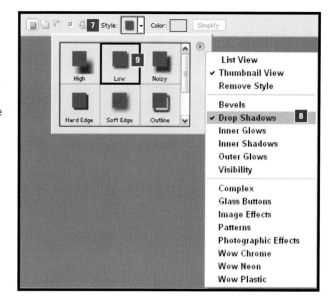

10. **Click in the image near the back end of the skis, and drag down and to the right to draw an ellipse shape. The shape automatically fills with the color and layer style that you selected in the Options bar.**

    The Ellipse tool begins drawing from an outside edge, making it difficult to precisely position and scale the shape as you draw. Don't worry if your shape doesn't match the illustration exactly. You move and rescale this shape later in this session.

    < T I P >

    You can move a shape as you draw it by keeping your mouse depressed while pressing the spacebar on your keyboard and dragging to move the shape. With the mouse still depressed, release the spacebar to continue drawing the shape.

    < N O T E >

    Notice a new layer in the Layers palette, labeled **Shape 1**, which contains the shape you just drew. This is a special shape layer, made up of a color fill and a mask with a vector outline, as described in the earlier Discussion on the anatomy of a shape layer. The default behavior of all shape tools is to create a new shape layer for each shape you draw.

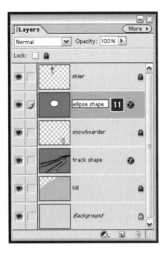

11. **Double-click directly on the** Shape 1 **layer name in the Layers palette, and type** ellipse shape **to give this layer a more meaningful name.**

12. **The dark line around the shape represents the vector outline of the shape.**

    To make the outline invisible, so that it doesn't interfere with your view of the shape, press the Enter (Macintosh: Return) key on your keyboard.

13. **Click the Geometry options arrow just to the right of the shape icons on the Options bar to open the Ellipse Options palette.**

14. **In the Ellipse Options palette, select Circle (draw diameter or radius) to constrain the Ellipse tool so that it draws a perfect circle rather than an ellipse shape.**

    Another way to constrain the Ellipse tool to a circle is to hold the Shift key while you draw. This technique can also be used to constrain the Rectangle and Rounded Rectangle tools so that they draw squares.

15. **Still in the Ellipse Options palette, select From Center to draw the circle from the center out.**

    You'll probably find it easier to draw a circle from the center out than to draw it starting from an edge as you did for the ellipse shape.

16. **Click in the vicinity of the skier's belt in the image, and drag out from that center point to create a shape that's automatically constrained to a circle.**

    Don't worry about precisely matching the circle in the illustration. You have a chance to resize and reposition the circle later in this session.

<CAUTION>

The circle you just drew has the same color and layer style as the ellipse you drew earlier because the Options bar is sticky—it retains the settings last used. Sometimes this can lead to unanticipated results. If you ever wonder why all your shapes have a drop shadow, for example, the first place to check is the Options bar, which probably has settings left over from a previous shape.

17. **Click on the** Shape 1 **label on the new shape layer in the Layers palette, and rename the layer** circle shape.

18. **Select File→Save as. In the Save As dialog box, make sure that Format is set to Photoshop and that a check mark appears next to Save→Layers. Navigate to your ccproject folder, and click Save to save** 09_snow.psd **with the changes you made in this tutorial. Leave the file open for the next tutorial.**

    In this tutorial you were introduced to shapes and shape layers in the course of creating two geometric shapes—an ellipse and a circle—in the greeting card you're creating in this session.

<TIP>

To retain the vector information in a shape, save it in PSD, Photoshop PDF, or Photoshop EPS format before flattening the file. Keep in mind that if you reopen a Photoshop EPS file in Photoshop Elements 2, the vector information is converted to pixels (rasterized).

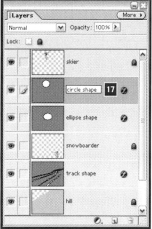

Shape Geometry Options

Each of the shape tools has specific Geometry options. Some options are common to a number of tools, like the Fixed Size setting in the Ellipse, Rectangle, Rounded Rectangle, and Custom Shape tool Geometry options palettes. You can use some unique options to draw specialty shapes. For example, the Polygon Options palette has settings for creating a star and controlling

its shape, with the number of points on the star determined by the Sides setting in the tool's Options bar. The Rounded Rectangle tool, which is great for making buttons for the Web, includes a Radius field in its Options bar that controls the roundness of a rectangle's corners. And the Line tool has an Arrowheads palette that has settings for creating assorted arrowheads.

Tutorial
» Creating Custom Shapes

Custom shapes are just like geometric shapes except that custom shapes are pictorial. Photoshop Elements 2 ships with more than 300 custom shapes, including animals, fruits, musical notes, signs, symbols, and more. In this tutorial, you learn how to create custom shapes, switch between sets of custom shapes, and load custom shape sets that you might acquire from other sources all to enhance the graphic look of this greeting card.

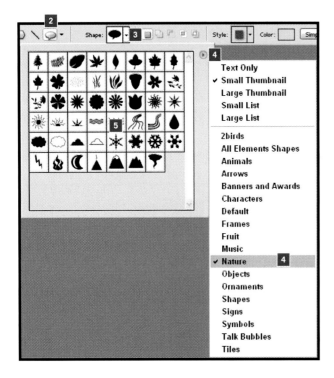

1. **With 09_snow.psd still open from the previous tutorial, check that the following settings are as you left them at the end of the last tutorial:**

   » The **circle shape** layer should be selected in the Layers palette.

   » The Ellipse tool should be selected in the toolbox.

   » The Color field in the Options bar should be set to light blue.

   » The Style field in the Options bar should be set to Low drop shadow.

<NOTE>

If you closed 09_snow.psd at the end of the previous tutorial, navigate to your ccproject folder, and open 09_snow.psd from there.

2. **Click on the Custom Shape tool icon on the Options bar.**
   This is a quick way of switching between tools in a tool group. Alternatively, you could select the Custom Shape tool from the flyout menu of shape tools in the toolbox.

3. **Click on the down-facing arrow on the Shape field in the Options bar to open the Custom Shape picker.**
   The Custom Shape picker displays all the custom shapes in the currently loaded set of custom shapes.

4. **Click the right-facing arrow on the Custom Shape picker to display its palette menu, and choose Nature.**
   This replaces the current shapes in the Custom Shape picker with a set of Nature shapes that ships with Photoshop Elements 2.

5. **Click on the Snowflake 1 thumbnail in the Custom Shape picker to select that custom shape.**
   The selected shape appears in the Shape field on the Options bar.

<NOTE>

The palette menu on the Custom Shape picker has two parts. The items at the top offer different ways of viewing available shapes in the picker—text only, small thumbnail, large thumbnail, small list (text and icon), large list. The items at the bottom are available sets of custom shapes.

<TIP>

Hold your mouse over any thumbnail in the Custom Shape picker to reveal the name of that custom shape.

6. **Click in any blank space on the Options bar to close the Custom Shape picker.**

<NOTE>

The Custom Shape tool, like the geometric shape tools, offers options on the Options bar and in a Geometry options palette. Leave all options as they are for now.

7. **Click and drag in the light blue area at the top left of the image to create a light blue snowflake shape with a drop shadow style similar to that in the illustration.**
   You can scale the size and proportions of a custom shape as you draw, creating many variations on a single custom shape.

8. **Double-click on the Shape 1 label on the new shape layer in the Layers palette, and rename this layer** snowflake shape.

<NOTE>

When you create a custom or geometric shape, it is automatically located on its own new shape layer. If you add lots of shapes to an image (for example, lots of little snowflakes), you can end up with a Layers palette cluttered with individual layers. To avoid this, you can place multiple custom and/or geometric shapes on one shape layer.

9. **Click on the Add to Shape Area button in the Options palette.**
   Make sure that the **snowflake shape** layer is still selected in the Layers palette.

<CAUTION>

The Add to Shape Area button is grayed out on the Options bar if you select a layer other than a shape layer.

10. **Click and drag in the top left of the image to create a second, smaller snowflake on the** snowflake shape **layer.**

    If you look closely at the thumbnail on the snowflake layer, you see the outlines of two snowflake shapes.

11. **Choose File→Save to resave** 09_snow.psd **in your ccproject folder. Leave the file open for the next tutorial.**

    You now have two variations of a star custom shape in your greeting card.

A Treasure Trove of Custom Shapes

You are not limited to using the 300+ custom shapes that ship with Photoshop Elements 2. The Web is a treasure trove of down-loadable homemade custom shapes. Try entering "Photoshop custom shapes" in a search engine to find sites that offer shapes. Most homemade custom shapes are made in and intended for use in the complete version of Photoshop, because that program has a feature for saving shapes that is not available in Photohop Elements 2. However, many custom shapes made for Photoshop work fine in Photoshop Elements 2.

One source for homemade custom shapes (as well as other items like brushes and patterns) is the Adobe Studio Exchange (http://share.studio.adobe.com). Register at the site, and follow directions there to locate and download Photoshop custom shapes in archived (.zip or .sit) format. If the archived files don't automatically expand on your hard drive, use a utility like Winzip (Macintosh: Aladdin Stufflt Expander). The expanded custom shape files should have a .csh extension.

To install a custom shape, move a .csh file into the Custom Shapes folder buried in the application folder on your hard drive.

The typical path is C:→Program Files→Adobe→Photoshop Elements 2→Presets→Custom Shapes (Macintosh: Applications→Adobe Photoshop Elements 2→Presets→Custom Shapes). Restart Photoshop Elements 2 after installing a custom shape file.

To use your new custom shapes, select the Custom Shape tool. Click the arrow on the Shape field in the Options bar to open the Custom Shape picker. Click the arrow at the top right of the Custom Shape picker to open the palette menu. The newly installed custom shape set should appear in that menu. Select that set to view its contents in the Custom Shape picker. Select one of the new shapes in the Custom Shape picker and click and drag in an image to create a custom shape.

However: Downloading and using homemade files can be a risky business. Any resulting damage is not the responsibility of the author or publishers of this book. It is strongly suggested that you download only from reputable sources and comply with all copy-rights and use restrictions.

Tutorial
» Moving and Transforming Shapes

In this tutorial, you learn how to move and transform shapes. You use the Move tool to move and scale the contents of shape layers, the Shape Selection tool to move individual shapes, and a Transform Shape command to distort a shape. In the process, you resize and change the form of several of the custom shapes in this greeting card.

1. **With** 09_snow.psd **still open from the previous tutorial, select the Move tool in the toolbox.**
   If 09_snow.psd is not open, reopen it from your ccproject folder.

2. **In the Options bar, deselect Auto Select Layer and make sure that Show Bounding Box is selected.**
   Resetting all tools, as you did at the beginning of this session, reactivated the Auto Select Layer option even if you turned it off in the past. Deselecting the Auto Select Layer option whenever you see it activated is a good idea, because it can be more hindrance than help.

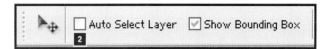

3. **Select the** ellipse shape **layer in the Layers palette.**
   A bounding box with anchor points appears around the ellipse shape in the image. Anchor points can be moved to scale and otherwise transform a shape.

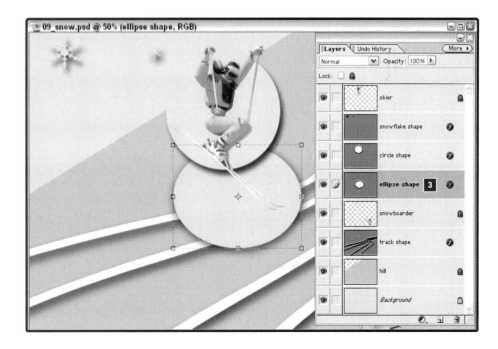

4. **If your ellipse shape is not positioned like the one in the illustration, click inside its bounding box and drag the shape into position.**
   Alternatively, use the arrow keys on your keyboard to nudge the shape into position one pixel at a time. Hold the Shift key to nudge the shape ten pixels at a time.

5. **If your ellipse shape is not shaped just like the one in the illustration, click on a corner anchor point of the bounding box and drag to scale the ellipse shape until it resembles the illustration.**

6. **Click the large check mark on the Options bar to accept the transformation.**
   Until you accept the transformation, you won't be able to use certain other features. Other ways to accept a transformation include clicking on a different layer in the Layers palette or pressing the Enter (Macintosh: Return) key on the keyboard.

Scaling by Numbers

In your own work, you'll most often rescale a shape by visual reference, as in Step 5. However, Photoshop Elements 2 does offer more precise techniques. For example, to precisely replicate this ellipse shape, click on an edge of its bounding box to change the Options bar so that it displays the transform options. Enter 1.75 in in the Width field and 1.5 in in the Height field in the Options bar. (It's important that you specify inches [in], because these fields default to percent as the unit of measurement.)

Alternatively, you can use the Info palette as a scaling guide. Choose Window→Info to open the Info palette. (If the Info palette opens in the Palette Well, drag it into your work area so it stays open.) As you scale the ellipse shape, keep your eye on the bottom-right quadrant of the Info palette and try to approximate these dimensions: W: 1.750 and H: 1.500.

7. **Repeat Steps 3 through 6 on the** circle shape **layer if the size or position of your circle shape differs from the illustration.**
   Scaling can change the proportions as well as the size of a shape. Hold the Shift key as you drag to resize the circle shape while maintaining its proportions. If you're scaling by numbers, as described in the Scaling by Numbers sidebar, set both the width and height of the circle to **1.6 in.**

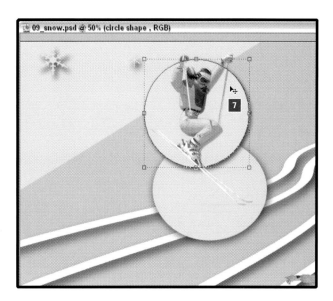

<NOTE>

Moving and transforming shapes can be accomplished with either the Move tool or the Shape Selection tool. The difference is that the Move tool affects all the artwork on a layer, while the Shape Selection tool affects individual shapes even if they are located on the same layer. In most cases, these tools are interchangeable; but the Shape Selection tool is the tool to use if you have multiple custom or geometric shapes on a single shape layer and you want to move or transform the shapes independently of one another.

8. **Click on the Shape Selection tool icon (the black arrow) in the Options bar to select that tool.**
   Alternatively, choose the Shape Selection tool from the flyout menu of shape tools in the toolbox.

9. **Double-click on one of the snowflake shapes in the image to display a bounding box around that snowflake only.**

   The selected snowflake is one of two custom shapes that you added to the same shape layer in the previous tutorial.

10. **Click inside the bounding box to move the selected snowflake shape to the right to match the illustration.**

    Notice that the other snowflake shape on the same shape layer is not affected. Similarly, you can transform an individual shape. For example, to scale one snowflake shape without affecting the other shape on the same layer, you would click and drag a point on the selected snowflake's bounding box.

<TIP>

You can rotate or skew a shape from the bounding box, in addition to scaling it. To rotate a shape, move your cursor outside the bounding box until it changes to a double-pointed arrow; then click and drag. To skew a shape, click on the edge of the bounding box to display transform options in the Options bar, select the Skew icon in the Options bar, then click on a corner anchor point and drag either horizontally or vertically.

<NOTE>

More complex transformations require use of transform commands accessed from the image menu on the menu bar. These include changing the perspective of a shape and distorting a shape (slanting it vertically and horizontally).

11. **Select the Shape Selection tool in the toolbox.**

12. **Double-click on the white ski tracks shape in the image to activate a bounding box around that shape.**

    You can't see all the anchor points around this bounding box because this shape is so big. The next step remedies this problem.

<NOTE>

The ski tracks shape was created for you using the River 1 custom shape from the Nature set of custom shapes.

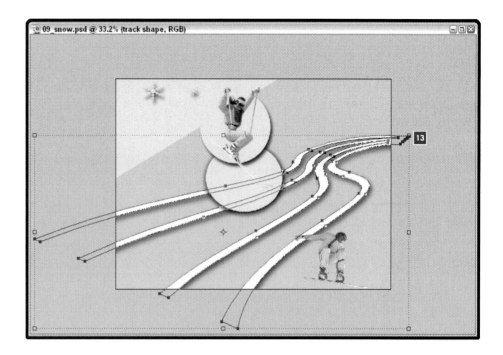

13. **Press Ctrl+0 [zero] (Macintosh: ⌘+0) on the keyboard.**

This useful shortcut zooms out and expands the document window just enough so that you can see all the anchor points of the bounding box in the gray area of the document window.

14. **Choose Image→Transform Shape→Distort from the menu bar.**

The Distort command allows you to slant an image vertically and horizontally at the same time.

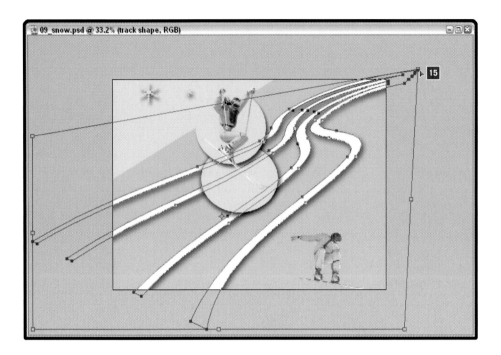

15. Click the anchor point at the top-right corner of the bounding box, and drag up and slightly to the right until the tracks look like those in the illustration.

16. Click the check mark on the Options bar to accept the transformation.

17. Choose File➔Save to save 09_snow.psd into your ccproject folder with these changes. Leave the file open for the next tutorial.

    In this tutorial you transformed the size and form of several custom shapes in this greeting card.

Tutorial

» Changing Shape Attributes

This tutorial covers several ways to change the appearance of shapes by changing attributes of the shape layer. You learn how easily you can modify the color, layer style, and even the basic content of a shape layer, changing the look of the geometric and custom shapes contained in your ski greeting card.

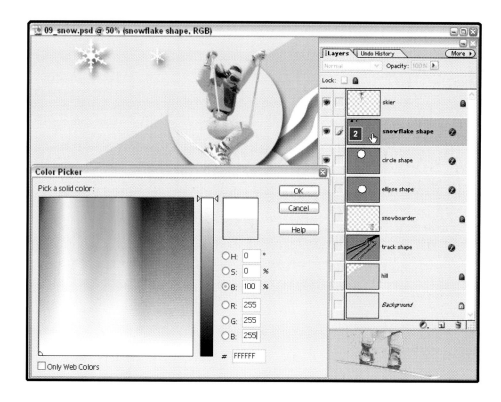

1. With 09_snow.psd **still open from the previous tutorial, double-click directly on the thumbnail on the** snowflake shape **layer to open the Color Picker.**

2. **In the Color Picker, choose white (R:** 255**, G:** 255**, B:** 255**) and click OK to change the color of both shapes on the** snowflake shape **layer.**
   This is a quick way to change shape color that you might not uncover on your own. You can't limit a color change to just one shape on a shape layer. Color affects all shapes on a shape layer because it's an attribute of the underlying fill on the shape layer.

< N O T E >

Shape layer styles are just like regular layer styles, except that they can be applied from a shape tool's Options bar. When a layer style is applied from the shape tool Options bar, its appearance is limited to its default settings. Typically, you want to modify those settings to suit your design.

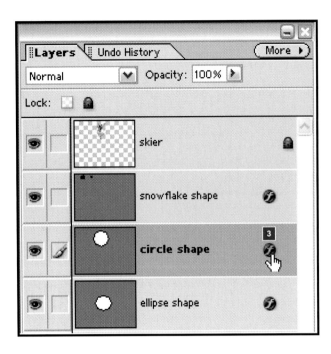

3. **Double-click the _f_ icon on the** circle shape **layer to open the Style Settings dialog box.**

   The _f_ icon identifies this layer as having a layer style.

<N O T E>

Each layer style has specific Style settings. The active fields in the Style Settings dialog box are the settings for the Low drop shadow style that you applied to the **circle shape** layer when you created the layer. The grayed out settings are relevant to other layer styles.

4. **In the Style Settings dialog box, click on the Shadow Distance slider and move it from its default setting to 9 px.**

   With the Preview box checked, you can see the shadow on the circle shape change in the image. This changes the appearance of the drop shadow on the circle shape, creating a separation between the top of the circle shape and the background of the image.

5. **Click OK.**

   The Style Settings dialog box closes and applies the setting.

<N O T E>

The sticky settings on the shape Options bar can result in a layer style intended for one shape automatically attaching itself to subsequent shape layers. In the next step, you learn how to delete an unwanted layer style from a shape layer.

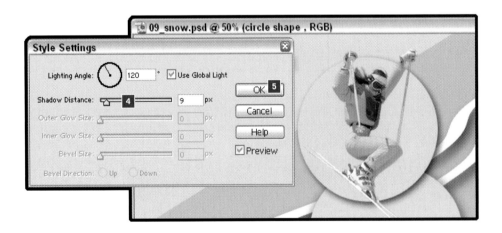

6. **Select the** snowflake shape **layer in the Layers palette.**
   When you created this layer, it automatically acquired a Low drop shadow layer style from a sticky Style setting.

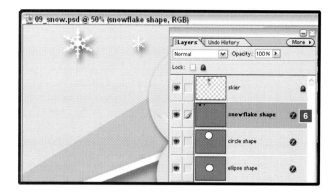

7. **Choose Layer→Layer Style→Clear Layer Style from the menu bar.**
   This removes the layer style from both shapes on this shape layer. This command is hard to find, so try to commit it to memory. Keep in mind that all shapes on a shape layer are affected by deleting or modifying a layer style.

< N O T E >

When you create a shape layer, its content consists of a solid color fill under a vector mask. You can change the appearance of a shape by changing the underlying content of the shape layer. In the steps that follow, you change the content of the **circle shape** layer from its initial solid color to a gradient.

8. **Press D on the keyboard to set the Foreground and Background Color boxes in the toolbox to their default colors—black and white.**
   This is a quick way to set the Background color to white for use in the gradient that you create.

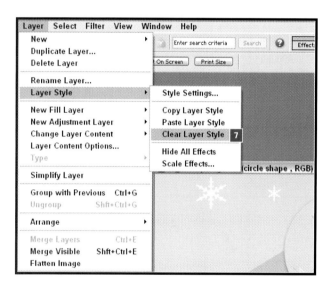

Changing Layer Content

The Change Layer Content command is a powerful creative tool. This feature uses the vector outlines on a shape layer as a mask to limit the area affected by fills (Solid Color, Gradient, and Pattern fills) and adjustments (Levels, Brightness/Contrast, Hue/Saturation, Gradient Map, Invert, Threshold, and Posterize adjustments). This offers many fresh ways to change the look of an image. For example, you could add a shape (perhaps a custom shape from the frame set) to a photographic image and turn the area under that shape to grayscale (by changing layer content to Hue/Saturation and lowering the Saturation control in the Hue/Saturation dialog box to 0), or to a photographic negative (by changing layer content to Invert), or to a graphic (by changing layer content to Posterize). Try applying various content changes to a shape to see the effects that are available.

9. **Select the Eyedropper tool in the toolbox. Click on the light blue background at the top left of the image.**
   This changes the Foreground Color box to light blue.

10. **Select the** circle shape **layer in the Layers palette.**

11. **Choose Layer➔Change Layer Content➔Gradient from the menu bar at the top of the screen.**
    This applies a gradient with default settings to the circle shape. It also opens the Gradient Fill dialog box, where you can make changes to the gradient.

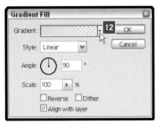

12. **In the Gradient Fill dialog box, click the down-facing arrow to the right of the Gradient field to open the Gradient Picker.**

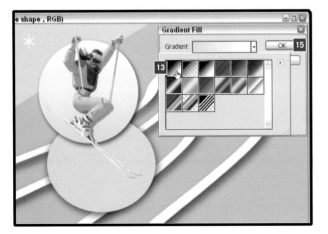

13. **Click on the first thumbnail in the Gradient Picker.**
    If you hold your cursor over this thumbnail, you can see that it's labeled Foreground to Background. This changes the gradient in the circle shape to a Foreground color to Background color (light blue to white) gradient.

14. **Click anywhere in the Gradient Fill dialog box to close the Gradient Picker.**

15. **Leave the other settings in the Gradient Fill dialog box at their defaults, and click OK to close the Gradient Fill dialog box.**
    The circle shape in your image fills with a light blue to white gradient.

16. **Choose File➔Save to resave** 09_snow.psd, **and leave the file open for the next tutorial.**
    In this tutorial you changed the style, content, and appearance of the shapes in your ski greeting card.

Tutorial
» Combining Shapes to Create a Unique Shape

You can combine any geometric or custom shapes to create a shape of your own. This feature opens endless possibilties for creating unique shapes. You get a taste of those possibilities in this tutorial in which you combine custom shapes to create a mini-mountain range in your greeting card.

1. With 09_snow.psd **still open from the previous tutorial, select the** *Background* **layer in the Layers palette.**
   This ensures that the shape layer you create is located just above this layer.

2. **Select the Custom Shape tool in the toolbox.**
   In the next steps, you create and position a custom shape, using skills you learned earlier in this session.

<NOTE>
You are not limited to using custom shapes to create a combination shape. Combinations can be made from geometric shapes (for example, you could combine circles and rectangles to create a realistic looking pipe). Or you can combine custom shapes with geometric shapes.

3. Click the arrow on the Shape field in the Options bar to open the Shape picker. Click the right-facing arrow on the Shape picker to display the palette menu. Select the Nature set of custom shapes if it's not already selected.

4. Click on the Mountain 1 shape in the Shape picker. Click anywhere in the Options bar to close the Shape picker.

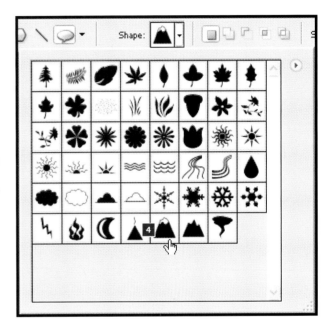

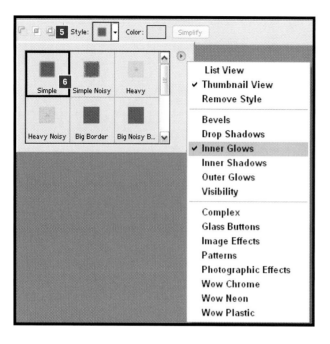

5. **Click the arrow on the Style field to open the Style picker. Click the right-facing arrow on the Style picker to open the palette menu. Choose Inner Glows from the palette menu to load the inner glows style set.**

   The Inner Glows style set offers variations on glow effects located inside the shape to which they are applied.

6. **Select the Simple style from the menu of inner glow styles displayed in the Style picker. Click anywhere on the Options bar to close the Style picker.**

   The Simple style is what it sounds like—a simple inner glow effect. You can get a sense of what each style looks like from the style thumbnails displayed in the Style picker.

7. **Hold the Alt (Macintosh: Option) key to temporarily change the cursor to the Eyedropper tool. Click on the light blue area at the top left of the image to make sure that the shape Color is set to light blue.**

8. **Click in the top left of the image, and drag to create a mountain shape with a Simple inner glow layer style.**

9. **Press the V key on your keyboard to select the Move tool.**

10. **Click inside the bounding box in the image and drag to move the mountain shape into position to match the illustration.**

    If necessary, click on the anchor points of the bounding box and drag to scale the mountain shape to match the illustration.

11. **Click on the Custom Shape tool in the toolbox to display shape options in the Options bar.**

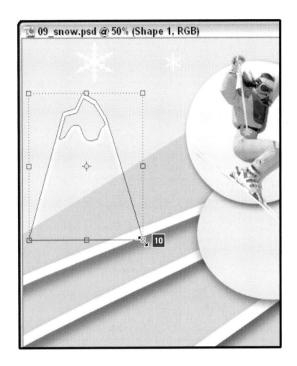

12. **Click on the Add to Shape Area button on the Options bar, and make sure that the** Shape 1 **layer is selected in the Layers palette.**

    This allows you to add another shape to the **Shape 1** layer that contains your first mountain shape. The next mountain shape you draw is added to that layer, rather than appearing on a shape layer of its own, which is the default behavior.

13. **Click in the top left of the image, and draw another mountain shape.**

    Notice that this shape is on the same **Shape 1** shape layer in the Layers palette as your first mountain shape.

    < N O T E >

    If for any reason your second mountain shape did not end up on the same layer as the first mountain shape, follow these steps to try again: Click the Step Backward button on the Shortcuts bar. Select the Shape Selection tool, and click on the first mountain shape in the image. Repeat Steps 11 through 13.

14. **Select the Shape Selection tool in the Options bar.**

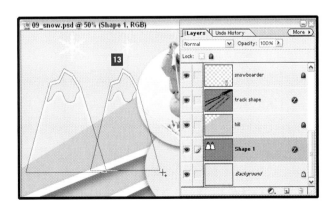

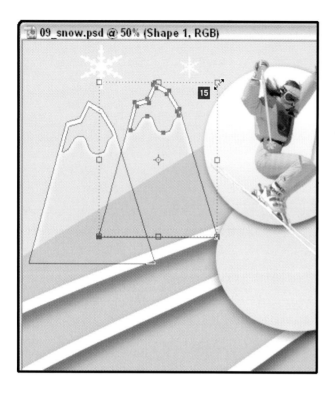

15. **Click on your new mountain shape in the document window to select that shape. Click inside the bounding box, and drag the shape into place to match the illustration. Click on the anchor points of the bounding box and drag to scale the image to match the illustration.**

    After you finish moving and scaling, the second mountain shape must overlap the first mountain shape as in the illustration.

16. **Click the large check mark on the Options bar to accept the transformation.**

    In the next steps, you combine your two mountain shapes, adding one shape area to the other.

Shape Area Options

In this tutorial, you combined two shapes by adding their shape areas together. Selecting one of the other Shape Area Options before clicking the Combine button on the Options bar creates different results:

» The Subtract from Shape Area deletes one shape from the other, leaving a hole in one shape.

» The Intersect Shape Area option deletes all but the overlapping areas of two shapes.

» The Exclude Overlapping Shape Areas combines two shapes, deleting their overlapping areas.

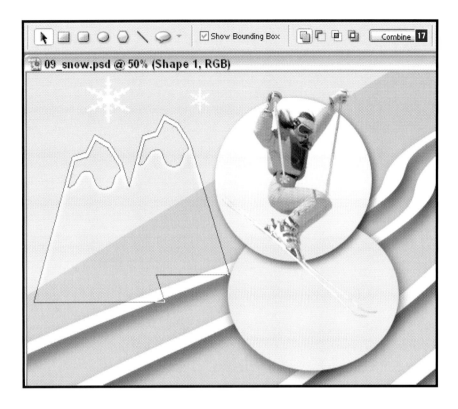

17. **Make sure that the Add to Shape Area box is still selected in the Options bar, and click the Combine button in the Options bar.**

    This adds the two mountain shapes together to create a mini-mountain range.

18. **Click on the Shape 1 label on the new shape layer, and rename the layer** mountain range**.**

    Don't bother adding the word "shape" to the layer name because in the next tutorial you change this layer to a regular layer so you can paint on it.

19. **Choose File→Save to resave** 09_snow.psd **with these changes. Leave the file open for the last tutorial in this session.**

    In this tutorial you combined two mountain shapes that shipped with the program to create a unique, customized shape—a small mountain range—that adds visual interest to this greeting card.

Tutorial
» Simplifying a Shape Layer

Certain actions, such as filtering, painting, and filling, cannot be performed on a shape layer because it is partially vector-based. In this tutorial, you simplify (rasterize) the mountain range shape layer in your greeting card, changing its contents to pixels, so that you can fill part of the layer with color, creating white mountain peaks.

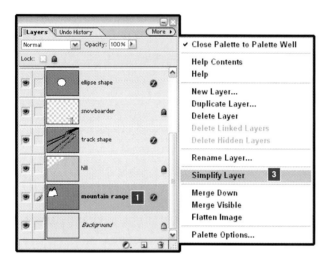

1. **With** 09_snow.psd **still open from the previous tutorial, select the** mountain range **shape layer in the Layers palette.**

2. **Click on the Edit menu on the menu bar, and notice that the Fill and Stroke functions are grayed out. Then click on the Filter menu to see that the filters are all grayed out.**

   These functions are unavailable because the selected layer is a shape layer, which is vector-based in part.

3. **Click the More button at the top right of the Layers palette, and choose Simplify Layer from the palette menu.**

   Alternatively, you can simplify a layer by choosing Layer→ Simplify Layer from the Layers palette or by selecting a shape tool with the layer selected and clicking the Simplify button on the Options bar.

The Effects of Simplifying a Layer

The outline that defines a shape is a vector-based, or mathematically generated, element, as you learned in the discussion at the beginning of this session. This vector component of a shape layer prevents you from using certain pixel-based editing tools—filters, fills, and paint—on a shape layer.

Simplifying (sometimes called rasterizing) a shape layer changes it from a partially vector-based layer to a regular layer composed entirely of pixels. The graphics on the layer are no longer shapes, but images built from pixels (sometimes called bitmapped images). Unlike shapes, these bitmapped images cannot be sized up or

reshaped at will without degrading their appearance. And they no longer retain their crisp edges for printing to a postscript printer.

However, after you take advantage of the ease of drawing with the shape tools, and you're satisfied with the size and position of your shapes, you may decide to simplify a shape layer for the purpose of using a filter, fill, or painting tool on the contents of the layer. Keep in mind that after a layer is simplified, you cannot re-vectorize its content. So you may want to duplicate your original shape layer before simplifying, turn off the visibility of the duplicate layer, and retain it in the file as an invisible backup layer.

4. **Select the Magic Wand tool in the toolbox. Click inside the snow-cap of one mountain to select that area. Shift+click inside the snowcap of the second mountain to add that area to the selection.**

5. **Choose Edit→Fill to open the Fill dialog box. Click on the Use field, choose White from the menu, and then click OK.**

The dialog box closes, and the snowcaps fill with white. This action was not possible until you simplified the mountain range layer.

6. **Choose File→Save As. In the Save As dialog box, rename the file 09_snow_end.psd. Make sure that Format is set to Photoshop and Layers is checked, and click Save to save the file to your ccproject folder.**

You continue with this same file in the next session on creating and editing text.

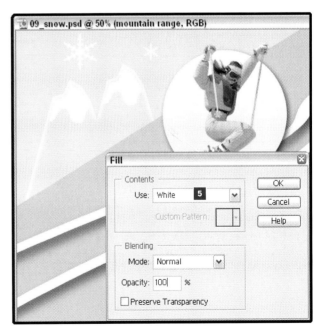

» Session Review

This session covered shapes and shape layers. You learned about the nature of a shape layer, which contains vector-based and pixel-based components. You created geometric shapes and custom shapes in your ski greeting card. You learned how to move and transform shapes layers with the Move tool and individual shapes with the Shape Selection tool. You changed the color of shapes, modified layer styles on shape layers, and changed layer content. You learned how to combine shapes into one-of-a-kind shapes and how to simplify shape layers in order to apply pixel-based editing features. The shapes you created in this greeting card create a unique backdrop for the text you add to this card in the next session.

1. Name two special qualities of shapes. (See Discussion: The Anatomy of a Shape.)

2. Describe the vector component of a shape layer. (See Discussion: The Anatomy of a Shape.)

3. Name three shapes that you can create with the geometric shape tools. (See Tutorial: Creating Geometric Shapes.)

4. Explain the difference between the Ellipse tool and the Elliptical Marquee tool. (See Tutorial: Creating Geometric Shapes.)

5. When you draw a shape, with what does the shape automatically fill? (See Tutorial: Creating Geometric Shapes.)

6. Name two ways to constrain an ellipse shape to a circle. (See Tutorial: Creating Geometric Shapes.)

7. What's the only way in which a custom shape differs from a geometric shape? (See Tutorial: Creating Custom Shapes.)

8. When you create more than one shape, by default do both shapes appear on the same shape layer or do they appear on separate shape layers? (See Tutorial: Creating Custom Shapes.)

9. What feature do you use to create multiple shapes on the same shape layer? (See Tutorial: Creating Custom Shapes.)

10. What is the difference between the way the Move tool and the Shape Selection tool work to move and transform shapes? (See Tutorial: Moving and Transforming Shapes.)

11. Name one kind of transformation that requires you to use a transform shape command. (See Tutorial: Moving and Transforming Shapes.)

12. Explain how to change the color of a shape. (See Tutorial: Changing Shape Attributes.)

13. How do you remove a layer style from a shape? (See Tutorial: Changing Shape Attributes.)

14. What does the Change Layer Content command do? (See Tutorial: Changing Shape Attributes.)

15. Name two ways that you can combine shapes using Shape Area Options. (See Tutorial: Combining Shapes to Create a Unique Shape.)

16. Name three editing actions that you can't perform on a shape layer. (See Tutorial: Simplifying a Shape Layer.)

17. When you simplify a layer, what is the resulting layer composed of? (See Tutorial: Simplifying a Shape Layer.)

Session 10

Creating and Editing Text

Session Introduction

The type features in Photoshop Elements 2 are easy to use. Although they're not designed to handle long paragraphs of text, they're ideal for embellishing an image with short strings of text, like photo captions, copyrights, headlines, or decorative type elements. In this session, you create vector-based type on type layers. You set the font, size, color, and other attributes of type, and you add type to a document in horizontal and vertical formats. Type remains editable in Photoshop Elements 2, which you see as you make changes to text. Although the program doesn't have extensive formatting controls, you can work around this by formatting manually as you do in the tutorial on kerning by hand. You also learn some special techniques for working with text—warping the shape of text, displaying images inside text, and simplifying type in order to apply pixel-based effects like filters. You apply what you learn about text to the winter sports greeting card you started in the preceding session. The combination of shapes created there and text effects added in this session creates a card with a clean graphic appearance that distinguishes it from the photo-based cards you make in other sessions.

TOOLS YOU'LL USE
Horizontal Type tool, Vertical Type tool

CD-ROM FILES NEEDED
10_snow.psd, 10_snow_end.psd

TIME REQUIRED
30 minutes

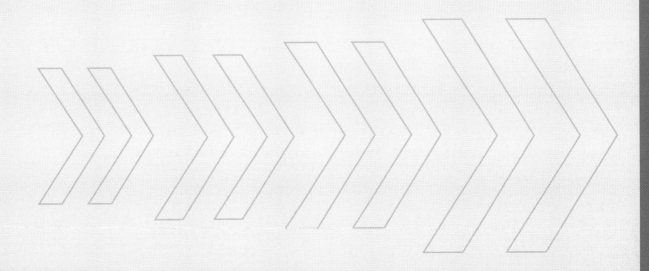

Tutorial
» Creating Horizontal Text

This tutorial walks you through the easy process of creating horizontal text on an editable type layer. You select a type tool, choose type attributes (font family, font style, font size, text color, and aliasing) in the Options bar, and enter text directly into the document window. The resulting copy is the first of several text treatments you add to the winter sports greeting card you created in the preceding session on shapes.

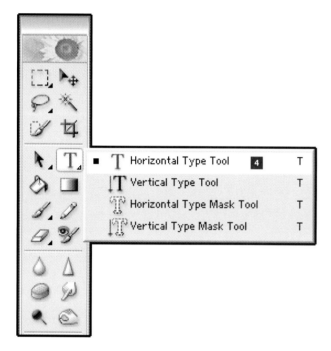

1. **Make sure that you are working with the file you saved to your ccproject folder at the end of the last session,** 09_snow_end.psd.
   Alternatively, if you prefer using a fresh file, open the iteration file 10_snow.psd from the Tutorial Files→Session 10 folder on your hard drive.

2. **Click the tool icon on the far left of the Options bar, and choose Reset All Tools.**

3. **Select the** skier **layer at the top of the Layer stack in the Layers palette.**
   This ensures that the type layers you create are located above that layer.

4. **Select the Horizontal Type tool in the toolbox.**
   If a different type tool is showing in your toolbox, click on that tool icon and choose the Horizontal Type tool from the flyout menu.

5. **In the Options bar, click the arrow to the right of the Font Family field to display a list of available fonts. Choose Courier New.**
   This sets the typeface of the text you're about to create. Many typefaces come with built-in styles, which you choose in the next step.

6. **Click the arrow to the right of the Font Style field, and choose Bold from the menu.**
   Font Styles are variations (for example, italic, bold, oblique, condensed) that are built into particular fonts.

< T I P >

If a particular font doesn't have a built-in bold or italic style, you can simulate that style by selecting the Faux Bold button or the Faux Italic button on the Options bar.

< T I P >

Another way to select a Font Family or Font Style is to start to type its name into the corresponding field. As you type, the program displays the closest match in the field.

7. **Click the arrow to the right of the Font Size field in the Options bar, and choose 12 pt from the menu.**

   Alternatively, you can type a point size into the Font Size field.

8. **Click inside the Text Color field in the Options bar to open the Color Picker, choose white (R:** 255, **G:** 255, **B:** 255), **and click OK to set the type color to white.**

   Another way to set the initial color of type is to change the contents of the Foreground Color box in the toolbox using the Color Picker or the Eyedropper tool (or by pressing D followed by X on your keyboard for white). The Text Color field in the Options bar changes automatically to match the Foreground color.

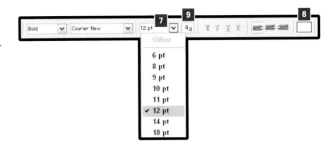

<NOTE>

All the type on a type layer starts out the same color, font, and size. Changes can be made to some or all of that type after it's created.

9. **Leave the Anti-aliased button on the Options bar selected, which is the default behavior.**

   This ensures that the edges of the type gradually blend into the background color when viewed on screen or printed to an inkjet printer.

<NOTE>

The default unit of measurement for type is points. If you type a different unit of measurement (px, pica, in, cm, or mm) into the Font Size dialog box and press Enter (Macintosh: Return), font size is automatically recalculated in points. If you want to change this behavior, go to Edit→Preferences→Units & Rulers (Macintosh: Photoshop Elements→Preferences→Units & Rulers) and change the unit of measurement in the Type field.

<NOTE>

Anti-aliased and aliased were explained in Session 5.

<TIP>

When you create type for the Web or other on-screen viewing, keep in mind that small type often looks blurry on screen if it has anti-aliased edges. That's because the gradual transitions at the edges of anti-aliased characters appear to blend into one another. The solution is to deselect the Anti-aliased button. This aliases the type, giving it stair-stepped edges that can make small type easier to read on screen.

Adding Fonts

You can add to the fonts available in Photoshop Elements 2 by installing new fonts into your operating system. To install a font into Windows XP, click the Start button at the bottom left of your monitor and choose Control Panel→Fonts. Choose File→Install New Font from the menu bar at the top of the Fonts window to open the Add Fonts dialog box. In the Add Fonts dialog box, navigate to the directory that contains the font to be installed and select the font from the font list. (If you want to install all the listed fonts, choose Select All. If you want to install multiple fonts, Ctrl+click their names in the font list.) Click OK to install the selected

font(s). Click the red button on the top right of the Fonts window to close that window. (To install a font in a Macintosh OS X operating system, drag the font to the Library→Fonts folder to make it available to all users. If you want the font to be available to you only, drag it to the Users→[your username]→Library→Fonts folder.)

Launch or restart Photoshop Elements 2. In Photoshop Elements 2, select a type tool and click on the arrow to the right of the Font Family field in the Options bar to open the font menu. The new font should appear in the font menu.

10. **Click on the right side of the document window. The cursor changes to an I-beam. Type the word** white.

The word white appears in the image with the attributes you set in the Options bar.

11. **Click the big check mark at the right of the Options bar to commit (confirm) your type entry.**

You can commit type in a number of other ways: click on another layer, select another tool, or just click in the image.

<CAUTION>

Each time you enter or edit type, you have to commit the type or you are prevented from performing other operations. If you find that a command is unavailable or a shortcut doesn't work, odds are good that you forgot to commit a type layer. You'll know that's the case if you see the big check mark on the type tool Options bar. As soon as you click that check mark, it disappears from the Options bar and the program works as normal.

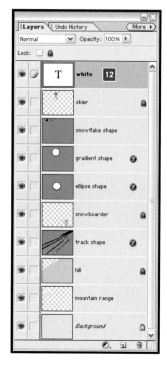

12. **Notice that a new layer, labeled** white, **appears in the Layers palette.**

The T icon on the layer indicates that this is a type layer. Each use of the Horizontal Type tool or Vertical Type tool automatically creates a new type layer that takes its name from the layer's content. This automatic naming feature makes identifying a particular type layer in the Layers palette easy.

13. **Click away from the word** white **in the document window to start a new type layer.**

It's good practice to locate individual pieces of type on separate layers so that you can move and edit them independently

<CAUTION>

Be sure to click far away from existing text if you want to enter text on a new type layer. Otherwise, your new text ends up on the same layer as the existing text. This can lead to typeovers and other inadvertent changes to the existing text..

14. **Type the phrase** bright•soft•fresh. **To insert a bullet point between the two word pairs, follow these instructions:**
Windows: Press the Num Lock key on the numeric keypad on your keyboard. To insert each bullet point, hold the Alt key, enter 0149 on the numeric keypad, and release the Alt key. When you finish typing the entire phrase, click the Num Lock key again to deactivate it.
Macintosh: Press Option+8 on your keyboard to insert each bullet point.

15. **Select the Move tool. Click and drag the words** bright•soft•fresh **on top of the ellipse shape in the image.**
Selecting the Move tool commits the type, displaying a new layer in the Layers palette labeled **bright soft fresh**. Notice how easy it is to move this phrase because it's on its own separate layer.

16. **Choose File→Save As. In the Save As dialog box, navigate to your ccproject folder, rename your file** 10_snow.psd, **and make sure that the Layers option is checked. Click Save. Leave the image open for the next tutorial.**
In this tutorial you used the Horizontal Type tool to add a Type layer to your winter sports greeting card that contains text and special characters.

<NOTE>

If you started this tutorial with the 10_snow.psd file from the Session 10 tutorial files, then you won't need to rename your file, just save it.

Type Layers

A type layer contains vector-based type, which is mathematically described rather than pixel-based. Consequently, you can rescale type without harming its appearance. And if you print to a post-script printer, the edges of the type are relatively crisp and smooth. (This isn't true, however, if you print to an inkjet printer, which converts type from vectors to pixels.)

Type layers are unique because their contents are completely editable. You can change the font, color, size, and even the wording of a type layer at any time. However, if you simplify (rasterize) a type layer, its content is no longer editable.

A type layer acts like a regular layer in most other respects. You can change its blending mode, vary its opacity, turn off its visibility, and even give it a layer style.

Finding Codes for Special Characters

Photoshop Elements 2 has no built-in way to insert special characters (like bullet points, mathematical symbols, foreign accents, and more) into text. Instead, follow the procedure in Step 14, substituting the code that corresponds to the character that you want to display. To find a particular code, consult the character map contained in your operating system.

To see the character map for a particular font in Windows XP, click the Start button at the bottom left of your screen and choose Run. Type charmap in the Run dialog box, and click OK. In the Character Map window that opens, click in the Font field and choose a font. Click on the desired character to display the code

for that character in the bottom-right corner of the Character Map window. Jot the code down, and click the red button to close the Character Map window.

To see the codes for a particular font in Macintosh OS X, open the Key Caps application from the Applications→Utilities folder. Choose a font from the Font menu at the top of the screen. Click and hold the Option key to see a visual representation of the key that generates the desired character. Hold the Option+Shift key combination to see keys for more characters. Jot down the key combination you need, and click the red button to close Key Caps.

Tutorial
» Creating Vertical Text

In this tutorial, you learn how to create text from scratch with a vertical orientation and how to convert existing horizontal text into vertical text. The resulting decorative vertical text in your greeting card brings to mind falling snow.

1. **With** 10_snow.psd **still open from the previous tutorial, select the** bright soft fresh **layer in the Layers palette if it's not already selected.**
   This ensures that the next type layer is located directly above this layer.

2. **Click on the type tool that's showing in your toolbox, and choose the Vertical Type tool from the flyout menu.**

3. **Leave the fields in the Options bar as they were at the end of the last tutorial (Courier New, Bold, 12 pt, Anti-aliased, and white).**

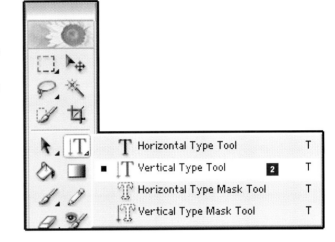

4. **Click in the top right of the image, and type the word** cold.
   This creates a layer of vertical type. The type runs from top to bottom, and each letter has a vertical orientation.

<NOTE>
You can create vertical type from scratch or change the orientation of an existing layer from horizontal to vertical.

5. **Select the** white **type layer in the Layers palette.**
   This layer contains horizontal type.

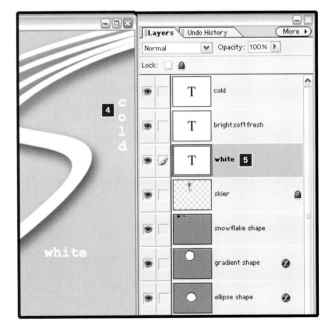

6. **With any type tool selected, click the Change Text Orientation button on the Options bar.**

   This converts the contents of the **cold** layer from horizontal to vertical orientation.

7. **Choose File→Save, and resave** 10_snow.psd **to your ccproject folder. Leave the image open.**

   Your greeting card now contains two layers of vertical text, one made with the Vertical Type tool (**cold**), and one converted from horizontal text (**white**).

Tutorial

» Working with Multiple Lines of Text

In this tutorial, you learn to create and align multiple lines of text on a single layer. Your greeting card is embellished with multiple lines of vertical type extolling the virtues of snow.

1. **With** 10_snow.psd **still open from the previous tutorial, make sure that the** cold **type layer is selected in your Layers palette.**
   This ensures that the next layer is located above it.

2. **Select the Horizontal Type tool in the toolbox, and click inside the image.**
   Click away from the existing text in order to generate a new type layer.

3. **In the Options bar, set Font Family to Courier (T1), Font Style to Medium, Font Size to 14 pt, and Text Color to dark gray (R:**93**, G:**106**, B:**96**). Leave the Anti-aliased button selected. Select the Underline button to add a design element to your type.**
   The first tutorial in this session covers setting font attributes, if you need a refresher.

4. **Make sure that the Center Text button is selected in the Options bar.**
   This centers each line of text that you enter on this type layer relative to the initial position of your cursor when you begin to type on the layer.

<NOTE>

The horizontal alignment buttons align the left edge, horizontal center, or right edge of each line of type on a layer to the initial position of the cursor.

5. **Create the first line of type on this layer by typing the word** crisp, **pressing the spacebar twice, and typing the word** dry.

6. **Press Enter (Macintosh: Return) on your keyboard to move the cursor to a new line on the same layer.**
   A hard return like this is necessary if you want to create another line of text on the same type layer.

<NOTE>
In this program, text does not automatically wrap at the end of a line as it does in word processing programs or when you create paragraph type in the full version of Adobe Photoshop. If you were to continue typing without a hard return, the text would run off the screen in Photoshop Elements 2.

7. **Press Enter (Macintosh: Return) again to add an additional space between the two lines of type. Make a second line of type by typing the word** clean, **pressing the spacebar three times, and entering the word** light.

8. **Click the check mark on the Options bar to commit the type.**
   The Layers palette now displays a type layer labeled **crisp dry clean light**. This layer contains two lines of text, both centered horizontally on the initial position of your cursor.

9. **Click the Change Text Orientation button on the Options bar.**
   This converts the two lines of text to vertical type, centering them vertically on the initial position of your cursor. Lines of vertical type are read from right to left.

< N O T E >
The alignment buttons that appear in the Options bar when vertical type is selected align the top edge, vertical center, or bottom edge of each line of type on the layer to the initial position of the cursor.

10. **Choose File→Save to resave** 10_snow.psd **to your ccproject folder. As usual, leave the file open.**
    Your greeting card now has another Type layer containing multiple lines of vertical text (crisp dry clean light).

Tutorial
» Formatting Text Manually

Photoshop Elements 2 doesn't have sophisticated controls for formatting text. So performing a formatting task like adjusting the space between individual type characters (traditionally known as kerning) requires a manual workaround like the one you learn in this tutorial. You type the letters s-n-o-w into your greeting card in a large font, with each letter on an independent type layer. Then you simulate kerning by manually moving the contents of each layer with the Move tool.

1. **With** 10_snow.psd **still open from the previous tutorial, select the** track shape **layer in the Layers palette.**
   This ensures the layers you create are located directly above that layer.

2. **Select the Horizontal Type tool, and click in the image away from other text.**

3. **In the Options bar, set Font Family to Arial Black and Font Style to Regular. Click in the Font Size field and type** 170 pt. **Leave the Anti-aliased button selected. Deselect the Underline button if it is selected. Click in the Text Color field, and choose gray blue (R:**144, **G:**155, **B:**179).

4. **In the Options bar, select the Faux Bold button.**
   This adds a simulated bold style to the typeface.

5. **Type a lowercase letter** w **in the image.**
   This letter is very large due to the large font size and the heavy font.

6. **Click the check mark in the Options bar to commit the type.**
   A new **w** layer appears in the Layers palette.

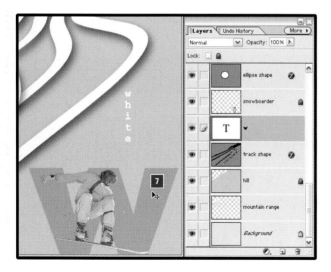

7. **Hold down the Ctrl (Macintosh: ⌘) key to temporarily switch your cursor to the Move tool. Click in the image, and drag the letter w into position so that it touches the bottom edge of the document window and encompasses all of the boy's snowboard, as in the illustration. Release the Ctrl (Macintosh: ⌘) key.**

8. **Click in the image, away from existing type, to start a new layer. Type a lowercase letter** o.

9. **Click the check mark in the Options bar to commit the type.**
   A new **o** layer appears in the Layers palette.

<TIP>
If you have trouble moving a letter, it's probably because it's not on a separate layer. If two letters are sharing a layer, delete that layer from the Layers palette and re-create each letter on a separate layer by following Steps 8 and 9.

10. **Hold the Ctrl (Macintosh: ⌘) key to temporarily switch to a Move tool cursor. Click in the image, and drag the letter o to the left of the letter w.**
You can move this letter independently because it's on its own separate layer.

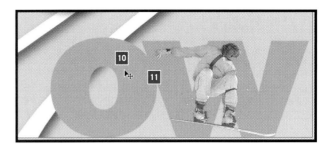

11. **With the Ctrl (Macintosh: ⌘) key depressed, use the arrow keys on your keyboard to nudge the letter o into place, overlapping the letter w slightly.**
Setting the spacing between letters in this manner—positioning letters on individual layers manually with the Move tool—is a workaround for the lack of more sophisticated kerning controls. You can use a similar technique to simulate leading (setting spacing between lines of type) and baseline shift (creating superscripts and subscripts).

12. **Repeat Steps 8 through 11 with the letters n and s, moving each letter into position manually.**
Your final result should resemble the illustration, and your layers palette should contain a separate type layer for each of the four letters of the word snow.

13. **Choose File→Save, and resave** `10_snow.psd` **to your ccproject folder. Leave the image open for the next tutorial.**
The greeting card now contains the word snow in large decorative letters that you positioned manually.

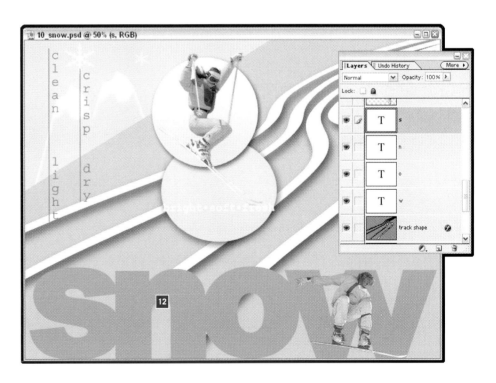

Tutorial
» Editing Text

The most useful feature of a type layer is that its contents are editable. In this tutorial, you learn how to edit an entire layer of text, as well as a selected portion of text on a layer. You change font family, style, size, and color of various pieces of text in your snow greeting card.

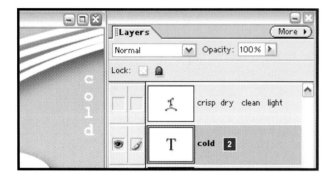

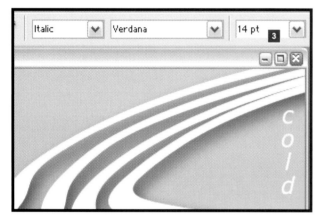

1. **With** 10_snow.psd **still open from the previous tutorial, select the Horizontal or Vertical type tool from the toolbox.**
   You can use either tool to edit text; the cursor automatically changes to the orientation of the text that you are editing.

2. **Click on the** cold **layer in the Layers palette to select that layer.**
   This selects the entire type layer for editing, without adding a highlight to the layer (which makes it easier to preview your edits). Another way to select an entire type layer is to double-click the T icon on that layer in the Layers palette. This method works even if you have a tool other than a type tool selected, but it has the disadvantage of adding an inverse highlight that obscures your edits.

3. **In the Options bar, choose Verdana from the Font Family menu, Italic from the Font Style menu, and 14 pt from the Font Size menu.**
   All the text on the **cold** layer changes accordingly.

<TIP>
If you want to change the contents of a type layer, but you're not sure which font to choose, you can see how each font looks on the text in your image. With a type tool selected in the toolbox and the type layer selected in the Layers palette, click in the Font Family field on the Options bar. Then use the arrow keys on your keyboard to cycle through the fonts, enjoying a live preview of each in your image. You can do the same thing in the Font Style field.

4. **With a type tool, click in your image just above the word** light, **and drag down to select and highlight that word from the** crisp dry clean light **layer.**

   You can use this click and drag method to select a single character or any neighboring characters on a type layer. The selected characters have an inverse highlight.

<NOTE>

A quick way to select one word from a type layer is to select a type tool, click inside that word in the document, and double-click. Triple-clicking selects a line of text.

5. **Click the Text Color field in the Options bar to open the Color Picker. Select pale blue (R:** 241, **G:** 243, **B:**251), **and click OK to recolor the selected text.**

   Choosing a color from the Swatches palette or clicking the Foreground Color box in the toolbox and choosing a color from the Color Picker also changes the color of highlighted text.

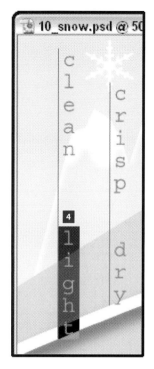

6. **Click the check mark on the Options bar to commit this type edit.**

   The highlight on the text disappears, and you can see your change. Recall that other ways to commit a type edit include clicking in the image.

7. **Double-click on the word** dry **in the image to select that word. Repeat Steps 5 and 6 to change the color of this selected text.**

8. **Choose File→Save, and leave** 10_snow.psd **open for the next tutorial.**

   In this tutorial, you had only a taste of the many ways that you can edit text on a type layer. You can change any of the type attributes on the Options bar, rotate text, or scale it up or down with transform commands. You can even change the words on a type layer while maintaining the layer's type attributes by simply typing over the existing words. This gives you lots of flexibility when you're adding text to a project like this series of greeting cards.

Tutorial
» Simplifying a Type Layer

Certain changes cannot be made to text unless the layer on which the text is located is simplified—converted from a vector-based type layer to a regular, pixel-based layer. For example, you can't apply a filter to text, paint on text, or apply a gradient to text unless you simplify it first. In this tutorial, you simplify a type layer in your winter sports greeting card in order to apply a filter to its contents.

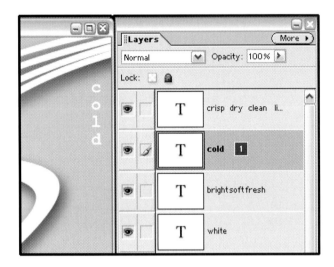

1. **With** 10_snow.psd **still open from the preceding tutorial, select the** cold **type layer in the Layers palette.**

2. **Click the Filters tab in the Palette Well on the Options bar to open the Filters palette.**

<NOTE>
Photoshop Elements 2 ships with a variety of prebuilt filters that you can use to apply special effects to your images.

3. **Choose Stylize from the category menu at the top of the Filters palette.**

4. **Select the Wind filter thumbnail, and click the Apply button at the top of the Filters palette.**

5. The program warns you that this type layer must be simplified before proceeding. Click OK to simplify the type layer.
Simplify is the Photoshop Elements term for rasterize. Simplifying or rasterizing type changes it from editable, vector-based type, to graphic images of text that are made up of pixels. After you simplify type, it loses its inherent editability, scalability, and ability to produce crisp edges on a postscript printer.

<NOTE>
If you know that an operation requires type to be simplified, you don't have to wait for a warning from the program. You can simplify a selected layer in a number of ways. You can click the More button on the top right of the Layers palette and choose Simplify Layer. You can choose Layer➔Simplify Layer from the menu bar at the top of the screen. Or you can right-click (Macintosh: Ctrl+click) on the layer in the Layers palette and choose Simplify Layer from the contextual menu.

6. Click OK in the Wind dialog box to apply the Wind filter with its default settings. Click on the Options bar to close the Filters palette into the Palette Well.

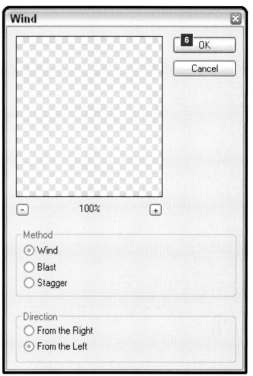

7. **Choose Filter➔Wind from the menu bar at the top of the screen to apply the filter again to intensify its effect.**

8 Notice that the cold **layer in the Layers palette no longer displays the T icon that identifies a type layer.**
This layer has been simplified—converted to a regular pixel-based layer.

<TIP>
After you simplify text, you can't convert it back to vector-based type. So if you ever simplify in error, be sure to undo that operation before you exhaust your 20 default Undo History states.

9. **Choose File➔Save to resave** 10_snow.psd **to your ccproject folder. Leave the file open for the next tutorial.**
The word "cold" in your winter sports greeting card is no longer editable type. It has been simplified to a regular layer with a windblown filter effect.

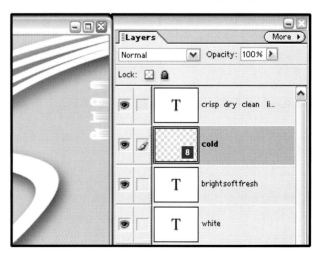

Tutorial
» Warping Text

The warp text feature bends and distorts the shape of text so that it looks more dynamic. In this tutorial, you apply a flag-shaped warp to vertical text in your winter sports greeting card to convey the illusion of motion. You also warp some horizontal text to follow the curve of an ellipse shape.

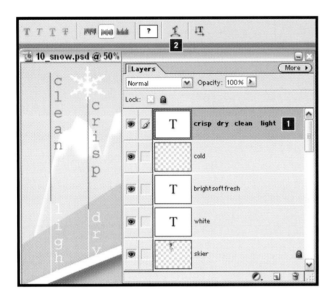

1. **With** 10_snow.psd **still open from the previous tutorial, select the** crisp dry clean light **layer in the Layers palette.**

2. **Select the Vertical Type tool in the toolbox, and click the Warp Text icon on the Options bar.**
   The Warp Text dialog box opens.

< T I P >
Another way to invoke the warp text feature is to choose Layer→ Type→Warp Text from the menu bar at the top of the screen.

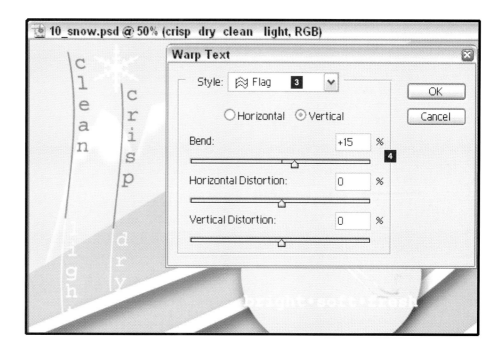

3. **In the Warp Text dialog box, click the arrow at the right of the Style field, and choose Flag from the Warp Style menu.**
This bends the text to mimic the waves in a flag flying in the wind.

4. **Move the Bend slider in the Warp Text dialog box to +15 to give a slight wave to both lines of vertical text on the selected layer. Leave the other settings at their defaults, and click OK to apply the warp effect.**

5. **Notice that the T thumbnail on the** crisp dry clean light **layer in the Layers palette has been replaced with a special warped text thumbnail.**

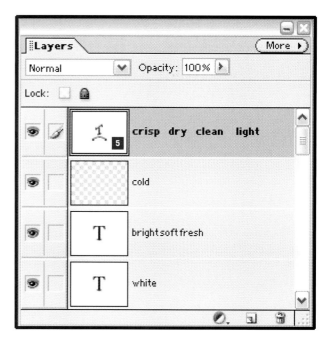

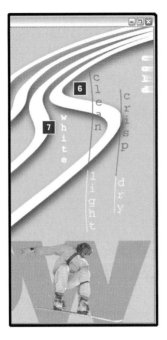

6. **Select the Move tool in the toolbox. Click in the image, and drag to move the warped text into position to match the illustration.**
   You edited and warped this layer before moving it into position to avoid accidentally selecting other nearby text layers as you worked on this layer.

7. **Select the** white **type layer in the Layers palette. Click and drag in the image to move the word** white **into position to the left of the warped text to match the illustration.**
   In the next steps, you apply a warp effect to a horizontal text layer, bending the text around the curve of an ellipse shape.

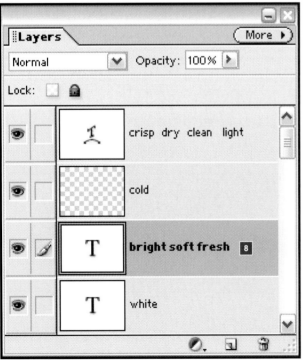

8. **Select the** bright soft fresh **layer in the Layers palette.**

9. **Select the Horizontal Type tool in the toolbox.**

10. **Click the Warp Text icon on the Options bar to open the Warp Text dialog box.**

11. **In the Warp Text dialog box, choose Arc from the Style menu. Select the Horizontal radio button if it's not already selected. Move the Bend slider to -66% and the Vertical Distortion slider to +3%.**

    I recommend experimenting with the settings in the Warp Text dialog box until you get a result you like in the image, rather than trying to understand the engineering logic of each setting.

12. **Without closing the Warp Text dialog box, click in the image and drag the words** bright•soft•fresh **to the bottom of the ellipse shape, as in the illustration.**

    Being able to move type with the Warp Text dialog box open comes in handy for positioning type as you distort it.

13. **Click OK to apply this text warp and to close the Warp Text dialog box.**

14. **In the type tool Options bar, change the Font Size of the** bright•soft•fresh **layer to 10 pt.**

    The type attributes of a warped type layer remain editable just like those of a regular type layer. Reducing the size of the type helps fit the text to the shape of the ellipse.

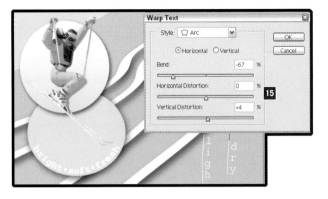

15. **Click the Warp Text icon on the Options bar again to reopen the Warp Text dialog box. Tweak the settings as necessary to bend the text so that it matches the curve of the ellipse. When you're satisfied, click OK to apply this warp effect.**

< N O T E >

One of the most useful qualities of a warp text effect is that it remains editable. You can reopen the Warp Text dialog box at any time by selecting a warped layer in the Layers palette, selecting a type tool, and clicking the Warp Text icon on the Options bar. In the Warp Text dialog box, you can tweak any of the warp settings or choose None from the Style menu to eliminate the warp effect entirely.

16. **Choose File➔Save, and leave the file open for the last tutorial in this session.**

In this tutorial, you applied the Warp text feature to text in your winter sports greeting card, coming up with two different looks—wavy text that suggests motion and text that wraps around a curve.

Tutorial
» Grouping Text and Image

In this tutorial, you learn a special text effect. By grouping a type layer with an image layer, you can create the illusion that the image is part of the type. In your winter sports greeting card, you limit the visibility of a photograph of a snowboarder to the confines of the large text at the bottom of the image.

1. **With** 10_snow.psd **still open from the previous tutorial, select the** s **type layer in the Layers palette.**

   If the stacking order of your **s, n, o,** and **w** layers doesn't match this illustration, click and drag each of the layers to reorder them. Recall that each of the large letters in the word **snow** is currently on an independent layer. The grouping effect requires that this type be on a single layer. So your first task is to create a composite layer of the contents of the **s, n, o,** and **w** layers.

   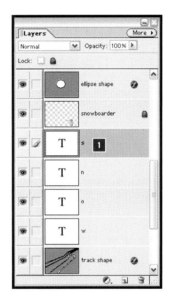

2. **Click the Create New Layer icon at the bottom of the Layers palette to make a new layer just above the** s **layer and below the** snowboarder **layer. Double-click on the** Layer 1 **label on the new layer, and rename the layer** snow.

3. **Click in the link field to the left of each of the** s, n, o, **and** w **layers to link those four layers to the new** snow **layer.**

   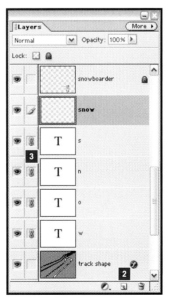

4. Hold the Alt (Macintosh: Option) key as you click the More button on the Layers palette, and choose Merge Linked.

This copies the content of the individual letter layers into the composite **snow** layer.

5. Click in the Visibility field to the left of each of the s, n, o, **and** w **layers, removing the Eye icons from those fields.**

Although these individual layers are no longer a necessary part of the image, it makes sense to keep them in the document because they are editable type, whereas the **snow** layer is not. In the next step, you group the composite **snow** type layer with the **snowboarder** image layer, so that the snowboarder appears to be part of the type.

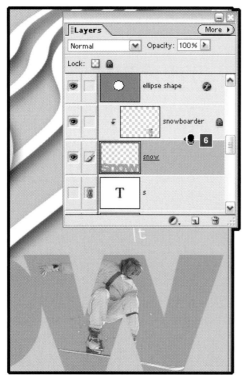

6. Hold the Alt (Macintosh: Option) key over the border between the snowboarder **and the** snow **type layer until the cursor changes to a double circle. Click on that border to group the two layers.**

The arrow and indent on the **snowboarder** layer indicate that that layer is masked by the content of the **snow** type layer. The image of the snowboarder now appears only where content appears on the **snow** type layer.

< T I P >

An interesting variation on this technique is to group a very large photograph with a type layer, creating the illusion that all of the type is filled with the photographic image.

< T I P >

The hardest part of replicating this technique is remembering the order in which to put the grouped layers. The layer that is acting as the mask (usually the type layer) should be below the layer that is filling the mask (usually the image layer).

7. Save this final image to your ccproject folder by choosing File→Save As. In the Save As dialog box, rename the image 10_snow_end.psd. **Make sure that Layers is selected, and click Save.**

You completed another collage for your greeting card series. This piece uses lots of shape and text techniques that you learned over the last two sessions.

» Session Review

The focus of this session was text. You created horizontal and vertical type layers, learning how to control font, color, size, and other type attributes. You learned the special procedure for inserting symbols and characters into text. You were able to work around the lack of formatting controls in Photoshop Elements 2 by kerning type manually. You saw how easy it is to edit a type layer, and you learned how and when to simplify a type layer. You filtered and warped text, and learned a technique for grouping text and image. This resulted in several layers of decorative type in your winter sports greeting card, in addition to the shapes you added to the card in the last session.

1. What's the difference between Font Family and Font Style in Photoshop Elements 2? (See Tutorial: Creating Horizontal Text.)

2. What is the function of the large check mark on the type tool Options bar? (See Tutorial: Creating Horizontal Text.)

3. What icon identifies a type layer in the Layers palette? (See Tutorial: Creating Horizontal Text.)

4. Name at least one special quality of type layers. (See Tutorial: Creating Horizontal Text.)

5. How do you create vertical text from scratch? (See Tutorial: Creating Vertical Text.)

6. Can horizontal text be converted into vertical text? (See Tutorial: Creating Vertical Text.)

7. Does type wrap from line to line automatically in Photoshop Elements 2? (See Tutorial: Working with Multiple Lines of Text.)

8. Describe how to kern text in Photoshop Elements 2. (See Tutorial: Formatting Text Manually.)

9. Describe at least one way to select all the text on a type layer for purposes of editing. (See Tutorial: Editing Text.)

10. What does it mean to simplify a type layer? (See Tutorial: Simplifying a Type Layer.)

11. Can you edit the font, size, color, and other type attributes of text that has been warped? (See Tutorial: Warping Text.)

12. Can you reopen the Warp Text dialog box to make changes to warped text? (See Tutorial: Warping Text.)

13. How do you group two layers together in the Layers palette? (See Tutorial: Grouping Text and Image.)

clean

white

light

crisp

dry

bright·soft·fresh

snow

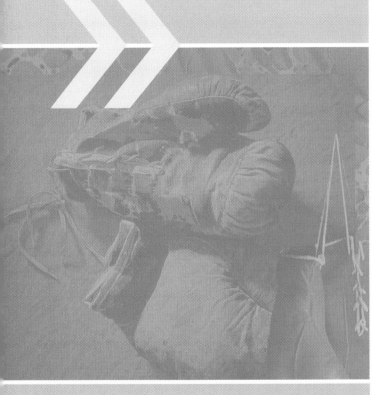

Part VI

Outputting

Session 11

Printing

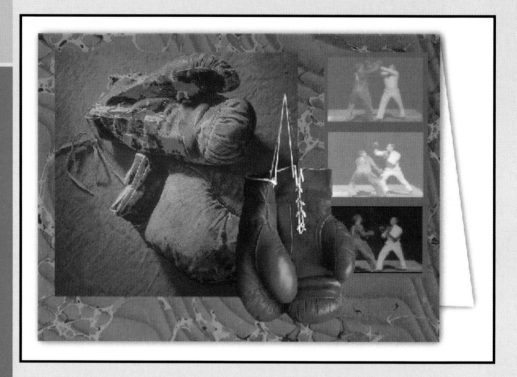

Session Introduction

In this session, you learn how to print from Photoshop Elements 2. You prepare and print the greeting cards you've been creating throughout this course. Then you tackle some special print layouts made with the automatic Picture Package, Contact Sheet, and Photomerge features of the program.

TOOLS YOU'LL USE
Print command, Picture Package, Contact Sheet, Photomerge

CD-ROM FILES NEEDED
Final greeting cards folder (climber_end.psd, 01_boxing_end.psd, 02_biking_end.psd, 04_stopwatch_end.psd, 05_graffiti_end.psd, 06_baseball_end.psd, 07_racecars_end.psd, 08_ride_end.psd, 10_snow_end.psd, BS02_basketball_end.psd); 11_01stadium.psd, 11_02stadium.psd, 11_03stadium.psd, 11_panorama.psd.

TIME REQUIRED
30 minutes

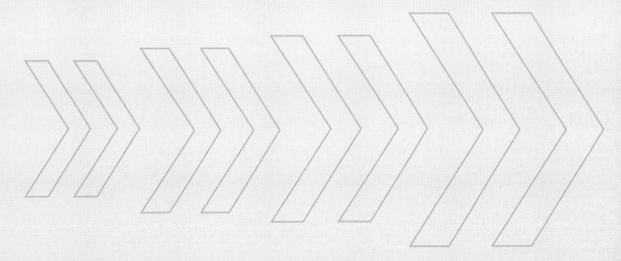

Tutorial
» Preparing Files for Printing

Photoshop Elements 2 was designed for easy desktop printing. So preparing files for printing is a straightforward process, as you discover in this tutorial. In addition to learning about printing in general, this is where you find instructions for laying out the greeting cards you've been preparing throughout this book and for printing those cards on your desktop printer.

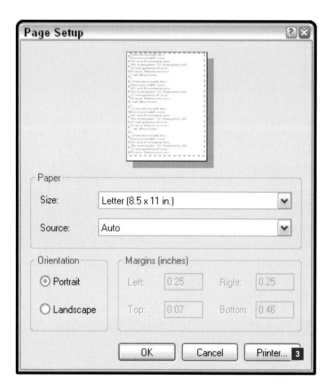

1. **Choose File→Open from the menu bar at the top of the screen, navigate to the Final Greeting Cards folder inside the Session 11 Tutorial Files folder on your hard drive, and open** `01_boxing_end.psd`.
   This is a flattened copy of the greeting card image that you created in Session 1. Alternatively, you can use the layered file of the same name that you created and saved to your ccproject folder at the end of Session 1.

<NOTE>
The files provided for you to print in the Session 11 Tutorial Files folder have been flattened to reduce file size and to shorten your printing time. But keep in mind that you do not have to flatten files before printing. You can print directly from a layered file to your desktop printer. When you print from a layered file, make sure that an Eye icon appears next to every layer that you want to include in the print, because the program prints only visible layers.

<NOTE>
Photoshop Elements 2 was designed for printing to desktop inkjet printers rather than to commercial printers. Consequently, this program has no controls for proofing files in CMYK color mode or for converting files to CMYK, the color mode used in most commerical printing operations. Also you don't need to resave your files in special file formats like TIFF or EPS that are used in commercial printing processes and page layout programs.

2. **Choose File→Page Setup to open the Page Setup dialog box.**
   The Page Setup dialog box looks quite different in Windows XP and Mac OS X, as reflected in the separate instructions and illustrations that follow. Mac users can skip to Step 7.

3. **Windows users only: Click the Printer button in the Page Setup dialog box to open a second Page Setup dialog box in which you choose your printer.**

4. **Windows users only: In the second Page Setup dialog box, choose your printer from the Name menu, and click the Properties button to open the Properties dialog box for your printer.**
   If your printer does not appear in the Name menu, go to the Windows Start menu→Printers and Faxes→Add a printer. The Add Printer Wizard walks you through the necessary steps.

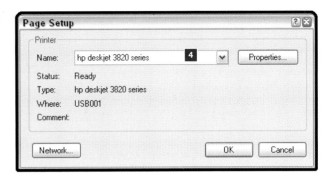

<**TIP**>

You can print these greeting card images on plain printer paper, but you may prefer special photo paper made for inkjet printers, water color paper, or card stock. The paper you choose affects the color and sharpness of the printed image. If you don't like the look of an image on one paper, experiment with another. If you find a photo paper you like that doesn't fold well due to its coating, consider cutting out an image printed on that paper and mounting it to a card with spray adhesive.

5. **Windows users only: In the Properties dialog box, set Print Quality to Best, choose the Paper Type on which you plan to print, and choose Letter (8.5 x 11 in.) as the Paper Size. Click OK in the Properties dialog box and again in the second Page Setup dialog box to get back to the original Page Setup dialog box.**
   Your particular printer may have other Property settings than those you see here. Consult your printer manual if you have questions about those settings.

6. **Windows users only: In the original Page Setup dialog box, make sure that the settings match those listed here and then click OK to close the dialog box.**

   » Size: Letter (8.5 x 11 in.)
   The available choices depend on the printer you identified in the preceding steps.

   » Source: Auto (or a particular feed bin from which your printer takes paper)

   » Orientation: Portrait
   This orients the image vertically on the page.

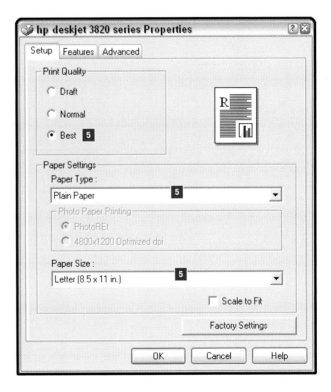

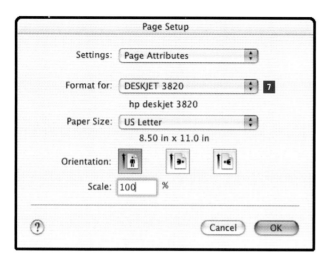

7. **Macintosh users only: Choose the following settings in the Page Setup dialog box, and then click OK to close the dialog box.**

   » Settings: Page Attributes

   » Format for: (your printer name)

   » Paper Size: US Letter
   US Letter is 8.5 in x 11 in. The available choices depend on the printer that you selected in the Format for field.

   » Orientation: Portrait (the button on the far left)

   » Scale: 100%

<NOTE>
After defining basic settings in the Page Setup dialog boxes, move on to Print Preview to position your printed image on the page. The following steps apply to both Windows and Macintosh users.

8. **Choose File→Print Preview to open the Photoshop Elements 2 Print Preview dialog box.**

More Print Preview Options

The Print Preview dialog box has another hidden function. This is the location of a buried setting for managing color during printing. You can use this setting to temporarily translate the colors in your document to the color space of your printer. Theoretically, this should result in more accurate printed color, although you may not always like the result. To try converting to your printer's color space, select Show More Options at the bottom of the Print Preview dialog box, and change the Options menu to Color Management. Click the Print Space Profile field to open a menu of printer profiles. If you see a profile for your printer, choose that one. If you don't see a profile for your printer, choose Printer Color Management to assign the printer driver to handle the color conversion. If you want to print with no color conversion, leave Print Space Profile at its default setting—Same as Source.

The Print Preview box also contains settings for changing the printed size of an image without affecting the actual size of the image. You can scale an image manually by clicking on the anchor points on the preview bounding box and dragging. Hold the Shift key to constrain proportions as you drag. Alternatively, you can enter a percentage or fixed dimensions in the Scaled Print Size fields. Or you can select Scale to Fit Media to automatically change the size of the printed image to fit the Paper Size you set earlier. Printing an image at less than 100 percent of its actual size is okay, but try not to scale an image up to more than 100 percent for printing.

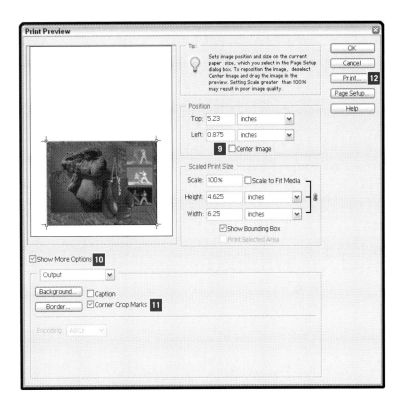

9. **In the Print Preview dialog box, deselect Center Image. Set the Top Position to** 5.23 **inches.**

   This moves the printed image down toward the bottom of the page, so that you can fold the top part of the page over to make a greeting card. Alternatively, you can click on the image and manually drag it to the bottom of the page preview in the Print Preview dialog box. The trick is to avoid moving the image so low that it interferes with the margin that your particular printer adds to the bottom of every page. If part of the image is cut off during printing, return to this dialog box and move the preview image up slightly.

10. **Select Show More Options.**

   This reveals additional settings at the bottom of the Print Preview dialog box.

11. **Select Corner Crop Marks to add crop marks at each corner of the printed image.**

   You use these crop marks as guides for folding and cutting around the greeting card.

12. **Click the Print button on the right side of the Print Preview dialog box.**

   This takes you directly into the Print dialog box. Alternatively, click OK to close the Print Preview dialog box, and choose File→Print from the menu bar. The Print dialog boxes for Macintosh and Windows are different, as evidenced by the following instructions and illustrations. Macintosh users can skip to Step 14.

< N O T E >

Click OK if you get a warning that Postscript specific settings will be ignored because you don't have a Postscript printer.

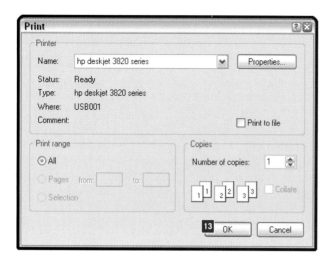

13. **Windows users only: Leave the settings in the Print dialog box as they are, and click OK to print the image.**
The Properties button in the Print dialog box is another way to access printer properties like Paper Type and Print Quality, which you Windows users adjusted earlier.

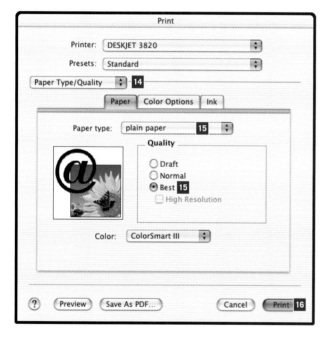

14. **Macintosh users only: In the Print dialog box, click the popup menu labeled Copies and Pages and choose Paper Type/Quality.**
A set of tabs appears in the dialog box.

15. **In the Paper tab, choose the Paper Type on which you plan to print, and set Quality to Best. Click the popup menu that's now labeled Paper Type/Quality, and choose Copies and Pages again to reveal the Print button.**

16. **Macintosh users only: Click the Print button in the Print dialog box to print this greeting card.**

17. **Fold the printed page horizontally along the top of the image, using the crop marks as a guide, to create a horizontal folded card. Open the card and cut around the edges of the printed image using a cutting blade and a sharp-edged ruler.**

    Congratulations! You've completed your first greeting card.

18. **Close** 01_boxing_end.psd **without saving.**

19. **Repeat this tutorial for each of the other final greeting card images listed in the CD-ROM Files Needed section at the beginning of this session.**

    You can use the final images you made and saved to your ccproject folder throughout the course, or the copies of those images located in the Final Greeting Cards folder inside the Session 11 Tutorial Files folder. Notice that you have fewer final images than the number of sessions in this course because some images took two sessions to finish.

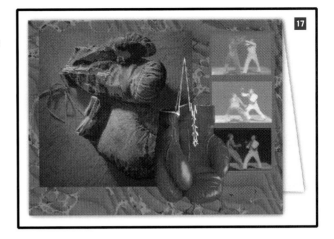

Tutorial
» Making a Contact Sheet

Traditional photographers use contact sheets, which are direct prints made from negatives, to keep track of the images they've shot. Digital photographers and imagemakers of all kinds can also benefit from a printed record of their digital images. With a simple automated command, you can create contact sheets that contain thumbnail representations of a folder full of images. In this tutorial you produce a contact sheet that displays all of the final greeting cards in this course.

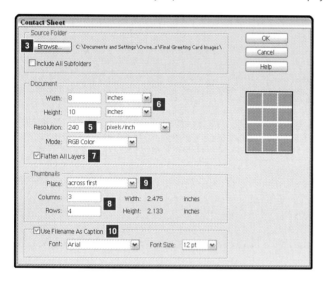

1. **Choose File→Print Layouts→Contact Sheet from the menu bar.**
   This opens the Contact Sheet dialog box.

2. **Make sure that the files you include in the contact sheet are closed.**

3. **Click the Browse (Macintosh: Choose) button in the Source Folder area of the dialog box to identify the folder of images that you want to include in this contact sheet.**
   This opens the Browse for Folder dialog box (Macintosh: Select Image Directory window).

4. **In the Browse for Folder dialog box (Macintosh: Select Image Directory window), navigate to the Final Greeting Cards folder inside the Session 11 Tutorial Files folder on your hard drive and click OK (Macintosh: Choose).**

5. **In the Document section of the Contact Sheet dialog box, set the parameters for the contact sheet that you are creating. Change its Resolution to 240 pixels/inch so that it prints well on an inkjet printer.**
   If you plan to use the contact sheet as a reference, leave the resolution at the default of 72 dpi to keep the file size down.

6. **Leave the Width and Height of the area that the thumbnails occupy at the default values of 8 x 10.**
   The contact sheet fits on a sheet of standard 8.5-x-11-inch paper. The diagram in the dialog box reflects these settings.

7. **Leave Flatten All Layers selected.**
   This creates a contact sheet with a background layer and a single image layer containing all the thumbnails and text. If you deselect Flatten All Layers, each thumbnail and caption are on a separate layer in the contact sheet, inflating its file size.

8. **Set the number of thumbnail columns to 3 and rows to 4.**
   You can see this layout in the contact sheet diagram in the dialog box.

9. **Leave the Place setting at its default—across first.**
   This instructs the program to arrange the thumbnails first from left to right and then from top to bottom, based on filenames.

10. **Leave Use Filename As Caption selected.**
    This adds the filename of each image below its thumbnail on the contact sheet. The filename is useful for identifying corresponding full-sized files. Leave Font and Size of the caption at the default settings.

<NOTE>

When you make a contact sheet, gather into one folder all the images that you want represented in your contact sheet. Rotate any vertical images that are displayed horizontally so that all images face the same direction in the contact sheet.

<NOTE>

The Width and Height of each thumbnail are noted in the Thumbnails section of the dialog box. Notice that the fewer the number of thumbnails, the larger each is.

11. Click OK to create the contact sheet.

If you're quick, you can watch the program create a new contact sheet document, open and resize a copy of each image, and place each in the contact sheet.

12. Choose File→Save, navigate to your ccproject folder, and save the contact sheet there.

You can print the contact sheet and save it as a catalog of your set of greeting cards.

Tutorial
» Creating a Picture Package

In this tutorial, you create a Picture Package of one image at different sizes. Then you swap out images to create a Picture Package of multiple images.

1. **Choose File→Print Layouts→Picture Package.**
   This opens the Picture Package dialog box.

2. **In the Source area of the Picture Package dialog box, set the Use field to File.**
   Choosing File tells the program to repeat a single image at different sizes on a single piece of paper. Choose File even if you want more than one image in your picture package.

3. **Click the Browse (Macintosh: Choose) button, navigate to the Final Greeting Cards folder inside the Session 11 Tutorial Files folder, and choose** 04_stopwatch_end.psd. **Click Open.**

4. **Leave Page Size set to the default values—8.0 x 10.0 inches.**
   This ensures that your Picture Package prints on a standard 8.5-x-11-inch page.

5. **Change Resolution to** 240 **pixels/inch so your Picture Package prints well on an inkjet printer. Leave Mode set to RGB Color.**

6. **Click in the Layout field to display a menu of layout presets. Choose (1)5x7 (4)2.5x3.5.**
   The selected layout is previewed.

7. **Leave Flatten All Layers selected to minimize file size.**
   This creates a Picture Package with a background layer and a single image layer for all the images and text. If you deselect this option, you get a larger file that has a separate layer for each picture and caption.

8. **Choose Custom Text in the Content field. In the Custom Text field, type** PROOF.
   The label feature offers the option to have text of your choice printed on top of the images in a picture package.

9. **Increase the Font Size to** 72 **pt. Set the Color to White, and decrease the Opacity to 60% so that the underlying image is visible.**

10. **Set Position to Top Left and Rotate to 90 Degrees Left.**
    You have a number of text placement options to choose from.

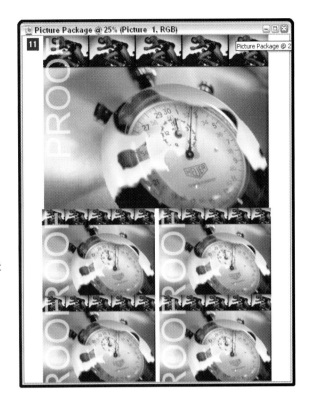

<TIP>

The Custom Text label feature is handy for marking images as nonreproducible proofs or for displaying copyright information to protect your printed images.

<NOTE>

If you choose Copyright, Caption, Author, or Title in the Label Content field, the program uses information that you enter into the File Info dialog box (File→File Info).

<NOTE>

The Souce area in the Picture Package dialog box includes two options in additon to File. Frontmost Document is available only if you have an image open and active. It tells the program to repeat that image at different sizes on a single sheet of paper. Folder creates a separate Picture Package document for each image in the selected folder. Each of the Picture Package documents repeats just one of the images at different sizes.

11. **Click OK to create a Picture Package of a single image at various sizes.**

12. **Choose File→Save, navigate to your ccproject folder, name the file Picture Package 1, and click Save.**
Now that you know how to create a Picture Package with a single image, it's a snap to create a Picture Package with multiple images.

<TIP>

If none of the choices in the menu of preset layouts suits you, you can create your own Picture Package layout with customized image sizes. Use a text editing program to open the ReadMe.txt file located in the Layouts folder inside the Presets folder in the application folder. That file contains detailed instructions for writing a Picture Package layout file. Follow those instructions, and save your customized layout file to the Layouts folder, being careful not to save over any original file. After you quit and relaunch Photoshop Elements 2, it appears in the Picture Package layout menu under the descriptive name that you include in the file.

13. **Repeat Steps 2 through 7, except this time set the Content field to None.**

14. **In the preview on the right side of the Picture Package dialog box, click in one of the smaller pictures.**
    This opens the Select an Image File dialog box.

15. **Navigate to the Final Greeting Card Images folder inside the Session 11 Tutorial Files folder. Choose an image other than the stopwatch image, and click OK.**

16. **Repeat Steps 14 and 15 with each of the other three small pictures.**

17. **Click OK. This creates a single Picture Package with multiple images.**

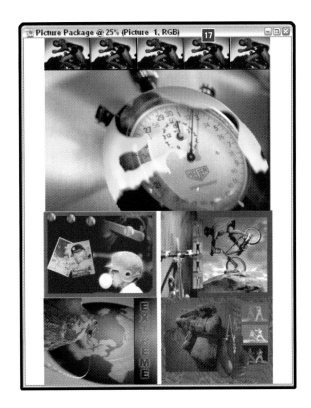

18. **Choose File→Save, navigate to your ccproject folder, name the file** Picture Package 2**, and click Save.**

In this tutorial you made two Picture Packages. The first displayed one of your greeting cards in several sizes. The second displayed multiple greeting cards.

Tutorial
» Creating a Panorama

Photoshop Elements 2 has a sophisticated Photomerge feature that you can use to stitch images together into a wide-angle, panoramic format. In this tutorial, you learn how to create a panorama, along with some tips on how to shoot photographs for use with this feature.

1. **Choose File→Open, navigate to your Session 11 Tutorial Files folder, and open three images:** 11_01stadium.psd, 11_02stadium.psd, **and** 11_03stadium.psd.

2. **Choose File→Create Photomerge.**
   This opens the PhotoMerge dialog box in which you identify the files to include in this Photomerge.

Shooting for Photomerge

Take a close look at the images that you just opened for use with the Photomerge feature. They illustrate some simple rules that you should follow when you're shooting images to use in a Photomerge. Observing these few rules can save you lots of time and effort.

Notice that the photographs are all shot from the same angle. The program can more easily merge photos that are level like these. This means that you should place your camera on a tripod, preferably one that has a smoothly rotating head (although any tripod is better than none at all). If you find yourself without a tripod, rest your camera on a steady surface, like the top of a wall, to try to make your photographs level.

Notice that the content of the images overlaps. For example, you see the same football player on the field on the right side of 11_02stadium.psd as on the left side of 11_03stadium.psd. A slight overlap of around 30 percent is a necessary ingredient for a successful Photomerge. The program needs the overlap to identify common areas among the photographs. You can calculate overlap by degree if your tripod has such measurements, but using your eye to overlap photos is much easier. Pick a spot on the right side of the first image. When you rotate your camera to take the

second image, place that spot in the leftmost 30 percent of the second image. Don't worry about being exact about this 30 percent figure. It's just a rough guide.

Notice that the exposure (the lightness/darkness) of the three photographs is the same. This is very important in order to avoid diagonal lines at the junctures between merged photographs. If you're using a camera that automatically adjusts exposure, the exposure is likely to change as you rotate to take a series of photos. The best way to handle this is to use a camera that has an auto-exposure (AE) lock. Set your exposure as you normally would for the first frame; engage the AE lock to take subsequent frames with the same exposure. If your camera does not have this feature, set the exposure of each frame manually to match the exposure of the others. If you don't have manual exposure settings, try not to turn into changed lighting conditions (for example, don't turn into and then away from the sun) as you shoot a series of photographs.

Here's a final tip that you won't see in these photographs. Take lots of photographs when you're shooting for Photomerge. The more photographs you shoot, the more you have to choose from and the more room you have to avoid errors.

3. **Notice that the three open files appear in the Source Files box:**
   `11_01stadium.psd`, `11_02stadium.psd`, **and**
   `11_03stadium.psd`.

   These are the files that will be included in the Photomerge. All
   open files appear in the Source Files box. Click the Remove
   button to remove any files that you don't want to use. You can
   include files that are not open by clicking the Browse button,
   navigating to those files on your hard drive, and clicking Open.

4. **Click OK to begin the automatic Photomerge process.**

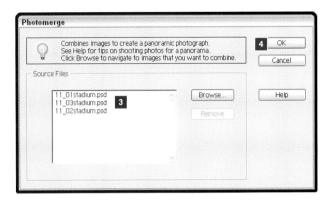

5. **In the Photomerge dialog box, drag the slider on the Navigator to
   the right to zoom in on the merged preview.**

   There may be small gaps between the photos, which need to
   be fixed. However, it's difficult to predict how well your
   Photomerge will work. If you're satisfied with the results you
   get, skip down to Step 12.

   < T I P >

   Dragging the red box in the Navigator repositions the merged preview so you can see the area that you want to fix. The Hand tool on
   the left side of the dialog box does the same thing.

   < N O T E >

   This is a relatively successful Photomerge. Sometimes the program
   is unable to include a particular photo, so it leaves it in the lightbox (the white band) above the merged preview. Or the automatic
   Photomerge may create a jumbled result. You can try to fix these
   problems by manually clicking and dragging images into place
   from the lightbox or within the merged preview using the Select
   Image Tool that's located at the top left of the dialog box.

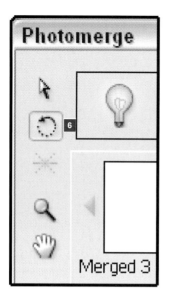

6. **Select the Rotate Image Tool at the top left of the Photomerge dialog box.**

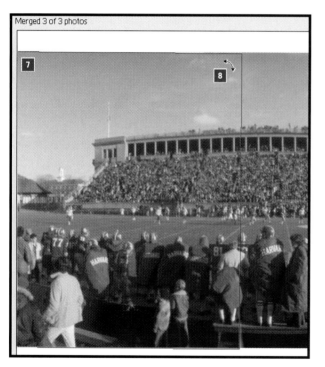

7. **Click on the left side of the merged preview to select the leftmost image.**

   The red border shows the edge of the selected photograph.

8. **Drag slightly clockwise to rotate the left image just enough to close the gap between it and the center image.**

   As you drag, the images become slightly transparent so you can match up their overlapping areas. Don't worry if you can't fix the gaps completely. After you finish with Photomerge, you can make further corrections with the Clone Stamp tool.

   <TIP>

   If you have trouble repositioning images manually in the Photomerge dialog box, deselect Snap to Image in the lower right of the dialog box. When this option is selected, Photomerge automatically tries to snap one image to another where they overlap.

   <NOTE>

   Moving and rotating parts of the merged image may cause the merged preview to have uneven borders. Don't worry about that. You can fix that with the Crop tool after the Photomerge is completed.

9. Select the Select Image tool at the top left of the dialog box, and click the rightmost image in the merged preview.

10. Select the Rotate Image tool again, and drag the rightmost image slightly counterclockwise to close the small gap between it and the center image.

   This gap is so small that it may not show up in your Photomerge. Skip this step if you don't see this gap.

11. Select the Select Image tool, and click outside of the merged preview to hide the red borders.

Additional Photomerge Settings

The Composition and Settings options at the bottom right of the Photomerge dialog box are useful on some, but not all, Photomerges. The Perspective setting can help counteract the tendency of merged photos to appear flat and lacking in perspective. This setting defaults to using the centermost photo as the vanishing point when it adjusts perspective, as indicated by the blue border you see when you click on the center image after applying the Perspective setting. You can dictate a different vanishing point by selecting the Set Vanishing Point tool (the star icon) at the top left of the Photomerge dialog box and clicking in the merged preview. If the Perspective setting causes distortion, try to correct it by selecting the Cylindrical Mapping option and clicking Preview. The Advanced Blending option is used to try to correct uneven exposure that causes blending problems. Keep in mind that these advanced settings do not work on every image. If you apply one of these settings and don't like the result, click the Undo button at the top right of the dialog box.

12. **After you're satisfied that no further adjustment is needed, click OK in the Photomerge dialog box to complete the Photomerge.**
The merged image in a wide panoramic format appears in a document window.

13. **Select the Crop tool, and use it to crop off any uneven borders. Use the Clone Stamp tool to fill in any gaps that may remain.**

14. **Choose File➔Save, navigate to your ccproject folder, name the file 11_panorama.psd, and click Save.**
A finished copy of the panorama is located in the Session 11 Tutorial Files folder. Print the panorama if you like.

15. **Close 11_01stadium.psd, 11_02stadium.psd, and 11_03stadium.psd without saving.**
That's all there is to creating wide-angle panoramic images in Photoshop Elements 2.

» Session Review

In this session, you learned how to print a document from Photoshop Elements 2, and you printed the greeting cards that you created throughout the course. You created some special layouts for print—a contact sheet of all your greeting card images, Picture Packages with single and multiple images, and a panoramic photograph.

1. Do you have to flatten a file before printing it? (See Tutorial: Preparing Files for Printing.)

2. What kind of paper can you use to print the greeting cards that you created in this course? (See Tutorial: Preparing Files for Printing.)

3. How do you position an image on a page in the printing process? (See Tutorial: Preparing Files for Printing.)

4. Should all files that you plan to include in a contact sheet be open or closed when you create the contact sheet? (See Tutorial: Making a Contact Sheet.)

5. What should you do to prepare for making your own contact sheets? (See Tutorial: Making a Contact Sheet.)

6. How do you include multiple images on a single sheet using the Picture Package feature? (See Tutorial: Creating a Picture Package.)

7. Which feature automatically creates a panoramic image from individual photographs? (See Tutorial: Creating a Panorama.)

01_boxing_end.psd

02_biking_end.psd

04_stopwatch_end.psd

05_graffiti_end.psd

06_baseball_end.psd

07_racecars_end.psd

08_ride_end.psd

10_snow_end.psd

BS02_basketball_end.psd

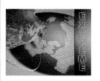

climber_end.psd

Outputting for the Web and Screen

Session Introduction

Print is not the only medium for sharing images from Photoshop Elements 2. The program has special features for preparing and outputting images for the Web and other on-screen media. The first tutorials in this session cover preparing image elements for a Web site that features photographs you used in your greeting cards. You learn how to optimize photographs, text, and graphic art for the Web; how to make the artwork for rollover buttons; how to prepare a large photograph for use as a Web page background; and how to create a GIF animation from layered artwork. Then you learn several quick and easy ways to display your greeting cards or other images on screen, using the automatic Web Photo Gallery, e-mail attachment, and PDF slideshow features of Photoshop Elements 2.

TOOLS YOU'LL USE
Save for Web, Web Photo Gallery, Attach to E-mail, PDF Slideshow

CD-ROM FILES NEEDED
12_web.psd, 12_web_end.psd, 12_anim.psd,
12_anim_end.gif, final greeting cards folder

TIME REQUIRED
90 minutes

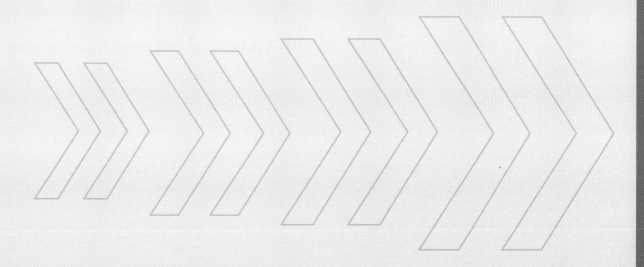

Discussion
Using Photoshop Elements 2 in Web Design

Photoshop Elements 2 is primarily an image-editing program. It cannot write JavaScript to make rollovers work, slice page layouts into HTML tables, or make working hot spots on an imagemap. However, it can be used for some important Web design functions: page layout, image optimization, and GIF animation.

Laying out a Web page in this program allows you to experiment with different compositions and decide on the size and position of graphic elements before you actually construct a site in a Web-authoring program. Placing individual pieces of artwork on separate layers in Photoshop Elements makes it easy to move items around, change their size, transform their shapes, recolor them, and give them various effects. The layout stage has been done for you in this session, because it's repetitive of the basic image creation skills that you've already acquired.

After you have a Web page layout, you can copy each graphic element to a new image file and use the Save for Web features in Photoshop Elements 2 to optimize the individual files (choose compression settings) and save them in Web compatible formats. This is what you concentrate on in this session. When you're finished, you'll have individual photographs optimized as JPEGs, a Web page background, a logo optimized as a transparent GIF, artwork for two states of rollover buttons, and a GIF animation. All of these Web-ready graphics could be brought into a Web-authoring application like Adobe GoLive or Macromedia Dreamweaver to be composed and programmed as a working Web page.

Tutorial
» Optimizing Photographs for the Web

In this tutorial, you learn how to optimize photographs as JPEGs for the Web.

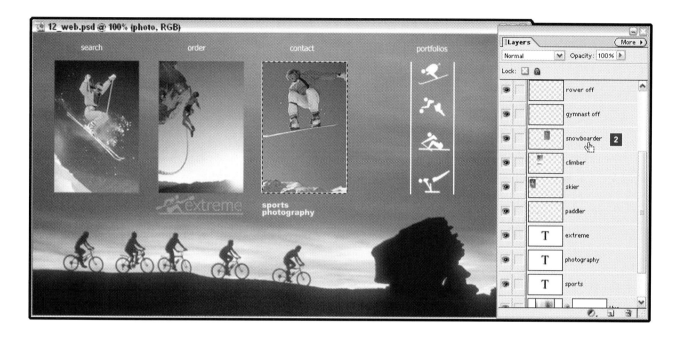

1. **Choose File→Open, navigate to the Session 12 Tutorial Files folder on your hard drive, and open** 12_web.psd.
   This is a layout for the home page of a photography portfolio site featuring the photographs used in your greeting cards.

2. **Ctrl+click (Macintosh: ⌘+click) on the** snowboarder **layer in the Layers palette to select all but the transparent pixels on that layer. Choose File→Copy.**
   This selects the photograph that is the only item on this layer and copies it to the clipboard. Another way to select all the artwork on a layer is to right-click (Macintosh: Ctrl+click) on the layer thumbnail and choose Select Layer Transparency.

3. **Choose File→New from Clipboard to create a new file that contains only the snowboarder photograph.**
   If you see any stray transparent pixels at the edges of this file, eliminate them by selecting the Crop tool, drawing a crop boundary just inside the checkerboard pattern, and pressing Enter (Macintosh: Return).

4. **Click in the new, untitled document window to make sure that it is active. Choose File→Save. In the Save As dialog box, name the new file** 12_snowboarder.psd, **make sure that Format is set to Photoshop, navigate to your ccproject folder, and click Save.**
   This creates a source file in PSD format. In the next steps, you optimize a copy of this source file as a JPEG for the Web.

<NOTE>
It's important to save the PSD source file from which an optimized file is made in case you need to make changes later. Rather than changing an optimized file, making changes to the source file and reoptimizing is best.

5. **Choose File→Save for Web.**
   This opens the Save for Web dialog box where you optimize a copy of this image.

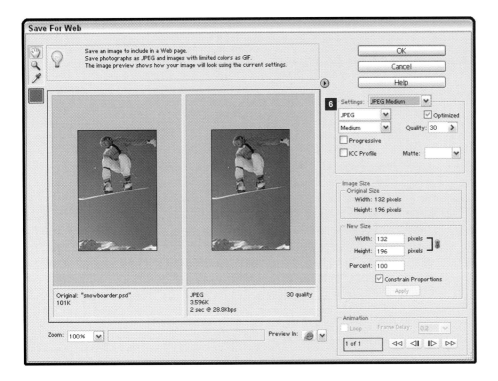

<NOTE>

Take a look at the two image panes in the Save For Web dialog box. The pane on the left is the original PSD image. The pane on the right is a preview of the optimized image. As you choose optimization settings on the right side of the Save For Web dialog box, you can visually evaluate the image quality of the optimized photo by comparing it to the original. You can also compare the file sizes of the original and the optimized files, which are reported at the bottom of the panes.

<TIP>

The optimized preview pane also displays an estimated time for downloading the file to a Web browser. Take this statistic with a grain of salt, because factors other than file size, like Web traffic, affect download time. For a better estimate of download time, click the small arrow by the top-right corner of the preview panes to open the Preview menu, and choose the speed of the modem or broadband device that you think is used by the viewers for whom you are designing.

6. **Click the Settings button to reveal a menu of optimization presets, and choose JPEG Medium.**

This sets the file Format field to JPEG and the Quality field to 30. The items in the Settings menu are presets that change other optimization settings on the right side of the Save For Web window. A preset is often a good place to start. You can then fine tune individual optimization settings as you do in the steps that follow.

What Is Optimizing?

Optimizing is the process of compressing images for travel across the Web. Choosing optimization settings is always a compromise between image size and image quality. You want your files to be as small as possible so that they download to a viewer's browser relatively fast. You also want the optimized image to look as close to the original as possible and be free of compression artifacts (which appear as blotches in a JPEG), dithered colors (which look like colored dots in a GIF), or untrue colors (caused by too few colors in a GIF).

7. **Select the Zoom tool at the top left of the Save For Web window, and click in either image pane to zoom in for a closer look.**
   Alternatively, use the Zoom menu at the bottom left of the Save For Web dialog box to change the magnification. Notice the compression artifacts (the blotchy areas) in the blue sky around the skateboarder. You reduce those by increasing compression Quality in the next steps.

<TIP>

Although optimizing photographs as JPEGs is usually best, there are two situations in which a photograph has to be optimized as a GIF—when it's to be included in an animated GIF, and when you want to retain transparent areas in a photograph (because JPEG format does not support transparency). When you optimize a photo as a GIF, set the Color field to a large number and turn the percentage of dithering up high to make the image look reasonably good.

<TIP>

Use the Hand tool at the top left of the Save For Web window to scroll around a magnified image.

8. **Double-click the Zoom tool to return to 100% magnification.**
   When you judge image quality, it's best to set magnification to 100%, because that's the view your users see.

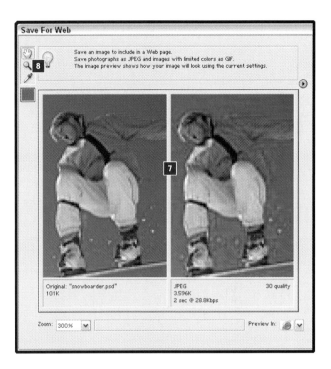

JPEG Format

Choosing a file format is the first decision to make when you're optimizing an image for the Web. You have two viable formats to choose from for optimizing a still image—JPEG and GIF. (It's best to avoid the PNG formats because Web browsers do not treat those formats uniformly.) JPEG stands for Joint Photographic Experts Group and is usually the best file format for optimizing photographs. In most cases, a photograph compresses to a smaller size and looks better when optimized as a JPEG rather than a GIF. JPEG is also the format to choose for a continuous tone graphic, like

one with a gradient or a beveled layer style. JPEG format works well for these kinds of images because it can display millions of colors.

JPEG is a lossy compression method, which means that it throws away image information. Therefore, you should save an image as a JPEG only once. Each time you resave, you lose more image information. If you need to change a JPEG, go back to the source file, make your changes, and reoptimize.

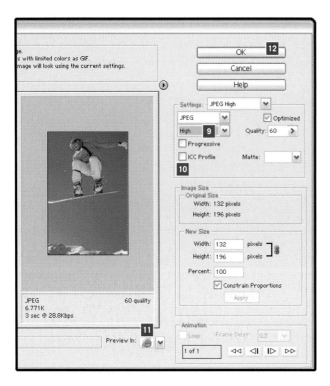

9. **Increase the Quality setting in the Save For Web dialog box to High.**
Alternatively, move the Quality slider in the dialog box to 60. This reduces the artifacts so that they are barely visible at the 100% view. The trade-off for this improved appearance is a slightly higher optimized file size.

< T I P >

Quality is the setting that has the largest impact on file size and appearance of a JPEG. The goal is to set Quality to the lowest number at which you don't see unacceptable artifacts. The lower the quality, the higher the compression and the smaller the file size.

< T I P >

You may be wondering how to determine an acceptable file size for an optimized image. There is no concrete answer because viewers' download capabilities vary so widely. As a rough guide, many Web designers try to keep the total size of all the images on a page below approximately 50K. Don't count any images you've included elsewhere in your Web site in that total, because a viewer's browser may reuse an image that's already downloaded.

10. **Leave the other optimization settings on the right side of the Save For Web window at their defaults.**
Leaving Optimized selected makes a JPEG slightly smaller. You don't need an ICC profile for color management. Color profiles increase file size and can't be read by most browsers anyway. A Progressive file, which downloads in black and white before the actual JPEG, is also unecessary. Matte color is not at issue because this image contains no transparent pixels. And the width and height of the optimized image do not have to be changed. (You can reduce the dimensions of the optimized file without affecting the source file with these Image Size controls. Reducing image dimensions decreases file size.)

11. **Click the Preview In button at the bottom of the Save For Web dialog box to preview the image in a default Web browser.**
The browser preview displays the image as it will look in that browser, descriptive information about the image, and some temporary HTML code for displaying the image in the browser.

< T I P >

You can preview an optimized image in any Web browser that's installed on your hard drive by clicking the arrow to the right of the Preview In field and navigating to that browser.

12. **Click OK in the Save For Web window if you're satisfied with the appearance and size of your optimized image.**
This opens the Save Optimized As dialog box.

13. In the Save Optimized As dialog box, navigate to your ccproject folder and click Save.

This saves the file as a JPEG optimized for the Web, 12_snowboarder.jpg. You'll find a copy of 12_snowboarder.jpg in your Session 12 Tutorial Files folder.

<NOTE>

This JPEG is ready to be brought into the program in which you are building a Web site (perhaps an HTML authoring program, like Adobe GoLive, or a text editor), for inclusion in one or more Web pages. If you try to re-create the page layout you use in this session as a Web page, repeat the steps in this tutorial on the skier and climber photographs that you find on separate layers in 12_web.psd in order to optimize those images for the Web.

14. Close the source file 12_snowboarder.psd.

It's not necessary to save this file again, because you haven't made any changes to it since you last saved it earlier in this tutorial. Leave 12_web.psd open for the next tutorial. In this tutorial you prepared a photograph for use on the Web, choosing optimization settings that balance the need for small file size against the desire for visual quality.

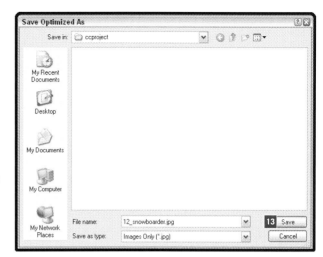

<TIP>

When you work on your own Web images, be sure to save the latest version of the source file. Otherwise, the source file and the optimized copy may not match, which can be confusing if you have to make changes to the source file later.

Tutorial
» Making a Web Page Background

Web page backgrounds come in several flavors—plain color backgrounds created in HTML, repeating patterned tiles, and photographic backgrounds. In this tutorial, you make a striking background from a large photograph, learning techniques for reducing the file size of a large photograph.

1. With `12_web.psd` still open from the previous tutorial, click Ctrl+D (Macintosh: ⌘+D) to eliminate any selection that may still be active from that tutorial. Select the photo layer in the `12_web.psd` Layers palette.

<NOTE>
If you closed `12_web.psd`, reopen it from your Session 12 Tutorial Files folder.

2. Choose Layer→Duplicate Layer. In the Duplicate Layer dialog box, type photo in the As field. Click the Document button and choose New. In the Name field, type a name for your new document— `12_photobg.psd`. Click OK to create a new document containing only this photograph.

This is a useful method for creating a new document that contains all the contents of the original layer and is the same size as the original document.

3. Click in the new `12_photobg.psd` document window to make sure that it's the active document. Choose File→Save, navigate to your ccproject folder, make sure that Format is set to Photoshop, and click Save.

This saves the source file in PSD format.

4. With `12_photobg.psd` active, choose File→Save for Web. In the Save For Web dialog box, notice that the file size of the original image is over 1 megabyte (M) and that, with JPEG Quality set to High, the optimized image is around 31K. Click Cancel to close the Save For Web window.

In the next steps, you learn how to reduce the optimized file size further by colorizing the source file.

5. In `12_photobg.psd`, click the Create New Fill or Adjustment Layer button at the bottom of the Layers palette and choose Hue/Saturation from the menu of layer types.

This creates a Hue/Saturation adjustment layer above the photo layer in this document and opens the Hue/Saturation dialog box.

6. **In the Hue/Saturation dialog box, select the Colorize option to tint the photo with the color in the Foreground Color box.**

7. **Drag the Hue slider to** 227 **and the Saturation slider to** 35 **to change the tint to a desaturated blue. Click OK to close the Hue/Saturation dialog box.**

8. **Choose File→Save For Web.**
   In the Save For Web dialog box, notice that the optimized file is now down to around 26.85K at the High quality setting.

Sizing a Background Image

An image that is designated as a background image in the HTML code for a Web page repeats horizontally and vertically to fill each viewer's Web browser. You can take advantage of this feature to create a patterned background from a small graphic image. But when you create a background from one large image, you don't want the viewer to see that image repeating in the browser. The way to avoid that is to make the background image larger in width and height than the screen area of the viewer's browser.

To determine the dimensions to use for a background image, you need to know the browser, platform, and screen resolution that your viewers are likely to use. (You might get this information from market research or general browser usage statistics.) On a computer with that configuration, open the target browser all the way and make a screen shot of the region in which Web content appears, not including menu bars and scrollbars. Open the screen shot in Photoshop Elements 2 and read the document dimensions in pixels from the status bar (Macintosh: document window). Make your background image at least as big as that screenshot so the background won't repeat in the target browser. For example, the background image that you're currently using was resized to 780 x 430 pixels so that it is just big enough to avoid repeating in the most popular current browser configuration—Internet Explorer 5 on Windows at a screen resolution of 800 x 600 pixels. (The remaining pixels are taken up by the browser's menu bars and scroll bars.)

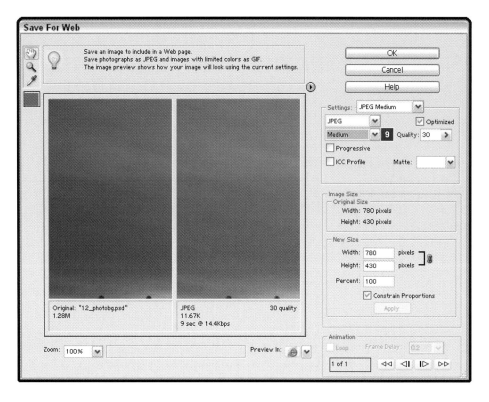

9. **Reduce the Quality setting to Medium. Click OK to accept these settings and to close the Save For Web dialog box.**
   You now have a full-sized background image that is only around 11.7K, saving your viewers from having to wait for a larger download.

<TIP>
You can shave even more file size off a JPEG by adding a slight Gaussian blur (Filter➔Blur➔Gaussian Blur) to the source image. In my view, this particular image suffers too much from added blur (the silhouetted bicyclists become too soft), but this technique works well on more abstract photographs.

10. **In the Save Optimized As dialog box, navigate to your ccproject folder and click Save to save your Web-ready background image 12_photobg.jpg.**
    You'll find a copy of 12_photobg.jpg in your Session 12 Tutorial Files folder.

11. **The file 12_photobg.psd remains open. With that document active, choose File➔Save to resave the source image with the blue color tint. Close this file.**

12. **Leave 12_web.psd open for the next tutorial.**
    In this tutorial you optimized a large photograph for the Web, giving it a monochrome tint in order to reduce its file size so that it is suitable for use as a Web page background despite its large physical dimensions.

Tutorial

» Optimizing Graphics and Text for the Web

In this tutorial, you make a logo from a graphic and text and save it for the Web as a GIF. This is an example of the type of graphic artwork that is best optimized as a GIF.

1. With `12_web.psd` open from the previous tutorial, in the Layers palette, select the paddler layer, and Alt+click (Macintosh: Option+click) the Create New Layer button at the bottom of the Layers palette.

   If `12_web.psd` is not still open, reopen it from your Session 12 Tutorial Files folder.

2. In the New Layer dialog box, type logo in the Name field and click OK.

   This makes a new **logo** layer above the **paddler** layer.

3. With the logo layer selected, click in the Link fields of the paddler layer and the three type layers—extreme, photography, and sports. Click the More button at the top of the Layers palette, and Alt+click (Macintosh: Option+click) Merge Linked in the palette menu.

   This creates a composite of the linked layers in the **logo** layer.

4. Ctrl+click (Macintosh: ⌘+click) the logo layer to select all the artwork on that layer. Choose Edit→Copy.

5. Choose File→New from Clipboard to create a new, untitled document that contains just the logo artwork.

6. Choose File→Save, navigate to your ccproject folder, name the new file `12_logo.psd`, and click Save to save this source file.

7. With `12_logo.psd` active, choose File→Save for Web.

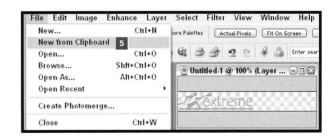

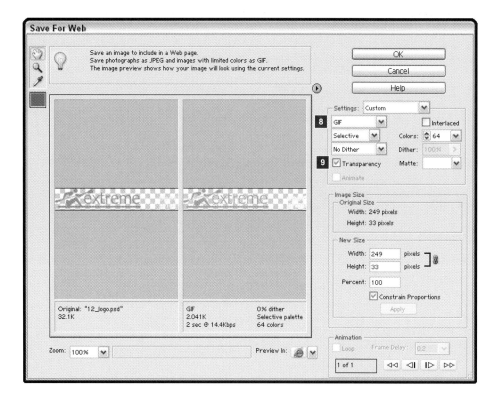

<TIP>

GIF is the best format (i.e., the format that makes the smallest and best-looking images) for flat art. This includes solid color graphics and icons and text that you save as a graphic.

<CAUTION>

If you add styles, effects, or gradients to flat art, it may optimize best as a JPEG rather than a GIF. When you're unsure which format to use, try both in the Save For Web dialog box and compare their size and appearance.

8. **In the Save For Web dialog box, set the Format field to GIF.**

9. **Make sure that the Transparency option in the Save For Web dialog box is selected.**
   This ensures that the transparent pixels in the source image are transparent in the GIF.

Making a Transparent GIF

Every image in Photoshop Elements 2 is technically rectangular or square (the shape of the document window). To simulate a non-rectangular graphic, create a source file in which the artwork is surrounded by transparent pixels. Optimize the file as a GIF, making sure to select the Transparency option in the Save For Web

window. If you do not select the Transparency option, the transparent pixels in the source image are filled with a solid color (the color in the Matte field) in the optimized image. Remember that only GIF, not JPEG, supports transparency.

10. **Click in the Matte field in the Save For Web window, choose Other, and select a blue color that's similar to the sky in the Web page background (try R:** 79, **G:** 94, **B:** 145**).**
Zoom in closer to see that this fills the semi-transparent pixels at the edge of the anti-aliased logo with blue so that the logo blends in with the matching page background when the page is built.

<CAUTION>
Some Web page backgrounds do not have just one predominant color. For example, imagine a striped yellow and red background. If you choose red as the Matte color of a foreground image with transparency, you'll see a red halo on the foreground image where it sits on top of a yellow background stripe, and vice versa. In that case, set the Matte color to None. This changes the edge of the foreground image to a stair-stepped anti-aliased look. You may miss the soft edge, but at least you won't see a halo.

11. **Set the Format field to Perceptual, Selective, or Adaptive.**
Do not be fooled into thinking that you should use the Web palette.

12. **Set the number of colors in the Colors field to** 64, **and take note of the file size in the preview pane. Click the arrow on the Colors field, and choose lower numbers in succession, noticing the reduction in file size. Continue until the previewed GIF changes color or just doesn't look good to you. Then move up one notch.**
This sets the number of colors that are used in this GIF. You may be satisfied with just eight colors for this particular image, which brings the file size to less than 2K. Choosing the number of colors for a GIF always requires subjective judgment and a compromise between lowering file size and maintaining authentic color in the optimized image.

<NOTE>
The number you choose for the Colors field is the most significant of the optimization settings when you're optimizing an image as a GIF.

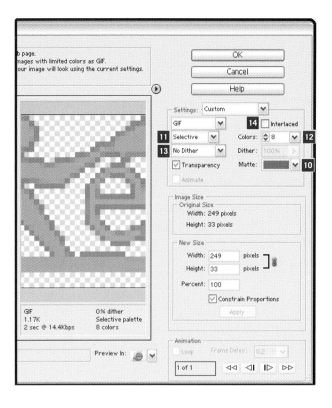

13. **Leave the Dither field set to No Dither.**
This tells the program not to use dots of color to try to simulate a color that's not among the eight colors used for this image.

14. **Leave Interlaced deselected.**
Selecting this option would create a low-resolution version of the image that would download before the actual image.

Choosing a Matte Color to Avoid Halos

The GIF format supports fully opaque or fully transparent pixels, but not semi-transparent pixels like those found around the edges of anti-aliased or feathered images or text. Semi-transparent pixels are filled in with the Matte color when you optimize artwork as a transparent GIF. The Matte color must match the predominant color in the Web page background to blend in with the background. For example, if the Matte color in this tutorial were set to white, you would see a thin white halo around the edge of the logo against the image of the sky in a Web browser.

If you're planning to use a plain color background created by HTML code and you know its hexadecimal identification code,

click on the Matte field in the Save For Web window to open the Color Picker, and type that code into the # box at the bottom of the Color Picker. If you're using an image as a page background and you need to discover the color of the page background, you have to exit the Save For Web window, use the Eyedropper tool to sample the page background, and click the Foreground Color box to open the Color Picker to see the RGB value of the sampled color. Then you can return to the Save For Web window for the transparent GIF, click the Matte field to open the Color Picker, and type the value into the RGB fields.

<NOTE>

Before completing optimization of any image, previewing how it looks in a browser is wise. You can preview in any browser that's installed on your own system by choosing from the Preview In menu at the bottom of the Save For Web dialog box, as you did in the last tutorial. But that won't tell you how your image looks on other platforms.

Choosing a Palette—Web-Safe Is Dead

A GIF, unlike a JPEG, can display only a limited number of colors—a maximum of 256 colors. The Palette setting determines the subset of colors from which a particular GIF's colors are taken. The Perceptual, Selective, and Adaptive palettes are all derived from colors in the image itself, each using a slightly different algorithm. You can't go wrong with any of these palettes. The Web palette, on the other hand, is a predetermined palette of 216 colors that are the only colors an 8-bit display system can replicate. This limited palette has no relationship to the actual colors in the image that you're optimizing, so selecting the Web palette can cause noticeable color shifts and dithering (dots of color) in your image.

The good news is that if you are designing for today's Web, you have no reason to limit yourself to the Web palette (sometimes called Web-safe or Browser-safe colors). That's because all but very old computers can now display millions of colors (24-bit color). So you can ignore the Web palette, except in the rare event that you're designing for a device that can display only 8-bit color.

<TIP>

To preview what your GIF will look like to any viewer still using an 8-bit color system, click the arrow at the top right of the preview pane in the Save For Web window and choose Browser Dither. If you zoom in, you'll see some dots of color. An 8-bit browser would use this dotting technique (similar to the traditional pointillist method of painting) to try to reproduce a non-Web-safe color from the limited Web palette. Note that this is different from the kind of dither discussed later in this tutorial. Browser Dither and regular Dither look similar, but they have different causes. Don't forget to deselect Browser Dither before moving on.

When to Dither

Dithering comes in handy when you want to keep the number of colors and resulting file size low (or when an original image, for example a photograph, has many more than the maximum number of 256 colors). When you choose one of the dither patterns—Diffusion, Pattern, or Noise—the program uses small dots of color to try to simulate an original color that is not among the limited colors that you've allowed for construction of the GIF. You can choose from three dither patterns that differ in the arrangement of those dots. If you choose the Diffusion dither pattern, you can also set the amount of dither.

Unfortunately, dithering has two downsides: It gives the image a spotted look that you may not like, and it increases file size.

15. **Click the right-facing arrow at the top right of the preview pane to open the Preview menu. Choose Standard Macintosh Color to preview how your image looks to viewers on most Macintosh computers. Click Standard Windows Color to see how the image looks to viewers on most Windows computers. Choose Uncompensated Color to return to the default option.**

    Notice that colors look darker to Windows viewers than to Macintosh viewers. The Uncompensated Color option shows the image as it appears on your monitor. It looks similar to the Use Color Profile option because this file is not tagged with a color profile.

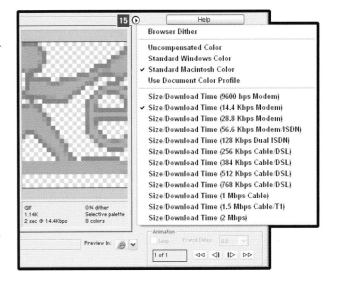

<CAUTION>

These built-in previews display only color differences. They do not show you other platform-specific differences, like the difference in HTML type size in Windows and Macintosh browsers. (The same size type looks larger on a Windows machine than on a Macintosh.)

16. **Click OK in the Save For Web dialog box to open the Save Optimized As dialog box.**

17. **In the Save Optimized As dialog box, navigate to your ccproject folder and click Save to save the optimized copy of the logo as** 12_logo.gif.

    This file, like the other optimized images that you made in this session, is now ready to be opened in a Web-authoring program to be included in a Web site. You can find a copy of 12_logo.gif in your Session 12 Tutorial Files folder.

18. **Close** 12_logo.psd **without saving it again. Leave** 12_web.psd **open for the next tutorial.**

    In this tutorial, you optimized graphics and text as a GIF for the web.

Text as Image versus HTML Text

When you create text in Photoshop and save it as a GIF (or less frequently, as a JPEG) for the Web, the text is in image format. The advantage of using text as an image is that you can dictate the font style and size. The disadvantage is that a text image has a larger file size than HTML text and must be downloaded like any other image. The alternative is to wait until you code a Web page to include text created by HTML code. That saves file size, but it detracts from the amount of control you have over the appearance of the text. If a viewer does not have a particular font on a computer, the browser changes the font of HTML text. In addition, HTML type size is relative, rather than fixed, so you can't control exactly how it looks.

You generally use image text for headlines and decorative type effects, and HTML text for paragraphs of text. You can dummy planned HTML text into your page layout so that you get a sense of its placement. Just don't bother to optimize that part of the layout. In this page layout, the small navigation text at the top of the page is intended as HTML text.

Tutorial
» Making Artwork for Rollover Buttons

In this tutorial, you prepare two transparent GIFs to be used as two states of a rollover button. You may be surprised to learn that a simple rollover is nothing more than a swapping of one piece of art for another upon the occurrence of a mouse event.

1. **With** 12_web.psd **open from the previous tutorial, Ctrl+click (Macintosh: ⌘+click) the** skier off **layer in the Layers palette to select the artwork on that layer. Choose Edit→Copy.**
   If 12_web.psd is no longer open, open it from your Session 12 Tutorial Files folder. In the next steps, you copy the white skier button from the page layout to its own source file and optimize it as a transparent GIF. This GIF can be specified as a rollover button's normal state in a Web-authoring program.

2. **Choose File→New from Clipboard to create a new file with just the white skier off artwork against transparent pixels.**

3. **Double-click the** Layer 1 **name, and rename the layer** skier.

4. **Choose File→Save, name the file** 12_skier_off.psd, **navigate to your ccproject folder, and click Save to save this source file.**

5. **With** 12_skier_off.psd **active, choose File→Save for Web.**

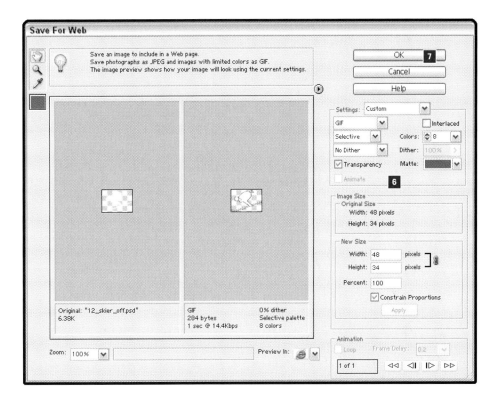

6. In the Save For Web dialog box, set the following options, which you learned about in the last tutorial:

>> Format: GIF

>> Palette: Selective

>> Dither: No Dither

>> Transparency: Selected

>> Interlaced: Deselected

>> Colors: 8

>> Matte: Blue (R: **1**, G: **95**, B: **159**)

7. Click OK in the Save For Web dialog box to open the Save Optimized As dialog box.

8. In the Save Optimized As dialog box, navigate to your ccproject folder and click Save to save 12_skier_off.gif.

This will be the normal state of a rollover button that can be used as a link to a portfolio of skiing photographs. You'll find a copy of 12_skier_off.gif in your Session 12 Tutorial Files folder. In the next steps, you make some simple changes to the skier artwork to create a second image of the same size that could be specified as the second state of a rollover button in a Web-authoring program. The second image might be programmed to appear in place of 12_skier_off.gif (the normal state) when a viewer moves the mouse over the button or clicks the button.

<NOTE>

A rollover is simply a set of JavaScript commands that swap one image for another upon occurrence of an event.

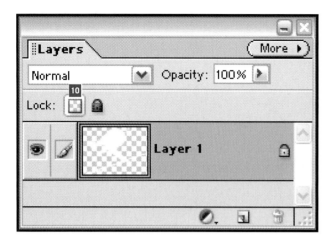

9. **Click on the source file** `12_skier_off.psd` **to make that document active.**

<TIP>
Creating the second state artwork by altering the first helps ensure that the document dimensions for both states are the same size. If they're not, one of the pieces of artwork will appear distorted when the rollover is programmed in a Web-authoring program. Note that one graphic can be a different size than the other, so long as the width and height of the Photoshop Elements 2 document windows (in other words, the file dimensions) are the same.

10. **Click the Transparency Lock in the Layers palette to protect the transparent pixels on the** skier **layer.**

11. **Choose the Eyedropper tool, and click on the extreme logo in the** `12_web.psd` **document window to set the Foreground Color box in the toolbox to orange.**

12. **Click Alt+Backspace (Macintosh: Option+Delete) to fill the skier artwork with the Foreground orange color.**
    If Transparency Lock was not selected, the entire layer would fill with orange.

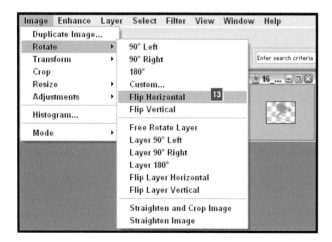

13. **Choose Image→Rotate→Flip Horizontal to change the orientation of the skier graphic.**

14. **Choose File→Save As.**

15. **In the Save As dialog box, change the File name to** `12_skier_on.psd`, **navigate to your ccproject folder, and click Save to create a source file.**

16. **Repeat Steps 5 through 7 using** `12_skier_on.psd`, **optimizing and saving a copy of this file as** `12_skier_on.gif`.
    You can find a copy of `12_skier_on.gif` in your Session 12 Tutorial Files folder.

17. **To get a sense of how the rollover will look when it's active, choose File→Open, navigate to the Session 12 Tutorial Files folder, and open** 12_web_end.psd**. Toggle off and on the Visibility icons on the** skier off **and** skier on **layers to simulate swapping the two image files in a rollover.**

18. **Close all the open files without resaving, except** 12_web.psd**, which you should leave open for the next tutorial.**

    You now have artwork for two states of a rollover button ready to be programmed with JavaScript in a Web-authoring program or by hand. If you plan to re-create the entire page layout in a Web-authoring program, repeat this tutorial on the other three portfolio rollover buttons—the basketball player, rower, and gymnast. (You don't have to do this to progress through the rest of this session.)

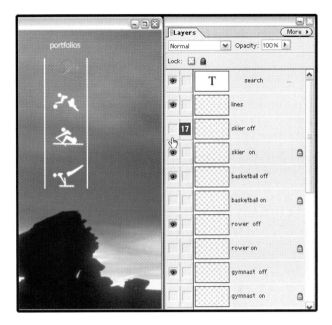

Tutorial
» Creating an Animated GIF

Animated GIFs are the simplest form of animation you see on the Web. Animated GIFs are easy to make; they don't require any additional coding to make them run, and they can be viewed in any Web browser. Photoshop Elements 2 has a feature that automatically turns artwork on separate layers into individual frames of an animated GIF. In this tutorial, you use this feature to create the artwork for an animated Web banner.

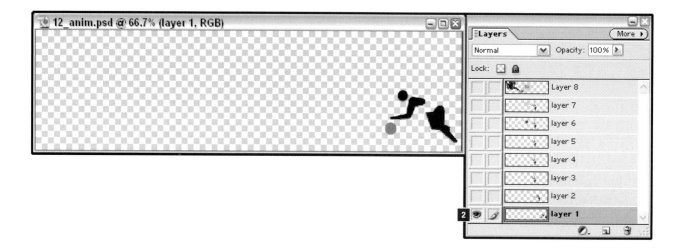

1. **Choose File→Open, navigate to your Session 12 Tutorial Files folder, and open** 12_anim.psd.

   This is a multi-layered file with different artwork on each layer. Follow the next steps to see how the file is constructed.

2. **In the Layers palette, Alt+click (Macintosh: Option+click) in the Visibility field of** layer 1 **to hide all the other layers so you can see what's on** layer 1.

   The artwork on this layer becomes the first frame of your animation.

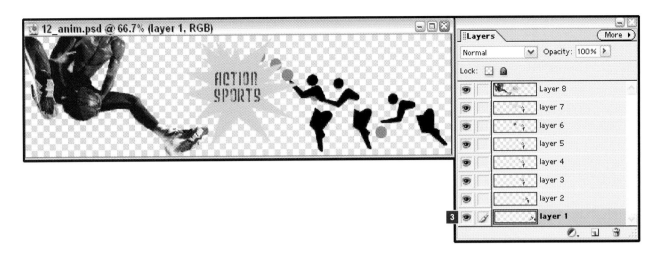

3. **Alt+click (Macintosh: Option+click) in that Visibility field again to turn the visibility of the other layers back on.**

4. **Repeat Step 3 on each successive layer in the Layers palette, observing how the artwork changes on each layer.**

5. **Choose File→Save for Web.**

<NOTE>

When you create your own animations, place individual graphics, photographs, or text on separate layers. Each layer becomes a separate frame in your animation. This layer-to-frame technique is similar to cell animation used by professional cartoonists. You can use it to create lots of different kinds of animations. Here are a few ideas:

- Place different photographs on separate layers to create a slideshow.
- Reposition a character in each layer to simulate motion.
- Change the size of an element on each layer to create a pulsating effect, or to make the element seem to grow or shrink.
- Vary the color of an element on each layer.
- Start with one letter and add another letter on each layer to simulate a typewriter.
- Use the Warp Text feature to change the shape of text on each layer.

<TIP>

When you create artwork for your own animations, you have to decide how many layers to include. The more layers there are, the more frames there are in the animation. The more frames there are, the smoother the animation appears, but the larger the file size of the animation is. I suggest you start with a few frames, check the file size in the Save For Web dialog box (with the Animate option selected), and add more frames only if the file size is reasonable when considered along with the size of all the graphics on the Web page or Web banner that you're creating. For example, if you want to keep the total size of all graphics on a Web page under 50K, a 35K animation may be too big depending on what else is on the page.

<CAUTION>

Animation is an attention-grabbing element, so I suggest that you use animation conservatively and wisely to emphasize without over-doing. An ill-considered animation on a Web page can distract the viewer and detract from the design. On the other hand, an animation in a Web banner is a good way to draw a viewer's attention to an advertiser's message.

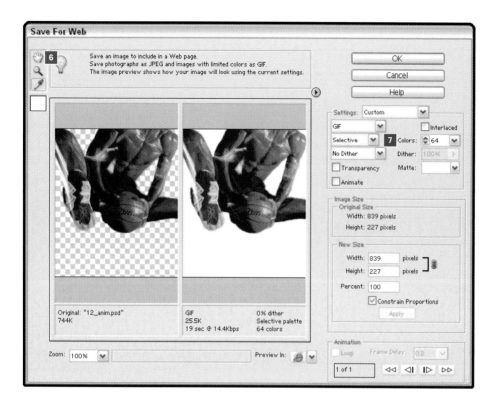

6. **In the Save For Web dialog box, select the Hand tool and move the image in the preview pane so that you can see the photograph of the basketball player.**

7. **Set the Format to** GIF **and the palette to** Selective. **Set the number of Colors to** 64. **Select No Dither, and make sure that Interlaced is deselected.**

   This is one of the rare situations in which an image containing a photograph must be optimized as a GIF rather than a JPEG. (You must set the Format field to **GIF** because you're making an animated GIF.) You can see some posterized areas in the photograph, but it looks acceptable alongside the flat art in this Web banner. The photograph would look better at 256 colors, but that would make the file size too high.

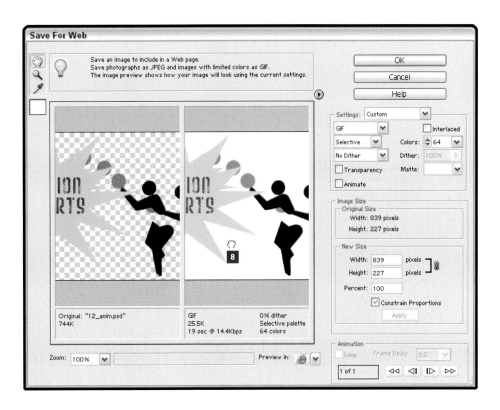

8. **With the Hand tool, move the image in the preview pane so that you can see the illustrations in this image. Check that they look acceptable at the settings that you chose in the preceeding step.**

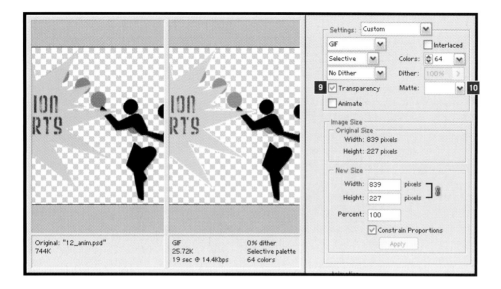

<TIP>

Not all animated GIFs require transparency. If you don't want to see through to the Web page background, surround the animated element with solid artwork that is repeated on each layer. (It's not sufficient to put the solid artwork on one layer at the bottom of the Layers palette. If you did that it would become just one fleeting frame in the animation.)

9. **Select the Transparency option in the Save For Web dialog box.**
   This allows the Web page background to show through around the animated characters.

10. **Click the arrow on the Matte field in the Save For Web dialog box, and choose White, if Matte is not already set to white.**
    This prepares the animated GIF for use against a white background, which could be created with HTML code in a Web-authoring program. Notice that the file size reported in the Preview pane is around 25K at this point.

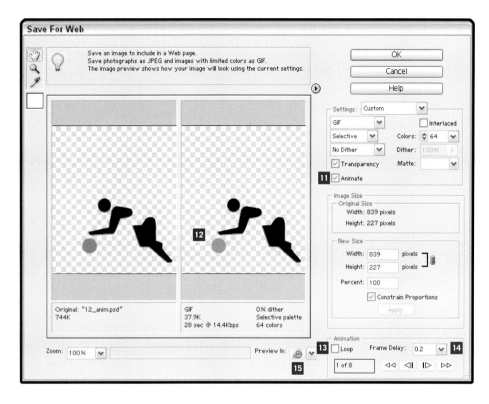

11. **Select the Animate option in the Save For Web dialog box.**

    This converts each layer in the source file to a separate frame in an animation. You may see only transparent pixels in the preview pane at this point because the preview pane is displaying the first frame of the animation, which is derived from the bottom layer of the source file, and the artwork on that layer and frame is on the right side of the document. This is addressed in the next step.

12. **With the Hand tool, click in the preview pane and drag to the left until you see the artwork on the first frame of the animation.**

13. **The Animation options at the bottom of the Save For Web dialog box are now active. Make sure that the Loop option is deselected so that the animation plays just once in a viewer's browser and stops.**

<TIP>

A looping animation can be annoying, so use this option sparingly. However, if you have only two or three simple frames in an animation, it may be necessary to select Loop. Otherwise, the animation might play through before becoming fully visible in a viewer's browser.

14. **Set the Frame Delay field to 0.2 seconds, if it is not already set to that value.**

    This controls the approximate amount of time between each frame in the animation. This number of seconds is not exact, because the timing of an animation depends in part on factors that you can't control, like the speed of a viewer's computer processor.

15. **Click the Preview In field at the bottom of the Save For Web window to preview the animation in your default Web browser.**

    You should see the player dribbling and shooting, followed by a burst of red and yellow. The yellow shape, the words *action sports*, and the photograph of a basketball player remain on screen at the end of the animation.

<NOTE>

You can preview the animation frame by frame in the Save For Web dialog box by clicking the arrows in the Animation area at the bottom of the dialog box. However, that's no substitute for viewing the working animation in one or more Web browsers.

16. **Click the Refresh button on your Web browser if you want to replay the animation.**

    Back in the Save For Web window, notice that the file size reported in the preview pane jumped from 25K to around 37K after you converted the layers in the source file to individual frames in the animation. In the next steps, you reduce the physical dimensions of the optimized file in order to reduce its file size. This is sometimes the last resort for optimizing a file to a reasonable size.

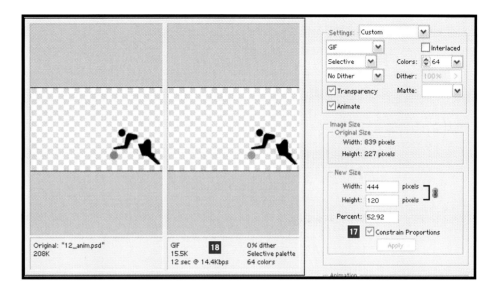

17. **In the Image Size section of the Save For Web window, make sure that Constrain Proportions is selected so that your image will not be distorted. Highlight the current value in the New Size→Height field, and enter** 120 **pixels. Notice that the Width and Percent fields are also reduced. Click Apply to reduce the dimensions of the optimized file, without affecting the source file.**

18. **Click in the preview pane to refresh the preview and reported statistics.**

    Notice that the total file size of the optimized animated GIF has been reduced more than 50 percent to around 15K.

19. **Click OK in the Save For Web dialog box to open the Save Optimized As dialog box. In the Save Optimized As dialog box, navigate to your ccproject folder, rename the file** 12_anim_end.gif**, and click Save to save the optimized animated GIF.**

    This file is ready to be brought into a Web-authoring program to be included as a banner in a Web site. You can find a pre-built copy of this final animated GIF in the Session 12 Tutorial Files folder on your hard drive.

20. **Close the source file,** 12_anim.psd**, without saving, because you made no changes to that file.**

    In this tutorial you learned how to make an animated GIF to include in a Web site.

<TIP>

If you want to play the animation outside of Photoshop Elements 2, drag 12_anim_end.gif on top of a Web browser's start icon (for example, the Internet Explorer icon on your hard drive). This opens the browser and plays the animation in the browser. A GIF animation does not need additional code or an external engine to play in a Web browser.

<TIP>

If you open any animated GIF in Photoshop Elements 2 (by choosing File→Open), the frames of the animation are distributed to separate layers in the Layers palette. This is a useful learning tool that you can use to deconstruct how other animated GIFs are made.

Tutorial
» Making a Web Photo Gallery Site

The Create Web Photo Gallery command is one of the most useful features in Photoshop Elements 2. It automatically creates a multipage Web site from any folder of images. This is a quick and easy way to display your portfolio, show proofs or design proposals to a client, or share photos with family and friends on the Web. In this tutorial, you make a Web Photo Gallery to show off the greeting card images that you created during this course.

1. **Choose File→Create Web Photo Gallery.**
   This opens the Web Photo Gallery dialog box where you can customize your Web Photo Gallery site.

2. **Click in the Styles field, and choose Spot Light from the menu of site styles.**
   A small preview of the style appears on the right side of the Web Photo Gallery dialog box. The styles are templates for various sites that you can create with the Web Photo Gallery. All the templates display thumbnails of each image, which can be clicked to display a larger version of the corresponding image. The Spot Light style is one of several that create a frames-based Web site, displaying the thumbnails and larger images at one time in separate frames.

3. **Type your e-mail address into the E-mail field.**
   This field, like many of the text fields in the dialog box, can be left blank or filled with any text you want, regardless of whether it's actually an e-mail address.

4. **Choose either .htm or .html from the Extension menu.**
   This designates the file extension to be added to each of the HTML files that are created automatically as part of this Web site. Either works, but if you plan to bring the files into a Web-authoring program for further modification, it makes sense to use whichever extension is the default for that particular program. (Adobe GoLive uses the the .html extension; Macromedia Dreamweaver uses .htm.)

5. **Click the Browse (Macintosh: Choose) button, and navigate to the final greeting cards folder inside the Session 12 Tutorial Files folder on your hard drive. Click OK (Macintosh: Choose) to select the folder of images to be displayed on your Web Photo Gallery site.**
   The final greeting cards folder has no subfolders. If it did, selecting Include All Subfolders would include the contents of those subfolders in the Web site.

6. **Click the Destination button, and navigate to the ccproject folder on your hard drive to create a subfolder in which to locate all the image, HTML, and other site files created by the Web Photo Gallery. In the Browse for Folder dialog box (Macintosh: Select Image Directory window), click the Make New Folder (Macintosh: New Folder) button. Name the new folder greeting card gallery, and click OK (Macintosh: click Create and then Choose).**
   You should create a separate folder for your Web Photo Gallery files so that they stay together. If they are rearranged or renamed, the links between the pages and their contents break.

7. Choose Banner from the Options menu if it's not already showing.

This changes the Options area of the dialog box to settings for a text banner that will appear in the top frame of the Web site that you're creating.

8. Type the following in the Options fields:

» Site Name: Sports Greeting Cards

» Photographer: [your name]
Note that this field does not have to contain the name of a photographer per se.

» Contact Info: [your phone, fax, or other contact info]
Including contact information in a prominent place on a Web site is important so your customers can get in touch with you. So be sure to fill in this field.

» Date: This field defaults to the current day's date. Delete the date, leaving this field blank.

» Font and Font Size: Ignore these options.
The banner font and size is a noncustomizable part of the Spot Light site style.

<NOTE>
You can type anything you want in the Site Name, Photographer, Contact Info, and Date fields of the site Banner, regardless of whether your text matches those labels. Alternatively, you can leave any of those fields blank.

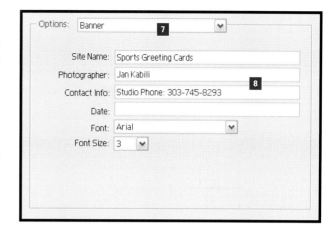

<CAUTION>
Many of the fields in the Web Photo Gallery that appear to be active have no effect when you choose a particular site style. Some fields are a noncustomizable part of the style; others are not relevant to the style. Unfortunately, you have no way to know which fields are inactive in any style until you finish creating the site and view it in a browser. The small warning on the right of the dialog box—"Some of the options may not apply to this style."—is the only information offered.

Preparing to Make Your Own Web Photo Gallery

Preparing to make a Web Photo Gallery of your own images is easy. The only thing that you must do is collect all the images in one folder. You don't have to worry about converting file formats or resizing images. The Web Photo Gallery feature does that for you automatically.

Beyond the required step of gathering images into a folder, you may want to take these additional, optional steps to prepare your images:

» If you plan to display copyright information or image captions in your Web Photo Gallery site, add that information to each image in your source folder. Choose File→Open to open an image, choose File→File Info, type the image information into the relevant fields, click OK, and close the image. Some of the Web Photo Gallery templates display information from these fields as image or thumbnail labels.

» If you plan to display filenames in your Web Photo Gallery site, you may want to change the filenames to something more meaningful than the names assigned by a digital camera. You can automatically change the names of a folder full of files by choosing File→Batch Process, selecting the source folder, designating a destination folder, setting File Naming options, and clicking OK. For example, if you choose Document Name and type the words greeting cards into the first name field, and choose 2 Digit Serial Number in the second name field, the images in the source folder will be renamed greeting-cards01.psd, greeting-cards02.psd, etc.

» If you are creating a Web Photo Gallery from digital photographs that you haven't yet corrected, check in the File Browser that all of the photographs are oriented in the right direction and rotate those that are not. Sometimes, vertical shots come into the computer with a horizontal orientation.

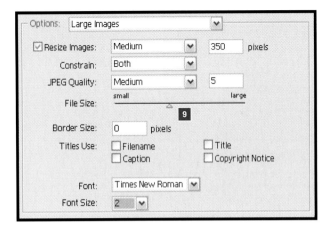

9. **Click in the Options field, and choose Large Images. Leave all these fields at their defaults.**

These fields govern the appearance of the large version of each image that displays in the top frame of the Web Photo Gallery site.

» Resize Images: Leave this option set to Medium (350 pixels wide).
This field determines the physical dimensions of the large images. You can choose a preset or enter a custom width in pixels. Leaving Constrain set to Both keeps the width and height of the images proportional.

» JPEG Quality: Leave this option set to Medium (5).
This sets the amount of compression quality, like the Quality field in the Save For Web dialog box. You can choose a preset, move the slider between small and large (small being the smallest file size and therefore the lowest quality level), or enter a number between 1 and 12 (12 being the highest quality and therefore the largest file size). Unfortunately, no preview of large image appearance or file size is available, so I suggest you leave these settings at their defaults for now. If you don't like the appearance or size of the large images in the final site, you can return to the Web Photo Gallery dialog box, change the JPEG Quality setting, and re-create the site.

» Border Size: Ignore this option. It has no effect in this style because the large images in this template have no border.

» Titles Use: These options have no effect on this style, which automatically labels each large image with the image filename minus the format suffix. (For example, if the filename is Selecting.jpg, the label Selecting appears above the large image.)
If you want to change the label that appears above a large image in this style, change the filename. When you're using other Web Photo Gallery styles, you can select a Title option (filename, title, caption, or copyright notice) to use as an image label. You create some of this information for a particular image file in the File Info dialog box, as discussed above.

» Font and Font Size: These options have no effect on this style. The font and size of the large image labels are hardwired into this style.

10. Click in the Options field, and choose Thumbnails. Set these options as indicated.

These options determine how the thumbnail version of each image appears in the bottom frame of the Web site.

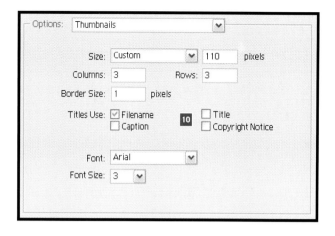

» Size: Type **110** pixels, which changes this field to Custom. This field determines the width of the thumbnail images. You can choose a preset or enter a custom width in pixels.

» Columns and Rows: Ignore these options. The Spot Light style doesn't use multiple columns or rows.

» Border Size: Enter **1** pixel to create a thin gray border around each thumbnail.

» Titles Use: Select Filename to add the full filename of each image under each thumbnail.
The other Titles Use options, which derive their content from data entered into the File Info dialog box, do not work with the Spot Light style.

» Font and Font Size: Ignore these options. The font and size of the thumbnails are hard-wired into this style.

< T I P >

If you're a photographer presenting images to a client in a Web Photo Gallery site, filenames can come in handy to identify particular images. In other cases, consider deselecting the filename option for a cleaner look to your site.

11. Click in the Options field, and choose Custom Colors.

These options have no effect on this style, so leave them at their defaults. With some styles, like the Table and Simple styles, you can use these options to customize the text, link, and page background colors in the site.

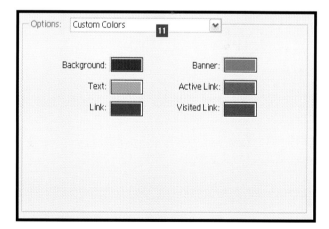

< T I P >

When you choose the Table site style, you can designate any image on your hard drive as the Web page background by clicking the Background button. This button is grayed out when any other style is selected.

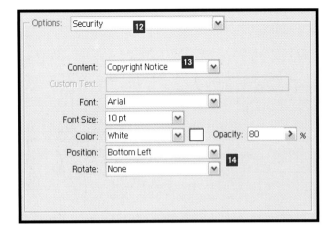

<TIP>
Leave Content set to None if you want no text on your large images.

<NOTE>
If you set the Security Options Content field to Custom Text, you can specify the message that displays across your large images in the Web site. This might come in handy for identifying images as proofs, copies, drafts, or samples. If you choose Caption, Credits, or Title in the Content field, that information would come from the File Info dialog boxes of the individual images.

12. **Click in the Options field, and choose Security.**
Use these options to add text on top of the large images in your Web Photo Gallery site to discourage viewers from downloading and misusing your images. You might also use this feature to identify images as proofs, samples, or drafts.

13. **Click in the Security Options Content field, and choose Copyright Notice.**
This causes the program to look for any information that has been entered into the Copyright Status and Copyright Notice fields of the File Info dialog boxes of the individual images that you're including in the site. (I entered the copyright notice **kabili 2003** into the File Info dialog boxes of the tutorial files that you're working with in this tutorial.)

14. **Set the other options in the Security area as follows to format the copyright notice that will appear on the large images in the Web site:**

» Font: **Arial**

» Font Size: **10 pt**

» Color: **White**

» Opacity: **80%**
This makes the text a little more subtle.

» Position: **Bottom Left**

» Rotate: **None**
Notice the 45° option. Use this option when you want text to cover as much of the image as possible.

15. **Click OK to create your Web Photo Gallery site.**
The program opens, resizes, optimizes, and saves a thumbnail and a larger version of each file in the source folder. It writes the HTML for the frameset and for each page in the site, and even opens your default Web browser to reveal the finished Web site.

16. In your default Web browser, click the image thumbnails to view each of the larger images in the top frame of the Web site.

<NOTE>

If you want to change anything in this Web Photo Gallery site, you have to return to Photoshop Elements 2, choose File→Create Web Photo Gallery again to reopen the Web Photo Gallery dialog box, make your changes in the option settings, and click OK to create an entirely new site replacing the old site.

Getting a Web Photo Gallery Site Online

You can put any Web Photo Gallery site online by uploading it to a Web server. If you already have an Internet Service Provider, check with them about how to upload a small Web site (less than 300K) to their server. Make sure that you confirm your username and password for logging on to the server, as well as the name of the host server and the directory to which you should upload your Web site. Ask whether you need an FTP program to upload to the server. If so, you'll find many FTP programs on the Web that you can download without charge. (Download the Windows FTP program WS-FTP LE from www.ipswitch.com/downloads, or the Macintosh FTP program Fetch from www.fetchsoftworks.com.) Connect to the Internet and upload to the Web server all of the Web Photo Gallery files and folders that Photoshop Elements 2 created for you, making sure not to rearrange any of the files and keeping the folders intact.

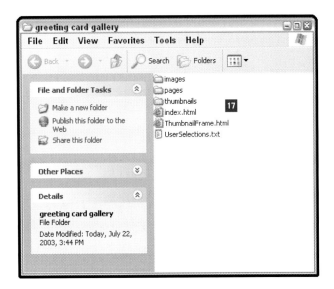

Windows interface

17. Close your Web browser, go directly to your hard drive, and open the greeting card gallery folder located inside your ccproject folder.

You see all the folders and files that make up your Web Photo Gallery site. A copy of the finished Web Photo Gallery site is in the greeting card gallery folder in the Session 12 Tutorial Files folder.

Macintosh interface

Tutorial
» Automatically Attaching an Image to E-mail

Photoshop Elements 2 makes sharing photographs and other images by e-mail easy. In this tutorial, you use the program's automatic Attach to E-mail feature to prepare an image for e-mail and attach it to a message in your existing e-mail program.

1. **Choose File→Open, navigate to your Session 12 Tutorial Files folder, and open** `12_boxing.psd`**.**
   This is a fairly large file (4.76Mb, and 1500 x 1110 pixels) in PSD format.

2. **Choose File→Attach to E-mail.**
   This displays the Attach to E-mail warning if the open file is in a format other than JPEG or is larger than 1200 pixels wide, as this one is. If the file is smaller than 1200 pixels, but is not a JPEG, the program asks whether you want to convert the file to JPEG. It is not necessary to do so. If the file is a sufficiently small JPEG to start with, your default e-mail program opens with the file attached to a new message in progress.

3. **Click the Auto Convert button in the Attach to E-mail window.**
   This causes Photoshop Elements 2 to do all of the following in the blink of an eye:

   » Make a copy of the open file `12_boxing.psd`.

   » Convert the copy to JPEG format, and compress it so that it is only 231K.

   » Launch your default e-mail program, and open a new message in progress.

   » Attach the compressed file to the new message as `12_boxingCopy.jpg`.

4. **All that's left for you to do is to fill in the recipient's e-mail address and the subject line, and write a brief message. Click the Send button in your e-mail program to send the message and the attached image file on its way.**

5. **Close** `12_boxing.psd` **without saving.**

<NOTE>
You could choose to send the file as is. However, e-mail is not a good medium for sending large files. A large e-mail attachment may be refused by an ISP, may clog up the recipient's e-mail pipeline, and is slow to download. Alternatively, you could convert the file to a compressed JPEG yourself in Photoshop Elements 2, using the opimization methods that you learned earlier in this Session. But using the program's automatic E-mail features is much faster and easier.

Tutorial
» Creating a PDF Slideshow

An elegant way to present a collection of images is as a slideshow. Creating a slideshow has never been easier than it is in Photoshop Elements 2. In this tutorial, you learn how to make a slideshow automatically, saving it in Adobe's Portable Document Format (PDF), which automatically plays on any computer on which Adobe's free software Acrobat Reader is installed.

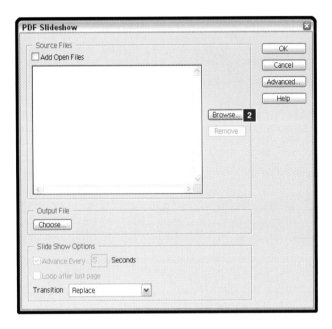

1. **Choose File→Automation Tools→PDF Slideshow.**

2. **In the PDF Slideshow dialog box, click the Browse button. Navigate to and open the final greeting cards folder in the Session 12 Tutorial Files folder on your hard drive.**

3. **In the Open window, Shift+click the first and last file to select all nine of the files in the final greeting cards folder. Click the Open button to add each of these files to the Source Files list in the PDF Slideshow dialog box.**

<TIP>

Images do not have to be in the same folder to be added to the Source Files list. You can navigate from folder to folder on your hard drive, selecting individual images to add to the list.

<TIP>

If a file is open, you can add it to the Source Files list by selecting Add Open Files in the PDF Slideshow dialog box.

4. **Click and drag any of the filenames up or down in the Source Files list to change the order in which images appear in the slideshow.**

Mac users will see colons rather than backslashes in the directory paths in this window.

<NOTE>

You can remove files from the Source Files list in the PDF Slideshow dialog box by selecting a filename in that list and clicking Remove.

<NOTE>

You can compress your slideshow more than the default by clicking the Advanced button to open the Encoding dialog box. Choose JPEG or ZIP compression, reduce the Quality level, and click OK.

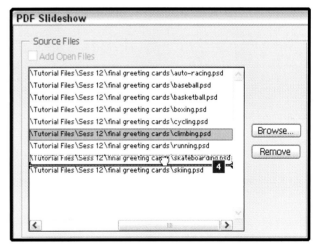

> **411**

<NOTE>
You do not need the full version of Adobe Acrobat to view a PDF slideshow (although the full version plays the slideshow). All you need is Adobe Reader, which can be downloaded for free from the Adobe Web site www.adobe.com. Older versions of Acrobat Reader will play a PDF slideshow, but to automatically advance the slides and display the transitions, the slideshow must be played in Acrobat Reader version 5.0 or above.

<TIP>
A PDF slideshow has lots of potential uses. It can be played unattended on a laptop computer parked at a trade show, a wedding reception, or an advertising venue. It can be burned onto a CD-ROM and distributed to family and friends. Or it can be uploaded to a Web site.

5. **Back in the PDF Slideshow dialog box, click the Choose button to set the destination for your slideshow. In the Save dialog box that opens, navigate to your ccproject folder, enter** card_slideshow **in the File name field, and click Save.**

6. **Turn your attention to the Slide Show Options in the PDF Slideshow dialog box, and set them as follows:**

   » Leave the Advance box selected.
   This ensures that the slides advance from one to the next automatically. If you prefer to manually advance the slides, leave this box unchecked, and during playback, click each slide to advance to the next.

   » Type **3** Seconds in the Advance field to set the time between slides.

   » Leave Loop after last page deselected so that the slideshow plays only once.
   Selecting loop sets the slideshow to play over and over on its own. This is a potentially useful way to present your images unattended.

   » Click in the Transition field, and choose Split Vertical Out to set the style with which one slide replaces another.
   You have lots of transitions to choose from, including Random Transition. If you don't want a stylized transition between slides, choose Replace.

7. **Click OK in the PDF Slideshow dialog box to create the slideshow.**

8. **Click OK when you see a message that the PDF slideshow was successful.**

9. **To view the slideshow, go outside Photoshop Elements to your hard drive, launch Adobe Acrobat Reader, and open** card_slideshow.pdf**.**
   The slideshow plays through once in full-screen mode, filling the screen with one big image after another separated by an effect. You can find a finished copy of card_slideshow.pdf in the Session 12 Tutorial Files folder.

10. **When the slideshow ends, press the Escape key on your keyboard to exit full-screen mode. Close Acrobat Reader.**
    Congratulations! You have now completed all the tutorials in this course. You got to know all the major features of Photoshop Elements 2, and you saw how powerful this program can be in skilled hands. Now it's up to you to practice and apply what you learned here. Keep this book near your computer as a reference and a practice guide. I hope you continue to enjoy using and learning about Photoshop Elements 2.

» Session Review

In this session, you learned about preparing images for output on the Web and in other screen media. You learned how to optimize photographs as JPEGs for display on the Web and how to make a large photograph into a Web page background of manageable size. You optimized graphics and text for the Web in transparent GIF format, creating a logo that could be placed on top of a Web page background. You made an animated GIF for use in a Web banner. Then you created an entire Web site from the greeting card images that you made during this course, using the automatic Web Photo Gallery feature. You made a slideshow of your greeting card images in PDF format, and you automatically prepared one of the card images to be sent as an e-mail attachment.

1. Name two Web design functions for which Photoshop Elements 2 is useful. (See Discussion: Using Photoshop Elements 2 in Web Design.)

2. When you optimize an image for the Web, you have to make compromises between two competing goals. What are those goals? (See Tutorial: Optimizing Photographs for the Web.)

3. What two file formats are currently best for optimizing a still image for the Web? (See Tutorial: Optimizing Photographs for the Web.)

4. What file format is generally best for optimizing photographs? (See Tutorial: Optimizing Photographs for the Web.)

5. What is the effect on file size of decreasing a JPEG Quality setting? (See Tutorial: Optimizing Photographs for the Web.)

6. Name one way to reduce the size of a large photograph so that it can be used as a Web page background. (See Tutorial: Making a Web Page Background.)

7. What file format is usually best for optimizing text and graphic art? (See Tutorial: Optimizing Graphics and Text for the Web.)

8. What is a transparent GIF? (See Tutorial: Optimizing Graphics and Text for the Web.)

9. How does the Matte feature improve a transparent GIF? (See Tutorial: Optimizing Graphics and Text for the Web.)

10. Is it important to stick to a Web-safe palette when you're creating graphics for the Web? (See Tutorial: Optimizing Graphics and Text for the Web.)

11. Name one advantage and one disadvantage of using text in the form of an image file on the Web? (See Tutorial: Optimizing Graphics and Text for the Web.)

12. What is the minimum number of pieces of artwork you need to create a rollover button? (See Tutorial: Making Artwork for Rollover Buttons.)

13. What must you do above all else to prepare to create an animated GIF in Photoshop Elements 2? (See Tutorial: Making an Animated GIF.)

14. If you resize an optimized image in the Save For Web window, what is the effect on the size of the original source file? (See Tutorial: Making an Animated GIF.)

15. What is the effect of setting Security Options in the Web Photo Gallery dialog box? (See Tutorial: Making a Web Photo Gallery Site.)

16. Do you have to convert an image to a small JPEG before attaching it to an e-mail message? (See Tutorial: Automatically Attaching an Image to E-mail.)

17. What software do you need to play back a PDF Slideshow? (See Tutorial: Creating a PDF Slideshow.)

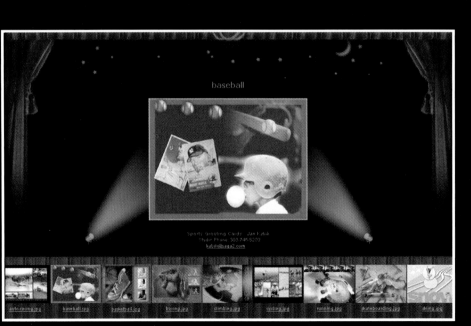

Part VII
CD-ROM Bonus Material: Enhancing Images

Bonus Session 1

Using Filters (CD-ROM)

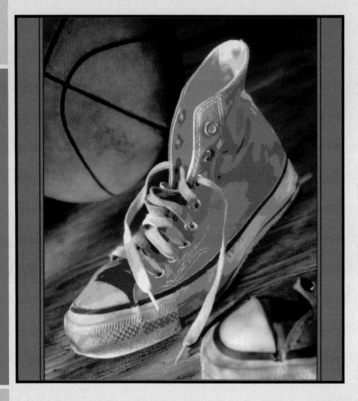

Tutorial: **Applying a Filter**

Tutorial: **Creating Selective Focus with a Filter**

Tutorial: **Filtering a Vector-Based Layer**

Tutorial: **Filtering with a Neutral Layer**

Tutorial: **Creating a Sketch from a Photograph**

Tutorial: **Creating Painterly Effects in a Photograph**

Session Introduction

Filters can change your artwork from ordinary to special with the click of a button. In this bonus session found on the CD-ROM, you learn the basics of applying filters, as well as some sophisticated uses for filters beyond the mere decorative. You apply the Gaussian Blur filter to simulate shortened depth of field in a photograph. You use filters to add texture and dimension to backgrounds. And you use filters to give a photograph the look of a sketch and to mimic painterly effects. Along the way, you learn how to apply a filter to vector objects like shapes and text, and you learn a special technique for filtering multiple layers with a neutral gray filter layer. Your work with filters in this session produces a unique, painterly collage on the subject of basketball for your final greeting card. You complete this greeting card in the following Bonus Session 2 (also on the CD-ROM), where you learn about the Effects features.

Applying Effects (CD-ROM)

Tutorial: **Applying a Text Effect**

Tutorial: **Applying a Frame Effect**

Tutorial: **Customizing Effects**

Session Introduction

Effects are similar to filters and layer styles in appearance and application, but they are more complex than both. Effects are a series of filters, layer styles, and related operations that are applied in quick succession to text, a selection, a layer, or an entire image. In this bonus session found on the CD-ROM, you use some of the unique items offered in the Effects palette to complete the greeting card you started in Bonus Session 1.

What's on the CD-ROM?

This appendix provides you with information on the contents of the CD-ROM that accompanies this book. For the latest and greatest information, please refer to the ReadMe file located at the root of the CD-ROM. Here is what you will find:

- » System Requirements
- » Using the CD-ROM with Windows and Macintosh
- » What's on the CD-ROM
- » Troubleshooting

System Requirements for using the CD-ROM

Make sure that your computer meets the minimum system requirements listed in this section. If your computer doesn't match up to most of these requirements, you may have a problem using the contents of the CD-ROM. Note that these are requirements for running the CD-ROM; they are not system requirements for Photoshop Elements 2. Those are covered in Part I, Project Overview.

For Windows 98, Windows 2000, Windows Me, or Windows XP:

» PC with a Pentium III class or better processor

» At least 64MB of total RAM installed on your computer, 128MB recommended

» At least 280MB of free hard drive space

» A color monitor with at least 800 x 600 resolution and a 16-bit video card

» A CD-ROM drive

For Macintosh:

» Macintosh OS computer with a G3, G4, or G5 PowerPC processor running OS 9.1, OS 9.2.x, or OS X 10.2.1 or later

» At least 64MB of total RAM installed on your computer, 128MB recommended

» At least 320MB of free hard drive space

» A color monitor with at least 800 x 600 resolution and a 16-bit video card

» A CD-ROM drive

Using the CD-ROM with Windows

To install the items from the CD-ROM to your hard drive, follow these steps:

1. Insert the CD-ROM into the CD-ROM drive.

2. The interface launches. If you have autorun disabled, click Start→Run. In the dialog box that appears, type D:\setup.exe. Replace *D* with the proper letter if the CD-ROM drive uses a different letter. (If you don't know the letter, see how the CD-ROM drive is listed under My Computer.) Click OK.

3. A license agreement appears. Read through the license agreement, and then click the Accept button if you want to use the CD. (After you click Accept, the License Agreement window never bothers you again.)

4. The CD interface Welcome screen appears. The interface coordinates installing Tutorial Files and programs. The interface basically enables you to click a button or two to make things happen.

5. Click anywhere on the Welcome screen to enter the interface. This next screen lists categories for the software on the CD.

6. For more information about an item, click its name. Be sure to read the information that appears. Sometimes a program has its own system requirements or requires you to do a few tricks on your computer before you can install or run the program. This screen tells you what you may need to do.

7. If you don't want to install an item, click the Back button to return to the previous screen. You can always return to the previous screen by clicking the Back button. Using this feature, you can browse, and then decide what you want to install.

8. To install an item, click the appropriate Install button. The CD interface drops to the background while the CD installs the item you chose.

9. To install other items, repeat Step 8.

10. When you finish installing, click the Quit button to close the interface. You can eject the CD now. Carefully place it back in the plastic jacket of the book for safekeeping.

< N O T E >

If you're on a Windows operating system other than Windows XP, you may have to change the read-only status of the copied tutorial files. Otherwise, you won't be able to write over the files as you work through the tutorials. To do so, select all the files in a folder that you've copied to your computer. Right-click one of the files and choose Properties. In the Properties dialog box, uncheck Read-only. Also, I suggest that you instruct Windows to display the filename extensions of the copied tutorial files (if it isn't already set up to show them) so that you can see the file formats (.psd, .tif, .jpg, and so on). Find your Folder Options dialog box. (It's located in a slightly different place in different versions of Windows; in Windows XP, it's in the Appearance and Themes Control Panel; in Windows 2000 and Me, in the My Computer→Tools folder; in Windows 98, in the My Computer→View folder.) Click the View tab. Uncheck Hide File Extensions for Known File Types, which is checked by default.

Using the CD-ROM with the Macintosh OS

To install the items from the CD-ROM to your hard drive, follow these steps:

1. Insert the CD-ROM into your CD-ROM drive.

2. Double-click the icon for the CD-ROM after it appears on the desktop.

3. Double-click the License Agreement icon. This is the license that you are agreeing to by using the CD. You can close this window once you've looked over the agreement.

4. To use the Tutorial Files, just drag the Tutorial Files folder, or any of its subfolders, from the CD-ROM onto your desktop.

5. Most programs come with installers; for those, simply open the Software folder on the CD-ROM and double-click the Install or Installer icon.

What's on the CD

The CD contains all of the author-created files and source materials for use in the tutorials in this book. The materials for each session are located in a corresponding Session folder inside the Tutorial Files folder. The Links file contains links to the author's Web sites and e-mail, along with some other links you'll find useful.

Applications

The following applications are on the CD:

Adobe Reader from Adobe Systems, Inc.

Freeware version—for Windows. This is the reader required to view PDF files. For more information, check out www.adobe.com/products/acrobat/readermain.html.

Adobe Photoshop Elements 2

Tryout version—for Windows. This powerful software is simple to use allowing you to do more with your photos, from quick corrections to creative editing, regardless of whether you use a digital camera or scan traditional photos.

Troubleshooting

If you have difficulty installing or using anything on the companion CD-ROM, try the following solutions:

» **Turn off any antivirus software that you may have running.** Installers sometimes mimic virus activity and can make your computer incorrectly believe that it is being infected by a virus. (Be sure to turn the antivirus software back on later.)

» **Close all running programs.** The more programs you're running, the less memory is available to other programs. Installers also typically update files and programs; if you keep other programs running, the installation may not work properly.

» **Reference the ReadMe.** Please refer to the ReadMe file located at the root of the CD-ROM for the latest product information at the time of publication.

If you still have trouble with the CD-ROM, please call the Wiley Publishing Customer Care phone number: (800) 762-2974. Outside the United States, call 1 (317) 572-3994. You can also contact Wiley Publishing Customer Service by e-mail at techsupdum@wiley.com. Wiley Publishing will provide technical support only for installation and other general quality control items; for technical support on the applications themselves, consult the program vendor or author.

Tools, Commands, and Shortcuts Lists

Here are some handy lists of shortcuts for tools and commands. The first table lists all of the tools in the toolbox, along with the keyboard shortcut for selecting each tool.

The second table describes each of the commands that have shortcut icons in the Shortcuts bar. Many of these commands also have keyboard shortcuts, which are included in this table. Photoshop Elements Help (Help→Photoshop Elements Help), contains several screens listing other popular commands and their shortcuts on both Windows and Macintosh computers.

If you don't have these lists with you, you can always move your mouse over a tool or command to invoke a tool tip to remind you of this information.

Table B-1: Tools and Their Keyboard Shortcuts

Tool Icon	Tool Name	Keyboard Shortcut
	Rectangular Marquee Tool	M
	Elliptical Marquee Tool	M
	Move Tool	V
	Lasso Tool	L
	Polygonal Lasso Tool	L
	Magnetic Lasso Tool	L
	Magic Wand Tool	W
	Selection Brush Tool	A
	Crop Tool	C
	Custom Shape Tool	U
	Rectangle Tool	U
	Rounded Rectangle Tool	U
	Ellipse Tool	U
	Polygon Tool	U
	Line Tool	U
	Shape Selection Tool	U
	Horizontal Type Tool	T
	Vertical Type Tool	T
	Horizontal Type Mask Tool	T
	Vertical Type Mask Tool	T
	Paint Bucket Tool	K

Tool Icon	Tool Name	Keyboard Shortcut
	Gradient Tool	G
	Brush Tool	B
	Impressionistic Brush	B
	Pencil Tool	N
	Eraser Tool	E
	Background Eraser Tool	E
	Magic Eraser Tool	E
	Red Eye Brush Tool	Y
	Blur Tool	R
	Sharpen Tool	P
	Sponge Tool	Q
	Smudge Tool	F
	Dodge Tool	O
	Burn Tool	J
	Clone Stamp Tool	S
	Pattern Stamp Tool	S
	Eyedropper Tool	I
	Hand Tool	H
	Zoom Tool	Z
	Set Default Foreground and Background Colors	D
	Switch Foreground and Background Colors	X

Table B-2: Shortcuts for Commands in the Shortcuts Bar

Shortcut Icon	Shortcut Name	Shortcut For	Keyboard Shortcut
	Adobe.com	Opens Adobe Systems Inc. Web site, www.adobe.com	—
	New	File→New	Ctrl+N (⌘+N)
	Open	File→Open	Ctrl+O (⌘+O)
	Browse	File→Browse	Shift+Ctrl+O (Shift+⌘+O)
	Import	File→Import	—
	Save	File→Save	Ctrl+S (⌘+S)
	Save for Web	File→Save for Web	Alt+Shift+Ctrl+S (Option+Shift+⌘+S)
	Save as PDF	File→Save As and choose Photoshop PDF from Format menu	Shift+Ctrl+S (⌘+Ctrl+S) + menu choice
	Attach to E-mail	File→Attach to E-mail	—
	Online Services	File→Online Services	—
	Print	File→Print	Alt+Ctrl+P (Option+⌘+P)
	Print Preview	File→Print Preview	Ctrl+P (⌘+P)
	Step Backward	Edit→Step Backward	Ctrl+Z (⌘+Z)
	Step Forward	Edit→Step Forward	Ctrl+Y (⌘+Y)
	Quick Fix	Enhance→Quick Fix	—
	Color Variations	Enhance→Adjust Color→ Color Variations	—
	Search Help	Help→Photoshop Elements Help and choose Search	F1 + menu choice
	Help Contents	Help→Photoshop Elements Help	F1

Index

About Seybold Seminars and Publications

Seybold Seminars and Publications is your complete guide
to the publishing industry. For more than 30 years it
has been the most trusted source for technology events,
news, and insider intelligence.

Produced by

PUBLICATIONS

Today, Seybold Publications and Consulting continues to guide publishing professionals around the world in their purchasing decisions and business strategies through newsletters, online resources, consulting, and custom corporate services.

- ### *The Seybold Report: Analyzing Publishing Technologies*
  The Seybold Report analyzes the cross-media tools, technologies, and trends shaping professional publishing today. Each in-depth newsletter delves into the topics changing the marketplace. *The Seybold Report* covers critical analyses of the business issues and market conditions that determine the success of new products, technologies, and companies. Read about the latest developments in mission-critical topic areas, including content and asset management, color management and proofing, industry standards, and cross-media workflows. A subscription to *The Seybold Report* (24 issues per year) includes our weekly email news service, *The Bulletin,* and full access to the seyboldreports.com archives.

- ### *The Bulletin: Seybold News & Views on Electronic Publishing*
  The Bulletin: Seybold News & Views on Electronic Publishing is Seybold Publications' weekly email news service covering all aspects of electronic publishing. Every week *The Bulletin* brings you all the important news in a concise, easy-to-read format.

For more information on **NEWSLETTER SUBSCRIPTIONS,** please visit **seyboldreports.com**.

CUSTOM SERVICES

In addition to newsletters and online information resources, Seybold
Publications and Consulting offers a variety of custom corporate services
designed to meet your organization's specific needs.

○ **Strategic Technology Advisory Research Service (STARS)**
The STARS program includes a group license to *The Seybold Report* and
The Bulletin, phone access to our analysts, access to online archives at
seyboldreports.com, an on-site visit by one of our analysts, and much more.

○ **Personalized Seminars**
Our team of skilled consultants and subject experts work with you to create a
custom presentation that gets your employees up to speed on topics spanning
the full spectrum of prepress and publishing technologies covered in our publications. Full-day and half-day seminars are available.

○ **Site Licenses**
Our electronic licensing program keeps everyone in your organization, sales
force, or marketing department up to date at a fraction of the cost of buying
individual subscriptions. One hard copy of *The Seybold Report* is included with
each electronic license.

For more information on **CUSTOM CORPORATE SERVICES,**
please visit **seyboldreports.com**.

SEYBOLD SEMINARS

EVENTS

Seybold Seminars facilitates exchange and discussion within the high-tech publishing community several times a year. A hard-hitting lineup of conferences, an opportunity to meet leading media technology vendors, and special events bring innovators and leaders together to share ideas and experiences.

Conferences

Our diverse educational programs are designed to tackle the full range of the latest developments in publishing technology. Topics include:

- Print publishing
- Web publishing
- Design
- Creative tools and standards
- Best practices

- Multimedia
- Content management
- Technology standards
- Security
- Digital rights management

In addition to the conferences, you'll have the opportunity to meet representatives from companies that bring you the newest products and technologies in the publishing marketplace. Test tools, evaluate products, and take free classes from the experts.

For more information on **SEYBOLD SEMINARS EVENTS,**
please visit **seyboldseminars.com**.

Wiley Publishing, Inc.
End-User License Agreement

READ THIS. You should carefully read these terms and conditions before opening the software packet(s) included with this book "Book". This is a license agreement "Agreement" between you and Wiley Publishing, Inc."WPI". By opening the accompanying software packet(s), you acknowledge that you have read and accept the following terms and conditions. If you do not agree and do not want to be bound by such terms and conditions, promptly return the Book and the unopened software packet(s) to the place you obtained them for a full refund.

1. **License Grant.** WPI grants to you (either an individual or entity) a nonexclusive license to use one copy of the enclosed software program(s) (collectively, the "Software" solely for your own personal or business purposes on a single computer (whether a standard computer or a workstation component of a multi-user network). The Software is in use on a computer when it is loaded into temporary memory (RAM) or installed into permanent memory (hard disk, CD-ROM, or other storage device). WPI reserves all rights not expressly granted herein.

2. **Ownership.** WPI is the owner of all right, title, and interest, including copyright, in and to the compilation of the Software recorded on the disk(s) or CD-ROM "Software Media". Copyright to the individual programs recorded on the Software Media is owned by the author or other authorized copyright owner of each program. Ownership of the Software and all proprietary rights relating thereto remain with WPI and its licensers.

3. **Restrictions On Use and Transfer.**

    (a) You may only (i) make one copy of the Software for backup or archival purposes, or (ii) transfer the Software to a single hard disk, provided that you keep the original for backup or archival purposes. You may not (i) rent or lease the Software, (ii) copy or reproduce the Software through a LAN or other network system or through any computer subscriber system or bulletin- board system, or (iii) modify, adapt, or create derivative works based on the Software.

    (b) You may not reverse engineer, decompile, or disassemble the Software. You may transfer the Software and user documentation on a permanent basis, provided that the transferee agrees to accept the terms and conditions of this Agreement and you retain no copies. If the Software is an update or has been updated, any transfer must include the most recent update and all prior versions.

4. **Restrictions on Use of Individual Programs.** You must follow the individual requirements and restrictions detailed for each individual program in the About the CD-ROM appendix of this Book. These limitations are also contained in the individual license agreements recorded on the Software Media. These limitations may include a requirement that after using the program for a specified period of time, the user must pay a registration fee or discontinue use. By opening the Software packet(s), you will be agreeing to abide by the licenses and restrictions for these individual programs that are detailed in the About the CD-ROM appendix and on the Software Media. None of the material on this Software Media or listed in this Book may ever be redistributed, in original or modified form, for commercial purposes.

5. **Limited Warranty.**

    (a) WPI warrants that the Software and Software Media are free from defects in materials and workmanship under normal use for a period of sixty (60) days from the date of purchase of this Book. If WPI receives notification within the warranty period of defects in materials or workmanship, WPI will replace the defective Software Media.

    (b) WPI AND THE AUTHOR OF THE BOOK DISCLAIM ALL OTHER WARRANTIES, EXPRESS OR IMPLIED, INCLUDING WITHOUT LIMITATION IMPLIED WARRANTIES OF MERCHANTABILITY AND FITNESS FOR A PARTICULAR PURPOSE, WITH RESPECT TO THE SOFTWARE, THE PROGRAMS, THE SOURCE CODE CONTAINED THEREIN, AND/OR THE TECHNIQUES DESCRIBED IN THIS BOOK. WPI DOES NOT WARRANT THAT THE FUNCTIONS CONTAINED IN THE SOFTWARE WILL MEET YOUR REQUIREMENTS OR THAT THE OPERATION OF THE SOFTWARE WILL BE ERROR FREE.

    (c) This limited warranty gives you specific legal rights, and you may have other rights that vary from jurisdiction to jurisdiction.